Suomalaiset:
People of the Marsh
by Mark Munger

First Edition
Copyright 2004 Mark Munger

ISBN 0-9720050-6-4
Library of Congress Number: 2004093033

Published by Cloquet River Press
5353 Knudsen Road
Duluth, Minnesota 55803

Edited by Scribendi (www.scribendi.com)

Visit the publisher at: www.cloquetriverpress.com

Printed in the United States of America
Cover Photograph by J.B. Kobe
Cover Design by Rene' Munger

2

ACKNOWLEDGMENTS

The author would like to thank the following individuals who served as readers for this project: Dr. Alexis Pogorleskin, Chair of the University of Minnesota-Duluth History Department; Ms. Renata Skube; Mr. Ken Hubert; The Reverend Stephen Schaitberger; Ms. Margaret Schaitberger; Mr. Keith Bosley; Ms. Miriam Toews, Writer in Residence, Winnipeg Public Library; Ms. Anita Zager, owner, Northern Lights Bookstore; Mr. Daniel Maki, Associate Professor, Finlandia University; Mr. Mark Rubin, J.D.; Ms. Phyllis Town; Ms. Susanne Schuler; The Reverend David Hill, Deacon, Trinity Episcopal Church; Ms. Rachel Martin; Mr. Richard Pemberton, JD; Dr. Joel Bamford, MD. Without these dedicated friends and professional scholars devoting their time and effort to reading the manuscript of this work, the content and flow of this novel might be vastly different, and, more than likely, vastly inferior.

I would also like to take this opportunity to mention two special friends from my youth. Wayne Rikala and Jeff Tynjala, two pure-bred third generation American Finns who grew up in my hometown of Duluth, Minnesota, provided me with my first glimpse into the fascinating world of Finnish heritage and culture. I am proud to still call them friends.

Lastly, a word of thanks to my wife, Rene', and my four sons, Matt, Dylan, Chris, and Jack. Many evenings have been lost to them while Dad types away at the keyboard, struggles with revisions, or sleeps in his chair because he has been up at five in the morning, struck by sudden inspiration. Their patience through the duration of this project is much appreciated.

Mark Munger
March 2004
Duluth, Minnesota

Dedicated to Judge Jeff Rantala:
The best damn guitar player
I've ever known.

Suomalaiset:
People of the Marsh

Stories from the Lake Superior Basin
Duluth, Minnesota

Prologue
(Part One)

Juho Stranden was thirty years old. The farmer had the misfortune of being forced to leave Kitee, in Eastern Finland. He was leaving his home for Duluth, Minnesota, in the United States. Stranden was a bachelor. He had never been on the Atlantic Ocean, the body of water that loomed before the ocean liner entrusted to carry the Finnish farmer and sixty-two of his countrymen to America.

Slate-colored water rolled beneath the steel plates of the ship as the vessel left the docks of Southampton. Stranden and his companions had landed at Hull, on the eastern coast of England, following a three-day voyage from Helsinki aboard the tramp steamer, *Polaris*. Along the way, the unemployed farmer chanced to meet two beautiful Finnish girls.

Aina and Katriina Jussila were single women from Paavola, Oulu, a city located just inland from the Gulf of Bothnia on the West Coast of Finland. They had captivated and engaged Juho during *Polaris'* crossing of the North Sea. Both women were starkly fair and blond, with eyes the color of Arctic ice. Outwardly, there was little to differentiate Aina, the older of the siblings by merely a year, from her younger sister, but Juho Stranden saw something, some rare spark of originality about Katriina, which compelled his attention. Perhaps it was her laugh, a timid gasp that allowed for a moderate escape of air. Perhaps it was the engaging pose she took at the rail of the great liner whenever Juho approached.

The three of them had spent a day exploring Southampton after arriving from Hull on the train. None of them spoke English, but several of the other young Finns accompanying them through the narrow streets of the harbor town possessed sufficient rudimentary English to communicate with shopkeepers and tavern owners along the way.

These Finns were not undertaking a voluntary exodus from Europe; they were leaving Finland out of necessity. It was the beginning of the Twentieth Century. Czar Nicholas II of Russia, the monarch who had direct control over the lives and welfare of the indentured Finns, had ordered all Finnish men to participate in the Russian military draft. Most of the emigrating Finnish men were like Juho Stranden: poor tenant farmers who owned no land, no oxen, no implements, no property of substance.

Young Finnish women like the Jussila sisters, girls of marriageable age, flocked to the United States on the heels of the emigrating Finnish men. The women sought steady employment as domestic servants, biding their time until they connected with eligible Finnish bachelors in America.

In addition to the onset of Russian military conscription, the population of Finland had grown exponentially, applying even more pressure upon Finnish men and women to emigrate. By the end of the 19th Century there was not enough land for those who wanted to farm, and not enough jobs for those who wanted to work. Finland, though beautiful geographically, presented nothing less than a financial wasteland for its impoverished citizenry.

Politics also played a part in the mass exodus of the Finns. Many Finnish immigrants to the United States were Socialists. Czar Nicholas II, confronted with the demands of industrializing an agrarian economy and intent upon the Russification of the Finns, found himself unable to temper the discontent of the landless Finnish peasants. This discord manifested itself in outright defiance among the leftists. Marxism and less drastic forms of Socialism spread like noxious political weeds throughout the Russian Empire. Some of the sixty-three Finns on board the ship headed to America were not only leaving economic hardship and famine, but they were escaping political persecution by the Russian authorities.

The Jussila sisters were bound for New York City where, under the care of an uncle, a man who owned an employment agency, they expected to find work as

8

housekeepers or nannies. For Juho Stranden, however, the future was far less clear.

Stranden's second cousin, Elin Gustafsson, lived in Duluth, along the shores of Lake Superior in Northeastern Minnesota. She had written to Juho about her friend, Anders Alhomaki. According to Elin, Anders knew how to secure jobs in the mines of the Vermilion Iron Range or along the wharves of Duluth's harbor. Elin's letter contained no promise of a job, no promise of a better life. Her letter contained only the promise of possibilities.

"Hello," Juho Stranden said, noting the appearance of the Jussila sisters in the vessel's third class dining hall.

Though the ocean liner's cheaper accommodations did not compare to the opulent upper realms of the ship, even the lowliest passengers aboard the vessel were afforded relative affluence. Juho carefully studied his surroundings as the ship steamed away from the Irish coast. Stranden came to the conclusion that it was his good fortune to have missed passage on *Lucarnia*, the original vessel he'd been booked on, and to have secured a third deck berth on the newest ship in the White Star Line.

"Hello, Mr. Stranden," Aina replied.

The woman's eyes darted to take in her younger sister's face, cognizant that affection simmered between the tall farmer with the uncharacteristically black hair and brown eyes, and her fair-skinned sibling.

"Please, have a seat. I was just going to order," Stranden replied, gesturing for the sisters to join him.

The women smiled and demurely claimed seats at the table. A waiter, a Lilliputian man with a manila cast to his skin, approached. The man addressed them in English, and so his words were completely lost upon the three Finns. Juho pointed to an overturned porcelain cup, indicating that he would start his morning meal with coffee. The two women gestured in similar fashion.

"Three coffees it is," the Englishman acknowledged through uneven teeth.

"Coffee, yes," Juho repeated in a thick accent, smiling brightly at his companions as he spoke English.

The waiter scurried away. Conversation at the table resumed in Finnish.

"Have you heard from your uncle in New York City?" the farmer asked.

Katriina nodded, but allowed her older sister to speak.

"Indeed we have. He's going to meet us at the dock when the ship arrives. I've been told we should get in sometime on the sixteenth," Aina said.

It was Sunday April 14th, 1912. They had left Southampton on the 10th.

"We've been making good time," Juho offered.

His face shone with excitement as he tried to subdue his enthusiasm for Katriina. He avoided making direct contact with her blue eyes. He concealed his admiration, limiting his glances in Katriina's direction.

The waiter returned and filled their cups with fresh coffee. All three of the passengers used their fingers to point out the items on adjoining tables that they were interested in. Juho ordered a muffin, two hard-boiled eggs, and English sausage. The women were content with marmalade and toast.

"Yes, very good time," Aina responded after the waiter had excused himself. "This ship is extremely fast."

"And safe; unsinkable, they say," Juho added.

Their meals came. Katriina took imperceptible bites of stale bread as Aina and Juho continued to converse. Katriina's eyes took in Juho Stranden's broad shoulders; his sinewy neck. Her mind began to speculate about him in ways that were not particularly genteel. A slight blush encompassed her face, vanishing before either her sister or the farmer could detect the sudden onset of color.

"So, you are going to Minnesota?" Aina asked.

"Yes. My cousin Elin lives in Duluth, on Lake Superior. She has a friend, Anders Alhomaki, who says that there are plenty of jobs for strong and willing men like me in Northern Minnesota."

"Many of our people have gone to Minnesota," Katriina interjected, becoming more comfortable with the situation. "What is the attraction?"

Juho smiled as he addressed the young woman:

"I've been told that Minnesota looks like Finland. Long winters with much snow. Many lakes and rivers. Pine and spruce forests; forests being logged for timber. Alhomaki has worked in the iron mines of Minnesota and the copper mines of Michigan. He's also worked as a stevedore."

"Stevedore?" Katriina asked.

"Moving cargo from docks to warehouses. The longshoremen bring the cargo off the ships. The stevedores haul the cargo from the docks to storage or to waiting railroad cars."

"Sounds like physical work," Aina said, interrupting her younger sister, intending the intrusion as a caution against Katriina becoming too familiar with their male companion.

Katriina recognized the authority behind her sister's comment and resumed eating, but the younger sister's blue eyes remained riveted on Juho Stranden's handsome face as she swallowed toast.

"It is. But what choice does a man like me have? I could have stayed in Finland, ended up impressed into the Czar's army or navy, to be used as a pawn in the Empire's game of chess with its enemies. Or I can take a short voyage on an elegant ocean liner with two beautiful ladies in the hopes of finding a new beginning. I will be thirty-one years old on the twentieth of April. I have no home, no fortune, no wife or family to hold me down. My back is strong. I am smart enough to know when I'm being misled and quick enough in my thinking to avoid disaster. If the work in Minnesota doesn't suit me, there are many other places in America waiting to welcome Juho Stranden."

"Perhaps New York City," Katriina whispered.

Stranden's smile returned.

"Perhaps," he answered quietly, his brown eyes locking on the pewter irises of the younger Jussila sister.

Aina's lips fluttered artificially.

11

"That's enough mooning, you two. My sister is such a child sometimes," the elder sister sighed. "Mr. Stranden, I must ask that you not encourage her behavior. She's only twenty. She has little experience with gentlemen.."

Katriina chewed in exaggerated fashion, glared at her sister, and finished the last of her toast. There was no mistaking the stern rebuke etched across Aina Jussila's brow. The younger woman knew better than to issue a challenge to her sister in the company of a stranger.

"I'll try to remember that," the farmer murmured, downing his coffee. "But I'm not so sure your younger sister is as easily directed as you might believe, Miss Aina."

Katriina smirked and shielded her eyes. Stranden stood up, intent upon leaving.

"May I walk with the two of you later this evening; that is, if the sky relents? There'll be no moon, but I hear the stars over the North Atlantic are not to be missed."

Aina Jussila studied Juho Stranden. She considered stating a strenuous objection to the budding flirtation between the Finnish man and her younger sister, but there seemed to be no fault in the farmer, no basis upon which to raise such a protest.

"We'll consider your offer, Mr. Stranden. Come by our cabin around nine and I'll let you know."

Juho smiled. The gesture revealed that the farmer had retained nearly all of his own teeth, save for two molars that had broken on the odd piece of gristle or bone over the years. He was cleanly groomed, educated, and obviously intelligent. Katriina could do far worse, in Aina's estimation. Still, there was a large discrepancy in age between the farmer and the younger Jussila sister. And soon there would be the entirety of the Eastern United States separating them. Aina set herself to weighing whether or not the girls should accompany Mr. Stranden for an evening stroll. There was much time to deliberate. There was ample time for contemplation. It was only morning.

"I'll do that. If you decide to go out, dress warmly. It will likely be quite cold," the farmer replied.

The women's eyes scrutinized Juho Stranden as he walked casually out of the dining hall. His berth, along with those of the other single men traveling in third class, was located in the bow of the ship.

Prologue
(Part Two)

Juha Niskanen sat on the edge of his bunk in the cabin he shared in third class with Juho Stranden. Niskanen's feet barely touched the floor as he studied the face of his companion.

"A walk on the upper deck? Are you crazy? It's freezing outside," Niskanen said in plaintive Finnish.

Stranden grinned.

"Ah," Juha noted, "so there is something more to your evening stroll than mere fresh air. A woman, I'll wager."

Stranden stood at a mirror above a small sink while arranging his heavily oiled hair.

"A possibility," Stranden replied. "Merely a possibility."

"That's what this trip to America is all about. The unlocking and discovery of possibilities," replied Niskanen. "Perhaps you might unlock something in this young woman's heart, eh, Stranden?"

The farmer nodded as he wiped excess hair tonic from his hand onto an elegantly stitched white towel that rested on a silver-plated towel bar. Stranden opened his mouth and inspected his teeth for particles of food by looking at a mirror fastened to the wall.

"Possibilities indeed," Juho Stranden agreed. "Katriina Jusilla presents an infinite number of those, I'll grant you. Trouble is, her older sister is a ferocious guardian. I doubt that I'll get close enough to smell Katriina's perfume on our walk. Aina will likely insist on placing herself between us for propriety's sake."

Niskanen thumbed through a book.

"You look fine," Juha Niskanen acknowledged. "You clean up well."

Stranden smiled, exposing white teeth.

"Don't wait up," the farmer added as he headed out the narrow door of their shared cabin. "Who knows what the night may bring?"

"Given that the chick is being watched by the hen, I'd take the cautious route, friend Stranden," the smaller man teased as he reclined in his bunk to read.

As Juho Stranden started out the door, his companion added, "Say, aren't you headed for Duluth, in Minnesota?"

The big man stopped in his tracks.

"You know that I am."

"Sometimes I forget the details of what I'm told," Niskanen admitted. "I met a Swede – big fellow, bigger than you – who lives there."

"In Duluth?"

"Yes, sir."

"He's on this ship?"

"Absolutely."

"I'd like to meet him, maybe confirm some of the information my cousin Elin has been passing along regarding job opportunities."

"Name's Karl Johansson. He's in Second Class. His fiancée is supposed to follow him over on the *Olympic* later this year. I'll see if I can't bring him by tomorrow."

"I'd appreciate that," Stranden said as he closed the cabin door.

They walked slowly around a promenade on the upper deck. Juho Stranden had been correct: Aina insisted on inserting herself between the two aspiring lovers. Katriina, familiar with her sister's resolve, acquiesced without a fuss. The women were dressed in long woolen skirts, heavy coats, mittens, insulated bonnets, and thick Laplander scarves. Their male companion wore a heavy storm coat, a garment originally worn by his father while serving in the Finnish Army. The coat's military insignia had been removed, leaving ghostly impressions behind in the wool. There was no wind. The air was frigid.

"New York sounds like a marvelous place to begin a new life," Juho Stranden said, adjusting his stride to that of the shorter women.

The sisters were five foot three and solidly built. Square, sturdy women, their bodies were roughly identical in shape; their faces were similar in detail. Both Jussila sisters had narrow jaws and prominent cheekbones, giving them classic beauty. When they spoke, their teeth were revealed as bits of ivory. Their eyes bore identical shards of indigo, though the expressiveness of Katriina's gaze was entirely unlike the somber analysis of Aina's stare.

"Once I've started work as a nanny," Katriina asserted, "I plan to use the money to take classes, to learn English, and then, once I've learned the language, to go to college."

Stranden looked across the torso of the older sister and addressed Katriina as they strolled:

"College? That seems ambitious. Me, I hope to get a decent job in the mines. Maybe spend winters working the woods. Save up enough to buy a small farm. I hear land in Northeastern Minnesota, ground that's been cleared of timber, is cheap, cheaper than the worst swamps of Finland."

Aina Jussila scowled.

"Once a farmer, always a farmer. I might have known," the older sister muttered.

Katriina glanced at the man and she smiled. "Don't mind my sister," she offered. "I happen to think that farming is an admirable occupation. There's much to be said for remaining connected to the soil. There's humility and honesty in what a man can grow and harvest by his own effort."

"And dreams of a better life buried beneath heaps of cow dung," Aina added with pique.

The insult didn't alter Juho's demeanor.

"I'll grant you that farming, especially in a place as cold and unforgiving as Northeastern Minnesota, is a gamble," Stranden admitted. "But I'm not a foolish dreamer. I know farming. I know hard work. I'm not the sort to try and reinvent myself by taking up further schooling. I learned enough in public school back in Muljula to know when I'm being taken advantage of. I'll learn to read and write in English. That's about it. Numbers – I'm very good at figuring. Beyond that, I'll have to rely upon my wits."

Katriina glared at her older sister. "There's plenty to be learned in life away from books and schooling. I expect Aina could use further educating in that regard."

An awkward silence imposed itself upon the three figures as they finished their tour of the deck. Stranden stopped and leaned against a railing overlooking the stern of the vessel. Electric lights cast a white glow across the ship's churning wake as the great liner sliced through black water. Salt permeated the air. Stars pulsed above the three Finns as they looked back towards Europe.

"We're nearing North America," Stranden finally said. "Another day or so and we should be on dry land."

"The ship seems to be traveling very fast," Katriina observed.

"She is indeed," Stranden said. "I'd wager twenty knots or more."

"There's no movement at all," Aina added. "It's like we're not even on the water."

"She's steady as a babe in a mother's arms," Juho agreed.

The North Atlantic spread out behind the ship as a vast watery plain. Beyond the illumination of the ship's lamps, sea and sky knitted together in a seamless mantle. The odor of burning coal intermittently touched their nostrils. The faint sounds of other passengers engaged in conversation reached their ears.

"I think it's time to retire," Aina urged after an appropriate interval.

There was a softening in her voice. She had spent most of her time at the railing surreptitiously considering the farmer. Her original impression seemed misdirected. Juho Stranden conveyed a kindness and a patience that would serve her somewhat impetuous younger sister well.

Perhaps, Aina thought, *being the wife of a farmer in Minnesota isn't the worst fate Katriina could realize.*

"May I walk you to your cabin?" Stranden asked.

Before Aina could interpose an objection, Katriina smiled and gushed: "That would be splendid, Mr. Stranden. I'd like that very much."

Aina held her tongue. She would discuss her sister's forward behavior with Katriina in the privacy of their cabin.

"How did it go?" Juha Niskanen asked when Juho Stranden returned.

"The older Jussila sister might be an impediment," Stranden acknowledged. "She really has it in for me."

"Maybe she's jealous that you're infatuated with little girls rather than mature maidens," Niskanen teased.

"They're only a year apart," Stranden advised.

"The older one, what's her name?"

"Aina," Juho Stranden replied as he removed his clothing, extinguished the light, climbed a ladder, pulled back the bed covers, and crawled between a wool blanket and linen sheets.

"And you say their surname is 'Jussila'?"

"That's right."

"Any relation to my friend Erik Jussila?"

"I inquired. They don't believe so."

"I'll see him at breakfast and ask him then. This Aina Jussila, she must be the evil, ugly, elderly sister, like in a children's tale," Niskanen postulated.

"Not at all," the farmer mumbled.

"She's attractive?"

"I guess so. Not so different from Katriina, as far as looks go. But testier. More resolute."

"You mean stubborn. A stubborn, attractive girl. Just my type. You know how I like a challenge."

"Like starting your own blacksmithing business in Vermont, when you can barely speak English?" Stranden quipped, alluding to the fact that this journey was Niskanen's second attempt to establish a new life in the United States.

"So you hold experimentation against a man, eh, Stranden? I did the best I could, but those damned conservative Yankees never gave me a fair chance. My work was lower-priced and of higher quality than any other forge

18

around Rutland, but it didn't matter. My accent did me in. They marked me as an outsider."

Juho Stranden was tired. His mind sought the solitude of sleep.

"All the same, Aina Jussila would be more of a challenge for you than trying to convince stodgy Vermonters to buy your horseshoes."

A period of silence ensued. There was no discernible motion to the ship.

"You say the older sister is beautiful?"

Stranden was near sleep and answered out of reflex. "They both are. Get some sleep. I'll introduce you to Aina in the morning," he whispered.

"A true friend, Juho Stranden. You are a true friend. Good night."

"Good night."

Prologue
(Part Three)

A raven-like shriek echoed through the interior compartments of the ocean liner. Steel objected as the ship's hull scraped against a submerged object.

"What the hell was that?" Juho Stranden whispered from his bed, an edge of concern overlaying his words.

Juha Niskanen awoke from a solid sleep, raised his head, and struck the top of his skull on the metal frame of Stranden's bunk.

"Goddamn it," the Finnish blacksmith cursed.

"What's wrong?" Juho asked as he tossed bed covers off his body, swung his legs over the edge of the bed, and dropped to the floor.

"I hit my goddamn head on your bunk," Niskanen muttered.

"We've got bigger problems, I'll wager, than whether you have a bump on your noggin or not," the farmer fretted. "Something's wrong." "Sounded like a collision to me," Niskanen observed. "Maybe we hit another ship."

Stranden fumbled in the dark for the light switch. His fingers found the button. Illumination flooded the chamber. The Finn pulled his trousers over his woolen underwear, tucked a wool shirt into the waist of the trousers, pulled on his socks and his shoes, and grabbed his coat.

"I'm going up top to see what happened."

"Not without me, you're not," Niskanen advised, swinging down from his berth. In quick succession, the smith donned pants, a sweater, a Mackinaw, and work boots.

The hallway was quiet. No other passengers stirred.

"Should we wake the others?" Stranden asked, his eyes riveted on the face of his companion as they walked the narrow corridor.

20

"Let's wait and see what's up," Niskanen urged.

"What about Erik?" Juho Stranden asked, referring to Niskanen's friend Erik Jussila.

"Him, I should wake."

Niskanen knocked on the door to Jussila's cabin. The portal opened slowly.

"Erik, something's happened."

Erik Jussila appeared in the doorway, his pale white wrists, feet, head, and neck the only portions of his body not covered by dingy long underwear.

"What's that you say?"

"Wake up and see your death," the blacksmith said with quiet authority.

"We think the ship hit something, or was hit," Stranden said hastily, glaring at Niskanen, unsettled that the man was inflaming the situation. "Get dressed. We'll meet you on the Boat Deck," Stranden added.

"I'll wake the others and then join you," Jussila replied.

Stranden nodded. He and Niskanen began to make their way up a series of ladders and stairways to the Boat Deck.

A significant crowd was milling nervously on an open deck near the vessel's stern. Stranden pulled out his pocket watch. It was shortly before midnight. He spotted the Jussila sisters.

"Katriina," the farmer shouted, advancing through the congregation of immigrants. Twenty or so Finns had gathered near the starboard lifeboats.

Stranden stopped next to Katriina and Aina Jussila. Aina looked at him. Fear clouded her face.

"Mr. Stranden," the older Jussila sister whispered.

Juha Niskanen followed his friend. The smith stopped behind the big Finn, looked at the two women, took in the beauty of Aina Jussila in the briefest of interludes, and nudged Stranden gently with an elbow.

"This is Juha Niskanen, a blacksmith. He's on his second trip to America," Juho advised, in response to his friend's prodding.

21

"Pleased to meet you," Niskanen said, removing his cap, a shabby stocking hat of distressed wool. "Juho has told me how much he admires you both," the Finn stammered. "For making this long journey alone," he added for clarity.

The women didn't acknowledge Niskanen's introduction. Their ears strained to hear news of the ship's condition. Another Finn, eighteen-year-old Anna Turja, was repeating news she had learned from one of the English officers:

"We've hit an iceberg. At full speed. They say we're sinking and that we'll need to take to the boats," Turja repeated to the small knot of Finnish passengers gathered around her.

"My boys," a middle-aged woman moaned, "my boys, Ernesti and Jaako, are not up here yet."

Aina stepped towards the distraught woman.

"Mrs. Panula, your boys are missing?" she asked.

"Only the two oldest. Juha, he's seven, Urho, he's two, and Eino, just a baby at eleven months, are all over there, with our babysitter, Sanni Riihivuori. She's a good girl. She's singing to them and playing games to keep them occupied. But my two oldest, they're not on deck."

The older woman broke down, sobbing. Aina and Katriina Jussila assisted Mrs. Panula into an empty deck chair. Anna Turja offered the stricken mother a clean linen handkerchief.

"Thank you," Mrs. Panula said, wiping her eyes. "I shouldn't be so worried. They say we have plenty of time, but I lost a son in Finland to the drowning. I don't want to lose another."

Katriina stood up.

"We'll find your boys, Mrs. Panula," Katriina said. "Mr. Stranden and his friend, Aina and I. We'll go back down and find them for you."

Aina grasped the sleeve of her sister's overcoat and whispered, "Do you think that's wise?"

Katriina nodded an affirmation and turned to Juho.

"What say you, Mr. Stranden? The boys are in the single men's quarters, back near where you and..." There was a pause. "What is your name again, sir?" she asked Niskanen.

"Juha Niskanen."

"Ah, yes, Mr. Niskanen. The boys are near where you were berthed. It shouldn't be too difficult a task to find them."

"The single men's quarters are at the other end of the ship and five or six decks down," Juho Stranden observed. "Do we know how long we've got?"

Aina looked at the farmer:

"They say several hours."

"All right, then, let's go," Niskanen interjected before Stranden could protest.

The older woman described her sons and advised the four Finns as to where her boys were berthed.

"You are angels," Mrs. Panula whispered. "Angels."

The search party was unable to return to the bow of the ship by the way Stranden and Niskanen had come up. Crew had been placed at the entrances to the upper decks. Gates had been locked in place to bar the panicked escape of second and third class passengers, nearly all immigrants, from below.

"Hurry," Niskanen urged. "I took this corridor a day ago. It avoids the regular stairways and ladders."

The women followed the men, their skirts shifting and bustling as they moved. The voices of other passengers, carried by the ship's ventilation system, reached the searchers as they negotiated their way towards the bow.

"Are you kin to a fellow by the name of Erik Jussila, from Elimaki?" Niskanen inquired of Katriina.

"Not that I know of," Katriina Jussila replied.

"I don't believe so," Aina added. "Why?"

"He's a friend, that's all. Thought there might be some connection."

"How will they get out?" Katriina asked, changing the subject, acknowledging the voices of other passengers echoing through the ship's vents.

"They won't. And we won't either if we don't hurry," Juho Stranden said.

They became lost. Niskanen's sense of direction was impaired by the urgency of their quest. The group came to a solid bulkhead, a dead end.

"You must return to the Boat Deck," Stranden directed the women. "We'll try to make it to the boys another way."

"Are you sure?" Aina asked. "I'm not certain Katriina and I know the way back."

She glanced at her younger sister. Katriina appeared confident: "I know the way."

"You're certain?" Juho Stranden asked.

"Yes. You find the boys and get them to their mother. We'll be fine. We'll meet you on deck and take the same lifeboat."

The vessel shifted.

"You better get back up top," Niskanen advised.

The group entered a hallway. The women moved towards a ladder.

"Wait," Stranden implored.

Katriina stopped. The farmer joined her.

"This ladder will lead you to the Stewards' Area. Take the stairway between the boilers to "A" Deck. You'll come to the Grand Staircase. That'll lead you to the boats," Stranden said.

The woman nodded.

"I'll be waiting for you," Katriina replied.

"This is no time to fawn over your farmer," Aina admonished.

Katriina Jussila kissed Stranden on the cheek, shrugged her shoulders, and began climbing the ladder.

"She's sweet on you, that's for sure," Juha Niskanen offered as the men entered a service corridor leading to the prow of the ship. "And her sister seems just my type."

"We better move if we want to find those boys," Stranden said, ignoring his companion's observation.

The Finns quickened their pace. A crowd of single men surged towards them. The sea of opposing passengers became impassable.

"We're never going to break through this throng. Look at their eyes: they know they're dead men. They'll do anything to get out."

Stranden flattened himself against a wall. A phalanx of immigrants from third class clogged the passageway.

"What'll we do?" Niskanen asked.

"Get the hell out while we can, and hope the Panula boys have the common sense to do the same," the farmer stated. "Stay close to me."

Stranden waded into the stream of men. Propelled by legs well-developed after years behind the plow, the farmer began to open a path through the panicked swarm. At the top of the Second Class Stairway, an ever-increasing crowd crushed two crewmembers that had been posted to hold back the passengers' exodus. The sailors were trampled in the melee, their cries drowned out by the murmuring unrest of immigrants fleeing towards open sky. Stranden forced his weary body, his thighs trembling from exertion, onto the Boat Deck, with Juha Niskanen right behind him.

Hundreds of nervous passengers, including Erik Jussila, congregated on the Lifeboat Deck. Despite an atmosphere of tension, the assembly of Finns remained calm, without evidence of panic, even as the vessel trembled; even as it became obvious that the ship was dying.

"Mrs. Panula," Stranden said upon locating the woman, surrounded by her three youngest sons and the nanny, Miss Riihivuori. "Have you seen your older boys?"

The mother, her face aged far beyond her forty-one years, shook her head sadly: "No, they've not made it up."

"I'm sorry," Stranden said. "We got close, but the crowd was stubborn. We had no means of breaking through their number."

"They may still make it out yet," Juha Niskanen added.

"Yes, that's possible," agreed Sanni Riihivuori. "They may be on another part of the ship, getting into another boat."

Mrs. Panula's mood brightened: "Sanni, would you take a look on the port side and see if they are there, by the other lifeboats?" the anxious mother asked.

"Surely. I'll take a look and be right back," the nanny responded.

"Make it quick," Niskanen urged the young woman. "Looks like they're getting ready to load the boats."

The crew worked feverishly. Officers brandished side arms, the weapons connected to their belts by lanyards, to dissuade violence. As the crowd moved towards the boat stations, the ship trembled so fiercely that the painted railings and lifeboat apparatus shook as if caught in a hurricane.

Sanni Riihivuori entered the crowd and disappeared.

Juha Niskanen turned to Mrs. Panula. "In the meanwhile, you best get your three youngest to the front of the line. Women and children go first. That's the law of the sea."

"I'll wait for my boys," Maria Panula said quietly.

"I'll wait too," Anna Turja added.

"Not a good idea," Juho Stranden advised. "From the looks of it, we're short on boats. You may only get one chance to escape."

"They said this vessel was unsinkable," Mrs. Panula lamented.

"They were wrong," Juha Niskanen said, bracing against the undulating horde of passengers. "They certainly and most assuredly were wrong."

Prologue
(Part Four)

"I thought you knew the way," Aina Jussila whispered as she followed her younger sister through a dimly lighted hallway.

Water dampened the women's stockings as they trudged towards the front of the ship, unaware that the vessel was sinking bow-first into the sea.

"Follow me," Katriina insisted, slogging through the icy water with determination. "There's a ladder up ahead that should lead us to the Boat Deck."

It was well after 1:30pm on April 15, 1912. The gash to the starboard side of the steamship had allowed millions of gallons of seawater to surge into the vessel's forward sections. While the Finnish women struggled to find a route to the lifeboats located many decks above them, significant numbers of second and third class passengers waited patiently in the common areas of the lower decks for evacuation.

A ladder. The women began to climb in anticipation of attaining the Boat Deck. Their progress was made more difficult by the angle of the ship's decline.

"This way," Katriina urged excitedly. "This is the way I remember."

"I hope so," Aina responded, her breathing labored, the hem of her skirt and petticoat laden with salt water.

"Where are my boys?" Mrs. Panula wailed. "Where are Ernesti and Jaako?"

The woman was seated on a bench with her three youngest children in close proximity. Sanni Riihivuori was not with the Panula Family. The young nanny had not returned from the port side of the ship. Anna Turja stood next to Mrs. Panula, holding the older woman's hand.

"You must enter a lifeboat," Juho Stranden urged Anna Turja. "There aren't many seats left. We can't find the Panula boys or the Jussila sisters."

Juha Niskanen and Erik Jussila arrived out of breath after inspecting the port side of the vessel.

"No luck. We couldn't find them," Erik Jussila observed.

Anna Turja glanced at the lifeboats.

"You best find a spot in one of the boats," Anna Turja urged Maria Panula. "We haven't much time."

Tears welled in the eyes of the older woman.

"I can't leave my boys," Mrs. Panula whispered. "I can't."

Anna nodded gravely before joining a line of passengers waiting to enter Lifeboat No. 15. One seat remained unclaimed when Miss Turja arrived at the head of the line.

"In you go, Miss," an Irish sailor said, lifting the woman over the wooden gunwale of the boat with ease.

"All clear," another deckhand shouted.

Steel cables began to lower Lifeboat No. 15 over the side of the stricken ship. The crowd pressed. An officer brandished a sidearm. An English businessman, his face pockmarked from long-departed acne, rushed towards the officer.

Crack.

The aggressor stopped in disbelief. Women wailed.

"Stand back, or my next shot won't be a warning," the officer commanded as he scrambled over the side of the departing lifeboat. "There'll be another boat available momentarily," the officer advised.

Stranden, Niskanen, and Erik Jussila watched the lifeboat descend. Most of the passengers on the Life Boat Deck remained calm. Occasionally, soft sobbing, followed by kind words and gentle admonitions to "be patient," could be discerned coming from the less stoic passengers.

"There's only one boat left," Juha Niskanen whispered. "Lifeboat No. 9."

"Let's go," Stranden urged.

"I'm not ready to drown," Erik Jussila said to no one in particular. "I don't know how to swim, and my life belt's back in my cabin."

"We're headed to Lifeboat No. 9," Niskanen advised Mrs. Panula.

"Thank you for your kindness. If you find my boys, send them to me, Mr. Niskanen," Mrs. Panula said. "Please send them to me."

The ship shuddered. Rivets popped free. The vessel was disintegrating.

"Don't forget to send Miss Riihivuori, my nanny, back to me as well," the stricken woman added.

"Yes, ma'am," Stranden promised, his words sounding confident despite his rising concern that they were too late to claim a seat on a lifeboat.

The men pushed their way through the crowd waiting to board Lifeboat No. 9. Miss Riihivuori and the Panula boys were not among those standing compliantly in line.

"Lifeboat No. 9 is being launched," Juha Niskanen whispered, "and I don't see another one."

"Then we need to get on this one," Juho Stranden replied.

The men raced down a stairway. As Lifeboat No. 9 passed them on its descent to the sea, Stranden, Jussila, and Niskanen mounted a railing, leaped through the night air, and landed on passengers already installed in the seats of the boat.

"Get the hell out of my lifeboat!" the officer in charge commanded.

The Finns remained in their seats. The officer removed his revolver from its holster.

"For God's sake, man," an American sitting with his wife and teenaged daughter urged, "let them stay. We've got room. We can take three more passengers."

The American girl began to sob. The girl's mother wrapped her arms protectively around the stricken child.

"I'm in charge here," the officer bellowed, his thumb contemplating the hammer of his gun; fear clearly etched in his voice.

29

"I agree with the Yank," added an Irishman sitting behind the Finns. "We've got space. Let the men stay."

Murmurs of agreement swept through the boat. The officer relaxed. The lifeboat continued its hurried descent.

An hour later, the occupants of Lifeboat No. 9 watched the disintegration of the once imperious ocean liner from a distance. Screams filled the night air. The lifeboat passed through desperate gaggles of passengers treading water. Those floating in the sea would eventually be recovered, but they would not be alive. Their bodies would remain accessible for retrieval and eventual burial by virtue of their life vests.

The officer commanding Life Boat No. 9 ignored the panicked entreaties of the people in the water, and the angry recriminations of the passengers in his boat. He refused to pick up survivors. The crew in the boat rowed with vigor until the vessel cleared the last of the dying. A short distance from the stricken ship, Lifeboat No. 9 stopped to witness the end. The aft portion of the luxury liner began to rise, cantilevered by the weight of the vessel's sinking bow. The entirety of the doomed vessel remained illuminated by the ship's electric generators, even as the ocean liner's stern broke free of the sea's grasp.

"My God," the wife of the American whispered from her dry perch in the lifeboat. "My God."

The three Finns in Lifeboat No. 9 watched helplessly as the inordinate weight of the vessel's bow fractured the ship in two. After separating, the stern bobbed in the cold water for a time before rising once more, forced upwards by the weight of the vessel's water-laden bow. The survivors gasped in unison as the ship's stern hesitated at its vertical apex before following the bow of the *Titanic* into unfathomable water.

Prologue
(Notes)

John Panula

John (Juha) Panula waited for his wife Maria and his five sons – Ernesti, Jaako, Juha, Urho, and Eino – in Coal Center, Pennsylvania. His family never arrived. Though the bodies of the six members of John's family were never found, a Canadian cable-laying ship, *Mackay-Bennett*, did retrieve the remains of an unidentified infant boy. The child was interned in Nova Scotia. The crew of the Canadian ship was so touched by the child's death that they constructed a stone memorial to the child and installed a copper medallion on his coffin, inscribed, "Our Babe."

John Panula was devastated by the loss of his family and returned to Finland. Some time later, he married Sannalissa Uprinen. Confronted by the same economic realities in Finland that had forced his original emigration, John Panula and his second wife returned to America. He settled in Northern Minnesota where he farmed and raised three children.

Susanna "Sanni" Riihivuori

Only twenty-two years old when she traveled on the *Titanic*, Sanni is often listed as the sixth child of John and Maria Panula. In reality, she was a neighbor of the Panulas. It is believed that Sanni agreed to serve as the Panulas' maid and nanny upon the family's reunification in Coal Center, Pennsylvania. Like many of the third class immigrant passengers of *Titanic*, her body was never recovered.

Juha Niskanen

Juha (John) Niskanen was thirty-nine years old when the *Titanic* sank. He remained in the United States following his treatment for exposure, eventually settling in Cazadero, California. Haunted by the events of April 15th, 1912, John Niskanen committed suicide on August 13, 1927.

Erik Jussila

Erik Jussila was, so far as the records show, no kin of the Jussila sisters. At the time of the *Titanic's* sinking, he was thirty-one years old and bound for Monessen, Pennsylvania, to work the steel mills located there. As a single man, he was denied access to three lifeboats before leaping into Lifeboat No. 9 with Stranden and Niskanen. Some accounts place him in Lifeboat No. 15 with Anna Turja. The voyage on the *Titanic* was Jussila's second across the Atlantic to America. After the sinking, Jussila convalesced at St. Vincent's Hospital before proceeding to Pennsylvania. Interviews given by Jussila to newspaper reporters reveal that Mr. Jussila disputed the time-honored notion that members of the *Titanic's* orchestra continued to play on the Lifeboat Deck as the vessel sank.

Aina and Katriina Jussila

The Jussila sisters perished in the *Titanic's* sinking on April 15, 1912. Their bodies were never found.

Anna Turja

Anna was eighteen years old at the time of the *Titanic* disaster. On the maiden voyage of the "unsinkable ship," she shared a cabin with Maria Panula, the three youngest Panula children, and Sanni Riihivuori. Anna did indeed make it into Lifeboat No. 15, while all of her traveling companions perished. After the sinking, Anna's family in Finland was advised that she was missing. It wasn't until six weeks later, after she'd safely reached her brother in Ashtabula, Ohio, that the mistake was corrected. Anna would eventually become one of the best known of the *Titanic* survivors. She settled in

Ohio, married Emil Lundi, and had seven children. She entertained John Panula on several occasions. What Anna and John discussed during those visits is not recorded.

Despite living a long and fruitful life in her adopted country, Anna Turja Lundi couldn't escape her history. Newspaper reporters routinely interviewed Mrs. Lundi on the anniversary of the *Titanic* disaster. She also recalled the tragedy for her seven children, always emphasizing that it was unclear to her "why God would spare a poor Finnish girl when all those rich people drowned."

Anna Turja Lundi died in Long Beach, California, in 1982. She was 89 years old.

Juho Stranden

After being rescued from Lifeboat No. 9, Juho (John) Stranden was treated at St. Vincent's Hospital in New York City. He returned to Finland after recovering from exposure and hypothermia. He moved from his hometown of Kitee, Finland to Pyhaselka, Finland, in 1925, where it is believed he lived out his days. Juho Stranden never made it to Duluth, Minnesota, and never met fellow Finnish immigrant, Anders Alhomaki.

Suomalaiset:
People of the Marsh

Prelude
September 30th, 1918

Autumn. Shadows sway back and forth, back and forth across the yellow grass of an open field one mile north of Lester Park in the East End of Duluth, Minnesota. The man's body forms a solid black silhouette against the gold, crimson, and brown foliage. He moves ably through the landscape on a well-traveled path. There is no sun. Gray clouds seal the dawn, trapping heavy air; air filled with the speculation of rain, against the barren escarpment rising above Lake Superior.

Water tumbles across the rocks and boulders of the Lester River, the quick-paced stream white and vibrant against the black basalt underlying its course. The wind quickens. Shadows dance. The man picks up his pace along the ridge overlooking the river because he senses rain. He knows the fickle climate of Northeastern Minnesota. For the entirety of his life he's faced the unpredictable patterns associated with living next to the largest fresh water lake in the world. He has no interest in slogging through a storm in a light jacket and his best shoes. He is not dressed for inclement weather. He is dressed for a casual stroll through the burgeoning aspen and birch forest that has established itself along the stream.

The man stops. Storm clouds pass overhead and cause an obliteration of light. The distraction draws the hiker's eyes away from considering his feet. As he approaches his destination, a tiny cabin hidden in the forest surrounding the Lester River, the man notes that someone has stolen the rudimentary clothesline running from his cabin to an adjacent spruce tree. The theft compels the man to gauge his surroundings. A short distance from the cabin, the man discovers a body dangling from a gnarled branch of a slender birch tree by the purloined rope. The stricken man's complexion matches the color of the sky framing the hangman's tree. The hue of the unfortunate soul's skin confirms that he is dead. The dead man's eyes are closed to the world. His narrow head rests upon his chest. His clothing is in disarray. The tips of the dead man's scruffy work boots tantalize recently fallen leaves, as the lifeless body moves to the cadence of the wind.

Chapter 1
August, 2001

Thunder Bay, Ontario, unlike Duluth, Minnesota, is not built upon the ridges and promontories of the Sawtooth Mountains. The Canadian city, located one hundred and thirty miles north of Duluth, occupies the flat, fertile plain of the Kaministiquia River. Hills rise in the distance and encircle the city. The Sleeping Giant and other bluffs of statuesque proportions stand imperiously above the shimmering waters of Lake Superior where the eastern edge of the city meets the lake.

Molly McAdams, a doctoral candidate at Lakehead University in Thunder Bay, unlimbers her arms and legs before straddling her mountain bike. It is near dusk. Shadows lengthen as the sun declines. The woman has put in an exhausting day examining DNA samples. A helmet dangles from the bicycle's handle bars by its webbing. Molly removes the headgear and places it firmly on her head. Strapping the helmet in place, the woman nods to a professor, someone she knows. The man, his head bald, the skin of his skull crimson from too much summer sun, waves in response. The professor does not stop walking. His pace remains quick, as if something of great importance propels him forward.

The young woman's house, a small frame cottage she shares with three other graduate students, is located on Rita, a side street located across town near the northern shore of Boulevard Lake. As Molly pulls out of the University parking lot she shifts gears and accelerates away from her work. Hot wind, air permeated with the sulfurous discharge of the local paper mill, greets the woman as she turns onto Oliver Road. She heads towards the business district of what was once the city of Port Arthur, which, now, along with the city of Fort William, forms the city of Thunder Bay.

Traffic is light until Oliver intersects with Court. Following Court through downtown Port Arthur past vintage buildings and vacant lots strewn with debris, the woman encounters a thoroughfare clogged with vehicles waiting to advance. She deviates onto the sidewalk, deftly missing a gaggle of children on their way to the Waverly Public Library, and scoots ahead of the traffic jam.

Molly rides like this, to and from the University, nearly every day of the year, excepting the days when the snow is too deep or the rain is too insistent. She does not own a car. She believes a car would impart too much freedom. Too much freedom would distract her from her goal. She is devoted to her pursuit of a doctoral degree at the University. The project she is working on weighs heavily upon her mind as she wheels north on Lyons Boulevard and follows Boulevard Lake's curving shoreline. Though her eyes are open and the scenery is lovely, she does not see.

I'm at a loss to understand why they came, the young researcher muses as she passes joggers exercising along the lakeshore and lovers embracing quietly on benches overlooking the calm green waters of the inland pond. *Why leave behind everything: your home, your family, your language, your culture, for the unknown?*

The work that captivates her, that occupies nearly every waking moment of Molly McAdams's life, involves solving a great mystery. Not the mystery of why her ancestors emigrated from Finland to North America, but the mystery of a dead child's lineage.

Perspiration slips down the angular structure of the young woman's face. She peddles faster. Tufts of long blond hair escape the confines of her riding helmet and flutter in the pungent air of the paper mill town. The young scientist achieves a cadence. She is near home. Tomorrow, she will delve further into the mystery. Tomorrow will bring her closer to unlocking the secrets of the child's tomb.

Chapter 2
Before

The river flows through a rugged canyon. Asphalt-colored water spreads out below the rapids like a shimmering blanket, before merging with the Earth's largest fresh water lake. Upon arriving at this confluence, the St. Louis River, a stream of foreboding content, has traveled nearly two hundred miles from its source and has drained nearly four thousand square miles of land.

This basin was once the home to the Dakota (Sioux) people. With the arrival of Europeans in what would become the United States and Canada, other indigenous tribes, most importantly the Six Nations of the Iroquois, were forced west. The Six Nations in turn displaced the Ojibwe (Anishinaabe). The Ojibwe themselves moved into what is now Wisconsin and Minnesota, where they collided with the Dakota, and where the tribes fought pitched battles for control of the St. Louis River Valley.

French fur traders and explorers, among them Daniel Greysolon Sieur du Lhut, arrived on the heels of the Ojibwe. Du Lhut sailed across Lake Superior, landing on a sandy spit of land, the natural barrier between river and lake that would became known as Minnesota Point. On June 27, 1679, Du Lhut claimed all of the Lake Superior Basin, including the St. Louis River Valley, for the King of France. The French explorer negotiated a peace treaty between the Dakota and the Ojibwe, which resulted in the further westward migration of the Dakota. Subsequent to the French and Indian War, all of New France, including the lands surrounding the St. Louis River, became British Territory.

As a result of a cartographer's error following the British defeat in the Revolutionary War the St. Louis River Valley came into the possession of the United States. British mapmaker John Mitchell described Lake of the Woods, a large body of water located to the north of the St. Louis River, as the source of Lake Superior via an estuary noted as "Long Lake." "Long Lake" is actually a river: the Pigeon River. Under the mistaken impression that "Long Lake" (the Pigeon River) was the source of Lake Superior, the Pigeon River became the international boundary between Canada and the United States at the conclusion of the War. This mistake designated the St. Louis River Valley as American soil.

Beginning with the French through their Northwest Trading Company, continuing with the English through the Hudson Bay Company, and eventually ending with John Jacob Astor's American Fur Company, fur-trading posts were established at the foot of the final rapids of the St. Louis River, in an area known as Fond du Lac. From antiquity, the watershed of the river was covered by white pine, red pine, spruce, and cedar forest. An abundance of fur-bearing mammals existed in these woodlands, resulting in profitable commerce between the Ojibwe and the white fur traders located at Fond du Lac. Moose and woodland caribou, along with black bear, otter, beaver, mink, lynx, martin, fisher, and the occasional cougar, occupied the forests and marshlands bordering the river. White-tailed deer would arrive in greater numbers only after the virgin forest was gone.

With the establishment of the American Fur Company's post on the banks of the river, Protestant missionaries arrived. The native peoples had been previously exposed to Catholicism during the French occupation of the area. Roman Catholic priests originally brought the Word to the indigenous Ojibwe and Dakota. In the middle of the 19th Century, Edmund Ely, a Presbyterian layman studying for his divinity degree, settled at Fond du Lac with his wife, Catherine. Their mission was to teach English grammar, arithmetic, and Protestant Christianity to the Ojibwe. Indian trader and surveyor George Stuntz arrived shortly after the Elys. Stuntz built a home on Minnesota Point, which he used as his base from which to survey the shoreline of St. Louis Bay and the surrounding area. The land Stuntz platted would eventually become the city of Duluth, named after the French nobleman who first claimed it for the Europeans, Daniel Greysolon Sieur du Lhut.

When Minnesota gained its statehood in 1858 the town site of Duluth claimed but a handful of residents. However, the village grew rapidly, fueled by a lumber industry that systematically clear-cut the great forests of the St. Louis River watershed.

The first trees felled were the magnificent white pines lining the hills overlooking St. Louis Bay. As late as 1870, the sloping shoulders of what in the prehistoric past had been the Sawtooth Mountains, retained virgin timber of gigantic dimensions. As Duluth grew, these legacy trees were cut. By the 1890s, the lumber industry was removing 150,000,000 board feet of lumber per year from the woodlands surrounding the St. Louis, Cloquet, Beaver, Otter, Paleface, Savanna, and Whiteface Rivers.

At the beginning of this great devastation, there were no Finns living in Northeastern Minnesota. Immigration from Finland to North America was rare prior to the 1890s. The first documented influx of Finnish men and women to the New World had taken place in 1638, at the end of the Thirty Years' War, when two Swedish vessels landed at what is now Wilmington, Delaware, proclaiming the area "New Sweden." Peter Minuit, the Dutch adventurer and businessman who had earlier coordinated the colonization of New York ("New Amsterdam"), had been enlisted by the Swedish government to found a colony in North America. Finland, being a province within the Kingdom of Sweden at the time, supplied a portion of the immigrants to New Sweden over the course of the colony's existence.

Pressure from competing Dutch and English settlers ended Sweden's North American experiment in 1655. New Sweden's remaining Finns were absorbed into the general population of the British Colonies. Today, a monument to this first wave of Finnish immigration remains in Philadelphia, Pennsylvania, where the congregation of Gloria Dei Lutheran Church, a church founded by Finnish Lutherans from Sweden in 1646, still holds services.

Despite being connected to the Swedes for over six hundred years (from the 13th Century until the conclusion of the Napoleonic Wars in 1809, when Finland became part of the Russian Empire), the Finns remained distinctly separate from the Swedes in language and culture.

The Finnish People belong to the Finno-Ugric ethnic group, a designation that places them linguistically with the Hungarians and Estonians. Genealogically, the Finnish people are believed to have originated near the Volga River, where an infusion of German, Scandinavian, and Slavic influences combined to form the Finns' unique heritage.

Another small wave of Finnish immigration to the United States took place in the 1860s. Clusters of Finnish farmers and their families settled on the prairie, founding New York Mills, Franklin, Holmes City, and several other small communities in Western Minnesota. However, the most significant influx of Finnish immigrants to North America took place after copper was discovered in the Upper Peninsula of Michigan, and after iron ore was found on Minnesota's Vermilion Range in the late 1860s.

Originally solicited by Norwegian mining interests to work in Norway, rural Finns, men largely unfamiliar with mining (being primarily farmers by occupation), were enticed by the Quincy Mining Company to emigrate from Norway to work the copper mines of Northern Michigan. What began as a trickle of Finnish men, and later, women, immigrating to the United States became, with the imposition of Russification upon the Finns by Czar Nicholas II, a tidal wave. No self-respecting Finn would kow-tow to the Czar and speak Russian. Czar Nicholas II's efforts to subdue the recalcitrant Finns by cultural erosion, at a point when Finnish music, art, and literature were beginning to blossom, reinforced the notion held by many Finns that emigration was the only viable alternative to the extinction of their independence.

Though primarily unskilled laborers, the emigrant Finns were, by and large, literate. Most adult emigrants from Finland had completed at least *Kansakoulu* (public elementary school) before arriving in the United States. The Finns were better educated and more independent of thought than many other immigrant groups. These cultural attributes came under attack when Nicholas II ascended the throne as Czar. Beginning in 1898, the Czar imposed restrictions upon the Finns' freedom of education, association, and political organization previously enjoyed by the Finnish people for more than seven hundred years.

Even after Finland's ties with Sweden were severed in 1809, the Finns had been allowed to function autonomously within the Russian Empire. Czar Nicholas II's Manifesto of 1898 eliminated this special status, however. Nicholas installed N.I. Bobrikov as Governor-General of Finland in the hopes of controlling the unpredictable Finns. This regime change, together with the Czar's abolition of Finland's military and the mandatory conscription of Finnish men into the Russian Army and Navy, resulted in furious dissent by the Finns. This dissent, accentuated by famine, crop failures, and severe unemployment, compelled a mass exodus of young men and women from Finland to America. By the time Bobrikov was assassinated on June 16, 1904 by a disgruntled Finnish revolutionary, emigration to the United States was already on the decline, having peaked in 1902 with the departure of 23,000 Finns.

The Finnish immigrants to North America, unskilled in trades or business but educated and idealistic, settled in great numbers in Upper Peninsula Michigan and Northeastern Minnesota. They settled in these inhospitable regions because economic opportunities abounded. It was here, amongst the tall timber and the iron- and copper-bearing rock, that a man could make a living without fear of being thrust into someone else's war. The Finns called themselves *Suomalaiset*; "people of the marsh" in the English language. One of these immigrants was a man named Anders Alhomaki. This, then, is his story.

Chapter 3
Spring, 1914

Wind lashed the rigging of the passenger ship *America* as it battled Lake Superior. Thirty-mile-an-hour gusts agitated the water. Thirty-three-year-old Anders Alhomaki held onto a brass rail with one hand and grasped a beer glass in the other. The Finnish immigrant miner had recently been terminated from his employment with the Quincy Mining Company in Houghton, Michigan and was now a passenger on the *America*, a packet steamer making slow progress from Isle Royale, the largest island in Lake Superior, to Duluth, Minnesota. It was a route well-known to the crew of the boat, a vessel whose primary mission was to transport supplies and passengers up and down Lake Superior's North Shore.

Thick smoke poured from *America*'s solitary stack as a coal boiler labored to push the vessel through troughs of black water. Anders Alhomaki's left hand held fast to the glass of People's Beer, a lager brewed in West Duluth, as the deck of the boat alternated between rising and falling with the seas.

"Rough go, eh?" said a big Canadian seated next to Alhomaki.

The stranger's broad shoulders crowded the miner as the two men nursed their beers.

Alhomaki nodded his long head. His black hair, coiled as tightly as an African's and worn short and plastered to his white scalp by hair tonic, shone in the gaslight. His brown eyes, so dark that they appeared as black ingots in the middle of his face, gleamed brightly. He was, like many of his Finnish countrymen, a quiet man, an unassuming man, when in the company of strangers.

"Cat got your tongue?" the Canadian continued, his enormous face turned towards the smaller man. "Where you from?"

"Finland. I came from Finland."

America's bow slammed down hard. Bottles rattled on the shelves, where wire mesh held the containers of liquor in place. The lights over the bar flickered, causing a momentary parade of shadows.

"No, not what country. I mean, now. Where are you from? Where are you headed?" the redheaded giant asked, wiping a hand on his woolen dress pants.

Both men were dressed for traveling in nearly identical black suit jackets, black trousers, and black dress shoes. Anders Alhomaki's clothing was inferior in quality, purchased at a local clothier in Houghton, Michigan, only a day before he had uprooted himself to return to Minnesota. Alhomaki's loss of employment in the underground copper mine had not compelled his move; he was not simply following the westward migration of his fellow miners. Other considerations, considerations that had nothing to do with economics, had forced the Finn to leave Michigan and return to Minnesota. In fact, the miner had by-passed newer mines located on the Gogebic Range near Hurley, Wisconsin, and Ironwood, Michigan, to make his way to Duluth.

Alhomaki had boarded the wooden passenger steamer, *Sailor Boy*, in Houghton. *Sailor Boy* had traversed the Keweenaw Waterway and ventured out into the lake, docking at Rock Harbor, Isle Royale. From Isle Royale, the largest island in Lake Superior and the site of several isolated Norwegian fishing villages, Alhomaki found passage on the *America* to Duluth. *America* was twice the size of the diminutive *Sailor Boy*, a statistic that would not save the *America* from joining *Sailor Boy* at the bottom of Lake Superior in the future.

"Houghton. I worked for Quincy," Anders Alhomaki finally replied.

Alhomaki's English was heavily influenced by his Finnish roots. His heritage, along with the heritage of other immigrants to the area – the Scandinavians, the Irish, the French, the Italians, the Slavs – would create the unique dialect of English spoken by those living in the Lake Superior Basin.

"I got laid off. It was time to move on."

The bearded Canadian's ruddy face broke into a smile.

"I'm George McAdams from Port Arthur," the stranger advised, extending his hand. "Got sidetracked in Copper Harbor chasing a skirt, if you know what I mean," McAdams said through a broad grin. "Caught a ride on a fishing trawler out of Copper Harbor to the island and then booked my passage to Duluth on this old tub."

Alhomaki nodded and shook the Canadian's enormous paw. The Finn studied the other man out of the corner of his eye.

I'd guess he's pushing fifty or better, the Finn surmised, *but he still has one hell of a grip.*

Anders Alhomaki didn't share with George McAdams his opinion as to the Canadian's age, or the rest of Anders Alhomaki's personal history. The Finn didn't relate, for example, that he had already tried his hand in Duluth, back when he had first arrived in America in May of 1908. There was no advantage, in the introspective Finn's view, to sharing too much information with a stranger. Still, Alhomaki's response revealed a sense of bitterness: "I've had enough of Houghton, enough of strikes and unions for awhile. It's time to leave when the children suffer for the sins of the fathers."

There was no need for Anders Alhomaki to explain to the Canadian what he meant. It was May of 1914. Recent events involving the Italian Hall in Calumet, Michigan, right down the road from Houghton, were well known to anyone living around Lake Superior. A predictable tragedy had occurred in the midst of a violent and bloody labor dispute between the miners and the managers of the underground copper mines.

Eighty percent of the hard rock miners working the copper mines in Michigan's Upper Peninsula were Finns. Initiated by the extremist Western Federation of Miners, supported by the American Federation of Labor, the copper miners in the UP went on strike for higher wages and better working conditions on July 23, 1913. In response, the mine operators brought in security guards – in reality, thugs hired to break heads – from

48

the Waddell-Mahon Agency in New York. The local sheriff blessed this incursion by deputizing the security force. Tensions mounted. A group of deputized strikebreakers armed with shotguns and rifles opened up on a Finnish boarding house that was occupied not by striking miners, but by women and children. Luckily, there were no casualties. The miners responded in kind. Two strikebreakers were killed. The resulting investigation determined that the newly deputized security officers had been killed by their own men. Escalating violence caused the Governor of Michigan to deploy artillery, cavalry, and other units of the Michigan National Guard to Houghton.

Talks between the strikers and management had stalled. By December 24, 1913, tensions were mounting, not only between the workers and the bosses, but within the Finnish community itself. Though the Western Federation of Miners had contributed $100,000.00 to a strike fund, most miners and their families were left impoverished by the walkout. A Christmas Eve party was held at Italian Hall in Calumet in an effort to comfort the children of the strikers. During the festivities, someone, no one ever discovered whom, yelled "fire" inside Italian Hall, setting off a panicked stampede. In the melee, a large number of children rushed down a stairway towards an exit door, only to find that the door was chained from the outside. Seventy-four people, mostly children, forty-seven of that number being Finns, were trampled to death on the stairway.

The unionists blamed the Italian Hall disaster on conservative elements in the local population, specifically those Finns sympathetic to the position of the mine managers. These anti-strike elements called themselves the Citizen's Alliance. The grief-stricken mining families refused compensation raised by the Citizen's Alliance. In the aftermath of the disaster, the President of the Western Federation of Miners was kidnapped from a local hotel, beaten, dragged, and shot in the back, before being thrown on a train bound for Chicago.

Anders Alhomaki had been relatively uninvolved in the 1913 strike. He was not a "Red Finn," the moniker given to

49

left-wing Finns of Marxist or Socialist persuasion. Anders was not a conservative, either. He was, like many others of his age and occupation, a trade unionist. He participated in the strike because he belonged to the Western Federation of Miners. He was not a leader. He was a follower. Though literate, having completed secondary school back in Finland, he was an unassuming man who simply refused to report for work. Yet, when the strike ended without resolution of the miners' grievances in March of 1914, Alhomaki had found himself blacklisted by the Quincy Mining Company. He was not alone. There were no longer any positions for Finns in the mines of Upper Peninsula Michigan. And so, Anders Alhomaki returned to Duluth.

Alhomaki had arrived in America back in 1908. He had traveled to Ellis Island by steamship from England, and then by passenger train to the Union Pacific Depot in Duluth, where sixty trains a day stopped to disgorge their human freight. Once in Duluth, he had found work in the underground iron mines of the Vermilion Range, working the Soudan Mine near the shores of Lake Vermilion in Northeastern Minnesota.

Restricted to narrow veins of high content ore by surrounding greenstone, the Vermilion Range sustained three productive mines. The Soudan Mine in Soudan, Minnesota, and the Chandler and Pioneer Mines in nearby Ely were the most successful iron ore mines on the Vermilion Range and remained in operation from the 1880s until the 1960s. All three operations employed immigrant Finns by the thousands. These men worked strictly underground, carving mine shafts through the unyielding basalt of the Canadian Shield.

Though the Miners' Strike of June 1907 had allowed Anders Alhomaki to find work in Soudan, the Strike of 1907 didn't originate in the underground iron mines of the Vermilion Range, but as a walkout at the Johnson/Wentworth Sawmill in Cloquet, Minnesota.

Cloquet was (and still is) a logging and lumbering town located on the banks of the St. Louis River, just above the site of the old Fond du Lac fur trading post. In 1907, the mill workers in Cloquet sought a twenty percent increase in their daily wages. When the employers balked at the workers' demands, the mill's employees left their jobs. This walkout was followed by sympathy strikes at the Duluth, Missabe, and Northern Railway (later the Duluth, Mesabi, and Iron Range Railway), a regional carrier of iron ore. Dockworkers and harbor men soon followed suit, closing down the ports of Two Harbors and Duluth, Minnesota, and Superior, Wisconsin.

By July 20th, 1907, the iron mines of Northeastern Minnesota were idle, the miners having joined the strike to improve their own wages; wages that averaged between two dollars and ten cents and two dollars and forty cents (less supplies) per day. The situation deteriorated when the management companies of the affected mines refused to enter into discussions with the fledgling Western Federation of Miners, or its spokesman, a twenty-four year old Finnish Socialist by the name of John Valimaki.

Instead of contract negotiations, the management companies, led by Oliver Mining, advertised for laborers in the mountainous regions of Croatia, Serbia, Slovenia, and Montenegro, promising high wages and steady work for those who would immigrate. The combination of an influx of Slavic strikebreakers, together with an absence of strike relief money in the coffers of the affected trade unions, caused workers to trickle back to their jobs. First to relent were the dockworkers, followed by the open pit miners of the Independent Mining Company in Mountain Iron, Minnesota, where, uncharacteristically, a compromise between labor and management was hammered out. In turn, the sawyers and railroad employees gave in. By November of 1907, as Anders Alhomaki was preparing to leave Finland for the United States, most of the strikers had returned to their jobs. One group, however, did not: Finns identified during the strike as Socialists or Marxists, the so-called "Red Finns," supporters of John Valimaki, were blacklisted, just as Anders Alhomaki was five years later in the copper mines of Upper Michigan.

This blanket prohibition was not limited to Northeastern Minnesota. In retribution against the Finns, the mining companies disseminated lists of banned Finnish miners throughout North America, as far east as the coal

51

fields of West Virginia, and as far west as the copper mines of Montana.

Many of the blacklisted miners sought work in the forests as loggers. Others bought cheap land in rural St. Louis County and adjacent Carlton County, where they attempted to farm infertile, rocky soil.

Anders Alhomaki was a new immigrant in 1908. He had not, as of then, been blacklisted. Thus, despite being a Finn, Anders found work in Soudan. For nearly four years, he labored beside recently arrived Balkan Slavs. Then, one day, he simply quit. Anders moved back to Duluth and worked for a time on the waterfront with his old friend and fellow Finnish immigrant, Olli Kinkkonen. Alhomaki's employment as a stevedore proved temporary, however.

Within the year, Anders found himself underground, working in the Quincy Copper Mine in Northern Michigan. He had fallen in love. Alhomaki was devastated when the woman he hoped to marry returned to Duluth from Houghton without him. The Strike of 1913 intervened, and when Anders was finally blacklisted from further work in the copper mines, he boarded America and left Hancock, Michigan, for Duluth.

True to his taciturn nature, Anders Alhomaki told George McAdams none of this as they drank together. The two men drained their beer glasses. The Canadian ordered another round as George McAdams and Anders Alhomaki steadied themselves against the violent pitch of the little boat.

Chapter 4

America's angular bow sliced through the stormy waters of Lake Superior, near the Minnesota entrance to St. Louis Bay. Above the steamship, the intricate metal work of the Aerial Bridge, the structure's moveable gondola suspended below the bridge's arch, suddenly appeared from inside a heavy sky. Rain pummeled the wooden superstructure of the *America*. The Finn and the Canadian stood on deck, exposed to the weather and clenching a railing as the boat plunged through tumultuous surf. Neither man was experiencing seasickness, despite the ample quantities of People's Beer they'd consumed the evening before. They were steady on their feet. They were, respectively, a timber cruiser and a miner, men used to hangovers far worse than the ones lingering in their brains that April morning.

"It's so damn thick, you can't even see the Incline," Alhomaki said quietly.

The Finn's observation referred to the most prominent of the City's two incline railways, tramways operated by the Duluth Street Railway Company. The best known of the City's inclines carried patrons and freight from Downtown Duluth to the residential neighborhoods being developed nearly seven hundred feet above Lake Superior. A smaller, less patronized incline operated between West Duluth and Bayview Heights. Alhomaki's reference was not lost on the big Canadian.

"I've taken a ride or two on the tram," McAdams offered. "Quite an impressive view from on top of the hill, but not much to see on a day like today."

Alhomaki didn't respond. His mind settled upon the reason he was returning to Duluth.

Although Anders had lost his job with the Quincy Mining Company and was unlikely to find work with any other mine in Michigan's Upper Peninsula (UP), he could have managed. There were positions open in the lumber mills and logging camps of the UP. However, the loss of his job in Hancock after two years of steady work gave Alhomaki an excuse to return to Duluth. The image of Elin Gustafsson, her auburn hair, the hue a striking balance between blond and crimson, her finely featured face, her small nose, her high cheekbones, her piercing blue eyes, eyes the color of stainless steel, occupied the foremost reaches of Anders's focus as the *America* worked its way into the Duluth harbor.

As the steamship passed beneath the Aerial Bridge, Alhomaki's attention shifted. He found himself studying the steel beams supporting the bridge's apparatus, fully cognizant that the ship canal the beams traversed was the result of civil disobedience.

The natural outlet for the St. Louis River is located in Superior, Wisconsin, across the bay from Duluth. Prior to 1870, ships visiting Duluth anchored out in Lake Superior. Vessels visiting Duluth were often damaged, if not completely destroyed, by fierce winds, winds that raged the entire length of the lake before colliding with the piers and docks located outside Minnesota Point.

Progressives in Duluth realized that the city would never reach its potential if Superior had the only entry into the calm waters of St. Louis Bay. Dredging had commenced on the Duluth side of the Bay during the summer of 1870. Duluthians were intent upon creating a breach through Minnesota Point, through which ship traffic could flow. The citizens of Superior became enraged and obtained a judge's order enjoining the work. The Duluthians, anticipating the arrival of the injunction, and aided by the steam dredge, *Ishpeming*, had worked throughout the night to open a channel from St. Louis Bay to Lake Superior. When George Stuntz arrived the next morning to serve the injunction upon Duluth's mayor, the canal was already completed. In addition, a small steamship had successfully negotiated the crude channel. The steamship's passage through the canal defined the waterway as "navigable," and rendered the injunction moot.

By the time Anders Alhomaki and George McAdams sailed into Duluth Harbor on the *America* in 1914, concrete piers had replaced the earthen banks of the primitive ship canal and the ornate superstructure of the Aerial Bridge had been erected to span the piers.

"I'm sailing home in a week, after I conclude my business in Duluth," the Canadian said as the steamship slowed to make its final approach.

The *America's* slip abutted Lake Avenue, an area known for its concentration of Finnish boarding houses, brothels, and taverns.

"I'm sailing from here to Ontario on the *America*," McAdams continued. "She stops in Two Harbors and Grand Marais before docking in Port Arthur."

Anders Alhomaki was quiet. The Finn studied the nuances of a landfall distorted by fog. As the steamship eased into the harbor, it passed the *Christopher Columbus*, a large passenger boat, steaming out of Duluth. Alhomaki knew the *Columbus* well. He and Elin Gustafsson had sailed on the unusual vessel, the brainchild of Alexander McDougall, in 1912, from Duluth across Lake Superior to Marquette, the largest city in Michigan's Upper Peninsula.

Alhomaki hadn't been impressed with the design of the *Christopher Columbus*, the only whaleback built expressly for passenger service. Due to their low profiles, blunt snouts, and rounded gunwales, critics derisively proclaimed McDougall's boats to be "cigar boats" or "pig boats." The trip across Lake Superior aboard the *Columbus* had been a rollicking, tossing, surging experience, which had convinced Anders Alhomaki that Alexander McDougall had never been a passenger on a boat of his own design.

Alhomaki managed a smile. Rainwater poured off the brim of his slouch hat and spattered the front of his canvas slicker. He wasn't attentive to the conversation at hand. He was thinking of Elin Gustafsson.

"I'm staying at the Spalding, on Superior Street," McAdams continued. "If you care to, I'd be honored to buy you dinner, once we've both cleaned up a bit."

Alhomaki's eyes shifted. "That's kind of you, but I've got plans. Maybe some other time."

The Finn opened a small pouch of tobacco and forced a plug of chew into his mouth as he watched dockworkers scurry across the wooden decking of the pier. The vessel slid noiselessly through the brown water of the Bay. The boat shuddered as its propeller reversed, slowing the boat until it was nearly stationary.

"I understand. Things to do, people to see," the Canadian said with acceptance. "If you ever get up to Port Arthur, make sure you stop in for a visit. There's many a fine Canadian woman that would strike your fancy, I'd wager."

"Don't know as I'll have occasion to get up your way, but if I do, I'll look you up," the Finn said, spitting tobacco into the copper-colored water.

"If you're ever in need of a job, you know where to find me," McAdams added. "Men who are unafraid of breaking a sweat can always find work with George McAdams."

The rain quickened. The men shook hands before gathering up identical rucksacks, canvas packs manufactured in Duluth by Poirer Pack Sack, bags commonly known amongst locals as "Duluth Packs." Hoisting his belongings over a broad shoulder, McAdams started down a set of narrow stairs leading to the gangway.

Once on land, McAdams tipped his fedora and vanished inside the gray veil. Anders Alhomaki followed the Canadian down the gangway, exited the boat, traversed the wooden pier, and stepped onto muddy ground. The Finn looked intently through the descending mist in anticipation of seeing a familiar face, but there was no one on the dock to greet Anders Alhomaki.

Chapter 5

Elin Gustafsson sat in the Mercury Café on St. Croix Avenue in Finntown studying her hands. A corset and a finely tailored women's suit confined her robust frame. Tobacco smoke filled the air of the crowded restaurant. Coffee cooled in a porcelain cup in front of the Finnish woman as she sat on a bench in a corner booth. As Elin's hazel eyes surveyed the junction of her hands and wrists, wind buffeted the plate glass windows of the café overlooking the avenue. She was waiting; waiting for the courage to face Anders Alhomaki. It was after six o'clock in the evening. It was Saturday. Anders would be slogging his way down the mucky alley from the pier towards his room at 237 South First Avenue East, near where the manufacturing and waterfront district of the city joined the retail shops and offices of downtown. He would be expecting her at the dock. In his last letter he'd requested that she meet him there.

It had been six months since Elin had left her job teaching English at Suomi College in Hancock, Michigan, to return to the Gustafsson Mansion located on the East Hillside of Duluth. Her father, Karl Gustafsson, an aristocrat of Swedish-Finn descent, was a prominent lawyer in town. Physically imposing at over six feet tall and two hundred pounds, the origins of Karl Gustafsson's jet-black hair, clean-shaven jowls, dark skin, and intimidating brown eyes were a mystery when one considered that he claimed to be one hundred percent Scandinavian. Elin's mother, Laina, a descendent of the Finnish middle class who did not speak Swedish, shared an austere complexion, auburn hair, blue eyes, and the traditionally high cheekbones of the Finns with the couple's only child.

Elin returned home from the Upper Peninsula of Michigan a week after receiving her father's telegram, making a quick transition from living with Anders Alhomaki in a rented cottage along a sharp bluff rising behind Hancock, Michigan, to reclaiming her childhood bedroom in the rambling mansion located on East Second Street, in the Ashtabula Heights section of Duluth. On the infrequent days when the wind was becalmed, the towering chimneys of the Markell House, a palatial estate located next door to the Gustafsson's expansive manor, belched coal smoke into the air, coating the turrets and gables of the Gustafsson home in acrid soot. Because Elin's bedroom faced the prominence of the Markell place, she kept her windows firmly fixed as she went about the untidy business of watching her mother die.

Elin had been twenty-three years old when she met Anders Alhomaki. She was college-educated, having obtained a Bachelor of Arts in English from Northern Indiana Normal School; an institution founded by Methodists in Valparaiso, Indiana (later acquired by the Lutherans and renamed Valparaiso University), the alma mater of both her parents. Elin had also earned a Master's Degree in English Composition from the University of Michigan, the institution where both her father and Oscar Larson, another prominent Finnish attorney living in Duluth, had attended law school. She began her teaching career as an English Instructor at the Duluth Normal School in the autumn of 1911. She first met Anders Alhomaki at a dance held in February of 1912 to raise money for the Finnish Women's Suffrage Society, a group organized by Elin's mother, Laina Gustafsson.

Following the lead of their counterparts in Finland, educated Finnish women like Laina Gustafsson began to vocalize their demands for universal suffrage. The dance where Elin Gustafsson fell in love with the quiet Finnish bachelor miner was held at the Work People's College in Riverside. The school was the nurturing place for Finnish radicalism in the city.

"Who's that handsome young man?" Elin had asked her friend Wendla Heikkonen at the dance, held two years before Laina Gustafsson's fatal illness.

"Anders Alhomaki," Wendla responded. "You're not thinking of swooning over him too, are you?"

Elin's impulsive nature was legendary amongst her friends.

"Oh, hush," Elin whispered. "I only want a dance."

"With you, it's never just a dance," Wendla observed. "With you, every dance is a prelude to something more significant."

Elin laughed.

"He's awfully striking."

"They're all awfully striking," Wendla said. "He looks like a laborer. Not the type of man your father would approve of. And he's at least thirty. He's likely only looking for an easy mark."

The women stood near a table displaying a punch bowl and assorted sweets in a dark corner of the school's meeting room. Couples and pairs of single Finnish women danced nearby, traversing the hardwood floor of the hall to traditional Finnish waltzes and reels. Three musicians, a guitarist, a fiddle player, and an old woman playing a decrepit button box occupied an alcove, filling the space with music.

"Give me a little nip," Elin whispered.

"I think you've had enough," Wendla Heikkonen replied, securing her free hand around a sash purse dangling from her shoulder.

"I've only had a swallow. Just one more sip," Elin urged.

Wendla glanced around the room. Though it wasn't yet Prohibition, the Work People's College was filled with temperance adherents. No one in authority, including Laina Gustafsson, a staunch prohibitionist, appeared to be watching them. Wendla's fingers worked the flap of her purse. Her eyes remained focused on the crowd. Her left hand withdrew a slender sterling flask filled with brandy from the depths of the bag. Elin grasped the silver container with clean white gloves, turned towards the wall, and raised the flask to her lips.

"That's enough," Wendla cautioned. "You don't want to be sick when that old man asks you to dance."

Elin Gustafsson smiled.

"Now I'm ready," Elin said in Finnish, dabbing her lips with a white linen handkerchief.

59

"Your father would tan your behind if he heard you speaking Suomi," Wendla admonished.

"My father isn't here," Elin replied as she began to walk across the room. "And neither is yours."

Anders Alhomaki stood in a small cluster of single men at the far end of the hall. The band played another waltz. The slight Finn watched in amazement as the most beautiful woman in the room floated across the floor towards him.

She must know someone in this group of men, the miner thought, *likely Oscar Ketola. He's been a consistent letter writer to the* Tribune *and* Herald *on behalf of women's issues.*

Ketola was a large-faced, broad-chested Finn who worked far less and talked far more than any other friend of Anders Alhomaki. Thick blond hair cascaded across Ketola's shoulders in Bohemian fashion, making the sometimes-employed stevedore look like a hero out of the *Kalevala*, the Finnish folk epic. Oscar's clear blue eyes fixed on the short, attractive woman walking deliberately towards the men. He was certain, as was Anders Alhomaki, that Elin Gustafsson was intent upon a dance with the tall stevedore.

"Hello," Ketola said in English, his hand extending to greet the woman as she stopped in front of the cluster of Finnish men engaged in heated debate.

Elin accepted the hand without conviction. Her eyes measured the faces of the other men before settling upon the face of the slender miner. She ended the exchange with Ketola and returned her gloved right hand to her side.

"I'm Elin, Elin Gustafsson," she said demurely, her eyes never leaving Anders Alhomaki's face.

The Finnish miner's cheeks turned crimson. He shifted his weight nervously before offering his hand to the woman.

"Anders. Anders Alhomaki," he mumbled.

Alhomaki knew, as every other male in the place knew, who Elin Gustafsson was. The daughter of Karl Gustafsson, one of Duluth's most prominent Finnish conservatives, and Laina Gustafsson, a radical feminist, whose political and social ideals were directly and concretely at odds with those of her husband. Elin was considered to be one of the most fetching and most desirable unmarried women at the dance. Her best friend and confidante, Wendla Heikkonen, was a close second.

Whereas Elin was robust, buxom, and fleshy, with an inordinately handsome face, Wendla was delicate, thin and, despite her apparent edges, pleasingly sculpted, with long blond hair tied up off her shoulders, and penetrating brown eyes set deep in her face.

"Pleased to meet you, Mr. Alhomaki," Elin replied, shaking the miner's hand.

There was an interval of awkward silence. Olli Kinkkonen, a logger and stevedore who shared Alhomaki's dark complexion and jet-black hair, leaned over and whispered, loud enough for the woman to hear, "I think she wants to dance."

Anders turned in puzzlement. "With me?" he asked Kinkkonen in Finnish.

"With you," Elin interjected in their language.

The miner's face flushed again.

"Go on," Matti Peltoma urged. "You'll never have a better offer."

"He's right, you know," Wendla Heikkonen encouraged after joining her friend.

The miner sheepishly extended his right arm to Miss Gustafsson.

"Don't step on her feet," Olli Kinkkonen chided as the couple moved out onto the crowded dance floor.

They danced two straight reels, whirling and twirling across the hardwood. Exhausted, they retreated to the punch bowl.

"You dance well," Anders said in English as he poured a cup of hot cranberry cider for the woman.

"So do you," Elin agreed, downing the liquid in one swallow.

Sweat leaked from the miner's scalp and dripped down his neatly trimmed black sideburns. Unlike many of his companions, Alhomaki did not wear a moustache. His face was cleanly shaven. Although Anders Alhomaki's chin was exceedingly narrow, Elin found the overall effect of the miner's features to be handsome.

"Would you like to get a bit of fresh air?" the woman asked. "You look like you could use it."

"I am a bit overheated," Alhomaki acknowledged. Certain that his innocent remark was about to be misconstrued, he quickly added, "From the dancing, I mean."

Elin laughed.

"I knew what you meant, Mr. Alhomaki. I can tell you're a gentleman and not some cad."

Anders smiled, the first hint of emotion he'd displayed since asking Elin to dance.

The two talked quietly and with easy familiarity as they wandered South 88th Avenue West, passing construction that would eventually become United States Steel's factory town, the Model City (later renamed "Morgan Park" in honor of J.P Morgan), a community being built to supply housing for workers in the company's steel plant in Gary-New Duluth.

Anders Alhomaki impressed Elin Gustafsson with his knowledge of world politics, women's issues, and Finnish history. He was deeply passionate in his beliefs, views that transcended easy labels. In addition to being a union man, he was an occasional Lutheran and a Populist who believed, after benefiting from the aftermath of the ill-advised labor strike of 1907, that the working man's best hope for fair treatment was to organize and gain access to the political process by electing sympathetic men into office.

Their long walk that first evening together, both of them bundled in winter clothing against the cold wind sweeping down from Bardon's Peak, a prominent bluff of exposed gabbro overlooking the far western edge of Duluth, convinced Elin that Anders Alhomaki was a kind and thoughtful man, a man who supported efforts to improve the political and social status of women.

Laina Gustafsson witnessed her daughter's flirtation with the little Finn from a distance. She stood in the shadows of the Work People's Hall and scrutinized the couple's interaction when they returned from their walk and resumed dancing. Laina, though exceedingly liberal in the raising of her daughter, a trait that annoyed her socially rigid husband to no end, understood the dangers presented by Elin's interest in men of lesser standing.

One never knows a man's motivation, Laina Gustafsson thought, watching her daughter and Mr. Alhomaki step slowly through a waltz, linked as if they were one, their bodies pressed tightly together. *Elin knows the dangers of revealing too much of herself to a man before she's certain of his intentions. I've at least taught her that much.*

"This is Mr. Anders Alhomaki. Mr. Alhomaki, my mother, Mrs. Laina Gustafsson," Elin said as she presented the Finnish miner to her mother later that evening.

"Pleased to meet you, Mrs. Gustafsson," Anders Alhomaki replied, extending a calloused hand.

"Likewise," Laina responded, offering her hand to the miner.

"Mr. Alhomaki is a firm believer in a woman's right to vote and to work outside the home," Elin continued, her words rushing out breathlessly as she attempted to convince her mother of her new beau's worth.

"I see," Laina Gustafsson answered, her faint blue eyes locked upon the dark irises of the miner. "And what does Mr. Alhomaki do for a living?" the mother asked, switching her inquiry to Finnish.

"Right now, I'm working a temporary job in a warehouse with my cousin, Reino Maki, but that work will eventually end. When it does, I plan on traveling to Houghton, Michigan to work in the copper mines," Alhomaki answered in perfect Finnish.

Laina Gustafsson studied the man's face as he answered her questions.

He seems genuine. He's articulate, Laina thought. *Still, Karl would have a heart attack if he saw his little girl dancing intimately with a laborer.*

"It was nice to meet you, Mr. Alhomaki. I'm afraid it's late and my daughter needs her rest. Tomorrow is Monday. Elin needs to be fresh and alert to teach her students at the Normal School," Laina advised, reverting to English.

"I understand," Anders replied. "May I escort the two of you to the streetcar? It's snowing. You never know when you might need a strong arm to lean upon."

The mother looked at her daughter. Urgency and expectancy were clear on the younger woman's face.

"I'm the head of the cleaning committee," Laina answered. "I'll be staying long into the night. Why don't you walk my daughter to the trolley stop? You never can tell what sort of fellow might be lurking in the dark after a dance."

"It would be my pleasure. Is that all right with you, Miss Gustafsson?"

Elin smiled. Her white teeth reflected the heightened lighting of the hall.

"That would be very nice, Mr. Alhomaki."

A light snow had fallen. The wind had ceased. The temperature was timid for February. The miner and the teacher stood beneath the clouded sky in near-perfect darkness at the trolley stop. There were no street lamps near the streetcar station. No automobiles or carriages braved the slippery streets.

"It's a lovely evening," Elin said as they waited for a trolley beneath a sentry white pine, a remnant of the forest that once covered the St. Louis River Valley.

"I'm glad you introduced yourself," Anders replied, his eyes focused upon his black dress shoes, the toes of the footwear covered with snow.

"Would you have walked across the floor to ask me to dance?" the woman inquired boldly.

The Finnish miner thought for a moment before responding.

"I'm afraid I don't have that kind of courage," Anders answered through a weak grin, his eyes concentrating on his shoes.

Chapter 6
1912

It had caused a rift between father and daughter as wide and deep as the Baltic Sea. Romance had blossomed after Elin Gustafsson and Anders Alhomaki met at the Suffrage Dance. The schoolteacher and the miner became inseparable. However, the first meeting between Anders Alhomaki and Karl Gustafsson had been nothing short of disastrous, the aftermath of which drove a wedge between the lawyer and his only child.

"I forbid you to see that illiterate vagabond of a man," Karl Gustafsson had hissed at his daughter following a family dinner in their palatial home, during which Anders Alhomaki had first become acquainted with the attorney. "I absolutely forbid it."

By inviting Anders Alhomaki to the Gustafsson Mansion for a pleasant evening of roast beef and quiet discussion, Laina Gustafsson had thought to soften the blow of her daughter's liaison with someone her husband would clearly see as socially and intellectually inferior. Upon the miner's arrival, however, Karl Gustafsson retreated to his study, where he remained, unwilling to acknowledge Alhomaki's presence in the house until the evening meal was served.

"He'll warm to you, Mr. Alhomaki," Laina Gustafsson said. "Once you two get to talking, he'll warm to you. He'll see that there's more to you than meets the eye."

"I hope so, ma'am. Right now, I feel more than a bit awkward," Anders confided, replied nervously in their native tongue.

"Oh, Anders, please don't speak Finnish," Elin interjected. "Father will explode if you speak Suomi."

"Sorry. It was an inadvertent lapse, a bad habit from working in the mines. You either speak Finn or Serbo-Croatian. Only a few of the men speak English, and most of that's impossible to understand," he said apologetically, reverting to English.

"Dinner is served," the cook announced from behind a closed door that led to the mansion's massive kitchen.

The door to the study opened. Karl Gustafsson walked unashamedly to the head of the table and waited for his family and their guest to join him.

Sofia Wirtanen, the family's maid, a striking single woman of twenty, bustled in and out of the dining room with plates heaped with food. Anders watched with covert understanding. Karl Gustafsson smiled involuntarily as the attorney watched the girl distribute the evening meal.

There's something between them, the miner thought. *Maybe flirtation; maybe something more. I wonder if Mrs. Gustafsson knows. Probably not. If she suspected that her husband was interested in a servant Elin's age, that servant would likely be on a boat back to Helsinki.*

"Thank you, Sofia," Laina Gustafsson said tersely as the maid left the room.

There's an edge to her voice, Alhomaki observed. *There's knowledge behind that tone.*

Karl Gustafsson's face resumed a prominent scowl. Anders Alhomaki couldn't discern whether the grimace was due to his presence or the inflection of Mrs. Gustafsson's remark.

"Let us pray," the lawyer began. "Dear Lord Jesus, please accept our thanks for this bounty, for the Grace revealed in your suffering, for the precious gift of salvation, and for the gathering of this family. Amen."

There was no mention of the family's dinner guest in the prayer. The absence of such a reference increased the tension in the room.

Throughout the meal, Karl Gustafsson made it a point to direct his comments towards his wife and daughter. The patriarch ignored remarks made by the miner in response to conversation around the table. Finally, his dessert plate scraped clean, his coffee cup empty, Karl Gustafsson retired to his study, never having said a single word to his daughter's guest.

"That didn't go so well," Anders offered to Elin as they stood on the mansion's concrete front porch. "And I didn't even speak Finnish," he added wryly.

It was June. They'd been together as a couple, never intimate but on the verge of intimacy, for four months.

"He's an old fuddy-duddy," Elin remarked, tightening her grip on the sleeve of Anders's suit coat, the garment newly purchased from Dove Clothing, a shop on Superior Street owned by Alex Kyyhkynen, a local Finnish merchant. There was quality in the stitching and the fabric of the coat and trousers. Still, Alhomaki's off-the-rack purchase had been no match for the hand-tailored pinstriped business suit worn by Karl Gustafsson, the product of hours of diligent labor by Finnish tailor Peter Sikkio, clothier to the wealthiest elite of Duluth.

"He is your father. I doubt he'll let you see me after tonight."

"I'm twenty-two years old. I can make my own decisions about whom I should and should not see."

The miner looked down the hill towards Lake Superior. The avenue's paving bricks glistened. Precipitation had circulated above the town that evening; not enough to make an umbrella necessary but enough to wrinkle Alhomaki's carefully pressed suit. Anders's eyes refused to consider the woman standing next to him as he watched isolated droplets of cold rain strike warm pavement.

"I'm leaving for Houghton tomorrow," the miner disclosed.

"Tomorrow?" Elin asked, her eyes opening wider. "Because of tonight?"

"No, my job in the warehouse is finished. There's no work around here. A Croatian fellow I know from Soudan, Stanley Cukela, dropped me a postcard. Stan says there are jobs in the copper mines if a man's willing to work hard and put up with the bosses. I've done it before. I can do it again."

"What about us?"

Anders had refused to succumb to the pleading tone of Elin's voice.

"Us? After what we just went through you still think there can be an 'us'"?

"You must have wax plugging your ears. I told you I don't care what my father thinks. I love you; that's something even a dull-brained immigrant Finlander should understand," the woman whispered, no rancor in her voice, the use of the derisive "Finlander" meant to add emphasis to her words.

Alhomaki kicked the toe of his finely polished dress shoe against the concrete stoop.

"Well? Don't you have anything to say?" Elin asked.

The miner tilted his head and took in the beauty of the woman's wide face.

"I need to work. You know why. I've told you I want to have enough saved up to buy a farm, like we've talked about. I need to work."

"Then take me with you."

Anders's eyes widened.

"You're crazy. You're father will hunt me down like a dog."

"I'm an adult woman. My mother will support my decision. She likes you. Karl will just have to get used to the idea of us being together."

"El, I'm not ready for marriage," Alhomaki advised in English. "It's not that I want to be with someone else. You know how I feel about you. But I'm not ready to marry you unless I can make a life for us away from laboring in the mines. I need some time to put together enough money to buy land. I don't want a little forty carved out of some swamp. I want at least two hundred acres, if not more, of good, level farmland. That'll take time."

Elin had moved closer, had raised her right hand to the man's face and stroked the edges of his cheek.

"Did I say anything about marriage? I'm a modern girl. We can live together until you're ready. It'll be all right."

Later that evening, Karl Gustafsson had remained impassively rooted behind his oak desk. His voice, while full of anger and hostility, had never increased beyond a conversational tone as he addressed his daughter once Anders Alhomaki was gone.

"You will not, under any circumstances, ever see that worthless piece of cow dung again, understand?"

Elin sat in an oak side chair in front of her father. Her mother stood at Elin's side. Laina Gustafsson's considerable strength of character proved to be utterly useless against her husband's venom.

"As you say," Elin replied, her voice quiet, her hands folded calmly across the lap of her dress.

"My sources tell me he's a Syndicalist."

"That's not true. He doesn't belong to the IWW. He belongs to the miners' union."

"Same thing. Unionist, Communist, Syndicalist. You know I represent timber interests and mine owners. You know how sensitive those folks are to the threat of organized labor and the attempted uprising of the ignorant unwashed."

Elin's cheeks flushed. She pursed her lips but held her temper.

"Anders isn't ignorant. He's intelligent."

"He's a filthy, uneducated laborer who will never amount to a hill of beans," the lawyer responded, choosing an American expression to emphasize his rancor.

The daughter turned her head and sought her mother's support. There was only a blank, defenseless look on Laina Gustafsson's face. Riled but unwilling to reduce the discussion to a shouting match, the young woman relented.

"As you say."

"As I say," Karl repeated, his eyes turning to his wife. "And you, Mrs. Gustafsson, will in no way countenance or encourage any further communication between our daughter and that loathsome immigrant."

Laina's eyes averted as she obediently nodded acquiescence.

"Good. That being understood, Elin, you may retire to your bedroom. I've got some other matters to discuss with your mother."

Early morning, the day following Karl Gustafsson's rebuke, magenta beams of sunlight had climbed above the Wisconsin shoreline, across the calm silver water of Lake Superior. A double-paned window in Elin's bedroom overlooked the roof of an attached carriage house. The young woman dropped her valise onto the slate roof of the carriage house, waited a sufficient interval to ensure that her departure wasn't detected, and eased herself out the window. It was a short drop to the slate roofing, an easy fall from the carriage roof to the ground, and an exhilarating walk down Lake Avenue to where Anders Alhomaki waited. A few days later, the two lovers rented a small bungalow in Hancock, Michigan, where they lived together in intimacy until Elin Gustafsson received her father's curt telegram summoning her home.

Chapter 7
Spring, 1914

Elin Gustafsson downed the last of her coffee, slid her winter coat over her shoulders, and gathered her purse and umbrella. She left a Liberty quarter on the smooth maple surface of the table, trudged across the planked floor of the Mercury Café, and opened a wooden door, its surface shiny with new varnish, before extending her umbrella against an intermittent downpour.

It was a short trek to the Talonen Boarding House. As Elin Gustafsson skirted the muddy alley, she battled visions of her mother's death by recalling happier times spent with Anders Alhomaki in Northern Michigan.

They had forged a good life in Hancock. The underground copper mine operated year-round, providing Anders with steady employment. Elin's application to teach English at Suomi College, a Lutheran seminary founded by the Finnish Evangelical Lutheran Church of America, had been readily accepted. The small cottage she and Anders rented was at the top of the bluff rising behind the city of Hancock, overlooking the Keweenaw Waterway, the canal cutting between Houghton and Hancock. The dwelling was within easy walking distance of both the Quincy Mine and the College.

Intimacy had been a problem for the quiet miner. When they shared a cabin on the *Christopher Columbus* as "Mr. and Mrs. Rikala," it had been Elin, not Anders, who had left her berth for his on the second night of their voyage from Duluth to Marquette. Having been surreptitiously educated from an early age by her Suffragette mother about human reproduction and sexuality, Elin had been a curious but careful young woman as she reached maturity. An affair with a married professor in Valparaiso, Indiana, while obtaining her

71

English degree, had left her educated in more than vowels and consonants. Dr. Victor Pula had been a kind and gentle lover. Concerns over unwanted pregnancy had compelled them to explore the twists and turns of innovative amore until Elin was fitted with a "womb veil," an early form of diaphragm. The awkwardness of the device and the difficulties she had encountered in obtaining one from a doctor recommended to her by another girl at the Northern Indiana Normal School had compelled Elin to begin her own personal study of woman's rights and birth control.

During their two years together in Hancock, Elin had educated Anders, as she herself had been educated by Victor Pula. The miner offered no recriminations or inquiry as to where she'd obtained her knowledge of male anatomy. He simply accepted her gifts, the wonder of her mouth, the rounded curves of her small breasts, the fiery heat of her thighs, and learned.

Their last night together in the tiny frame cottage had been one not of wondrous exploration and tenderness, but one of anxiety and tears. Elin clung to Anders's warm body, his skin clean and smelling of homemade soap, his curly hair freshly washed and brushed smooth against his scalp, for the better part of the long night. She buried her face in the coarse fibers of his chest hair and wept for hours on end. The miner simply held her and allowed her to use his body for protection, as an ineffective shield against the world.

When the telegram came in October of 1913, Elin Gustafsson was left with no choice.

Daughter:

Regardless of how you feel about my rules or how I feel about your unspeakable relations with that illiterate miner, you must return to Duluth immediately. There is no kind or soft way to tell you this. Your mother has been diagnosed with the cancer. It has spread from her female organs to her brain and it is unlikely that she will survive the winter. If you wish to see her and comfort her before she passes, you will be on the next train out of Houghton for Duluth.

Sincerely,
Karl Gustafsson

"I'll go with you," Anders Alhomaki had offered.

"No. This is something I must face alone," Elin had replied. "Besides, there's no telling what father would do if he learned you were back in town. It's best that you stay here for now. You have steady work. You can save money for that farm you're always talking about buying. I'll write you every week. I'll keep you up-to-date on what's happening. But it's best that you remain here, at work, with your mind focused on our future."

Her right hand grasped the handle of the door. She pulled hard, dislodging the heavy wooden portal from the threshold, and entered the boarding house.

Inside, a fire raged in a pot-bellied stove in the corner of the building's lobby. A well-used roll-top desk sat against a far wall. The chair to the desk was unoccupied. An obese man, the proprietor of the place by his attitude, sat in an overstuffed chair in front of the stove, reading a magazine. The smell of over-percolated coffee rode a current of warm air.

"Can I help you, ma'am?" the man said, shifting his eyes from the magazine to take in Elin Gustafsson's face.

"I'm here to see Anders Alhomaki."

"Ah. You must be Miss Gustafsson," the man replied, his thick lips audibly smacking together as he spoke.

"I am."

"Anders thought you might be stopping by. I'll go see if he's decent. Rules, you know. No women in the rooms," the man added, his left eye winking provocatively.

Elin studied the man as he labored to rise from the chair. His legs were large and insulated with fat. Once upright, he ambulated by swinging his entire torso, advancing in the manner of elephants. His blond hair was thick with sweat. His face was apple red and streaked with moisture. The white linen shirt he wore was ringed with perspiration under his pendulous breasts.

73

"Charles Talonen," the man said, extending a meaty hand to the woman. "I own the place," he added in Finnish.

She felt as if he was testing her, trying to determine her ethnicity and whether she had lost her native tongue to assimilation.

"Pleased to meet you, Mr. Talonen," she responded in perfect Finnish, removing her mittens to shake the man's sweaty hand.

Talonen smiled.

"Have a seat. I'll go see if Mr. Alhomaki is receiving visitors."

Charles Talonen gestured to an empty sofa. Elin sat easily on the fabric, the blue velvet of the davenport soft against the back of her stocking-covered legs, and watched the man struggle down the hallway towards the sleeping rooms.

Her face warmed. She folded her umbrella. Wind buffeted the clapboard siding of the rickety frame building. Rain pelted the windows lining the street. Newly installed electric streetlamps cast shallow light on the sidewalk outside. Gas lamps illuminated the lobby of the boarding house. A log in the stove cracked. A tear hung from Elin Gustafsson's left eye. She reached into her purse, removed a clean linen handkerchief, and dabbed the descending moisture. Mr. Talonen re-appeared. Anders Alhomaki followed the landlord into the parlor.

"Miss Gustafsson," the miner said, his emotions concealed as he stopped and extended his right hand.

"Mr. Alhomaki," she replied, standing to greet him, grasping his palm in her own.

"I'll leave you two alone," Talonen said, shifting his weight in an effort to begin walking. "I've got some work I can do in the office. Just keep it in the lobby, Anders," the fat man added with a knowing smile.

The miner didn't respond. His heart raced with anticipation. He bent close to Elin, close enough to smell her perfume and to note the tiny pores of her skin.

"I've missed you," he said, leaning in to kiss her small lips.

She drew back. Not defensively, but to create distance.

74

"Mother died," she whispered, challenged by the enormity of what those words meant.

Chapter 8

Meager precipitation fell as Elin Gustafsson and Anders Alhomaki climbed towards the Gustafsson mansion. The couple passed Sadie Salmela's place, a whorehouse frequented by Finnish men from the Canal Park district of the City, a tidy three-story brick building that, unless one knew from personal experience the business conducted inside, looked for all the world like a boarding house for day laborers, dock workers, and out-of-work miners and loggers. No prostitutes plied their wares on the street outside the building. The women remained inside, out of the weather, playing cards, dealing with the boredom of an off day in their chosen profession.

Anders's bare hands remained inside the pockets of his slicker. Elin closed her umbrella as the rain turned to mist. Their faces moistened with drizzle as they labored up Lake Avenue.

"I'm sorry to hear about your mother," the Finnish miner began after an interval of silence. "She was a fine woman."

Elin looked straight ahead as she answered, "It was a horrible death. Even with morphine, the headaches raged so fiercely that she wanted to be taken months ago. But she was so strong, so vital. She fought far longer than the doctors believed she could."

Anders nodded. Another period of silence ensued.

A tall man approached them, carrying a young child in his arms. The little girl, no more than two or three years old, slept soundly, tufts of a dirty dress protruding from her patchwork coat, her face protected from the weather. A strong odor of alcohol wafted from the stranger as he passed. His facial features were consistent with Italian or Slavic heritage. The man stumbled, fell headlong onto the paving bricks and dropped the child to the pavement in the ensuing tumble.

Cursing in a language Anders Alhomaki knew to be Slovene, the stranger brushed dirt from his frayed dungarees, picked up the bawling child, and stood unsteadily beneath the aura of a streetlamp.

"Drunk," Anders observed. "Drunk and caring for his child," the miner added, watching the stranger resume his stagger.

Elin didn't respond. The couple continued their climb towards East Second Street. Newly installed electric lights blazed from inside the Markell Mansion and the Gustafsson home next door. A gas street lamp on the corner flickered. Anders looked into the soft blue eyes of his companion as he spoke in Finnish:

"When is your mother's funeral?"

"Monday. At the Finnish Church," Elin replied, referring to the Independent Finnish Evangelical Lutheran Church (later known as Messiah), which was located on St. Croix Avenue, just a stone's throw from Talonen's Boarding House.

"What time is the service?"

Elin took in Anders's kind brown eyes and the dark features of his thinly handsome face as she replied, "Eleven. But you're not thinking of attending, are you?"

The remark stung the miner. His eyebrows raised in apprehension.

"Of course. Your mother was a woman of compassion and quality. After all she did for us while we struggled in Hancock, why shouldn't I pay her my last respects?"

Laina Gustafsson had not only condoned the relationship between Anders Alhomaki and her only child, but she had insisted upon pilfering the Gustafsson household account to send money to Elin and the miner whenever they needed it. When the couple was short on funds for food or rent, Laina was always quick to wire an extra twenty or thirty dollars. The money was sent without any expectation of repayment. Karl Gustafsson, though suspicious of the absence of beefsteak on the family dinner table and his wife's sudden preference for chicken and whitefish, never learned of Laina's masterful deception.

And then there were the letters. Mrs. Gustafsson was, as a Suffragette, a most thoroughly modern woman. In her weekly letters to her daughter, she educated Elin on a myriad of topics, from voting rights, to the most recent advances in the knowledge of female contraception and fertility, to the likelihood of war in Europe. She made it a point to include copies of Margaret Sanger's column, "What Every Girl Should Know," clipped from the *New York Call* by her friend, Mrs. William Silvey, whenever Mrs. Silvey sent them from New York City.

Alice Munger Silvey had more than a casual acquaintance with life. The daughter of Roger Munger, one of the financial pioneers of Duluth, and the niece of world-renowned landscape artist Gilbert Munger, Alice Silvey and her husband, Duluth real estate magnate William Silvey, had been first class passengers, along with fellow Duluthian Constance Willard, on the *Titanic's* maiden voyage. William Silvey perished in the sinking and Alice, after returning to Duluth to conclude her late husband's affairs, settled in New York City. Despite the distance from her friends in Duluth, she remained in near constant correspondence with many of them, including Laina Gustafsson, with whom she shared a passion for women's health and social issues.

Elin stood next to the black wrought iron fence defining the perimeter of the Gustafsson property. The brown front lawn of the estate was speckled with shoots of new grass. She raised her hands and held the face of her companion in her woolen mittens.

"Mother would want you there," she whispered. "But I'm afraid that if you attend the funeral, father will come unglued. He's barely on speaking terms with me now. I think, for the time being, it's best you stay away."

Alhomaki's brown eyes flashed.

"Is there someone else?" he inquired in an accusatory tone.

Elin grimaced.

"How could you think that?" she asked, withdrawing her hands. "Because I'm an unmarried woman who shares herself with an unmarried man, you think I fall for whoever wanders by? How dare you."

A mitten-covered hand struck out. Anders's left hand darted upward and intercepted the blow. His reflexes were sharp, honed by years spent as a boxer in Finland. He'd been the welterweight champion of his country at sixteen years old. He'd retired at twenty-one, after beating a fair-haired Swedish boy into a coma, shortly before coming to America.

"Don't," he admonished. "I'm sorry."

Her eyes welled. His grip on her wrist was firm but non-threatening.

"I need to go inside," she said. "The wake begins at seven-thirty."

He released her.

"Elin, your mother wouldn't want you to yield your convictions to your father. She'd want you to stand up for us, with your chin held high."

Elin Gustafsson looked away from the miner.

"If Mother were here, I'd have that strength," Elin replied. "But she isn't. It will take time for me to be able to find that resolve. For now, I think it's best that you keep your distance."

"Why? Because your father's the best friend of Oscar Larson, the most powerful Finn in the city? What can he do to me that hasn't already been done to me by the mining bosses? I'm already using the name 'Andrew Maki' when I apply for work. I've been blacklisted by most of the mining companies in Minnesota and Michigan. And for what? I didn't engage in violence during the strikes. I simply refused to cross the picket lines. For that, the bastards deny me the ability to earn a living; a paltry, barely subsistence living at that."

Elin didn't admonish him for cursing. She allowed him his say. When Anders Alhomaki finished his diatribe, Elin Gustafsson pressed her lips into the soft skin of his cheek before withdrawing.

"I need to go inside."

The Finnish miner nodded.

"Have it your way, Miss Gustafsson."

Elin ascended the concrete stairway leading from the street to the house. As her boots reached the top stair, she turned and spoke in a conciliatory tone. "Maybe in a few days, when I've dealt with Mother's passing and my father is otherwise occupied, we could meet for a cup of coffee."

"Ordinarily I'd say 'yes' to your offer," Anders Alhomaki replied. "But I'm leaving at the end of the week for Virginia. A friend of mine, Tim Laitila, has some pull with the bosses at the Alpena Mine. It's a small operation but producing well. He's got a job lined up for me as a carpenter."

"I didn't know you were a carpenter," Elin replied calmly.

"I am if that's the only job available," Anders said with a bright grin.

The woman shook her head in understanding.

"Send me your address. Send it through the office at the Normal School," she added. She had been re-employed there as an English instructor. "That way, father won't know. I'll write as soon as I can."

Elin didn't wait for the miner to respond. Her feet moved cautiously across the wet concrete, uncertain of how she would react to seeing her mother's lifeless body on display in the parlor of the Gustafsson Mansion.

Chapter 9

He wasn't much of a drinker. Still, sitting across the table from George McAdams in the bar of the Spalding Hotel, Anders Alhomaki was intent upon getting drunk. The Finn had contacted the Canadian at the hotel after confronting the dismal prospect of spending his first evening back in Duluth alone.

The miner had forsaken his beverage of choice, People's Beer, for vodka. Straight up, without ice. He was on his fourth shot when a group of loud and obviously intoxicated young men entered the hotel tavern. From the cut of their expensive evening coats and their exaggerated swaggers, Alhomaki guessed they were sons of the lumber, banking, iron ore, and shipping barons in control of the city of Duluth: young men out on the town for a night of frivolity, likely a stop at one of the nicer houses of ill-repute located outside of Finntown, the Canal Park neighborhood Alhomaki and the majority of the single Finnish men called home.

George McAdams eyed the group of moneyed bonvivants as they claimed a large, round table across the saloon from the Canadian and his Finnish acquaintance.

"There's trouble, lad," McAdams asserted, sipping beer as he kept watch on the new arrivals. "They clearly can't hold their liquor and will likely end up causing some poor whorehouse a whole hell of a lot of misery."

Alhomaki nodded. His eyes surveyed the six men in the group. There wasn't a face at the far table he recognized.

"More whiskey," one of the young men shouted.

A Negro, his head bald and shiny as a new penny, entered the room and moved quickly towards the boisterous customers.

"Yes, sir," the man replied, his white uniform crisp and clean, his slight form straight and attentive as he spoke.

81

The waiter was young, shorter than Alhomaki, and frail. His face was cleanly shaven. Despite his stature and the incessant mumbling from around the table, the Negro maintained his poise.

"What the hell is this?" the largest man at the table asked. "Who the fuck gave Uncle Tom a job here? My old man is half-owner of the Spalding, and I don't recall him ever givin' a nigger a job."

"I sure enough don't know your father," the black man replied calmly, "but there's no call to insult me. I'm just here to do my job."

"Job? Your job is to lick my boots, you little monkey," the youth continued. Right boys? Africans are descended from apes. That's what Miss Pratt taught us in biology class at good ol' Duluth Central High School. Niggers can be trained to do anything, just like an organ grinder's monkey."

The Negro studied the faces of the men around the table. He looked across the room. Other than Anders Alhomaki and George McAdams, the only person in the bar on the inclement night was the bartender, a burly barrel of a man who stood behind the counter, wiping glasses, studying the encounter between the waiter and the young men.

"Say there, fellows. Why not tone it down a bit and try acting like the gentlemen we all know you are?" the barkeep asked, a hint of County Clare in his voice.

"Mind your own business, potato eater," another of the men, a small, pink-faced runt, responded. "Mr. Ellison's just having a little fun."

"His name is Cletus. Cletus Jones. And he's an educated man, graduated from Morgan State, in Baltimore, class of 1910. He has a degree, as I recollect, in the sciences," the barkeep replied. "He's working here to earn money for medical school. Howard University, as I recall, eh, Cletus?"

"That's right, Mr. O'Cochrane. Now how about you boys being respectful so I don't have to ask you to leave?" the black man asserted with confidence, his voice low, his eyes piercingly fierce.

"Ask us to leave? Hey, Ellison, you hear that?" the pasty-faced kid asked. "This Negro," the runt continued, elongating the word "Negro" with disdain, "wants us to leave your daddy's hotel."

Without warning, Ellison leaped out of his chair and struck Cletus Jones with a powerful left hook to the jaw. The waiter collapsed, knocked out cold.

"Toss that heap of trash out onto the sidewalk," commanded Ellison, obviously the ringleader of the group.

"Mr. Ellison, why the hell d'you do that?" the bartender, Dennis O'Cochrane, asked as he set his dishtowel on the finely polished surface of the bar. "There's no call for that sort of unprovoked behavior. Cletus is as gentle as a summer breeze. He's a Christian man. I'm afraid, father or no father, I'll have to ring the police."

The bartender reached for the telephone, raised the receiver, and clicked twice to reach the city switchboard. With a nod from the ringleader, two of Ellison's companions left the table and approached the Irishman.

"Hold on now," the bartender urged. O'Cochrane reached beneath the bar and withdrew an oak shillelagh. "You're just gonna have to cool your heels until the coppers arrive."

Ellison nodded again. Two more men doffed their winter coats, rose from the table, and moved across the hardwood floor of the Spalding Hotel tavern, towards the barkeep.

"Looks like that fellow needs some help," George McAdams whispered.

Anders Alhomaki surveyed the situation. He was cognizant that, if a fight broke out and he and the big Canadian were around when the police arrived, they'd be blamed for starting the ruckus. He wasn't interested in spending the night in the Duluth City Jail. He'd managed, through all the labor strife and nights of drunken excess he'd experienced working the mines, to keep his name off the police blotters of every little town in Minnesota and Michigan he'd visited. Still, his fists were already balled. His instincts told him that Ellison had been in the ring; that the blow the rich kid had delivered to the black man's jaw had not been lucky, but planned. The left had been executed with the precision of someone who'd sparred a few rounds, bloodied some noses, at the local YMCA. There was unfairness inherent in the assault, beyond the racial slurs and the ugliness of the crowd. Anders nodded. The two men rose from their chairs.

"What the hell you think you two timber dicks are doing?" Ellison asked as McAdams and Alhomaki stood up. "Sit down and drink your swill before you get yourselves hurt."

George McAdams smiled. He ignored the young man and moved towards the crowd assembling in front of O'Cochrane. Ellison and his last companion at the table stood up; Ellison's associate was a lean wisp of a boy, his wavy red hair parted in the middle, new auburn stubble visible upon his cheeks and jaw.

"Is that any way to talk to your elders? I was whipping lads twice your size when you were still taking milk out of your mother's teat. I'd suggest you fellows take a seat," McAdams observed over his shoulder as he walked towards the bar.

Anders Alhomaki moved across the floor and addressed Ellison and his companion:

"You heard the man. You're upsetting Mr. McAdams with your rude behavior. I'm certain you don't want to anger me as well," the Finn said.

A look of incredulity crossed Ellison's face.

"You must be joking. Didn't you see what I did to that monkey, you moronic Finn? Speaking of Finns, is it true Finnish boys sleep with their sisters and then turn them out as whores when they're tired of them?"

The young man advanced, his back protected by his red-haired companion. Ellison was a good six inches taller than Alhomaki and significantly heavier.

A light heavyweight, Anders thought, *if one wanted to categorize him as a fighter.*

Ellison raised his fists.

"You are one dumb mule," Ellison hissed scornfully through narrowly parted lips. "Prepare to meet the Marquis of Queensberry."

Ellison jabbed with his right, maintaining his hands high and away from his chest as he punched. Alhomaki shifted his weight and dodged the blow. Before the Finn could counter, Ellison launched a left cross that grazed Alhomaki's forehead.

He's quick, the miner thought. *I need to move in before he gets lucky.*

The two men circled.

"David, why don't you go help our pals?" Ellison suggested to the red-haired youth. "I've got the situation well in hand."

The redhead moved towards the bar, leaving Anders Alhomaki and Ellison alone. Ellison pawed at the air. Alhomaki saw a slight opening and feinted with his right before delivering a solid left uppercut into the young man's ribs.

Crunch.

The Finn knew he'd shattered at least one and possibly two ribs.

O'Cochrane brandished the cudgel above his head. Five men moved around the bar in a circle, looking for an opening. McAdams arrived, grabbed the pale-faced runt by the lapel of his expensive suit coat, and picked him up by one hand.

"Young man, this is a place for grown men, not little boys. I'd suggest you have a seat," the Canadian said, tossing the youth into a chair nearly ten feet away.

Two of the crowd turned on McAdams. The others, including the redhead identified as "David," attacked O'Cochrane. The club came down, smashing the back of David's head, knocking him to the floor, where he remained.

Ellison moved over the floor and threw a weak right. Alhomaki smiled. The injured ribs slowed the man. There was no power behind the punch. Anders feigned a left hook to confuse Ellison, to lure him in. The young man danced lightly on the balls of his feet and slipped his right hand through the Finn's defense.

85

The blow missed its intended target. Alhomaki followed up Ellison's errant punch with a crushing hammer to the side of the youth's left jaw. The strike splintered bone. Ellison groaned and fell unconscious to the hardwood.

George McAdams was backed up against the bar, his hands raised over his head in submission. One of the young men displayed a small revolver, a .22 from the size of the barrel, and waved the pistol at the big Canadian.

"You use that thing, sonny," O'Cochrane advised, noting that the kid's hand was trembling as it held the gun, "t'aint no one in the world that can help you."

"Stand back," the youth commanded, his free hand wiping nervous sweat from his forehead. "You bastards nearly killed my pals," he screamed. "Over what? Some useless nigger. Niggers are getting too plentiful, too cocky. Ever since US Steel started building the steel plant, they've been coming into town, stealing jobs from honest white men like yourselves. That little ape and all his kind should go back to Cleveland or Gary, wherever they came from. Leave the jobs for those that deserve them."

Anders Alhomaki approached the young man from behind. The youth detected the movement and trained the pistol on the Finn's chest.

"Stop right there. Are you too stupid to understand, Finlander? These niggers are taking jobs that you could have. Good paying jobs in the steel and wire mill. You're a fool if you don't see that."

Cletus moaned. The youth nervously shifted the barrel of the gun to cover the unconscious black man. George McAdams launched himself at the gun.

Crack.

The bullet passed through the Canadian's right shoulder without hitting bone. In a flash, the gun was in McAdams's left hand and the incident was over.

Chapter 10

St. Luke's, an Episcopal Hospital located on Duluth's East Hillside, between First Street and Second Street, was as quiet as a tomb. Two uniformed police officers escorted George McAdams into an immaculate reception area. The Canadian held his right arm close to his body to lessen the burden on his injured shoulder. Anders Alhomaki walked behind the officers.

"How's the shoulder, McAdams?" asked one of the policemen, a beanpole named MacIntyre.

"It's been better," the big man replied. "She's starting to throb something fierce."

"We called ahead. Doc Parker should be here to meet us," added MacInytre's partner, a cop named Fulton Andrews.

The men approached the reception desk. A matronly nurse scrutinized their arrival.

"You men bringing in the gunshot victim?" she asked, looking up from a pile of paperwork.

"Yes, ma'am," Andrews replied.

"Doctor Parker is waiting. I'll bring you to him," she added, rising from behind the desk, the starch of her white uniform crackling audibly with her movement.

Electric light undulated with unpredictable intensity as the woman led the men down a wide hallway. The heels of the nurse's white shoes clicked against the finely polished granite floor as she walked.

"In here," a male voice called out as the group approached the first examination room.

Inside the room, Dr. Joshua Parker, his white hair combed off his forehead, his white beard and moustache freshly trimmed, stood next to an oak examination table, awaiting the patient.

"Doctor Parker," MacIntyre said, extending his hand. "It's been a long time."

"Tim, my boy, aren't you due for a physical?" the physician replied, shaking the policeman's hand.

"You know I am," MacIntyre answered. "You also know how much I hate doctors."

Doc Parker smiled.

"So this big fella here is the patient?" he asked, gesturing towards McAdams.

"I am," the Canadian responded.

"Aren't you a little old to be roughhousing in a bar?" the doctor teased.

"By the outcome of tonight's encounter, I'd have to agree with you, Doc."

"You boys can leave us alone," Dr. Parker instructed, turning his attention to the wound. "By the looks of things, doesn't appear to be all that serious."

"Sure thing, Doc," Andrews said. "We'll wait in the lobby."

The three men found empty chairs in the reception area of the hospital and sat down to wait for George McAdams.

"Good thing for you, Finlander," MacIntyre said as he scanned a day-old copy of the *Duluth Herald*, the City's evening newspaper, "that Dennis O'Cochrane and me are lodge brothers. Without his say-so, I would have locked the two of you up for rioting."

Anders Alhomaki's narrow features were accented by shadow. He sat in an oak chair, his small weather-roughened hands on his lap, and studied MacIntyre with dark eyes.

"Those dandies you reduced to rubbish," Andrews added, "have some pretty prominent papas. Take young Horace Ellison, for example. His father, Eustace Ellison, not only owns half of the Spalding Hotel, the place you and the big Canuck busted up, but he also owns nearly all of the land at the top of the Incline. He's a wealthy man, a land speculator and lumberman; owns Amalgamated Properties. He's someone you don't want to get on the wrong side of."

"The boys started it," Alhomaki replied.

"That's the tale O'Cochrane tells. Don't know as I believe it," Andrews answered, looking at the Finn. "Could be the darkie was the cause of it all. Them folks don't know their places any more. Could have been he said something to provoke the boys."

"He didn't do anything," Alhomaki replied, his eyes locking with those of the cop.

"So you say," Andrews responded, disbelief behind his words.

"O'Cochrane backs him up," Tim MacIntyre inserted. "I'll take the word of my fellow Knight of Columbus brother any day."

"You would, you stupid Mick," Andrews said through a slight smile.

"Andrews, you dumb Englishman, what the hell would you know?"

A mechanical wall clock clicked off the time. In the examination room down the hall, the Canadian released howls of protest as Dr. Parker irrigated and cleansed the gunshot wound.

"The big fella is letting us know he's aggravated," MacIntyre observed, sipping on a cup of tepid coffee.

"It's gotta hurt somethin' fierce, having iodine poured into a gaping sore like that," Andrews agreed.

Anders Alhomaki remained silent. He closed his eyes and settled his chin against his chest.

Elin doesn't want me to attend the funeral, he thought. *But her mother was someone who deserves my respect. After all she did for us, I'm not certain I can just stay away.*

"Say, what happened to the Ellison kid?" Andrews asked his partner, interrupting the Finn's contemplation.

"Took him out to West Duluth, to the Duluth Hospital, for privacy," MacIntyre replied. "Less likely to be a reporter from the *Tribune-Herald* poking around out there in the late hours of the evening."

"Always said Eustace Ellison was a smart man," the Englishman asserted. "Smarter than his son, by a long shot. Doc Graham runs the West Duluth Hospital. Tight-lipped. Good choice."

The Irish cop nodded in agreement. A door opened. Doc Parker and George McAdams appeared in the reception area. McAdams's right arm was in a sling.

"He's all set to go," the physician noted as he entered the lobby.

"What do I owe you?" the Canadian asked, reaching into the rear pocket of his trousers for his billfold.

"Keep your money," Doc Parker replied. "Mr. Eustace Ellison is covering it."

The Canadian's face bore an element of confusion.

"Come on, you stupid Canuck," Andrews bellowed, rising from his chair. "You heard the man. The bill's been handled. Only thing that Mr. Ellison asks is that you keep this thing under your hat, understand? No one is to find out what happened tonight, least of all some snoopy ink dabber from the newspapers."

Anders Alhomaki forced himself to stand. His head began to pound from the after-affects of the vodka.

"You understand, Finlander?" the Englishman asked, a hint of derision in his tone. "Can you keep your ignorant mouth shut?"

Anders winced at the insult, clenched his fists, but said nothing. He found that, like so many times in his adopted homeland, his head nodded involuntarily and he held his tongue, allowing the indignity to dissipate.

"Good. Let's get these two brawlers home, shall we, Mac?"

The Ford Model T police cruiser bounced over Superior Street's rough brick surface. A set of trolley tracks ran down the middle of the broad street. The automobile surged west. It was well after midnight. Carriages full of late night revelers, pulled by well-groomed teams of light horses, rolled by. Teamsters and their mules stood patiently outside darkened storefronts on side streets and alleyways adjacent to the thoroughfare, waiting for laborers to unload or load their freight wagons.

"You staying at the Spalding?" MacIntyre asked George McAdams as the Irish policeman drove the black Ford.

"That's right," the Canadian replied.

"How's the shoulder?" Anders Alhomaki asked his companion as the car passed in front of the Lyceum Theater.

The automobile narrowly missed a group of patrons exiting the last show of the evening, before making a u-turn on Superior Street.

"Sore as hell but I'll live," McAdams said through a smile. "Like I said before, look me up in Port William," he added. "Stay in touch."

"You've got my word on it," the Finn replied, extending his right hand.

McAdams smiled. "I'm afraid I'll have to pass on the handshake, Mr. Alhomaki."

The Canadian raised his injured arm in its sling for emphasis.

"I understand," Anders replied through a grin.

Officer Andrews slammed the rear passenger door of the car and climbed back into the front seat.

MacIntyre accelerated the squad car away from the curb without waiting to ensure that George McAdams had made it safely inside the hotel.

"Talonen's Boarding House?" the Irish cop asked, looking over his shoulder as he drove.

Anders Alhomaki nodded.

"He doesn't say much," Fulton Andrews observed. "Cat got your tongue, Finlander?"

MacIntyre chuckled.

"Andrews, he's not going to rise to your bait. I'll wager our passenger is a lot smarter than you give him credit for, eh, Mr. Alhomaki? He's tired, a little hung-over, and looking for a nice warm bed is all, am I right?"

"Yes sir," Anders replied in a soft voice, carefully controlling his Finnish accent.

"See? Like I said, he's a lot smarter than he looks."

The police car pulled up in front of Talonen's. Andrews, who had taken pains to open the door for McAdams, didn't offer Anders Alhomaki the same courtesy. The miner exited the vehicle, the gasoline engine purring at idle, the movement of the pistons reverberating off the closely placed buildings, and shut the door.

"Have a good night," Officer MacIntyre advised through the open driver's side window, as Alhomaki began crossing the street.

"You also," the Finn replied as he hustled past a brownstone warehouse located next to Talonen's.

The vehicle's engine sputtered. Hard rubber tires bit into the bricked street. The vehicle shot forward. Anders Alhomaki walked at a deliberate pace. A near-summer wind blew in from the south. The Finn's head was bowed in thought. He didn't see the two men standing beneath the awning of the warehouse building until one of the men spoke.

"Finlander," a male voice, its texture rough and forbidding, called out. "A word with you."

Alhomaki stopped. His heart began to pound.

There's no good reason for someone to be waiting for me at this hour, along this street, Anders thought.

A huge figure moved under the canvas awning. Another man, whose presence Alhomaki merely felt but could not see, remained an insinuation.

"Yes?"

The Finn stopped on the sidewalk directly in front of his lodging place. An electric street lamp provided ancillary light, but did not reveal the details of the stranger's face. Alhomaki's left hand pushed aside the fabric of his suit coat. His fingers found the worn moose horn handle of a knife, resting in a scabbard against his left hip. The knife boasted a five-inch blade. Anders's blade was the type of weapon carried by nearly every Finnish male in the North Country; the type of knife banned by most logging outfits from their bunkhouses as too accessible and dangerous. Anders's fingers eased the handle free of the scabbard's grip but did not remove the weapon from its sheath.

The stranger quickly closed the space between them. He was larger and more imposing than George McAdams. The brim of a dress hat concealed his face. He wore an immaculate business suit, freshly polished spats that shone in the meager light, and a pressed white shirt beneath a vest. A gold watch chain intersected his ample belly and disappeared into a pocket.

"You don't need to know who I am," the man asserted, stopping a safe distance from the Finn. "All you need to know is that Mr. Eustace Ellison asked me to give you a message. You know who Mr. Ellison is, don't you, sir?"

"Sir" was said in such a way as to convey condescension.

"I know of him."

The stranger emitted a short laugh and turned slightly to the man in the shadows. "You catch that, Bud? He knows 'of him'."

The big man turned back to Alhomaki. "That's rich, that's rich. Mr. Ellison is particularly distressed about what transpired this evening, in regards to his son Horace."

The Finn's hand grasped the knife.

"Relax, Mr. Alhomaki," the stranger said. "That's not going to do you any good. My friend over there stays in the dark because he's a bad seed, a really sick man, in terms of his humanity. He's got a sawed-off ten-gauge pointed at you. And his trigger finger's a bit unsteady, if you get my drift. So just ease that blade back into its hiding place and listen to what I have to say."

The Finn withdrew his fingers from the handle of the hunting knife.

"Good. Now here's the thing. Mr. Ellison, the man I work for, now he's an understanding man. He can forgive most transgressions, even those against young Horace, who often has a big mouth and a quick temper. But, sir, he can't ignore the fact that you chose to do permanent injury to his namesake. A fight is one thing. Breaking a man's jaw and making him drink soup for a month... well, that, sir, is quite another matter."

The stranger shifted his weight.

"Bud, I think I've got his attention. For Chris sake's relax and lower that blunderbuss, would you?"

Alhomaki detected no movement in the shadows.

"Stubborn. Bud is one stubborn Norwegian," the stranger said. "Anyway, here's Mr. Ellison's proposal. He's willing to allow you to leave the city without any further recrimination, but you need to leave tomorrow morning. At first light. I've been authorized to pay your way on the first train out of town, wherever you want to go. But it must be tomorrow."

Anders Alhomaki's eyelids quivered.

"I have a funeral to attend on Monday," Anders whispered. "The mother of a significant friend."

"Oh, yes, Miss Gustafsson. Lovely girl. I'm afraid that won't be possible."

"Who are you to tell me what to do?" Anders hissed. The Finn's hand reached for the bone handle of his knife. The knife moved against its leather sheath.

"Unfortunately, you now find yourself in a bad situation, I'm afraid," the stranger continued, no emotion apparent in his voice. "And please refrain from doing anything foolish. As I've stated quite plainly, as plainly as I can, Bud would like nothing better than to pull the trigger on that big goose gun he's holding. I'm afraid there'd be precious little of you left if that happens."

The Finn relented and removed his hand from the knife's handle.

"Besides, how long do you think a powerful man like Karl Gustafsson is going to put up with the likes of you sniffing around the skirts of his only daughter? Take a look at the world, man. You've got nothing to offer the pretty Miss Elin. You're an illiterate, foul-smelling, hard-drinking laborer who happens to have been lucky enough to have spent some time with the most eligible single Finnish woman in the city of Duluth. Count your blessings, my friend, that you have sampled, as I understand it, the wonderful charms of that young matron. But don't deceive yourself. It can't and it won't continue."

Alhomaki's face flashed anger.

"I understand, friend. I understand you're upset. But do you really think that, with Laina Gustafsson gone, Karl Gustafsson will allow your little trysts to continue? Use your head, man. I know you may not be educated, but you seem to possess a modicum of intellect. Do I have to spell this out for you? Your time here in Duluth is up. You've managed to upset my employer and Mr. Gustafsson, a friend of Oscar Larson, the most powerful Finn in this town. You can't expect to avoid the consequences of your actions. Tomorrow morning, Mr. Alhomaki, you must not be found within fifty miles of Duluth. That's as plain as I can make it."

The Finn turned to escape further discussion. A hand reached out, extending further than Anders would have believed possible, given the distance between the two men, and grabbed Alhomaki's right shoulder with undeniable power.

"Don't be a fool," the stranger hissed.

The man shoved an envelope into the pocket of Alhomaki's coat.

"There's fifty dollars and an open pass on the Duluth, Missabe, and Northern in the envelope. I understand you've got the potential of a job up in Virginia. That meets my employer's requirement of being more than fifty miles away. Take the first DM and N train tomorrow morning, friend. That's the advice I'm here to give you."

Alhomaki's hand slid into his coat pocket. His fingers touched paper. The big man retreated, joining his companion beneath the canvas awning. Darkness prevented the Finn from witnessing detail. Anders's body shook from nervous tension as he watched the men retreat at a steady pace.

"Trouble?" Olli Kinkkonen asked as he stepped out of the shadows shrouding the entrance to the Talonen Boarding House, his eyes riveted upon the silhouettes of the departing thugs.

The miner nodded.

"I think it's best you come inside," Kinkkonen said.

Anders Alhomaki didn't object. He followed Olli Kinkkonen into the rooming house.

Chapter 11

Elin Gustafsson tossed and turned through the night. Visions of her mother's agonizing battle with cancer robbed the young woman of sleep. The prospect of her mother's still body, buried deep in the moist ground of Forest Hill Cemetery in the streetcar suburb of Woodland, stabbed at her mind like a brutal and persistent thorn.

At first, Laina had believed that she was only suffering from the after-effects of too much involvement in social and religious activities. She had secretly joined the Finnish Temperance Movement. Her involvement in the suffrage movement also continued, as did her weekly Bible studies with Reverend Heikki Sarvela, the pastor of the Finnish Lutheran Church on St. Croix Avenue. The effects of Laina's constant running, catching trolleys to make appointments with like-minded women located in the various neighborhoods of Duluth and the outlying communities of West Duluth, Proctor, and Gary-New Duluth took their toll. When she began to sag, presumably under the weight of fatigue, Laina believed that the remedy was simple: *I need rest*, she had thought. *I'm a little tired is all.*

Karl Gustafsson had noted the slowing of his wife's pace as she tried to self-diagnose and treat her loss of appetite and sudden lack of energy. He knew, through the extensive web of personal contacts he had woven through Duluth's citizenry, that Laina was in danger of becoming an outspoken radical. To the more conservative Finns in the community she appeared to be on the verge of joining the Socialists, at a time when the ascendancy of Karl's law practice was assured. Karl Gustafsson had allowed his wife her space, her privacy, in matters of politics and social issues, in an attempt to preserve a specter of a marriage between them. Despite these efforts, they were no longer occupying the same bed, their conjugal relationship having ended with Laina's discovery of a poem Karl had written to Sofia Wirtanen, the maid who shared their home. Laina had thereafter systematically accumulated sufficient evidence of Karl's indiscretions to demand the dismissal of the servant. A fictitious calm had asserted itself over the Gustafsson household but it was clear that, in return for this hesitant truce, Karl Gustafsson had given up any residual authority he had once claimed over his wife.

Discretion had not always accompanied the attorney's romantic liaisons. In addition to discovering Karl's sonnet to the servant girl slipped neatly between pages of Walt Whitman's *Leaves of Grass*, a first edition found by Laina in the maid's living quarters in the walk-up attic of the mansion, Laina had been privy to gossip. Rumors of excursions by Karl and the young maid along Skyline Parkway ("tally-hos" they were called in the vernacular of the day) with other rich and powerful men and their "escorts;" tales of Sunday picnics held while the men were supposedly engaged in business, all had reached Laina Gustafsson's ears shortly after Sofia Wirtanen began her employment with the family. Vapors of unpleasant innuendo eventually made their way to Laina, describing trysts at the St. Louis Hotel and the Spalding, conclusions to gay evenings spent by the couple at the Lyceum or the Orpheum, where Karl and Sofia watched vaudeville performances by visiting international stars. Laina was also made painfully aware of excursions made by her husband and his lover up the Incline to absorb the breath-taking views of the city, the bay, and the lake. All of this news, gathered as it was through the eyes and ears of women close to Laina Gustafsson, eventually found its intended audience.

The eruption took place two nights after Elin Gustafsson's return to Duluth. Elin had just settled into her room to unpack her trunk and valise, her clothing having been stuffed into her luggage in a desperate hurry to return, when she heard a debate raging several floors below.

"She must leave and she must leave now," Laina Gustafsson had protested, her voice strong and firm despite the disease. "I will not have that Jezebel living under my roof," Laina continued, her words crisp and determined in their delivery.

Elin's parents were in Karl's study. A fire smoldered in the fireplace, the logs damp with autumn rain. Karl sat dejectedly behind his ornate oak desk, hands pressed flat against an ink blotter covering the desk's wooden writing surface. His normally pale face was flushed with embarrassment at having his terminally ill wife discover his secret love affair.

"Laina, be reasonable. She'll never find another job working as a domestic if I release her outright. Give me some time to ease her into another position."

"Like you ease yourself inside of her?" Laina responded in a decidedly unladylike fashion.

"That's uncalled for. There's no reason to bring this discussion down to that level," Karl asserted, the lack of moral superiority apparent in his voice.

"Is it? A flirtation, I could understand. An occasional visit to a whorehouse, perhaps that could be forgiven if you were cautious and discreet. An affair with a twenty-two- year-old servant girl, conducted in open society? I doubt that anyone would disagree with my assessment of the vile nature of your conduct."

"Laina," Karl mumbled. "I never meant to..."

"Save the apologies. I'm not interested in the 'hows' or the 'whys'. And I'm not interested in discussing Christian forgiveness. I want that girl out of my house tomorrow morning. Period. End of debate. If you do not wish to accede to my resolution, then I will have no other choice but to take this discussion into the public realm."

Karl Gustafsson stood up and slammed his right fist, its flesh meaty and large, against the ink blotter.

"Damn you, woman. If you had been more interested in taking care of business at home instead of traipsing up and down this city on your urgent liberal errands, perhaps I would have stayed faithful. Did you ever think that your time away from this house, from your place at my side, might, in some fashion, be responsible for where we find ourselves tonight?"

Laina had batted her eyelids. The pain... The pain had returned despite the surgery she had endured at the West Duluth Hospital. Dr. Malcom Heitala had removed two tumors, one the size of a man's hand, the other the size of a plum, from her insides. He had also removed her ovaries and her uterus. Through the nausea caused by the anesthesia, through the long convalescence following the assault on her feminine organs, she had focused her mind upon her husband's dalliance. She had vowed, as she recovered, to regain control of her own home, to reclaim that space as her own, regardless of the cost. Her mouth turned upward in a sanguine grin:

"That's rich, blaming me for your inability to be true to our vows. My, what a fine lawyer you make."

Elin had eavesdropped on the conversation. Her parents' voices were carried to the third floor by the home's heating vents. Animosity rose in her mind against her father, like a tidal wave forming after a typhoon wind. Disgust colored her love and affinity for Karl Gustafsson. Despite his taciturn ways, despite his conservative bent, she had indeed, up until that moment in time, loved her father. But as she listened to her mother's anguished unraveling of the man's deceptions, Elin felt the natural affection she had always held for her father slip dangerously close to the precipice of hate.

The next morning, Sofia Wirtanen was gone. Her room in the attic of the mansion was empty and sparkling clean. No trace of the woman remained behind to rekindle bitter memories of the maid's unchaste alliance with the master of the house. Elin later discovered that her father had not sent the servant girl to Chicago, to which he had alluded in the days subsequent to his argument with his wife, but had instead installed Miss Wirtanen as a nanny with a Finnish client across St. Louis Bay in Superior. The woman remained close at hand, and in Elin's mind, accessible to Karl Gustafsson throughout Laina Gustafsson's illness.

Laina's end was grotesque and brutal. When Elin arrived from Houghton in October of 1913, her mother remained able to

99

accomplish the tasks of daily living. She was capable of bathing, combing her hair, of doing small chores around the home. Her social and political activities eroded slowly, beginning with an end to her attendance at Socialist meetings and ultimately culminating in an inability to attend Sunday worship at the Finnish church. With each small setback, with each minor disruption in her active calendar, Laina slipped deeper and deeper into depression. By March of 1914, she was essentially bedridden. Headaches, the result of an inoperable brain tumor metastasized from the cancer in her ovaries, made it impossible for her to concentrate. The mass also impinged upon her brain's ability to communicate with her body. Diapers were necessary. Laina's gait became unsteady, causing her to fall repeatedly between her bed and the master bathroom. Elin was forced to take a leave of absence from the Normal School to care for her mother. Karl was of little use. The few times that he felt compelled to visit his former bedroom and spend time with his wife, he sat silently in an overstuffed chair, staring at the flame of a gas fireplace across the room, his eyes closed in self-pity, his mind set in defeat.

During these rare visits by her father, Elin asked Karl to read to Laina from some of Laina's favorite books. Elin would encourage her father to pick up Laina's thumb-worn copies of *Pride and Prejudice* by Jane Austen, or Fyodor Dostoyevsky's *Crime and Punishment*, and read to Laina from her beloved novels. Laina's love of words, her need to revel in the humanity of these authors at the ending of her time, was patent. Though Elin saw glimpses of this need communicated by her mother's eyes, eyes increasingly glazed into vacancy by morphine, Elin could not compel her father to interact with her mother. If Karl Gustafsson spoke to his wife of twenty-five years in that bedroom, his words were idle representations of a day's work or bits and pieces of downtown gossip that did nothing to ease the pain of Laina's illness or the hurt of Karl Gustafsson's infidelity.

There was no great sigh, no revelation of fear or trepidation, during the last moments of Laina's existence. The day before Elin reunited with Anders Alhomaki upon the miner's return to Duluth from Michigan, Laina Gustafsson fell into a deep sleep. Elin was by her mother's side, reading the morning *Tribune*, seated in a chair in the master bedroom and carefully keeping watch. Elin had just completed the newspaper's section devoted to Northwestern Minnesota when she noticed that Laina's chest no longer labored against the soft linen sheets of the bed.

"Mother?" Elin had asked, placing the newspaper on an adjacent nightstand. "Mother?"

Elin leaned across her mother's frail torso, taking in the wasted skin, noting that the contours of her mother's once beautifully full face had become edged and bony. Laina's eyes were closed, as if she had simply drifted off to slumber. Laina's mouth was open, as it most often was when she slept on her back, under the influence of narcotics.

"Mother," Elin whispered as she crawled into bed with the dead woman. "Mother, I love you," Elin said in Finnish, drawing the warm body of Laina Gustafsson close to her as she spoke.

There were too many people at the funeral. Perhaps two hundred men and women, nearly all Finns, stood outside the Finnish Church, listening through the open front doors of the sanctuary to Reverend Sarvela's eulogy. Another hundred or so occupied pews inside the little chapel. Elin sat dutifully with Karl and other members of their extended family: cousins and assorted aunts and uncles from both sides of her lineage. Most were strangers to her, folks she'd met once or twice at infrequent reunions held by her father's side of the family, or at special occasions observed by her mother's side. Eight men carried Laina's casket, business associates and socially connected friends of her father.

If mother were here, Elin couldn't help but think as the pallbearers left the church with her mother's body locked inside an ornate black walnut coffin, *she'd be appalled that none of her women friends were asked to carry her on her last journey*.

Tears trickled down Elin's cheeks. Dense clouds drifted over the city as she walked limply beside her father, his enormous left arm around her waist, holding her up, compelling her along. Elin Gustafsson's eyes batted moisture.

The Gustafssons stopped in front of a horse-drawn hearse. Elin rummaged through her black patent leather purse for a handkerchief. Absorbing the tears with linen, she looked out into the crowd. Her eyes passed over scores of folks that meant nothing to her.

At the far end of the line of mourners, he stood with a felt hat held awkwardly in his hands. Her mouth inadvertently turned into a sad smile, a gesture that was not lost upon Karl Gustafsson as he pulled his daughter into the hearse.

"That Finn best be on a train out of here," Karl Gustafsson whispered under his breath. "He's no longer welcome in this town."

Chapter 12

Coal dust settled over the buildings of the village like fine ebony snow. Laundry left imprudently on clotheslines soiled quickly in the backyards of the little cottages lining the treeless streets. An early pioneer of the area had bestowed the name "Proctorknott" upon the town in honor of his friend, a senator from Kentucky. Proctor, Minnesota, as it came to be known, was built on the edge of the hill overlooking West Duluth, and served as the locus of the Duluth, Missabe, and Northern Railroad's main switching yard.

In 1914, steam-powered locomotives delivered load after load of high-grade iron ore mined from the Mesabi, Cuyuna, and Vermilion Ranges to ore docks located in West Duluth and Two Harbors. Trains destined for West Duluth traversed the Proctor yards, pulling upwards of one hundred open ore cars that were heaped full of iron-bearing rock. The ore, once loaded onto steamships, was bound for the blast furnaces of Cleveland, Pittsburgh, and Gary. In addition to carrying ore, the Missabe also provided a valuable ancillary service for residents of the area, by transporting passengers and freight between the cities and tiny mining locations scattered throughout Minnesota's Iron Ranges. Other than the occasional luxury dining car or elegant Pullman added to carry executives or politicians for special events, the Missabe passenger trains were strictly pedestrian.

Anders Alhomaki waited at the DM&N passenger depot in Proctor, protected from drifting coal ash by the building's eaves. He sat on a hard wooden bench, dressed in his one good suit and his one good shirt, waiting for the train to Virginia, Minnesota. He was to begin employment the following day as a carpenter in the Alpena Mine, working alongside his friend, Tim Laitila. As he waited in the late spring heat, watching dirty soot floating through clean air, white sunlight reflecting off row upon row of empty iron ore cars standing in the vast Missabe yard, Anders Alhomaki's mind began to wander.

Forest Hill Cemetery was and is located in a peaceful glade off Woodland Avenue in Duluth. Surrounded by Dutch-style gambrel-roofed homes, built for the employees of the Marshall Wells hardware empire, in essence a factory town located within the city, Morley Heights crowds the spines of steep pitches overlooking the cemetery. A branch of Amity Creek weaves through the graveyard, gurgling and bubbling as it falls towards Lake Superior. Geese and ducks, content in the knowledge that they won't be hunted within the city limits, still seek respite in the small ponds and pools located within the graveyard's iron gated perimeter.

The mourners had congregated beneath a regally proportioned weeping willow. Waves of heat shimmered off headstones. The pallbearers carrying Laina Gustafsson's casket struggled across the lawn to where Reverend Sarvela waited. The horses teamed to Mrs. Gustafsson's hearse stood patiently upon the cemetery's gravel access road. The animals twitched their ears and swished their tails in defense against early season deer and horse flies. The sky was serrated. White clouds interrupted the open blue vault above the cemetery.

Anders felt compelled to attend the burial. Laina Gustafsson had been a good woman, a faithful Christian and a devoted mother. Laina accepted Anders Alhomaki for what he was: a hard-working, honest immigrant, and had not held Anders's limited education or prospects against the man. For that, Anders was willing to risk whatever violence or recriminations Eustace Ellison might have had in store for the miner as a consequence for Anders's violating Ellison's edict to vacate the town.

The Finn surveyed the crowd. Amongst the well-dressed mourners, there were plenty of folks that Anders didn't know. Two or three of the men looked to be the size of the stranger who had threatened him in front of the boarding house. Unless he heard the men speak, however, he couldn't be certain. The voice. He'd never forget the texture and phrasing of the voice of the giant who had confronted him.

Olli Kinkkonen had agreed to attend the service with Anders. The dockworker wasn't exactly the sort of man one would select as a bodyguard. Kinkkonen was slight of build and nondescript in nearly every sense of the word, but he was a loyal friend, stubborn and unwilling to back down from a good tussle. He stood next to Alhomaki in the shade of an oak tree, some distance from the ceremony, maintaining a vigil to ensure there would be no surprises.

Elin Gustafsson's shoulders sloped in grief as she nervously shifted back and forth in front of her mother's crypt. Karl Gustafsson's massive forearm propped her up, kept her from tottering headlong into the pit. The lawyer's face was drawn, not, to Anders Alhomaki's observation, in upset, but in apparent aggravation. Karl Gustafsson glared at Alhomaki from inside the shadow cast by the lawyer's dress hat. There was no mistaking Gustafsson's intent. He was furious.

The pallbearers straddled the gaping hole and allowed the coffin a slow descent by maintaining firm pressure on the ropes cradling the walnut box. The casket settled evenly on cool earth. Their job completed, the pallbearers, including Karl Gustafsson's friend Oscar Larson, stepped behind the bereaved family to listen to Pastor Sarvela's words of committal.

A crow cawed. The creature rose from grass still wet with dew. The crow's flight disturbed the still air. Anders followed the bird's path as it sought a draft. Olli Kinkkonen nudged Anders Alhomaki with an elbow, causing Anders to return his eyes to the ceremony.

"I think he might be your man," Kinkkonen said, nodding slightly in the direction of the crowd.

"Where?" Anders whispered.

"There," the dockworker reiterated, pointing surreptitiously with an index finger.

A brawny gentleman in a finely crafted three-piece suit towered over the other men and women standing nearby. The man's wide-brimmed hat was tilted back on his head, allowing Anders to see the details of his large face.

"Why do you think that's him?"

"Because he hasn't taken his eyes off you since you arrived. And because the clean-shaven man standing next to him in the two-hundred-dollar suit is Eustace Ellison."

Alhomaki studied the big man. After an interval of scrutiny, Anders Alhomaki shifted his attention to Eustace Ellison's other companions.

"I don't see Ellison's kid."

"He's not in any shape to be seen, my friend. It'll be a good month before young Horace Ellison shows his battered face in public."

Alhomaki returned to his examination of the hulking stranger. The man returned Anders's look without yielding an indication of his thoughts.

"That might be him. Might not. I just can't be sure."

"I'll keep my eyes open and my ears peeled," Olli Kinkkonen advised.

The pastor concluded the committal service. Reverend Sarvela held a Finnish Bible firmly in his strong hands as he recited two passages: one from Joshua in the Old Testament, and one from the Gospel of John. Evidence of controlled weeping escaped the crowd. Some distance from the service, two gravediggers waited silently on a gentle knoll, their weatherworn work hats held tightly in their calloused hands, their eyes respectfully downcast, their shovels propped against nearby ash trees.

As Reverend Sarvela uttered his final words of consolation, Elin Gustafsson's sobs advanced. Her grief became audible to everyone in attendance. The young woman's father whispered in her ear, maintaining a careful vigil on Anders Alhomaki as he confided in his daughter.

"He's coming over to talk to you," Kinkkonen advised, locking his gaze on the big stranger's advance.

"It's a free country," Anders Alhomaki muttered in Finnish.

The giant ambled easily over uneven ground, the grace of his movement at odds with his physique. The mourners began to depart. Motorcars and horse-drawn carriages exited the cemetery. Anders Alhomaki lost sight of Elin Gustafsson as he concentrated his attention on the approach of the

106

stranger. Two men accompanied the giant. All three men moved with ease and confidence.

"Mr. Alhomaki, a word with you, if I might," the stranger called out as the Finn turned to avoid the impending confrontation.

Anders waited as the big man approached. Olli Kinkkonen leveled his fedora on his head and plunged both hands nervously into the front pockets of his dress trousers. The stranger stopped short of the two Finns. The two henchmen remained behind the stranger.

"Apparently I was not clear in my instructions," the man began. "I thought my advice to you was succinct and direct."

Anders's heart raced. He listened to the soft voice of the intruder, the quality of the man's diction betraying intellect and education.

"It was."

The stranger smiled, exposing a large overbite that disrupted the handsome lines of his face.

"You ignored my warning."

Anders grinned nervously. His left hand searched along the seam of his dress slacks for the knife scabbard, but came up empty. He remembered he'd left his knife in his room out of respect for the departed.

"Before we discuss the matter, might we have the benefit of an introduction?" Olli Kinkkonen inserted, reflexively balling his fists in his pockets as he eyed the stranger.

"Ah, yes. Where are my manners? My name is William Burnside. These two fellows in my company – well, it's best you don't know their names, though Mr. Alhomaki has already met Bud, the man to my right; at least, in a manner of speaking."

"What business do you have with Mr. Alhomaki?" Kinkkonen continued, emboldened by Burnside's placidity.

The big man's lips parted, displaying the pink lining of his mouth.

"That's between Mr. Alhomaki and myself."

"Whatever you have to say to me, you can say in front of Mr. Kinkkonen."

Burnside glanced over his shoulder, monitoring the exit of the crowd.

"Mr. Alhomaki, you were told to relocate yourself at least fifty miles from here. You were told that your presence wasn't welcome at this service. I thought I made that exceedingly clear to you on Saturday night."

"You did."

"Then why this disobedience? There's no reason for you to ignore my admonitions, unless to convey disrespect. And when you show disrespect to me, you show disrespect to Mr. Ellison. And that's not something Mr. Ellison tolerates well."

Anders shifted his weight.

"Relax, Finlander," Bud whispered. "No one's going to start anything at a funeral."

Burnside nodded.

"He's right, you know. This is neither the time nor the place for us to deal properly with your disrespect."

"Maybe you fellows should march yourselves back across the grass, get in your Tin Lizzy, and get the hell out of here," Olli Kinkkonen sneered, the excitement of a looming physical altercation palpable in his words.

Burnside frowned.

"As I stated plainly when we first began this dialogue, little man, this discussion is none of your concern," William Burnside said with measured patience.

"It is if three men confront a friend of mine," Kinkkonen replied matter-of-factly.

"'Confrontation' is such a strong term," Bud interjected. "We're merely having a serious discussion."

A large man, dressed in a well fitted three-piece-suit, separated from the mourners and advanced towards the group.

"I'd say this discussion is coming to a close," Burnside noted.

The man's stride claimed yards of earth with each step. When he arrived, he inserted his ample body between the two camps.

"Gentlemen," Karl Gustafsson said quietly. "Is this really necessary? My wife is barely in the ground and here you are, posturing like schoolboys. Out of respect for Laina and my daughter, would you please disperse and take your argument elsewhere?"

Burnside and Gustafsson stood nearly eye-to-eye.

"But my instructions from Mr. Ellison were to ensure that this Finlander left the city on yesterday's train. I thought you were in agreement," Burnside replied, no trace of emotion in his steady voice.

"I am. But there are some things that are better left for another time and place. This is one of those things," the lawyer said.

Anders Alhomaki relaxed.

"There will be a time and a place when we address your disrespect, Mr. Alhomaki, Mr. Kinkkonen," Burnside continued. "Until then," he had advised, tipping his hat. "My deepest sympathies to you, Mr. Gustafsson, and to your daughter."

"Your concern is much appreciated, as is your discretion," Karl Gustafsson responded.

William Burnside and his companions retreated toward an idling Ford motorcar. Gustafsson held his ground.

"You're not welcome here," the attorney began. "You've never been welcome here."

Alhomaki returned Gustafsson's keen gaze with defiance.

"I don't think it's your place to say," Anders replied.

"It is. It is when your presence disrupts the orderly and secure future of my only child," Karl Gustafsson added. "What have you to offer Elin, Mr. Alhomaki, beyond a life of poverty, ignorance, and uncertainty? My daughter is an educated woman. Granted, some of that education has instilled so-called 'modern ideas' in her head, ideas that are troubling and devious. But, after all is said and done, she is a bright, educated, lovely young girl, from a part of society that you will never attain." Gustafsson paused. "You may think that because I have intervened here, on the grounds where my wife now rests, I somehow condone your presence; I accept your unhealthy interest in my daughter. Rest assured that such is not the case. I despise the illicit and Godless time you spent with Elin in Northern Michigan. I should have sent men to bring her back, men like Mr. Burnside, dozens of whom Eustace Ellison and I have access to at the drop of a dime. Men, who would have left you rotting in some nameless, abandoned copper mine at the end of some desolate trail. I don't know why I allowed your immoral conduct. I should have stopped it then. I am stopping it now."

Anders Alhomaki squinted. He tried to make out the beautiful face of the lawyer's daughter as she sat in the rear seat of the funeral carriage. His fingers dug into the soft wool of his trousers, manipulating the seams to steady his nerves.

"She's an adult woman. She can make her own choices."

"She's my daughter. You, a man of your age, and childless at that, cannot understand what such a connection entails. I've made it clear that you will not see her. This is the only conversation I will have with you on the subject. I will not waste words or time on the likes of you, Mr. Alhomaki. I trust you understand. It is over. You will leave the city of Duluth today, or you may not like the outcome of the situation."

"Who are you to threaten, Mr. Gustafsson?" Olli Kinkkonen interrupted. "Anders is a free man, in a free country. Your daughter, as Anders points out, is an adult woman, free to make her own decisions."

"Shut your mouth," Karl Gustafsson retorted, his voice rising in anger. "This is none of your concern."

"It's my concern when big shots start to threaten my friends."

Anders raised his hand to silence Kinkkonen.

"This isn't the time or the place, as you so aptly stated, Mr. Gustafsson. It so happens that I'm leaving Duluth this afternoon for Virginia. I have a position that requires me to move to the Iron Range. Does that satisfy you?"

Gustafsson studied the face of his adversary.

"That's acceptable, so long as you don't contact Elin in any fashion. No messages, no letters, and, most important of all, no clandestine visits."

Alhomaki had nodded.

"We have an understanding, then, Mr. Alhomaki? That you will henceforth remain out of my daughter's life?"

"We have an understanding, Mr. Gustafsson."

The trip up the Western Incline, known as the Belt Line Railway, had presented a glorious view of the City. Duluth's broad-shouldered hills rose above the St. Louis River Basin and spread out north to south in an orderly fashion. The noonday sun cast fierce yellow light across the forest of new aspen and birch, sprouting along the logged-off hillside. Here and there, the occasional remaining white or red pine stood tall and solitary against weedy second growth. The iron wheels of the trolley carriage had clanked as the car passed over gaps in the Incline's steel rails. As cables pulled the conveyance up two miles of steep slope, away from Grand Avenue and 61st Avenue West and towards the Village of Proctor, Anders Alhomaki studied the landscape. His eyes closed inadvertently. The Finn fell into a light sleep before a jolt announced the tram's arrival at the top of the bluff. The sudden stop had roused Anders from his slumber.

Alhomaki spent the afternoon traversing the dirt streets of Proctor before settling in at the DM&N depot to wait for his train. Sitting on the pine bench beneath the sloping roof of the terminal, the bustle of arriving and departing ore trains prominent in the background, Anders Alhomaki's hands nervously folded and unfolded a printed train schedule. The address of the Duluth Normal School, the place of Elin Gustafsson's employment, had been written in Anders's hand upon the reverse of the train schedule.

Chapter 13
June, 1916

Unrelenting mud confronted Anders Alhomaki and Tim Laitila as they sought to shore up a narrow gauge railroad trestle leading to the Alpena mine.

"Shit," Laitila muttered in English as the claw hammer he was swinging slipped in his gloveless hand, occasioning him to strike his thumb with the head of the hammer.

The carpenter's mistake sent a searing pain through his thumb and into his wrist.

"Keep her level, man," Laitila observed, referring to the rough sawn cross-member that Anders Alhomaki was trying to hold in place against a steady downpour.

"Johnson has no business sending us out in this crap," Alhomaki observed, his woolen shirt and dungarees soaked through, his woolen long underwear clinging to the skin of his thighs. "It's unhealthy and dangerous."

"Isak Johnson could give a good Goddamn about his men," Laitila stewed. "He's a boss, one of them. Used to be you could trust the man to do the right thing, but with the mine playing itself out and jobs disappearing like water on a hot stone, he's changed. He'll do anything to please the bosses, anything to squeeze another ton of iron out of this shit hole."

Tim Laitila swung his hammer through seemingly impenetrable rain. Steel connected with steel, driving a twenty-penny spike through the white pine support into a red pine upright.

"That'll hold 'er," Laitila said, sucking hard on his injured thumb in an attempt to draw the swelling down. "Let's hit the break shed and get some hot coffee. Our pay envelopes should be ready. Maybe Freda will come around with them like she did last week. She's one gorgeous piece of flesh," Laitila said dreamily.

"She's only seventeen years old," Alhomaki admonished. "She's Elmer Henderson's daughter. I doubt that the boss of the Alpena mine would be happy knowing you covet his little girl. You're old enough to be her father. You're nothing but a common laborer. One finger on her lovely patrician skin likely gets you sacked, or worse yet, buys you a prison cell," Anders added, concluding the conversation in Finnish.

"Touching the likes of Freda Henderson might be worth getting sacked," Laitila mused. "I'd be free of this mud and slime. Getting sacked might make me settle down and find a job worth my considerable carpentry skills."

"You're a married man. And, according to that Bible you carry in your back pocket, one of religious conviction," Alhomaki replied in Finnish. "I'm shocked, Mr. Laitila. Shocked and scandalized by your lust."

As the men stepped under the protective eaves of the break shed, Tim Laitila pulled out the tattered copy of the Finnish-language Bible he carried with him wherever he went and recited aloud:

> I compare you, my love,
> to a mare of Pharaoh's chariots.
> Your cheeks are comely with ornaments,
> your neck, a string of jewels...
> Behold, you are beautiful, my love;
> behold, you are beautiful;
> your eyes are doves...

"Song of Solomon, Chapter 1, verses 9-15," Laitila added.

"Wonderful. But how does that change the fact that you're married, have two children, and have no business giving the bosses' daughter the once-over?"

"There's no harm in looking," Laitila advised. "It's the acting upon what you see that leads a man to spiritual decline."

Alhomaki chortled and continued, "You need this job more than I do. I'd keep my thoughts about little Freda to myself, if I were you."

"My mind is blank on the subject," Tim Laitila said through a smile.

Anders Alhomaki had been working in Virginia at the Alpena mine with Tim Laitila for nearly two years. The job had been steady. As carpenters, Anders and Tim Laitila remained on the job even during periods of layoff. They spent their time erecting and repairing trestles, fences, buildings, dams, and other structures on mining company property. Every day except Sunday, the men either walked or bummed rides from town, from their modest rooms in the Ukkula Boarding House at the east end of Chestnut Street in Virginia, to the mine. The two men received their weekly wages every Saturday at the rate of two and a half dollars a day. Their boss, Isak Johnson, scrutinized every hour of their work experience.

Johnson was a tough Norwegian, over sixty years old, and missing three fingers on his dominant right hand, the result of a band saw accident. The only saving grace to Johnson was his tendency to tip the bottle, a trait that generally left him incoherent by midday. This gave the carpenters under his charge free reign until Johnson sobered up the next morning, when he generally arrived at work hung over and pissed-off, a combination that begged silence and acquiescence from his men.

The door to the break shed was warped. It took all of Anders Alhomaki's considerable strength to pull the portal open. A wave of hot dry air and the smell of wood smoke greeted the men as they entered the building. Freda Henderson sat behind a desk, facing the door, her back to a pot-bellied stove roaring in the corner. An Italian miner by the name of Joe Greene stood in front of the girl, his arms crossed defiantly over his chest as he debated the amount of his paycheck with the female clerk.

"This ain't right," Greene said with a thick accent, his left hand shaking an open pay envelope in the warm air, his other hand clamped tightly to his crumpled paycheck. "This mine is stealing from the men who create its profit. This ain't fair, this thing that you do, Miss Henderson."

"Mr. Greene, the amount is correct. The cost of blasting caps and dynamite has to be deducted. You know that. The other supplies, they too must be accounted for. Be glad that the war has shut off immigration or you might not be working at all," the young woman responded calmly, obviously aware of the protections afforded her as the manager's daughter.

Mike Montgomery, head of mine security, stood behind the woman, his hands on his hips, his eyes riveted on the Italian miner. Other men filtered into the shed and stood behind Joe Greene. A small crowd gathered around the payroll desk. Montgomery shifted his right hand along his belt. A Colt Peacemaker revolver rested on his hip in a battered leather holster. Montgomery's fingers tapped expectantly on the weapon's steel hammer as he studied the faces of the men across the room.

"This is bullshit," one of the new arrivals shouted, his tone accusatory and angry. "We're getting crapped on again."

Montgomery extended to the limits of his six-foot frame and cleared his voice. "There'll be none of that. There's a lady present. Another outburst and you can all wait until next Saturday to get paid," the security guard announced, his voice barely rising above the noise of shuffling feet.

"To hell with this," Joe Greene hissed, tearing his paycheck in half and tossing it back onto the desk. "To hell with this. It's time the IWW took over."

Montgomery smiled. For months the more vocal miners on the Mesabi Iron Range had bandied about the threat of another strike. An undercurrent of discontent simmered all winter long, fermenting to a boil in the spring but never erupting into a walkout. It was June 3rd, 1916. Organizers from the IWW, the International Workers of the World, a Syndicalist group to the left of the more moderate Western Federation of Miners, had been instigating discontent in the iron mines for months. Joe Greene wasn't a member of the IWW. He wasn't a leader in the union. He was simply a man upset about his pay.

Greene pushed his way past the other miners and stepped out into the rain. His voice was loud and clear as he walked away from the shed: "To hell with this bullshit. Better to starve to death than to work for nothing," Joe Greene shouted as he walked off the job.

Alhomaki stepped forward.

"Andrew Maki," he said, using the name he had assumed and worked under on the Mesabi Iron Range.

Alhomaki stared at the woman. Freda Henderson's eyes appeared colorless and cheerless, empty of any sign of sympathy for the position of the working men standing in front of her. Her face was pale and without blush. Her lips were drawn in seriousness and absent color.

Why does Laitila think she's attractive? the Finn thought. *She's nowhere near as beautiful as his wife Mara. Or Elin.*

Anders Alhomaki still carried a torch for Elin Gustafsson after two years of forced separation. Despite his promise to Karl Gustafsson that he would not attempt to contact the lawyer's daughter, he had attempted to send messages detailing his life, his love, and his dreams to Elin. The messages were addressed to Elin in care of the Duluth Normal School. The envelopes were not returned by the post office, yet despite forwarding over a dozen letters, Anders never received a single response.

It is over, Anders Alhomaki finally realized. *She is moving on with her life. Probably for the best,* he thought the evening he decided to cease his futile entreaties. *She is from another world, another class. Eventually, she would have wanted more than an ignorant miner for a husband, more than a houseful of squalling children tugging at her skirts. Her upbringing and heredity would have pushed me out. Better now than later.*

The emptiness in Anders's gut caused by their break-up hadn't abated with the passage of time. Thoughts of the fair-haired woman with the steely eyes and full hips caught him unawares, at the oddest moments, defeating his best intentions to forget.

On a visit to Duluth in 1915, a year after he left Duluth on the heels of Karl Gustafsson and Eustace Ellison's threats, Anders Alhomaki had encountered George McAdams at the Dove Clothing store on Superior Street. The big Canadian had looked fit and trim as he tried on a new pair of Red Wing work boots in the store. The reunion between the men had been entirely unplanned.

"Anders," McAdams had exclaimed, as the Finn stood behind the Canadian, Alhomaki's reflection visible in a full-length mirror on the opposing wall.

McAdams turned and extended his hand, nearly tripping on untied bootlaces in the process.

"Good to see you, man."

"Likewise, George. It's been a long time. How's the shoulder?"

McAdams winked and rotated his right arm. "Like new. That old sawbones knew what he was doing. Haven't had a lick of trouble with it since. What brings you to town?"

Anders smiled.

"Land."

"Here, in Duluth? "

"There's nothing for me in this town. It's over between Elin and me."

"Elin?"

"Gustafsson."

"Karl Gustafsson's daughter?"

"The same."

"You're in love with Karl Gustafsson's daughter? I never knew."

"Was. Was in love. But it wouldn't have worked. She's an educated, modern woman. I'm just a miner trying to make a day's wages. It wouldn't have been a good match."

McAdams nodded.

"Let me square myself up on these boots and then you can fill me in on what brings you back to Duluth."

Outside the clothing store, a cool autumn wind had surged across the open water of the Big Lake as the men walked side by side down a cement sidewalk. Entering Smith's Cafeteria, the men stood in line behind other patrons, patiently waiting to place their orders. Sitting behind a plate glass window that overlooked a newly installed concrete sidewalk on Superior Street, Anders Alhomaki devoured an enormous slice of apple pie topped with a slab of sharp cheddar cheese. The Finn braced himself with sips of thick coffee and pondered how much of his dream he wanted to share with the Canadian.

"So tell me about this land," McAdams had begun, his wide mouth full of cheese and pie, his massive right hand curled around the handle of a porcelain coffee mug. "I know some folks in the land acquisition business in town. Maybe they can help."

The comment occasioned Anders's interest, but another thought intruded, taking the discussion in another direction. "Say, how is it that you're here today, George? Shouldn't you be back up in Port Arthur, keeping a watchful eye on your interests? I should think you're coming into the busy time of year for anyone associated with logging and timber."

"That's true. But one might say that other matters, matters closer to a man's heart, have taken over since we last spoke."

Alhomaki studied George McAdams's face. The Canadian had shaved off his trademark scarlet beard. The Finn stared at the deep cleft in the center of the Canadian's chin. The dimple blessed the foreigner with a certain aristocratic aura that defied his easy-going manner.

"What the hell's that supposed to mean?"

McAdams smiled. "I've taken a liking to a certain Finnish girl."

Anders winced. The miner suspected that McAdams's statement was a veiled reference to Elin Gustafsson. It made sense. McAdams was a man of means. George McAdams was handsome, well-mannered, and articulate, possessing qualities that would endear the Canadian to Karl Gustafsson, if not to Elin herself.

McAdams sensed the Finn's unrest. "Don't worry, my friend. I'm not after Miss Gustafsson, though I have some troubling news to report on that score."

"News? What news? She didn't respond to a single letter I sent. I gave up writing to her. Though the letters never came back, she never answered."

"I'd suggest it's not because of a want of trying on her part. Her father has, so far as I'm aware, kept her under a sort of perverse house arrest ever since her mother's passing. I'm not sure that any mail ever gets to her."

Alhomaki pushed himself back from the edge of the table.

"What's the news?"

The Canadian looked away from his companion to watch a small boy and a large mongrel dash across Superior Street through traffic. McAdams sighed.

"She's been seeing Horace Ellison."

McAdams's revelation slammed into Alhomaki's innards like a sucker punch. Still, the Finn maintained an outward calm.

"How do you know all this? You seem to possess a wealth of information about the intimate goings on of Duluth society, for someone who lives north of the border."

A smile returned to McAdams's face. "I neglected to tell you. I moved down here. Bought a small outfit north of town. I've been logging off some old mining company stumpage. Norway pine for telephone and telegraph posts, cedar and tamarack for fencing, that sort of thing. Been here about a year."

"Amazing."

"Not so much. Love will do that sort of thing to you."

McAdams finished his pie, wiped his hands on a white linen napkin, and taken a draw of coffee.

"Love?"

"I hired a fellow by the name of Henri Heikkonen as camp boss."

"I know the name. His daughter Wendla is a friend of Elin's. Her closest friend."

"Exactly."

Anders's mouth formed a grin.

"Now you understand, Finlander," the Canadian said, intending no derision in the term 'Finlander'.

119

"You and Wendla? That's rich."

"We're planning on getting married in a year. Unfortunately, her father had a heart attack and no longer works for me. I need a new camp boss for the upcoming season. I pay the crew by the piece, but the boss, the blacksmith, the cook, and the camp clerk are all on salary. If you hear of anyone interested in a fair wage for some hard work, let me know."

"I will. I'm content, at least for now, working for Alpena."

"Unlikely you'll stay put for long," McAdams observed, musing on the propensity of inquisitive men to give in to wanderlust. "Anyway, once the paperwork clears, I'll be an American."

"You're going to give up your Canadian citizenship?"

"No. I'll hold dual citizenship. I want to keep my Canadian credentials for business purposes. My main interests are still in Port Arthur, at least those involving money," McAdams said with a wink. "Oscar Larson is helping me work through the details."

"Larson, eh? You are getting into bed with the powerful. Can't think of a more influential man in Duluth than Oscar Larson. I hear he's in line for a run at the Governor's mansion."

"They tell me it'll likely be for a seat in Congress."

Alhomaki whistled.

"Amazing. A Finn in Congress. Less than a decade ago, the boys in Washington were trying to kick us out of the country."

"Pray tell," the Canadian prompted.

Anders's reference was not entirely lost on George McAdams. Though a Scotsman by heritage, McAdams employed upwards of one hundred Finns in his logging and sawmill operations in Ontario. He made it his business to understand the men who worked for him, to understand not only their basic needs but also to comprehend their culture and their upbringing. He was one of the few members of the Port Arthur Board of Trade who could claim to have taken a sauna in February and jumped into the frigid waters of Lake Superior off the Sleeping Giant. McAdams knew the story of John Svan of Eveleth, Minnesota, but he allowed Anders Alhomaki to relate the details of the tale as the men stood up from their table and exited the café.

"Time for a drink and a cigar?" the Canadian asked.

"Yes, but only if I buy," the Finn responded

"If you insist. Get back to what you were saying," McAdams encouraged as the men walked.

"John Svan was an immigrant from Finland like myself. He had his first papers, as I do. He wanted to obtain his second papers, to be able to vote, to run for election, to hold office. In short, he wanted to become an American citizen."

"I've heard bits and pieces of this before, but do go on."

"This was in the winter of 1907-1908. The Strike of 1907 was fresh in the bosses' minds. I was still in Finland but ready to leave and, in fact, ended up getting a job in Soudan, working underground, because the Finns involved in the 1907 Strike were blacklisted. Anyway, Svan completed his application for second papers, for citizenship. The United States Attorney in St. Paul, a son of a bitch by the name of John Sweet, denied the papers. Denied them, Goddamn it, for no legal reason."

The men had continued west on Superior Street towards the St. Louis Hotel. Alhomaki took a deep breath and continued, "Well, Svan wasn't about to give up simply because some governmental bureaucrat told him to. He hired Victor Gran, a Finnish lawyer here in Duluth... "

"I've met him," McAdams interjected.

"He's also a son of a bitch. But at least, in this instance, he was Svan's son of a bitch. So Gran files a petition, not in United States District Court in St. Paul, but here, in Duluth, in State District Court in front of Judge Cant."

McAdams held the Finn back at an intersection, preventing Alhomaki from being struck by an accelerating Hudson.

121

"I've met Cant. Good head on his shoulders," the Canadian observed as the men crossed the avenue at a brisk pace.

"So it turns out. Cant denied the motion to dismiss and insisted on hearing the case, which forced Sweet to come up with a reason to deny Svan citizenship. Svan had a job. He'd been here the requisite time and had no blight on his record. Not so much as a vagrancy charge. So what does Sweet come up with?"

"I'll give. What?" McAdams asked.

"The Oriental Exclusion Act. Sweet claimed that, because some anthropologists' believe that Finns are descended from Genghis Khan's invaders, Finns are Mongolian, which, of course, means we're Oriental. And as Orientals, we don't meet the requirements for citizenship."

"How's that?"

"Apparently white and Negro races are allowed citizenship under the law, but not Orientals."

"I'm sure there's something similar on the books in Ottawa."

Alhomaki smiled.

"Except no white Canadian was ever crazy enough to think that it applied to Finns."

McAdams laughed. "You give my country too much credit."

"Well, Judge Cant, he entered his order after hearing from Gran and Sweet, released it right to the newspapers. His decision was simple. Finns had always been considered 'white people' before Sweet went off on his tangent. Nothing, other than the Strike of 1907, intervened. Judge Cant ruled that Finns were white before the strike and remained white after the strike."

"Interesting. This was decided when?"

"January of 1908. Just before I came to America. I have a copy of the newspaper story in my Duluth Pack. I carry it with me, to remind me of what might have happened had John Svan been before a different judge."

The men slowed for a group of young boys playing marbles against the side of an empty storefront. Both men watched as the smallest boy in the lot repeatedly confiscated the marbles of his larger comrades.

"Tell me about this land," McAdams said as they continued west, the sting of a Nor'easter buffeting them from behind.

Alhomaki kept his eyes riveted on the smoothness of the newly poured walkway as he again considered how much he was willing to reveal.

"I've been looking around Virginia and the East Range for cutover land owned by the mining companies. I hadn't found a parcel that met my needs," Anders replied.

"But something has struck your fancy?"

Alhomaki continued to mull over how much detail he should share with McAdams; how much passion he should express. There was a pause in the conversation as the men entered the St. Louis Hotel, passed through the lobby, and found a table in the saloon. A piano player massaged an upright grand. Chopin challenged the din of clanging glassware and muted conversation. The men sat down and ordered two cigars and two tap beers from a waiter before Anders Alhomaki drew a deep breath, cast caution to the wind, and answered the Canadian's question: "I found a piece, a hundred and sixty acres, near the Duluth, Missabe, and Northern tracks, close to Brimson. Beautiful high ground surrounding a little lake – Papoose Lake they call it, bordered to the east by railroad right-of-way and to the south by the Cloquet River. It's just what I've been looking for."

"I know the parcel. Logged off by Oliver Mining, as I recall."

"That's the piece."

"What in hell's name are you going to do way out there, in the middle of nowhere?"

Alhomaki had hoisted his mug and downed his beer in a single swallow before answering George McAdams's question: "Farm."

Joe Greene walked to Virginia, paid his twenty-cent fare, and boarded a car on the Mesabi Electric Railway. Heading east on the trolley, Greene aroused the passions of his fellow Italian miners, who in turn, conveyed his message to the Slavs, Cornishmen, and other immigrants working the iron claims, until the entire labor force between Virginia and Gilbert, a labor force made ripe for a strike by the constant propaganda of the IWW, walked off the job. From Gilbert, the eastern terminus of the intercity trolley, to the St. James Mine near Aurora, the eastern limit of the Mesabi Iron Range, Joe Greene walked to mine after mine, location after location, hamlet after hamlet, engaging the miners with his impassioned plea to strike. Within days, the hierarchy of the IWW arrived to coordinate the strike effort. Led by Sam Scarlet, Carlo Tresca, and Elizabeth Gurley Flynn, the walkout spread throughout the three Iron Ranges of Minnesota and into the lumber camps, camps predominantly manned by Finns who had lost their positions in the iron mines after the strike of 1907. But, as with the General Strike of 1907 and the Copper Country Strike of 1913, Joe Greene's noble effort in 1916 to secure better wages and working conditions ended without success. The miners who returned to work after the Strike of 1916 earned the same low wages and faced the same outlandish prices in local shops that were present before they had gone out on strike. Inflation precipitated by World War I had caused the retail prices of essential goods to skyrocket, while the daily wages of the miners remained at pre-war levels.

Once again, those who participated in the strike, the miners working the mines of Northeastern Minnesota and the Finns working the forests, found that they had been blacklisted. And once again, Anders Alhomaki found that he was without a job.

Chapter 14

Elin Gustafsson held a handkerchief close to her bosom as she exited a rented carriage alongside Horace Ellison. The rig, an exquisitely crafted coach of black walnut, drawn by matching ebony American Saddlebred geldings, was parked on Superior Street in front of the Lyceum Theater in downtown Duluth. The fetching young woman and the well-proportioned young businessman climbed out of the carriage and made their way beneath the bright electric lights demarcating the theater's entrance. Horace Ellison brazenly guided Elin past a pair of stone lions standing guard at the base of the theater's ornate staircase and to the head of a line of customers waiting to enter the venue through the theater's main entrance. Other patrons, full of the knowledge of whom Horace Ellison was and the economic power he represented, didn't object to the young man's cavalier advance.

"I hope this play is as good as you say it is," Ellison remarked as the couple passed beneath the center arch of the Lyceum's main entrance, walked through a bronze door, and entered the building.

"The production is supposed to be simply marvelous," Elin replied in a sugary tone. "*The Garden of Allah* has received rave reviews wherever it has played. The *News Tribune* simply gushed over the play's staging."

The couple crossed the elegant mosaic floor of the Lyceum Block's outer lobby. Modern elevators and open stairways led from the main floor of the structure to the building's upper levels, where professionals and business concerns leased office space. A brass-framed directory, surrounded by gray granite trim, hung heavily from a wall of finely polished white marble. The headquarters of Amalgamated Properties, the holding company coordinating the business affairs of Eustace Ellison's burgeoning empire, occupied the entire top floor of the Lyceum Building. Horace

Ellison's office faced east. He had a profound view of the North Shore of Lake Superior. His father's suite overlooked St. Louis Bay and the city's bustling waterfront. The muddle of grain elevators, ships, piers, and warehouses strung out between Canal Park and Rice's Point provided Eustace Ellison with an accounting, on the days when coal and wood smoke or weather didn't obscure the scene, of the commercial heart and soul of Duluth.

The couple nodded and smiled mechanically as they passed people they knew or recognized. They entered the interior lobby of the Lyceum Theater. Opulent wall coverings, fresco accents, and finely turned oak woodwork set against puritanical white marble greeted their arrival. Electric chandeliers dazzled with light. Horace Ellison handed an usher two tickets. The man, a smallish figure in a bright gold uniform, his military-style tunic buttoned from his waist to his throat and embellished with far too much embroidery, assisted them to their seats.

Inside the theater proper, the elegance of the lobby was repeated and magnified. Frescoes adorned the walls. The ceiling soared above the plush seats of the theater's general admission sections to a height in excess of seventy feet. Three balconies of successively small dimensions cantilevered towards the rear of the hall. Six private boxes hung from the theater's terracotta walls, suspended above the auditorium as if by magic. The stage was gigantic; large enough to accommodate the spectacle of the Arabian world that Horace Ellison and Elin Gustafsson were about to view.

"Thank you kindly," Elin said as the usher assisted her into her box seat.

"Yes, here you go," Ellison said through a smile that appeared forced, though in actuality, Horace was genuinely appreciative of the deference the theater employee had shown them. "Something extra," the young businessman added, stuffing a five-dollar bill into the usher's gloved hand.

"I'm much obliged, Mr. Ellison," the man said. "Will you or Miss Gustafsson be requiring anything else?"

"Not just yet. If this thing becomes too boring, I may ask you to bring us a bottle of father's reserve," Horace whispered conspiratorially.

"I understand, sir. I'll check back after a bit."

The usher turned stiffly on his heels and left the couple alone in the box.

"You say this play is about the Arabs?" Horace Ellison said loudly.

"Yes. But it's so much more than that," Elin replied. "Remember, I showed you the advertisement from the *Tribune*? A cast of over one hundred. Live camels, horses, and donkeys on stage. Billed as 'Bigger than *Ben Hur*'."

"I loved *Ben Hur*," Horace Ellison said, his eyes riveted on the face of his date.

"I know," she whispered.

Elin Gustafsson silently lamented the fact that Anders Alhomaki had never once, in the two years he'd been exiled from Duluth, so much as written a note, much less attempted to telephone or visit. During the first six months following her mother's funeral, Elin Gustafsson had remained a prisoner in her own home, strictly watched and supervised by her father or one of his loyal servants. Elin's personal errands were accomplished under the watchful eye of Mrs. Bester, the spinsterly maid hired to replace the departed Miss Wirtanen. Visits to the library, or to museums, or art galleries, were conducted under the tutelage of Karl Gustafsson himself, Mrs. Bester, or not at all. Elin received, over her protest, an unsolicited two-months' leave of absence from her teaching position at the Duluth Normal School. When her father finally allowed her to return to work, believing Anders Alhomaki had written to her in care of her employer, Elin was fully expectant that there would be a stack of messages in her mail slot at the school for her to consider and cherish. In actuality, there were no letters waiting for her when she returned to work.

The austerity of Anders's cowardice, the impact of his spineless capitulation to her father's desire, broke Elin's resolve. Anders's presumed neglect fractured her self-esteem

127

into smithereens of self-doubt and guilt. All the days and nights she had spent with Anders; all the giving of her body and her love; all the moments spent holding the miner's hands in hers were dashed to nothingness by his betrayal. For months after her return to teaching, Elin searched her heart for an answer, looking, prying, trying to uncover what she had done to culture such distance from someone she had been intimate with. Elin replayed the final scene of their relationship in her mind, watching it over and over and over again like a silent picture show at the Lyric, one of the more ostentatious moving picture houses in town. In the scene, at least as it played out in memory, she sat dejected and deflated in the rear seat of the funeral carriage while her father and Eustace Ellison's men confronted Anders Alhomaki and Anders's friend, Olli Kinkkonen, across the green lawn of Forest Hills Cemetery. She did not hear her father's words. She did not hear Anders's response. Nevertheless, it was clear that, whatever had been said between the two men, her father had convinced the Finn to give up, to yield love to power. Over time, after nights of sleepless consideration and internal debate, Elin Gustafsson came to the recognition that her mother was not going to rise from the dank earth to care for or protect Elin from the ideals and constraints of her father. And over the same span of time, Elin concluded that Anders Alhomaki had abandoned her. She determined that, having been forsaken by her mother and her lover, God could subject Elin Gustafsson to whatever fate God himself chose for her.

The orchestra began to warm up. The house lights dimmed.

"Elin, are you all right?" Horace Ellison asked, his eyes expressing a level of concern that was, against the flat aspect of her recent past, somehow comforting.

"I'm fine."

"Are you certain? You're crying."

Elin hadn't noticed the tear descending her powdered cheek. Somehow reality had been suspended as she wrestled with memory. Horace passed her a clean linen handkerchief, the initials "H.E.E." (Horace Eustace Ellison) monogrammed in gold across the cloth. She dabbed at the moisture. A notion of what was possible, of what was preordained, began to form in her mind. She smiled and returned the handkerchief to Horace as a battalion of stringed instruments commenced an orchestral fanfare.

Chapter 15

"Damn the Germans," Oscar Larson muttered, holding the front page of the *Duluth Herald* in his ample hands, mounds of boiled whitefish, cabbage, potatoes, and carrots resting on the china plate in front of him.

"How's that?" Eustace Ellison asked, his mouth stuffed with leg of lamb; mint jelly sliding off the meat in dollops before coming to rest on the white Irish linen tablecloth covering the oak dining table.

"You've left a bit of your dinner in the corner of your mouth," Karl Gustafsson advised, pointing to the left side of his face in an attempt to assist Ellison in locating the offending mutton.

Ellison removed the debris with his napkin.

"Much better," Gustafsson observed.

"Pass me the wine, would you, Karl?" Eustace Ellison asked.

Gustafsson leaned over his plate, the surface devoid of food, no remnants of the liver and onions he'd devoured left behind as evidence, and retrieved a bottle of white dinner wine, a domestic brand from California, which he passed to his companion.

"What about Germany?" Gustafsson asked as Oscar Larson's face flushed.

"Goddamn it to hell. We're going to have to get into it," Larson said with authority. "The French and British are stuck behind their trenches. They haven't moved a lick in two years."

"The way I hear it, it's the Russians who are hurting the worst," Ellison observed, smacking his thin lips as he savored a second glass of wine. "The Bolsheviks are getting the peasants and factory workers upset. The Reds are calling for a revolution."

Oscar Larson placed the newspaper to one side, stared out a second-floor window and watched a Canadian steamboat seek a clear line of entry through the Duluth ship canal. The three businessmen were eating dinner at the Kitchi Gammi Club. Once a week, usually on Wednesday evenings, a group of like-thinking gentlemen gathered to discuss current events, business strategies, and Oscar Larson's political ambitions. Some evenings, six or seven businessmen supped together. Other evenings, as this one, there were only three.

Larson's anticipated entry into electoral politics was becoming a prevalent topic of conversation at the gatherings. It was assumed that he would run for a seat in the United States House of Representatives. It was July 15th, 1916. The election in question was still three years away, giving Oscar Larson plenty of time to secure the backing of the moneyed interests in Minnesota's Eighth Congressional District, the District covering Northeastern Minnesota. He would run as a moderate Republican, as a foil to the more vocal elements within the Finnish immigrant community, elements attempting to carve out a niche for the Finns on the radical left. Oscar Larson was willing to work hard at cultivating the support of non-Finns and non-Republicans to ensure that he would be the first native-born Finnish immigrant to hold federal elective office. As part of his worldview, something on which an immigrant candidate needed to be crystal clear, Larson had no qualms about involving the United States in the Great War. Had he been in Congress in 1916, when the issue was first discussed with vigor, he would have urged America to step in.

"Wilson," Larson mumbled as he forced Lake Superior whitefish into a corner of his mouth. "That's what you get with a Democrat. Timid. Unable to make decisions. Teddy Roosevelt wouldn't waste time. Abe Lincoln wouldn't wring his hands. But Wilson, he ponders and contemplates and frets while the Germans sink ton after ton of our cargo, goods bought and paid for by America. It's time we rolled up our sleeves and got into it."

"I'm not so sure that's in our best interests, at least right now," Karl Gustafsson observed.

Gustafsson was also a Republican. He harbored no sympathy for the workingmen who would end up fighting any war in which America chose to engage. Gustafsson's law practice was based upon his representation of the mining, timber, manufacturing, and shipping corporations that made commerce in the port cities of Duluth and Superior hum. The owners, shareholders, and upper level managers of these concerns came to Karl Gustafsson for their personal legal work. At any given moment, Karl Gustafsson and Oscar Larson represented nearly all of the financial institutions located in the city of Duluth, save for those entities loyal to Chester Congdon, another local attorney with a vast personal fortune and ready access to political power.

Although Karl Gustafsson and Oscar Larson generally agreed on most matters, Gustafsson believed that the sinking of French and British freighters by German submarines, and the loss of American products being carried to Europe that such attacks entailed, were insignificant when compared to the overall profit being generated by the war. American military and consumer goods were in great demand across the Atlantic. The loss of a ship or two in the process of transferring those goods to European customers was, in Karl Gustafsson's mind, simply part of the cost of doing business.

"I'm with Karl on this one. Let the English and Boche blast each other into dust. Then we'll sell them whatever they need to rebuild Europe," Eustace Ellison added.

Oscar Larson pushed his ample belly away from the table, struck a match, and lit a Cuban. His jowls quivered as he drew heavily on the end of the stogie to create flame.

"Russia will fall. The Czar has no hope of coming out of this war with an empire. He may not even be able to keep his own head. Lenin and his boys are gaining strength. It's only a matter of time before unpaid Russian soldiers and sailors turn their guns on the ruling class. We can't afford to allow France or England to lose any more men. The more French and English soldiers who die in the trenches, the more unrest their deaths breed at home. The more the French and English newspapers clamor, the more the liberals organize.

No, I'm afraid that isolation isn't the panacea that Woodrow Wilson would have us believe."

"What's got you started tonight, Oscar?" Ellison asked.

"Since Sarajevo, the Allies have been content to hold the Germans at bay by standing firm in the Allied trenches in Northern France. Apparently, that hasn't been sitting well with the war hounds in London. The French and the British have just launched an offensive near the Somme, hundreds of thousands of troops supported by new-fangled mechanized armored vehicles. Tanks, I think they call them."

"Why's that so upsetting?" Gustafsson asked.

"There's no real hope of breaking through the German line at the Somme. It's doomed, logistically, to failure. Another failure may push the English working man to consider more drastic remedies."

"Such as?" Ellison asked.

"Such as sacking the whole English commercial system. Marx lived in England, remember. Marx's ideals still have sympathizers there. That's why we need to get America into the war, to prevent a German success, or an Allied failure. Such an outcome would destabilize Europe. The Europeans are becoming our most lucrative trading partners. Without Europe, the United States economy will stagnate. Many of the corporate clients that Karl and I rely upon for our retainers will stumble, maybe fail. That's what has me concerned."

Karl Gustafsson stood up from the table, lit a cigar, and released a cloud of acrid smoke into the warm air of the private dining room. The Finnish attorney's face broke into a broad smile. "Always the worrier, Oscar. Relax. Have a glass of wine. Let's talk about how we're going to get you elected to Congress."

"One last thing," Eustace Ellison interjected.

"Yes?" Larson asked.

"The reason I'm dead set against the war is simple. I've only got the one son. I'll be damned if I want to see Horace shipped overseas to fight England's war."

"There are ways of dealing with the draft, if and when it's instituted," Oscar Larson reminded the businessman. "I'm sure we can make an appointment with the right fellow on the draft commission to discuss a classification that coincides with your son's limitations."

Ellison's face broke into a grin.

"By then, we might be in-laws," Eustace said, directing his newfound cheer at Karl Gustafsson. "To my son and your daughter," Ellison added, raising his wine glass.

"Give them some time, Eustace," Karl Gustafsson advised. "They've barely started dating. Not that I'm ungrateful for your son's interest. Keeps her pretty head from wandering into places it ought not go."

Silence intruded. The subject of Elin's breach of decorum by running off to Northern Michigan and living with Anders Alhomaki was not something the men in the room felt comfortable discussing. Recognition of Elin's indiscretions would not, under any circumstances, be verbalized. To do so would break the code of honor binding the men. Though all of them suspected that Karl Gustafsson's wayward daughter was no longer a virgin, and therefore, less marriageable, such a topic would never come up.

Eustice Ellison was mindful of the need to avoid this subject as he offered a toast:

"To Elin and Horace. May they find love and happiness."

The awkwardness in the room subsided. The men raised their glasses and drained the last of the wine.

Chapter 16
October, 1916

George McAdams followed Andrew Maki, as Anders Alhomaki was now known after the Strike of 1916, through a landscape reduced to scrub. The men hiked a trail skirting white pine stumps, the remnants of colossal trees that had been logged off. Piles of decaying limbs, discarded and useless as lumber, littered the countryside. Stands of immature jack pine, their trunks coated with running pitch, their fronds extended spindly and snake-like against the distant sky of late autumn, crowded the trail. To the left, the oily waters of the Cloquet River oozed slowly through high banks of reddish sand. The flood plain of the river was similarly barren. All of the cedar trees had been harvested from the stream bottom. The valley appeared desolate and empty.

"This is quite a hike," McAdams observed, his leather boots slipping on discarded bark and brown pine needles as the men trudged along.

"At least there aren't any bugs. Last month, when I was out here working, the horse flies and deer flies were so thick I nearly went out of my mind," Maki responded without casting a glance back at his companion.

Both men wore thick Pendleton wool work shirts, the sleeves of the shirts closed at the wrists, the collars open, the white of the men's woolen underwear exposed at the base of their necks. Maki wore the traditional summer clothing of a logger: Chippewa brand rubberized shoes, suspenders, a black Stetson, a red plaid shirt and brown wool work pants. McAdams wore more expensive Red Wing sportsman boots, purchased from Dove Clothing in Duluth, a blue plaid woolen shirt, black wool pants, and a belt, an item of clothing that loggers rarely wore in the woods. Andrew dug his left hand into the front pocket of his shirt, removed a tin of Weyman, and stuck a wad of chew into his mouth.

"Want a plug?" the Finn asked, never breaking stride as he offered the canister to the Canadian.

"No thanks. I'll load a pipe when we get there," McAdams replied.

The trail followed the steep sand bank of the river for a mile or so from where the men had disembarked from the Duluth, Missabe, and Northern ore train they'd hopped near Aurora. It was Sunday. The men had spent Saturday night in Virginia. They had left work early Saturday evening after paying the crew at the Wolf Lake Logging Camp. They had spent a good portion of Saturday night and early Sunday morning playing poker in a Virginia saloon. McAdams lost a bundle. Maki broke even. The men then paid for soft hotel beds and female companionship.

What Wendla doesn't know won't hurt her, George McAdams had thought as he climbed the stairs with Flora, the prostitute he'd retained for the evening. *This is the last time. That's a promise, Lord. The very last,* McAdams had pledged before sleeping with the whore.

The path turned west, away from the river, and began to follow a series of hog-backed ridges towards Papoose Lake. No original forest remained. Entire groves of white and red pine had been eliminated. There had been no replanting of the pines once Weyerhaeuser's loggers cleaned up what harvestable timber Oliver Mining had missed. The pitching, rolling, undulating landscape looked like an impressionistic painting of another world as the men moved easily through the beginnings of a second-growth forest of junk trees. Aspen, birch, and jack pine sprouted like uncontrolled weeds against piles of pine boughs, rotting stumps, and the occasional abandoned logging shack.

Papoose Lake became visible long before the men reached its swampy shoreline. A brief shelf of dry, level land extended to the south of the marsh surrounding the open water, and allowed an undisturbed view of the landscape. A log cabin, the walls constructed of straight tamarack trees logged off the swamp that surrounded Papoose Lake, reinforced the fact that the men had arrived at Andrew Maki's farm.

Andrew stopped on top of a small rise overlooking empty country. Off to the west, the barren hills lolled and scalloped towards McAdams's Wolf Lake Camp. Potholes and marshlands interrupted vacant forest. The Finn spat a wad of phlegm onto the soil and covered his spittle with sandy humus, nudged into place with the toe of a Chippewa. Maki's eyes surveyed the one hundred and sixty acre tract that was his and his alone.

"She's coming along," McAdams remarked as the men arrived at Maki's cabin. The Canadian drew flame into the bowl of his wooden pipe, puffing smoke into the air as the tobacco ignited. "You should be ready to break ground next summer."

Andrew Maki smiled, leaned against the incomplete wall of his cabin, and considered his boss. Winter wasn't far away. The structure wasn't even half-finished.

"That's an optimist's view of things," Andrew suggested. "I don't even have a stove for the place, much less a roof."

"You told me you'd give me a good year on the job when I hired you," McAdams replied, his lips clamped tight against the stem of the pipe as he spoke. "You haven't even given me three months."

Anders grinned.

"I said what I said. You know I'll stand by my word. One year. One year of being Camp Foreman. It's beyond me why you hired a miner to run your logging camp, in any event."

McAdams turned his attention to the lake.

"You're one of the few honest men I've come across, is why," the Canadian replied. "Seems to me that you've been under-employed, working the mines and the docks. You've got a good head on your shoulders. Except, of course, when it comes to women."

Maki laughed, a great gasp of air erupting from his mouth and inadvertently propelling his chew onto the sandy ground.

"I wouldn't say that old Flora was anything to write home about," Maki retorted.

"Who's that?"

"The old biddy you took up with last night."

"Sorry, I'm engaged to a lovely Finnish girl by the name of Wendla, Wendy to her friends. Don't know as I've ever been introduced to 'Flora'."

"I see. A new leaf," Maki replied in Finn.

"I hate it when you talk gibberish," McAdams said, a touch of annoyance to his voice. "Mr. Maki, I'm not sure I can trust you."

"You just told me I was the most honest man you knew," Andrew Maki replied in English.

"Just because you're honest doesn't mean I have to trust you."

"That's an interesting distinction."

A moment of quiet ensued. A pair of wood ducks, the drake's head a brilliant display of color, streaked by, headed towards the river. A myriad of blue jays, anxious to claim the forest as their own for winter, flitted across open country.

As the men stood contemplating the landscape, Andrew Maki silently evaluated his position, his place in America. Other than the contract he carried on his land, the title of which was held by McAdams Forest Products, Inc., of Minnesota, and the twenty dollars a month he paid George McAdams towards satisfaction of that contract, Maki was beholden to no one. His infatuation with Elin Gustafsson remained a discreet, sour little sore at the base of his soul. But it was a sore that, over time, stung less. His visits to the whorehouses in Virginia and Biwabik weren't salves against the pain of Elin's departure from his life; they were transitory physical distractions, necessary interventions to prevent him from falling in love all over again. His was a single-minded determination. He would complete the construction of the cabin on Papoose Lake over the winter of 1916-1917. He would work like a dog for George McAdams until the summer of 1918. And then he would farm. He envisioned a barn, a sauna next to a patch of firm ground bordering the lake, a root cellar, fencing, a machine shed, each improvement made slowly, deliberately, crafted lovingly by his own hands. He saw, in the not-too-distant future, a herd of beef cattle, a team of Percherons, an assortment of pigs, chickens, and a milk cow, grazing, scratching, wandering the fenced confines of his farm. And acres of barley and alfalfa hay, the heads of the grasses gently swaying in the breeze of upcoming summers. Somewhere in that future, the face of another woman would emerge, but not until he had worked his shoulders into an ache, until the land was cleared of stumps and planted in grasses, until wood smoke curled from the stone chimney of his sauna.

"What in the devil are you thinking about?" McAdams finally asked, the Canadian's inquiry interrupting Anders's whimsy.

The Finn didn't reply.

"You're not mooning over that Gustafsson girl again, aren't you?"

Maki shook his head in the negative.

"I hope you're not taking a shine to that whore, Madeline. I told you to spend time with someone else. You can't spend every night in a brothel with the same whore. It's bad for the psyche."

"I am not mooning over Elin Gustafsson. And I am not 'sweet on' Madeline DeBoer."

"That's a good thing. Wendy tells me that Elin and young Ellison are getting on fairly thick these days. And as for Madeline, while she may be a fine lay, I doubt you'd want her carrying your seed. You being candid about Miss Gustafsson?"

Andrew felt jealousy stab briefly at his façade.

"She's no longer my concern," Maki replied dryly, searching his tobacco tin for another plug.

A slight wind broke across the lake, creating small whitecaps on dark water.

"Seems to me it would be better for you to deal with the issue than bury it," McAdams added, tapping the bowl of his pipe against the log wall of the partially finished cabin.

"There's nothing to bury."

"So you say, Mr. Maki."

Andrew glanced at the Canadian. The Finn's face flushed. He pulled a watch out of the front right pocket of his trousers.

"We'd better be getting back to camp," Maki observed, his eyes fixed upon his watch.

"You're changing the subject, aren't you?"

The Finn's natural complexion returned.

"You might say that."

Chapter 17

Horace Ellison drove slowly. The Model T's wood spoked wheels spun gravel at every hairpin corner of Skyline Drive as the automobile headed west on the boulevard overlooking the placid waters of St. Louis Bay. Whiteside Island was visible intermittently through gray sheets of harvest rain across a narrow channel of red water. There was, Elin Gustafsson knew, a lovely farm and home on the island, owned by the wealthy Whiteside family. She had been there, had picnicked there innumerable times with her parents as a young child, having taken a ferry to the island from the Minnesota side of the river.

The young woman stared blankly at the barren hillside rising next to the passenger side of the automobile as Horace Ellison cautiously negotiated each curve and twist in the gravel path. There were no other revelers on the road. No tally-hos were in progress on that dismal, foggy day. They were alone, snaking their way through the aspen and birch woodlands that had claimed the rocky precipices above the city after the demise of the pines.

"How's this for a place to stop?" Horace asked, his voice slightly edgy, his hands quivering nervously against the mahogany steering wheel of the Ford.

"On a clear day, it would be perfect. Today, it will simply have to do," Elin replied.

The motorcar pulled into a turn-around and came to a stop with the windshield facing east, overlooking the slow waters of the river. West Duluth and Riverside spread out below the crest of the hill. Homes, businesses, and industrial buildings fanned out across the flat bottomlands to the east and west. Coal smoke poured from the stacks of the United States Steel Plant in Gary. Smog billowed upward, becoming suspended in the rain-sodden clouds.

Horace Ellison set the handbrake and turned off the Ford's gasoline engine.

"I wish it were a better day," the young man said plainly.

"It's fine, though it could be ten degrees warmer," Elin replied, her gloved hands pressed against her chest.

Ellison turned in his seat and moved to kiss the woman. Elin Gustafsson tensed momentarily before forcing the rigidity from her limbs. She turned to accept the kiss. Unexpectedly, Horace forced the tip of his tongue into her mouth.

"What are you doing?" she asked in surprise.

The young man's eyes flashed something.

Anger? Elin guessed.

Horace's facial grimace disappeared.

"I thought you'd done this before."

An awkward thought passed through Elin Gustafsson's mind.

So, he expects that I have experienced everything there is to experience in the way of lovemaking, she postulated. *How to handle this without getting him angry?*

"I haven't. I've been honest with you about my past. That's not something I've ever experienced," she explained. "It's not that I'm not willing to try it. You simply caught me off-guard."

Ellison leaned back in his seat and considered a response.

She's been with that Finlander and expects me to believe she's never tasted his tongue? If that's the case, Anders Alhomaki is nothing more than a clod. And if she's lying, I'll soon know. One way or another, Elin, I will find out your secrets, Ellison thought as he studied the gossamer skin of the young woman's face.

"I'm sorry," Horace responded in moderate apology. "I really thought you'd French-kissed before."

"Well, I haven't. Is it something that you enjoy?"

Careful, Horace, Ellison said to himself. *Don't fall into her trap. She wants to know how experienced you are. She can't ever know about the whores...* Horace stopped his thought before it

142

fully formed, cognizant that Elin was studying him carefully, as if she could read his mind.

"It is."

Elin shifted in her seat and placed her moist lips on Horace's. Her mouth opened. Horace touched the enamel of her small teeth with the tip of his tongue. She drew his tongue into her mouth. His hands began to fumble with the buttons of her dress coat. She stroked the edges of his jaw, touching the lobes of his ears, the fibers of his thick brown hair, as her breathing began to intensify. His fingers opened the fasteners of her coat and dug expectantly inside the protection the wool afforded.

This is what I must do, she confided to herself. *There is no other path left to me.*

They were silent as the Ford lumbered east across the boulevard towards the Gustafsson Mansion. Elin's thighs were wet with Horace Ellison's seed. She had not allowed him to release inside of her. She had resumed some semblance of control over her own destiny. There was little to be gained by allowing Eustace Ellison's son to impregnate her before they were married. When Anders Alhomaki had left, she had discarded the womb veil as being unnecessary. She had given herself twice to men and twice they had disappointed her. Victor Pulla, understandably, had not been able to break away from his marriage of twenty years to marry her. Anders Alhomaki, on the other hand, couldn't be forgiven. He had capitulated to her father and Eustace Ellison with nary a protest. No, she had given herself freely to a man for the last time.

Her hands had found Horace as he sought to enter her. She had coerced him into allowing her to caress him with her fingers, manipulating him to climax. There would be no pregnancy, no need of a shotgun marriage. She had a future planned for them, a future that did not include a hasty ceremony driven by social necessity.

"It was an interesting afternoon," Elin said with a smirk, as she stood expectantly at the front entry to the

Gustafsson home. "Will I see you during the week?" she asked.

Horace's eyes darted. He sought to disquiet the guilt he experienced after Elin's mechanical release of his desire. The young man shifted his weight on the balls of his feet as he pondered an answer.

I let her control the outcome, he thought, a slight cold rain soaking his head as he stood on Elin Gustafsson's front porch. *Father would never understand.*

"I'm heading to St. Paul to appear before the Tax Commission tomorrow morning," Horace explained. "I won't be back until Saturday."

"May I see you off?" the woman asked.

I've upset him. It's as plain as the nose on his face, she thought. *How long can I play this game of cat and mouse?*

"I'm leaving at six o'clock in the morning. There's no need. Get your rest. You have to teach tomorrow."

She smiled. The tension cleared.

"I'll see you next weekend, then?"

Horace Ellison considered a response. His gaze took in the agreeable contours of the woman's face and her full figure.

There are worse things than coming on a beautiful woman's leg, he admitted to himself.

"I'll telephone you when I get in," he replied, pecking Elin's smooth cheek to emphasize that the crisis had passed.

Chapter 18

"The Suomi involved in the IWW are a thorn in the Governor's side," Victor Gran said to the gathering of conservative Finns in the boardroom of the American Exchange Bank at 230 West Superior Street in Duluth. "Governor Burnquist is anxious for our support. He's counting upon us to mobilize the more reasonable elements of our people. He'll be relying upon our efforts to counter the anti-war attitude displayed by the Red Finns."

"The last labor dispute spilled over into the lumber camps," Oscar Larson lamented. "It's time we put an end to this foolishness and prove to the American people that Finns are hard-working, loyal, trustworthy citizens."

A murmur of acceptance surged around the table. The Finnish businessmen in the room nodded their heads in agreement between draws on their cigars and pipes. Tobacco haze hung heavy near the ornately plastered ceiling, the surface's new paint already stained from cigars smoked at previous meetings.

"I propose that we form a loyalty league," Alex Koivisto, a gangly stockbroker and futures trader announced. "We need to create a group of dedicated Finns ready, willing, and able to challenge the Marxists and Socialists on key issues, such as the right to require an honest twelve-hour workday from employees, and the providence of entering the Great War."

"Hear, hear," Victor Gran agreed. "Why not call it the 'American Loyalty League'?"

There were over twenty prominent Finns in attendance. As the war in Europe dragged on, as the attacks by German submarines and surface warships against French and English merchant vessels increased, sending millions of tons of American goods bound for Europe to the bottom of the North Atlantic, it became more and more apparent that

America would enter the war on the side of the Allies. Canada had already sent men. The other Commonwealth Nations, including New Zealand, Australia, India, and South Africa, had made contributions. At Gallipoli the attempted Allied invasion of the Isthmus controlling the Black Sea had resulted in the slaughter of thousands of British, Australian, and New Zealander troops. The Somme Offensive, as predicted by Oscar Larson, had resulted in mass slaughter and no improvement in the Allied position along the Western Front. Despite Woodrow Wilson's vehement objection to the war, the entry of the United States into the fray was, at least in the minds of the men assembled in the boardroom, a looming inevitability.

"Wilson is coddling dissenters and slackers," Eino Laine, the owner of a number of rental properties and, off the public record, the largest proprietor of brothels in Finntown, added with disdain. "Federal protections for the Syndicalists, Communists, and agitators seem downright un-American, given the fact that our boys will soon be dying in the trenches."

Victor Gran nodded his head and sat heavily in an oak chair at the head of the table. The lawyer listened attentively to the most investigated man in all of St. Louis County. Laine's money had effectively buffered the enterprising Finn from serious trouble with the law; a twenty here, a fifty there, strictly cash, strictly under the table to a Duluth police officer or St. Louis County Sheriff's deputy at the right moment. Three times criminal indictments had been sought against the tenement lord; three times the grand jury had returned "a 'no' bill".

The fact he's hired William Burnside and Peder "Bud" Nordquist, enticed them away from doing Eustace Ellison's dirty .work, Gran mused, *is not comforting. Hopefully, Eino has the common sense to keep his muscle away from politics.*

Victor Gran mulled over these thoughts as Eino Laine completed his diatribe.

"You're right, Eino," Victor Gran agreed. "But all Wilson's Executive Order does is preclude violence being advanced against those opposing the war. There's nothing in the order that prevents our banding together, as suggested by Governor Burnquist, to give voice to an opposing view. So long as we avoid direct physical confrontation with the Reds, the IWW, and the others agitating against the war, the Governor pledges his utmost and sincere support."

Oscar Larson hunched over the edge of the conference table, chewed the inside of his cheek, and addressed the group. "I agree that we should call ourselves the 'American Liberty League.' I nominate Victor Gran to chair the group. I also move that each man at this table contribute $5,000.00 to the effort, payable by the first of December."

"I second the nomination and the motion," concurred Reino Carlstrom, a raw-boned Swedish Finn who owned the largest dredging company at the Head of the Lakes. "And I will personally write my check before we leave here this evening."

Gran resumed standing at the head of the table. "I'm flattered by the nomination. I will also write my check as soon as our business is concluded. I'd suggest we appoint Juda Tylla as our treasurer. He can open an account in the name of the League at his bank," Gran advised, referring to the owner of the Finnish-American Bank, located in Duluth's West End.

"I call the question," advanced John Rantala, the lone Finnish pharmacist in town.

"All in favor of Victor Gran as chairman of the American Liberty League and Juda Tylla for treasurer, say 'aye'," Oscar Larson proclaimed.

There was a unanimous chorus of "ayes".

"Looks like you've got your organized resistance to the slackers," Reino Carlstrom said, slapping Victor Gran on the back as the group dispersed. "Here's my contribution," Carlstrom added, handing a check for $5,000.00 to Tylla.

"The League appreciates your prompt donation, Reino. We've got to make the non-Finns in this community understand that the radicals who oppose the war do not speak for all of us," Tylla advised, slipping the check into the inside pocket of his blue pinstriped suit jacket.

Others walked up and presented personal checks to Tylla on their way out the door. Within minutes, only Victor Gran and Karl Gustafsson remained in the conference room.

"You don't look too happy, for someone who just got his way," Gustafsson observed, downing a glass of tepid whole milk as he sat heavily in his chair. "I went along with your scheme, even though you and I don't see eye-to-eye on the war."

"I respect that, Karl, I truly do. I'm cognizant that you're not in favor of the conflict in Europe."

"And yet..."

Victor Gran looked out the window. It was winter. Christmas Eve, 1916. Snow fell lightly from a claustrophobic sky, covering downtown Duluth in a loose mantle of white. Pedestrians scurried along un-shoveled sidewalks in their last-minute haste to buy Christmas gifts. Automobiles spun their narrow rubber tires fruitlessly on inclined avenues, the drivers of the autos eventually yielding to gravity and parking their motorcars on the level surface of Superior Street. Trolleys rolled on, unaffected by the storm. Carriages and wagons, the horses' hooves clip-clopping against the wet paving bricks, negotiated the roads without hesitation. Electric streetlights began to glow as dusk settled swiftly over the cityscape.

"I'm troubled. It's Eino Laine. I know he's basically a businessman like the rest of us..."

There was another pause.

"You suspect that he might, shall we say, deviate from the non-violent premise of our new organization?" Gustafsson asked.

Gran nodded an affirmation.

"I have a similar inkling," Karl Gustafsson agreed.

Victor Gran sipped hot tea and looked Karl Gustafsson in the eye. The tea was made from red sumac berries picked by Victor's wife Helvi during the past summer. Helvi insisted that her husband drink the natural tea and abstain from coffee, on the premise that the tea controlled Victor's gout.

"Eino Laine employs men who are extremely dangerous. I think you know the gents I'm referring to," Gran said.

Gustafsson stood up.

"I do. Let's just hope he uses some common sense when the situation heats up."

Victor Gran reached over and shook Gustafsson's hand.

"Merry Christmas, Karl," Gran said.

"Merry Christmas to you too, Victor. Say hello to Helvi, will you?" Karl Gustafsson added.

"I will. Wish that lovely daughter of yours a 'Merry Christmas' from the Grans."

Karl Gustafsson nodded and followed his friend out of the boardroom. The men avoided any further mention of Eino Laine as they left the American Exchange Bank in time to attend Christmas Eve service at the Finnish Evangelical Lutheran Church on St. Croix Avenue.

Chapter 19
December, 1916

Andrew Maki worked his crew hard during the week leading up to Christmas. Unbeknownst to the loggers, they were going to be given both Christmas Eve and Christmas Day off. With George McAdams and Wendy Heikkonen traveling to Port Arthur to spend the holidays with George's brother, Adrian, the Vice President of McAdams Forest Products and the man in charge of running the Canadian side of the brothers' lumber and logging interests, George McAdams had determined his crew deserved an extended holiday.

The war had been a boon for the McAdams brothers. American companies cried out for the cedar and tamarack that was logged from the land surrounding Wolf Lake. George McAdams had purchased the tract at a significant discount at a time when the market for such secondary woods was depressed. To complement the Wolf Lake operation, the Canadian arm of McAdams Forest Products worked the last remaining stands of white pine remaining in Northwestern Ontario. These combined operations catapulted the McAdams family business into prominence, simultaneously in Duluth and Port Arthur. Though Adrian McAdams was a competent accountant, he had no self-control, a deficit that required his older brother to make frequent trips to Canada to ensure the future success of the company.

With the ground frozen, the loggers working at Wolf Lake Camp used sledges pulled by solidly built Percheron and Belgian draft horses to move logs out of the woods to the shores of Wolf Lake. To facilitate an easy haul, a water tank was installed on a camp sledge. Water was hand-pumped from a large hole cut through the thick ice of Wolf Lake into the tank on the sledge. The sledge was then drawn by a team of draft horses along the primitive logging roads leading from the forest to the shores of Wolf Lake, where the logs were stacked for storage. The water from the tank was spread evenly along the roads, where it froze, reducing friction and making it possible for a two-horse team to haul a mountain of timber.

A crude earthen dam and a timbered sluice controlled the level of Wolf Lake. In the spring, once the thaw was on and the lake free of ice, the logs would be rafted together and floated to the south end of the lake. After the winter's harvest had been made ready, men from the McAdams Camp would remove the timbers that constituted the sluice at the center of the earthen dam, and allow a torrent of stored spring melt and rainwater to flush the logs down a creek towards the West Branch of the Cloquet River. Andrew Maki and a select group of his men, including the cook, Iner Halvorson, would precede the logs in a Wanigan, a twenty-four foot houseboat with an eight foot beam and a shallow draft, crafted from slab lumber, canvas, pitch, and tar paper. The loggers working out of the Wanigan, derisively denoted "pig men," would eat, sleep, and live on the flat-bottomed boat and earn double wages as they guided cedar and tamarack logs down the Cloquet River. The pig men would bring the harvest to Island Lake, some forty miles to the south, constantly battling rapids, boulders, and snags to keep the logs flowing.

At Island Lake, the logs would be loaded onto Duluth and Northeastern Railroad flatbeds by a steam crane, before being hauled by locomotive to the city of Cloquet. By using streams, rivers, and the Island Lake Reservoir to transport the harvested timber along the majority of the distance from stump to mill, George McAdams was limiting his shipping costs. It was Andrew Maki's responsibility to ensure that the shoreline of Wolf Lake was piled high with product before spring breakup. It was a responsibility that Maki took seriously.

"Get those nags moving, Alex," Andrew Maki shouted to one of the camp teamsters, Alex Rutanen, as Maki approached the latest stand of tamarack being harvested from the swamp surrounding Wolf Lake.

Maki's feet were attached to crude maple skis by leather thongs looped across his winter boots. He wore ankle-high Chippewas with impervious rubber soles and leather uppers. Maki's breath was suspended above his head, seemingly frozen in place. It was cold: fifteen below zero. Hoarfrost covered the nostrils, eyes, and snouts of two Belgians straining to pull a sledge load of logs out of the woods and onto the iced roadway. Rutanen yelled at the horses in Finnish and snapped the reins. The animals pulled harder.

"You men lend a hand," Andrew Maki shouted, noting that six of his loggers stood idly by, axes and saws in hand, watching the horses struggle mightily to move the load. "Get behind that sled and put your backs into it."

The men looked at Maki like he was insane. No one moved. Though there was no wind, it was brutally cold. The loggers uniformly shrunk into the meager warmth of their wool mackinaws, mittens, and fur hats as they stood shivering in place, their backs to the wind. Vapor rose from the loggers' mouths and noses, adding a layer of ice to their hats.

"Here now, give me a hand," Maki reiterated, stepping out of homemade leather ski bindings, stabbing the iron tips of his ski poles, tips forged by the camp blacksmith over the past autumn, into thigh-deep snow.

Maki's boots promptly sank through the accumulated snow until he was waist-deep in a snowdrift. Fighting the snow's grip, the Finn trudged forward. Upon reaching the ice road, Maki moved with determination towards his crew.

"Let's give Old Blue and Little Bob a hand," Maki insisted, naming the horses in the process of directing his men in Finnish.

The crew reformed behind the wooden platform of the sledge and began to push.

"Hey, now," Alex Rutanen encouraged the team, snapping the stiff leather reins with more vigor.

The runners of the sled moved. Progress through the deep snow was marginal until the sled claimed the ice road, at which point it glided forward with ease.

"Much obliged, boss," Alex called out as the Belgians leaned easily into their work.

The crew picked up their tools and formed a circle around the camp boss.

"That's the last load of the day," Andrew Maki revealed. "Mr. McAdams is giving you Christmas Eve and Christmas Day off this year," Maki added, taking special note of the men's appreciative reaction as he announced the unusual two-day respite from work. "Make the most of it and come back on the 26th, sober, refreshed, and ready to go."

"Thanks boss," the group said in unison.

"Don't thank me, thank Mr. McAdams. You can hitch a ride to Aurora on the DM and N tomorrow morning. Find a place to bunk there or catch another train to Virginia or Duluth, but whatever you do, be ready to work bright and early on the 26th."

The crew dispersed. The single men talked excitedly about the prospects of women, liquor, and a hot bath in an inexpensive hotel. The married crewmembers quietly considered McAdams's gift of two days with their wives and children, a generous circumstance given that it was the height of the logging season.

"One more thing," Maki called out as he attempted to slide his boots into the bindings of his skis. "The Sky Pilot's in camp. He brought along his accordion and wants to sing a few hymns, say a prayer or two, and pontificate a while after chow."

A collective groan went up from the band of departing men as they shuffled down the ice road towards the camp. The crew was tired, cold, hungry, and desperate with anticipation. They were not interested in singing religious songs with an evangelical preacher in the middle of a below-zero night in the wilderness.

Chapter 20

Maki flicked the reins of the harness. The sleigh, a small and delicate cutter used to deliver supplies to the logging camp, flew over the snow-packed roadway towards Palo-Markham, a tiny hamlet founded by the Finns that was located some distance to the northwest of Wolf Lake Camp. Two black grade geldings, their backs shiny beneath the light of the full moon, pulled the rig with easy confidence.

"I appreciate the lift," Pastor J. Rankila said as the sleigh sped over the frozen surface of the rough gravel road. "The regular pastor at the church is still recovering from a deer-hunting accident."

"Accident?" Maki asked, while keeping his eyes straight ahead, maintaining his concentration on the darkened path leading west.

"Shot himself in the foot climbing over deadfall," the pastor answered. "He's a city boy," Rankila added with a chortle.

Maki laughed softly, emitting wisps of vapor as he exhaled. The sleigh was not equipped with lights. Andrew Maki navigated by the moon's illumination, thankful that there were no clouds in the sky. Somewhere off in the distance, a Canada lynx, a large cousin to the more familiar and numerous bobcat, let out a piercing scream.

"What in God's name was that?" the reverend asked, obviously unnerved by the intensity of the cat's call.

"Lynx. Must have killed a snowshoe hare," the logger advised, slowing the rig to round a ninety-degree bend in the road.

Silence imposed itself for a period of time. The only sound to be heard was that of the horses' labored breathing and the rhythmic beat of their shod hooves striking frozen ground. Pastor Rankila drew his winter coat, a long formal affair, tight around his rotund body, as the shadows of frozen aspen and birch saplings passed over the advancing sleigh. The reverend ducked his chin into the coat's collar and forced his mittened hands deeper into the pockets of the garment.

"I enjoyed your sermon," Andrew Maki said, interrupting a long silence between the men.

"Well, unfortunately, if you were coming to the evening service, you'd hear it again," the cleric advised. "I haven't had time to prepare anything fresh."

Maki smiled and cast his eyes over the short, round pastor's form as the sleigh bounced across a crude bridge, spanning a frozen creek.

"It was good enough to hear again."

The members of the Brimson Finnish Evangelical Church congregated at the Farmers' Cooperative Association store for Christmas Eve. A church building was in the planning stages, but would not be completed for two years. The Cooperative building was aglow with candles. Flickering yellow light from a hundred flames danced across the wind-smoothed snowfield surrounding the makeshift chapel. Rigs and horses of every discernible shape and size stood idle outside the building, the animals patiently awaiting the culmination of the evening service. Maki drew his sleigh close to the front door of the building and eased the team to a stop. Leather and metal creaked in the cold as the pastor climbed off the rig, releasing tension from the iron springs beneath his side of the sleigh as he departed.

"Thanks again for the lift," the Sky Pilot said with sincere gratitude. "It was a pleasure riding with you. Merry Christmas."

"Merry Christmas to you too," Andrew Maki replied.

Another sleigh arrived as Maki snapped the reins and urged his team into motion. A family, consisting of the parents and four children under the age of ten, scrambled out of a battered sledge, a device more appropriate for hauling freight than passengers, and followed Reverend Rankila into the Cooperative store. Maki watched wistfully as the family entered the warm building, the smell of wood smoke escaping as the pastor held the door for the worshipers.

It was too cold to try and spend the night in his unfinished cabin on Papoose Lake. The town of Aurora was twenty miles away, a trek of several hours in daylight, more at night by the light of the moon. Maki checked his pocket watch. It was six o'clock.

"Plenty of time to make the last train," the logger observed, referring to the Duluth and Iron Range Railroad service from Two Harbors to Aurora. "I'll need to board the team for the night at Olga's," Maki said. Olga Petrell was the local postmistress who manned the Brimson post office.

The logger sent a snap through the leather harness to alert the team of his intentions. In a matter of minutes, the horses were boarded with Olga, a dollar exchanged for the privilege, and he was seated in a passenger car of a D& IR train, headed north.

Maki strolled a cement sidewalk in downtown Aurora, his face turned into his Mackinaw against the bitter cold. His mind wandered as his feet drew him along. Elin Gustafsson and Horace Ellison were engaged to be married. That was a fact he could not change, a fact he had learned from George McAdams before the Canadian had gone on holiday. Elin, according to the version of the tale passed on to McAdams through Wendy Heikkonen, believed that Andrew, because he'd not written to Elin while working in the Alpena Mine, had simply lost interest in the relationship. Wendy's admonitions to the contrary, her attempts to convince Elin that letters had been sent, only to be intercepted at the Normal School by staff paid to do so by Karl Gustafsson, fell upon deaf ears. There was no amount of cajoling or haranguing that could move Elin to reconsider her views. It was over. Most completely and assuredly, it was over.

Olson's Café was nearly deserted. Two other patrons, an elderly miner and his wife, sat in a far corner of the little restaurant and ate their Christmas Eve dinner in silence. Andrew Maki stood patiently while the only waitress in the place filled the couple's coffee cups with steaming black liquid. The smells of fried beefsteak and baking bread merged to form an odoriferous bouquet. Andrew's eyes were drawn to the woman waiting tables. He took in her hair, long strands of blond fibers tied up in a tight bun against the base of her agile neck. Her narrow hips shifted as she conversed with the elderly couple. As the waitress turned towards Andrew Maki, the logger inadvertently smiled.

Her eyes were a ballet of blue. Sloping cheekbones accented the contours of her face. Her lips, though absent of lipstick, were as red as a fresh apple. There was a spark, a genuine flash of intellect about the way she considered him.

"May I help you?" she asked in English.

"I'd like dinner," Andrew Maki replied in Finnish.

The woman, looking to be near thirty, approximating the logger's own age, smiled, exposing clean white teeth and the soft pink of her mouth.

"I'm sorry, but the kitchen is closed," she advised, speaking their language without hesitation.

Maki's eyelids batted nervously.

She's a delightful woman, the logger thought as he stood near the doorway. *But she's wearing a wedding band*, he noted with disappointment.

"I've come in from the woods," Maki stated, trying to restrain his anxiousness, "from Wolf Lake Camp."

She studied him with a steady look, a look of intense scrutiny.

"Father," she called out in Finnish, "do we have anything left to feed a hungry logger?"

An older gentleman stepped out of the kitchen. The man's frame blocked the portal. He was tall, stoop-shouldered, and rugged. His face boasted a pink complexion. He wore a patch over one eye.

"Who wants to know?" the cook asked, yelling across the nearly empty café.

"This gentleman," the woman said, pausing. "What is your name, sir?"

"Andrew Maki."

"Ah. Mr. Maki has come in from the woods. He's tired, hungry, and, by the look of things, in need of a hot bath," the woman observed through a smile.

"Maki, eh? Got any relatives here in Aurora?"

"A cousin. Helmi. Works as a trackman on the D and IR."

"Helmi's a good sort," the cook stated without emotion. "We can fry up something. Nothing fancy. We need to close down in time for midnight service at Holy Rosary," the old man advised.

"A couple of eggs, some toast, a beef steak on the side?"

"That I can do," the cook answered, closing the distance between the men and extending a long, narrow hand and spidery fingers to Maki. "Jerome Seppo. This is my daughter, Heidi."

Maki shook the man's hand and smiled at the waitress.

"Pleased to meet you both."

The cook grunted and shuffled back into the kitchen.

"Please take a seat. Coffee?" Heidi asked.

"That'd be fine."

The couple across the room paid the logger no attention. The waitress brought Maki a cup and saucer, set them on the table, and poured hot coffee into the cup.

"I've been in here before but never seen you," Andrew said, trying to conceal his fluttering heart from the woman.

"We bought the restaurant two weeks ago. Father lost his eye in an accident in the Mohawk Mine. My husband died in the same explosion. We sold both of our homes, pooled the little money we cleared, and bought this place. My father wasn't able to go back to working with just one eye, and I needed to earn a living."

The logger avoided looking directly at the woman. Maki didn't want her to see the appreciation in his eyes, created by the news of her single status.

"I'm sorry to hear about your husband," he said.

There was a slowing of the dialogue between them as the woman struggled to avoid tears.

"Don't cry," Maki said, handing the woman his cloth napkin.

She refused the gesture. As quickly as the upset had come upon the woman, it vanished.

"Thanks. I'm OK. It's been three months and I'm still not used to talking about it. One moment, you're in love with someone, sharing your life, your house, a child, and the next moment, the local policeman is on your front porch, telling you that your life has changed, changed unalterably for the worse."

Maki considered the information. *Heidi had a child?*

"Joseph Genelli was a good man. A wonderful father. He was gone before I could tell him those things," Heidi Genelli observed quietly, forming a weak grin as she turned to retrieve the logger's food.

Chapter 21

Andrew Maki lingered at Olson's Café. Maki sipped coffee while the old man and his daughter cleaned up the place. Finally, to avoid an awkward exchange in which Mrs. Genelli would be forced to ask him politely to leave, the Finn counted out enough money to pay the bill and leave a significant tip. His belly full of eggs, steak, fried potatoes, toast, and coffee, Maki stood up and made for the exit door.

"Thank you for stopping in," Heidi Genelli called out, wiping sweat from her brow with a dishrag as she stood next to the kitchen sink, scrubbing pots and pans.

Andrew nodded. A sudden urge to say something untoward and foolish interrupted his thinking. He thought better of it and simply smiled before stepping outside.

New electric street lamps gaily illuminated Aurora's main street. The Finn trudged through the bitter cold towards the bus depot. The forerunner of what would later become the Greyhound Bus Line ran from Hibbing, its birthplace, to every city, mining location, burgh, tavern, and town on the Mesabi Iron Range. The last bus from Aurora was scheduled to leave at eight. Andrew pulled out his watch. He had five minutes to make the bus station. He doubled his stride and made it to the station in time.

Bouncing along the rutted gravel road between Aurora and Virginia, the logger found himself thinking about Heidi Genelli. She was not educated, like Elin Gustafsson, though she surely possessed a quick mind. She was older than Elin, had been married, and was caring for a child, all circumstances with which Andrew Maki was wholly unfamiliar. Her face, though benefiting from her blue eyes, long blond hair, and rounded cheekbones, was, in the abstract, rather ordinary. Her hips, despite having given birth, were straight, like a man's, without the curves normally assigned to an adult woman. Her bust, from what Andrew could detect through the apron and the dress Heidi wore as she worked, was modest at best. Again, the distinctions to be drawn between the waitress and Elin Gustafsson were striking.

Still, Andrew Maki thought as he rode the bus to Virginia through a dark and lonely Christmas Eve, *she has managed to stir something inside me that I thought had died when I was banished from Duluth.*

The logger placed the back of his head against the unforgiving oak of his seat and soon fell fast asleep. When he awoke, the bus was in front of Yodoski's Saloon on Chestnut Street in Virginia. Zordick Yodoski, the Polish proprietor of the saloon and the two-dollar-a-night rooms that were rented out on the second and third floors of the building, had anticipated Maki's arrival. Madeline DeBoer, a full-figured whore who lived at the tavern, sat at Maki's usual table, flushed with excitement. She had a bottle of vodka open and two glasses ready when Andrew Maki walked into the bar.

"Hello, stranger," Madeline said, her faint hazel eyes scrutinizing the miner as he stepped into the warmth.

"Miss DeBoer," Maki responded with a weariness that caught him off-guard.

I don't want to do this, he thought to himself. *I don't want to wake up on Christmas morning in Madeline DeBoer's shabby little room above this shabby little saloon.*

The whore poured the logger a drink. She shifted her thick body on a wooden chair. A complicated series of undergarments and the stiffly ironed dress she wore rustled in the process. Despite the cold, her upper arms were exposed, the pink flesh jiggling and quivering as she reached across the table and poured two glasses of vodka.

"You look done in," the woman offered, pulling an empty chair out so that Andrew Maki could sit beside her at the table.

There were several clusters of single men and drunkards stationed at various places around the interior of the saloon. Gaslight exposed the rough edges of the space, revealing the dirt and filth that Zordick had allowed to accumulate in the corners. The mirror behind the bar, once magnificently reflective, was clouded from a decade of tobacco smoke. A radiator hissed and dispensed wet heat. Zordick himself was off, attending Christmas Eve Mass with his wife and three daughters at the local Roman Catholic Church. Hans Englemeyer, a German bricklayer who spelled the Polish bar owner from time to time, manned the bar. Hans nodded noncommittally to Maki as the logger sat down beside the prostitute.

"I am. It was a long, cold ride from Wolf Lake," Andrew Maki said, removing his rabbit fur hat, woolen mittens, and his Mackinaw. Snow melted off his Chippewas. Water ran down the rubber surface of the boots and pooled on the dirty floor.

"You look like you could use some company," Madeline said through a bright smile, as she touched the bare skin of the back of his hand with her thick fingers.

Maki studied the woman. He had visited her regularly since being hired by McAdams to run the Wolf Lake Camp. He'd met her on a Friday night, when he and George McAdams had stopped into the bar for a quick bump. George had struck up an immediate conversation with Flora Gibbons, a tall, raw-boned, unattractive tart with fire in her eyes and agony in her loins. George had been in a desperate way. Wendy, his betrothed, though not a virgin, was insistent that they "wait" until their marriage night to consummate their love. By the time McAdams and Maki first wandered into Yodoski's Saloon in Virginia, it had been months since George McAdams had been with a woman. Now George was calling it off, vowing to stop spending Saturday nights in Flora Gibbons' creaking iron bed on the third floor of Yodoski's.

I need to make the same commitment, Andrew Maki thought as the whore stroked the dark hairs on the back of his arm. *If I want to have a chance at a real life, with a real woman and a family, I need to stop this nonsense.*

Maki smiled a tired smile as he took in the sagging skin of his companion's jowls. There was nothing about Madeline DeBoer's face that was endearing. Her skin was worn and used up, the result of too much booze and not enough sleep. Though he guessed she was not yet thirty years old, the creases around Madeline's eyes made her appear to be at least fifty.

How many times has she visited the doctor to get rid of an unwanted child? To buy powders for the clap? To treat other female maladies that I cannot name, but know to be the consequences of the life of a whore? Andrew Maki asked himself.

"What's on your mind?" the woman asked.

Andrew raised the shot glass and downed the liquor. Madeline's hand stopped stroking his arm.

"That you've had a hard life," he whispered.

She was taken aback by the remark. The prostitute's upper lip, the surface painted red with too much lipstick, quivered nervously.

"What's that supposed to mean?"

Maki poured himself another shot and tossed it down. The woman removed her hand from his skin.

"You're too good a woman to be here, doing this," he responded with little conviction.

"Bullshit," Madeline DeBoer replied. "There ain't nothin' good about me, sweetheart, except what's hiding in my skirt."

The crass talk solidified his resolve. Though he'd felt himself stirring when the whore had stroked his arm, whatever animal lust had been awakened was now reposed.

"You've got a good heart. You're not stupid. You can't be over thirty years old. There are hundreds, if not thousands, of lonely, single miners roaming the Mesabi Iron Range who would consider themselves blessed to be your husband," Maki said with assurance.

The frown on Madeline's face abated.

"You askin'?"

The woman sipped vodka from a tall water glass devoid of ice as she stared at the logger. Maki shifted his weight in his chair and touched the woman's hand with his own.

"'Fraid not, Maddie. I'm not in the mood for marriage."

The woman nodded her head.

"Still carryin' the torch for that little Finnish girl, ain't you? You know, her daddy ain't gonna let you within a hundred miles of her. You got no chance there, you know that, don'tcha?"

Maki smiled and pushed his glass away.

"You're very perceptive, Maddie. That is one thing I love about you. Cut to the chase. Tell it straight. I think I've gotten over Elin Gustafsson," he replied, the words trailing off as he stopped himself from saying more, from revealing his newfound infatuation with a waitress.

"Come upstairs," Madeline urged, oblivious to Maki's unspoken interest in Heidi Genelli. "I promise to make you forget about that little girl," the whore added with a mischievous wink.

Despite his resolve, the logger hesitated. His eyes took in the exposed flesh of Madeline's lovely bosom, the flesh of her breasts pink and satiny. He knew the pleasures buried deep behind the façade of fabric covering the whore. He knew the ravishment the woman was capable of releasing. Andrew Maki knew all these things, desired them at that moment more than could be ciphered by the most diligent accountant, and yet, he declined.

"Not tonight, Madeline. I'm afraid I'll have to pass."

Snow swirled 'round the windows of the saloon overlooking Chestnut Street. Wind buffeted the building. Steam percolated through the cast iron radiators in a futile effort to abate the migrating chill. Madeline DeBoer's face pouted in disappointment. Tears began to stream from her eyes.

"It's Christmas Eve, Andrew. Christmas Eve and I'm all alone. I won't charge you a thing. I just don't want to spend the night by myself. You're the only one here that I'd offer this to. The only one," she whispered, wiping tears with the hem of her dress.

The garment she was wearing was a tattered old covering, salvaged from one of Virginia's second-hand stores. Someone, perhaps Madeline DeBoer, perhaps the prior owner, had repaired the various rips and tears in the dress with fabric that nearly, but not identically, matched that of the original.

The whore's silk stockings boasted numerous runs. Her hair, though, her hair, dark black and thick, was neatly combed and clean, as if she'd spent the entirety of the afternoon ensuring that her best attribute met expectations. Andrew Maki reached out to the woman with his left hand and touched her heavily rouged cheek with his index finger.

"I know, Madeline, I know. I'm lonely as well. But I don't think that spending the night together will make us feel any less lonely in the morning," he said.

She reached up with her hand and firmly grasped his wrist, pulling his hand away from her face with determination but not anger. She did not release her grip as she placed his hand on the table.

"Tomorrow is a long ways off," she whispered, her expression pleading for kindness.

His eyes became adjusted to the morning in stages. Dawn's obtuse light crept into Madeline DeBoer's bedroom through the room's only window. Gray gave way to hesitant yellow. Light infiltrated the space with carefully metered intensity. By the time Andrew Maki fully opened his eyes, the room was awash in stark light, the glory of an exposed Christmas sun repeated and intensified in the folds of snow that had accumulated outside the saloon over the evening.

Madeline slept on, her breath sour from booze, the unsheathed skin of her flabby upper back and the suggested contours of her breasts open to view as she slept face down on dirty sheets. Her sable hair fanned out across her broad back, the strands shiny in the daylight, before disappearing beneath the soiled woolen blanket covering her buttocks. The roundness of her hips and rear caused the bedcovers to rise significantly before sloping to her legs and feet.

Maki eased himself out of bed and stood naked in the magnificent light and considered the thick quilt of new snow choking Chestnut Street below.

"This isn't the sort of Christmas I expected when I left Finland for America," the logger mused, reaching over to retrieve his woolen union suit from the cold pine planking of the floor.

Chapter 22

Winter, 1916-1917. Forty men worked under the supervision of Andrew Maki at the McAdams's Wolf Lake Camp. Tim Laitila arrived in January, Finnish Bible and tools in hand, after the camp's blacksmith quit his post due to a disagreement over smoking cigarettes around camp, a habit precluded for camp safety in every logging camp in Northeastern Minnesota. Laitila had never worked as a blacksmith, but possessed skills in the craft after apprenticing under his father as a smith before coming to America from Finland twenty years before. Hiring Laitila was a major coup for Andrew Maki. Tim Laitila not only filled Jon Elmquist's position as blacksmith, but the camp also acquired an experienced carpenter in the bargain, although Laitila's hiring caused some small resentment amongst the men already in camp. Laitila was retained at the salary of forty dollars a month, a sum only twenty dollars below what Maki was being paid as camp boss. The forty-dollar salary was in line with what Maki paid the camp clerk. Laitila was also a vocal Christian, something that made the doubters and fence sitters in the camp nervous. Fortunately for Maki, it took but a few weeks of Laitila's industry to convince the other men that Tim Laitila was worth every cent he was paid. Hard work by the carpenter apparently more than made up, at least in the minds of the crew, for some occasional homiletics.

Over the winter months, Maki made weekly trips into Aurora on the camp delivery sleigh to retrieve mail, pick up supplies, and, on nearly every visit, share a cup of coffee with Heidi Genelli. A friendship blossomed between the widow and the logger. No kisses were exchanged, no dates were arranged. Heidi Genelli made it clear that she remained in mourning over the death of her husband, and Andrew Maki did not push the woman towards romance. He valued her companionship. His clandestine visits with her presented wonderful respites from the unrelenting monotony of camp life. He was biding his time, confident that there would be an opening for him to assert his growing affection.

Little Joey, as Heidi's son was called, took to the Finnish logger immediately. Though Andrew had never been much interested in children, Maki made a selfish effort to ingratiate himself with the boy in the hopes of improving his chances with the widow. At eight years old, Joey proved to be quick of mind, far sharper in mathematics and reading than any child of a similar age that Andrew had ever encountered. He was a serious boy, someone who considered and wondered at life, a trait that made him appear older than his years. The boy wasn't a recluse, however. He had a significant group of close friends, uncharacteristically ruffian and boisterous, a chorus of toughs and roustabouts distinctly at odds with Joey's personality. The other boys, however, respected the youngest Genelli's fists. Slow to anger, an obvious target for bullies, given his bookish looks and intellect, Joey made it clear, in one incident with a ten-year-old thug named Demetrius Allen, the son of Aurora's Chief of Police, that Joey Genelli was a boy to be reckoned with.

Joey had been walking home along Aurora's main street from school, his arms loaded with books, his blond hair waving in the spring wind, his blue eyes fixed on the sidewalk, when Demetrius Allen and a crowd of older boys blocked the path of Joey and two of his pals.

"Where you think you're goin', bookworm?" the older boy had asked, hands placed on his hips in the spitting image of a dime novel villain.

Demetrius was a well-built, thick-shouldered lad with a meaty face and small, nearly absent, cinnamon eyes. He wore his hair shorn to the scalp, like his father. He bore a cluster of vicious welts beneath his clothes, the result not of his father's anger, but that of his mother, a sour, angry woman who had no patience for the seven children she had birthed. Demetrius was the youngest of the seven and the only boy remaining at home. He was, in the eyes of his mother, shiftless and ungrateful, a combination that compelled her to reach for the short piece of leather oxen harness she hung on a nail in the pantry of their dingy little house perched on a ditch bank next to the D and IR tracks. Gertrude Allen was a woman whose ability to love had been drained away from her, sucked from her soul, by the still-births of four babies, the tragic deaths of two others in infancy, and the constant demands of the three daughters and one son still cloistered in her tiny house. Her rage was a well-kept secret. Chief Roger Allen had no inkling, no suspicion, that his wife was brutalizing his son, taking out her disappointments and frustrations on Demetrius' ten-year-old backside.

Joey Genelli had maintained a steady silence as he stared into Demetrius' face. There was no fear in the younger boy's eyes as he studied the features of the bully.

"Stupid wop," Demetrius had said, prejudice insistent in the remark.

The little boy didn't move. His companions began to cry.

"Crybabies," one of Allen's companions chided.

"Girls is what I'd call them," Demetrius added. "'Specially Genelli. What's wrong, Eyetalian? Don't you know how to speak English?"

Joey stood his ground.

"Stupid wop," the ten-year-old repeated as he placed his hands on Genelli's chest and shoved the boy backwards.

Books fell to the ground. Joey's lips parted in a crooked, knowing smile. The significance of the gesture was lost on the older boy.

"You are one stupid wop," Demetrius chided, kicking Joey's primer into the blacktopped street.

The bigger boy moved to grab his opponent's shoulders and press the child to the ground. Joey Genelli's fists rose.

"What, you think you can box me?" Allen asked, incredulity coating his words.

Joey Genelli didn't wait for Demetrius Allen to attack. Joey's fists lashed out with unexpected speed and fury. The blows drew immediate blood from the larger child's nose.

"Fight, fight," the other boys shouted, forming a ring around the combatants. The younger boys who had been with Joey Genelli took their leave, disappearing down the street.

"You little shit," Allen mumbled through surprise. "I'll teach you a thing or two."

Allen's first swing completely missed its mark. The second, a calculated low blow, landed in Joey's groin. Pain seared through Joey Genelli, buckling the boy in half. Demetrius followed up with a knee to Joey's face, which toppled the smaller boy onto the cement sidewalk.

Instantly the heavier boy was on top of Joey, his hands around Joey's throat. Joey raised his legs and kneed Allen in the stomach, to no effect.

"Nice try, baby," the bully said, his hands tightening around the child's windpipe, blood from Allen's nose dribbling down his chin, falling onto the clean white shirt Joey was wearing.

"Say there, young man," an adult voice cried out from the opposite side of the street. "Aren't you a little big to be picking on that boy?"

Bill Berquist, the owner of the local hardware store, advanced across the street towards the cluster of kids. Six foot three, lean as a lodge pole pine, Berquist's shop apron fluttered in the wind as he covered the distance in haste. His bald head shone in the spring sun, tufts of blond hair flowing behind as he walked between a parked Studebaker and a Monroe roadster, which had been left with its engine idling.

Demetrius Allen moved with deceptive speed. Before the shopkeeper's leading boot struck the cement sidewalk, the older boy rose from the ground and vanished, with his followers, into the alley behind Aurora's only movie theater.

"Are you all right, son?" Berquist asked as he knelt beside Joey Genelli.

The boy took time to regain his breath. His face was beet red. His eyes welled tears but he did not cry. He simply shook his head, grabbed the man's hand when offered, and stood in the shadow of the theater's marquee.

"You sure you're OK?" the man repeated.

"I'm sure," the boy whispered, wiping dirt from his cheeks.

"Those boys are way too old to be picking on someone your size," the shop owner offered as he assisted Joey in retrieving the displaced schoolbooks.

"I'm fine," Joey repeated. "Thank you," the boy added politely as he tucked his shirt into his trousers.

"You bleeding?" the man asked. "There's blood all over your shirt."

"Nope."

"From the other kid?"

"Yes, sir."

"You mean to say you bloodied someone twice your size?"

Joey Genelli forced a smile.

"You're Joe Genelli's son, right?" Bill Berquist inquired.

The boy nodded affirmatively.

"I should have guessed. Leave it to an ex-boxer to teach his son right," the man added, patting the boy on the shoulder. "Can you make it home?"

"Yes."

"Those boys aren't gonna bother you?"

Joey grinned.

"I think I broke Demetrius Allen's nose."

Indeed, Joey Genelli had broken Demetrius Allen's nose. When Rodger Allen found out that his ten-year-old son had picked a fight with a second grader, Demetrius spent a month restricted to the house. That was the overt punishment that the Chief of Police meted out. It was nothing compared to the clandestine whippings Demetrius received from his mother on a daily basis. He never again challenged little Joey Genelli to a fight.

Andrew Maki gave Joey further instruction in the art of pugilism. On his visits to town, when he had extra time while Bill Berquist was filling his order, when Heidi Genelli was too busy to chat, he took Joey to the high school gymnasium and taught him to weave, to hook, to counter-punch. The boy was quick with both his fists and his mind.

"Joey could be a great boxer," Andrew remarked to Heidi on the last visit he was able to make into town before spring break-up. "He's quick as greased lightning and tough as nails."

"You sound just like Joseph," Heidi had observed. "I'm glad you're taking an interest in Joey. He needs male guidance. My father's getting on in years and isn't very patient. He doesn't do well with children. Likely the reason he and Mom only had the one."

"Joey could easily turn professional when he's old enough," Andrew replied.

"Joey is going to be a doctor. Or a lawyer. He won't be boxing, if I have anything to say about it," the waitress had replied matter-of-factly. "It's good of you to teach him how to defend himself. Beyond that, I wish you'd work with his mind rather than his fists."

Andrew Maki studied the woman and smiled. She was right. Even if the boy steadied and matured his talent in the ring, the life he would lead as a boxer, a life Andrew Maki had left behind in Finland, was not the life of a gentleman. Education, not fisticuffs, would provide Joey with a stable future.

"I won't be back until sometime in May," Andrew replied after a moment of quiet.

"Break-up?"

"Yes. The frost will soon be out of the ground and the snow will be gone. The sleigh will be useless and the roads between Wolf Lake and here, such as they are, will be reduced to quagmires. I'll also be a bit busy. I need to get this year's harvest down the Cloquet ahead of our competition," the logger added.

"You're going with the Wanigan?" she asked, a hint of concern behind the question.

Andrew took in Heidi's plain, kind face, the sparse color of her eyes, and her stoic posture as she stood over his table, pouring coffee into his cup.

"Yes. As camp boss, McAdams expects me to ensure we don't lose logs on the way down."

Heidi's reference to the Wanigan evinced that she understood the dangers of Andrew Maki's occupation. The Wolf Lake Camp's Wanigan, a flat-bottomed raft equipped with a cabin for shelter, cooking, and storage, had been constructed by loggers out of scrap timber and logs several years before McAdams bought Wolf Lake Camp. Upon his arrival in January, Tim Laitila had set about rebuilding the vessel for the upcoming spring log drive. Most of the camp crew would receive their lay-off notices from the camp clerk once the harvest was stacked in place along the shores of Wolf Lake. Come late April, the cedar and tamarack cut that winter would be ready for the trip down the creek that drained the lake. The logs that formed the dam holding back the creek, creating the lake, would be removed, allowing the accumulated snow melt and spring rains to flood the creek bottom, creating enough flow for the Wanigan and the harvested logs to begin their journey towards Island Lake.

In the case of Wolf Lake Camp, the camp boss, the cook, the carpenter/blacksmith, and a handful of trusted men, including the two men who maintained the dam at Wolf Lake, would accompany the logs downstream to a tie lift located on Island Lake. There, men working for the Duluth and Northeastern, a logging railroad owned by the Weyerhaeuser Corporation, would load the cedar and tamarack posts onto rail cars and deliver the harvest to a tie and post plant located in the city of Cloquet. At Cloquet Tie, the largest logs would be barked and treated with creosote (coal tar) for use as telegraph and telephone poles, while the smaller logs would be barked and stacked for sale as fence posts.

During the journey downriver, a trip that would consume five weeks, from early May until mid-June, the Wanigan would be placed at the head of the floating harvest, to serve as cook station, storehouse, and bunkhouse for the pig men. The crew would work through all types of weather, battling rain, sleet, and the occasional late season snow squall during the early weeks, before fending off mosquitoes, blackflies, horseflies, and other biting insects when the waters receded and the eggs of the various pests hatched in the warming sun. Pig men often sustained serious injury or death even before they started downriver, crushed by out-of-control timbers rolling towards the water, buried by unstable stacks of wood that collapsed without warning. Pig men also died on the water, drowned in the surging, turbulent spring melt, their bodies trapped beneath a carpet of logs.

Island Lake, a reservoir originally formed behind an earthen dike to retain water for log drives, had grown considerably in size once Great Northern Power built a concrete dam to regulate the Cloquet River as part of Great Northern's effort to produce hydroelectric power. The Wolf Lake Camp's Wanigan would be pulled from the water at Island Lake by the steam hoist owned by the Duluth and Northeastern Railway. The Weyerhaeuser line had spurs running along the shoreline of Island Lake. Though other outfits operated Wanigans below the Island Lake Dam, McAdams's Wanigan would not be transported around the massive concrete structure located at the west end of the lake. The Wanigan would be shipped by rail back north to Brimson, where it would remain until loaded onto a horse-drawn freight wagon the following winter. Precariously balanced on the wagon, the Wanigan would be cautiously carted to Wolf Lake for repairs and for use on subsequent drives.

"I know it's part of your job," Heidi Genelli whispered, her mouth barely moving as she spoke, "but please be careful. I'll pray for you," she added, with the full knowledge that her conversion to the Roman faith had a deeper hold than Maki's adherence to Lutheranism.

"I appreciate that," Andrew answered, awkwardness coming between them.

Heidi Genelli nodded her head and turned to leave the table. Something about her concern, something about the tenuous way she sought to escape his presence, made Andrew call out: "I think it's time you and I went out to dinner," he said assuredly.

The widow stopped suddenly. Heidi Genelli hesitated, her back to the logger, as if she were taking a moment to steady herself. From his vantage point, Andrew Maki believed he saw the woman nod "yes."

Chapter 23

Elin Gustafsson's engagement to Horace Ellison was announced at a spring ball held at the Kitchi Gammi Club. In marked contrast to the Suffrage dance that had been the catalyst for Elin's relationship with Andrew Maki, the dance at the Kitch was a stuffy affair. The elite of the city, the women decked out in the newest fashions from New York, the men adorned in formal tuxedos, took to the hardwood floor of the second floor ballroom, sedately bowing and curtsying their way through boring waltzes. A chamber orchestra provided sedate music, while Elin and Horace moved in and out of other couples across the floor. As Elin danced, she was not thinking of her beau or her personal future. She was thinking about the recent disappointments that her mother's political allies had endured.

Suffrage had not been achieved. Marches in all of the major cities of the country had failed to move Congress to adopt universal voting for women on a national scale. Here and there, states such as California had opened the voting franchise to women on a local level, but the noise of the War Hawks crying out for American intervention in the Great War had drowned out the appeal for suffrage. Universally, America was clamoring for war. None other than former President Theodore Roosevelt was leading the debate, attempting to convince a reluctant Woodrow Wilson to intervene on behalf of America's European allies. The work done by women like Laina Gustafsson continued, despite the fervor of the War Hawks, though the voices of the suffragettes became less and less audible as they insisted that America retain its neutrality, a position at odds with the great weight of United States public opinion.

"You seem self-absorbed," Horace said as they finished a dance. "What, pray tell, has you so preoccupied?"

Elin simply smiled and patted her companion on the cheek, unwilling to engage in a political discussion in public.

"To our children," Eustace Ellison proposed, raising a glass of red wine in toast as his son and Elin Gustafsson resumed their places at the table.

Sofia Wirtanen Gustafsson, newly wed to Karl Gustafsson, sat with her husband and her stepdaughter Elin, along with Horace, Eustace, and Mia Ellison at a round table in a remote corner of the ballroom. When the toast was proposed, Horace's brother, Everett, and his date, Marjorie Eastman – of the camera family – were out on the floor, dancing, their chairs at the table empty

"To our children," Karl Gustafsson said agreeably, his face beaming from liquor and pride. "May they have long lives and make many children."

The reference to pregnancy caused Elin's eyes to shift and take in the face of her stepmother. Sofia's eyes didn't return Elin's gaze.

When Karl Gustafsson revealed his plan to marry Sofia Wirtanen, Elin met the announcement with, what Karl believed, was profound restraint. In truth, whatever spirit Elin had embodied, whatever resistance to her father she had once possessed, had collapsed and vanished with the death of Laina Gustafsson and the retreat of Andrew Maki. Though she continued her involvement in selected liberal causes, including the suffrage movement, Elin had lost the initiative she had evinced as the headstrong young woman who had run off with an immigrant miner to Northern Michigan. Life's unfortunate meanderings had restricted the spark that had once glowed within her, and rendered Elin Gustafsson internally distant and removed. Elin's soul had been left with a slightly mechanical quality, with the technical ability to live, to face the future, but there was no ethos; there was no great desire to celebrate life simmering inside Elin, upon which she could draw. And thus, when Karl Gustafsson disclosed his intention to marry his former maid, Elin had simply shrugged and responded, "I expected as much."

So, on the evening of her own engagement to a man that she clearly did not love, Elin Gustafsson joined the others at her table and raised her glass in recognition of her impending marriage to Horace Ellison.

The union of young Ellison and Karl Gustafsson's only child was the result of hard work by the involved fathers. Thrust together at numerous events, celebrations, and holidays due to the social and political positions of their families, the two young people had developed, over time, restrained respect and tolerance for one another. Horace Ellison came to love Elin Gustafsson. His attachment to her grew more solid and proprietary as he came to know the new, sanitized version of the woman. Despite her changed demeanor, despite the loss of her spirit, Elin retained extreme beauty and intellect, attributes that endeared her to the young business tycoon.

Although Elin Gustafsson did not love Horace Ellison, she accepted the eventuality of their relationship. There were things she wished to accomplish in life, things that required access to wealth. Vacations in New York, Paris, the Orient. Work with the poor through missionary visits to Africa and South America, coordinated by the Finnish Evangelical Lutheran Church through her mother's dear friend, Reverend Sarvela. Children would eventually be welcomed into the home. Not as a means to satisfy Karl Gustafsson's longing for grandchildren, not as a reply to Horace's entreaties for Elin to bear him an heir, but as a means to justify Elin's own existence.

"You were extremely quiet tonight," Horace remarked as he drove Elin home in his new Buick coupe, the vehicle recently purchased after a catastrophic crash between Horace's Ford and a lumber wagon.

Elin looked away, her thoughts concentrated upon mental images of her father and his former maid.

"I say," young Ellison repeated, "you certainly seem preoccupied."

She turned her face so that he could see her eyes as they passed beneath streetlights.

"I was just thinking about my stepmother."

"I thought as much," the businessman replied. "It must be somewhat awkward for you to have to take a meal with a woman of your own age, married to your father."

Elin nodded.

"'Somewhat awkward' would be putting it mildly," she whispered.

"I'd say that it's too late for you to intervene."

Elin grimaced at the remark but said nothing, returning her attention to the cityscape passing by, outside the automobile's plate glass windows.

"I'm awfully sorry that I never got to know your mother," Horace inserted, his tone conciliatory, the remark showing that he was improving his ability to read the young woman's moods.

Elin remained silent.

I'm not so sure Mother would have been enamored with you, she thought, careful to hide the notion from her beau.

Horace Ellison's patience began to wane.

"Elin, do you want to marry me?"

She sighed.

"Your father announced it to a room full of people and I didn't object. That's fairly clear, isn't it?"

He stopped the vehicle in front of the Gustafsson Mansion, turned off the key, and rotated his body to face the woman.

"Elin, do you love me?"

Silence.

"I've told you how much I love you; how much you mean to me. Do you share those feelings?"

She looked at him and patted his wrist with her gloved hand.

"Love is over-rated. I respect you, Horace. I think you've become a sober, thoughtful young man from the boy you were only two years ago."

The reference to Horace's period of sobriety, to his total abstinence from alcohol following the barroom brawl with Andrew Maki and George McAdams, was clear in her words. He had attempted to distance himself from the young men who had been with him that evening, seeking to correct his behaviors to coincide with his station in life. The turn-around had been remarkable, both to Elin Gustafsson, who had only known him as a spoiled, rowdy young braggart, and also to Horace's parents, who had long given up hope that he would follow his brother Everett's lead. Everett was a dentist, practicing in Hibbing, utilizing his one-half Finnish ethnicity, his mother Mia's heritage, upon which to build a clientele. Hopes that Horace would pursue a professional career or a career in business with Eustace Ellison had seemed extremely unlikely, until the evening when Andrew Maki broke young Horace's jaw. That seminal event had, at least to those paying close attention to the young man's life, seemed an epiphany.

"Is sobriety and respect enough to build a life upon?" Horace asked his betrothed, the chill of early spring creeping over them as they sat in the dark.

Elin leaned in and kissed Horace on the cheek. Her perfume found its way to the young man's olfactory nerves and aroused him. His hands moved to draw her into his body in a tight embrace, but she resisted.

"Not tonight, Horace."

He withdrew and studied the woman's face as best he could, given the defuse light.

"You didn't answer my question."

"I know. You're entitled to an answer," she replied, drawing a significant breath. "Yes, I think that respect is enough to build a life upon. I'll bear your children, Horace. I'll support your work. I will keep your home and make sure that you are content. Will I ever love you? That is something I cannot answer. We've had this talk before. I've told you that Mother's death was hard on me, and that the departure of Anders was a major blow. I will be faithful to you. I will care for you. More than that, at this moment, I cannot say."

There's hope, Horace Ellison thought. In time, she may come to love me. God, she is so beautiful, so poised, so brilliant. She is a woman any man would kill for. I cannot do better. Judging by where my former friends have chosen to hang their pants, I could do far worse. Time. Give her time. A child or two. Maybe then, she will learn to love me.

"Goodnight," she said, opening the door, leaving him the outline of her smile against the distant light emitted by her home.

Karl Gustafsson and Eustace Ellison sat, sipping vodka, at the bar in the basement Fireplace Room of the Kitchi Gammi Club. Other men sat at tables in front of a roaring fire in the basement fireplace, playing cribbage and chess. The dance was winding down. The men's respective brides were engaged in socializing with peers, a task made extremely difficult for Sofia, since she was far younger and less educated than the women around her. Mia Ellison took the young woman under her tutelage and protected her from the most vicious of the spinsters and hags patrolling the ballroom, as the men spent time discussing the American Loyalty League.

"Everyone has paid their contributions," Eustace Ellison began. "We've been able to take out several advertisements in support of the War in the *Herald* and *Tribune*. Hopefully, by reading our membership list posted at the bottom of the advertisement, folks will come to understand that the Finnish community in Duluth is comprised of more than Syndicalists and Marxists."

Karl Gustafsson smiled and sipped his vodka.

"Heady talk from someone who's not even Finnish," Gustafsson observed.

Ellison ignored the barb.

"Other communities are doing the same," Gustafsson continued. "Chicago will hold a meeting in the fall, a gathering of all similarly minded Finns. The Chicago group stole Oscar's original name. They're calling themselves 'the Lincoln Liberty League'."

"That does have a nice ring to it," Ellison observed. "I like the idea of using a Republican's name."

Gustafsson grinned. "So do I. Let's finish these drinks and see what the women are up to."

Ellison swallowed the last of his liquor and placed his glass on the bar. Gustafsson did the same. The men began to walk out of the room when Eustace Ellison said, "How's your daughter taking your marriage to Miss Wirtanen?"

"If you're asking, 'has she thrown a fit?' the answer is, curiously, 'no'. Since Laina's death and the departure of Mr. Alhomaki, Elin has been as compliant as an obedience-trained Newfoundland. It's a curiosity, that's for sure, but I'm not one to upset the apple cart."

"They do grow up, don't they? I'm amazed at Horace's sobriety. I don't know that I could make that choice and stick to it like he has. It's for the best, obviously. He simply can't remain in control when he drinks. But damn, I wish I had his resolute constitution! I'd be twenty pounds lighter if I could stay away from liquor," Eustace Ellison added, slapping his ample belly as the men climbed a stairway.

Karl Gustafsson remained silent. His mind wandered back to the days of his wife's dying. Though he had never openly expressed his feelings, he retained an unremitting aspect of disappointment in himself for the way that he had failed to honor Laina. She had birthed two stillborn babies before her pregnancy with Elin. Years of caring for the house and their daughter while Karl built his law practice. Nights spent beneath Karl's body, yielding herself to him to satisfy urges and lusts that she did not share, that were of little interest to her other than as a means to fulfill her marriage promise. Laina Gustafsson had never, not once, denied him his place at the head of the family in any discussion or argument, no matter how vehemently she may have opposed his views. And so, in return for all of Laina's obedience, respect, and yielding, Karl Gustafsson had slept with a twenty-year-old maid in the bed he shared with his wife. This was how he had repaid Laina's love. This was the sour, bitter bile that tainted Karl Gustafsson's soul and corrupted the honest and valid memories of time spent together in a marriage.

"Anything wrong?" Eustace Ellison whispered as the men reached the entrance to the ballroom.

Karl Gustafsson made no answer as the men crossed the threshold into the ballroom, which was filled with music, laughter, and celebration.

Chapter 24

"We've got an order to fill for the Cloquet Tie and Post Company," George McAdams advised as he and Andrew Maki sat in the dining hall of the kitchen building at Wolf Lake Camp.

It was April 14, 1917. In Washington D.C., Congress was debating the entry of the United States into the war in Europe. Rumors abounded that a massive conscription of men between the ages of eighteen and fifty would be passed by the lawmakers on the heels of a declaration of war. Business and industry, though ready to welcome the governmental procurement orders that were sure to spring from hostilities, nervously anticipated the depletion of the pool of inexpensive labor available to them as a result of the waves of immigrants who had flocked to the United States from the 1880s through the turn of the 20th Century. Without cheap labor, profit would be curtailed, with the result that war was welcomed by Chambers of Commerce throughout the country with a sense of nervous anticipation.

"We've got plenty of tamarack and cedar ready to go as soon as the ice is out," Andrew Maki replied, spitting a wad of chewing tobacco into a spittoon resting unevenly on the crude wooden floor of the building.

Iner Halvorson, the camp cook, and his two young apprentices worked in the well-appointed kitchen, a wood-fired cook stove surging with energy, cast iron pots of moose meat stew cooking in anticipation of a hungry crew at dinner time. Coffee pots, the blue and white enamel of the enormous containers chipped from hard use, simmered on the back burners of the stove. Sparks from the green balsam used to fire the cook stove erupted from the stove's metal chimney, presenting a constant danger of igniting the slash and waste covering the forest floor surrounding the camp.

"The man-catchers filled the crew right after the first of the year," Maki continued, referring to the paid recruiters who frequented Finntown in Duluth. "We've been going great guns all winter long, despite the snow."

The Cloquet River Valley was clogged with snow. Nearly every day, sixteen draft horses were hitched to a massive, wooden v-shaped plow used to clear the camp's logging trails and the road to Brimson. Fellers worked long hours taking down trees with bucksaws, so that skidders driving two horse sledges could transport the felled timber to the edges of Wolf Lake to await the spring melt. Wolf Lake Camp was one of many "piece" camps, outfits that paid their men – with the exception of the camp boss, cook, blacksmith, and camp clerk – a few pennies for each tree cut down and skidded out of the woods. The larger camps, those paying monthly wages based upon job classification, had all but disappeared with the last stands of white and red pine. Abandoned buildings from the ghost camps, long, low affairs built of logs or of slab lumber covered with tarpaper, dotted the landscape, inhabited and used by squirrels and mice as refuges from the weather.

Maki's reference to man-catchers was an allusion to the fellows who made their living grabbing out-of-work men from bars and brothels along Duluth's waterfront for delivery to the various lumber camps. These "recruits" nursed their hangovers, and the odd bruise from the persuasive fist, before returning somewhat reluctantly to the woods, carrying grain sacks filled with their clothes, a pair of summer shoes, and an odd assortment of personal items. These sacks uniformly came to rest on the well-worn wooden floors of rail cars owned by the Duluth, Missabe, and Northern, or the Duluth, Missabe, and Iron Range, or the Duluth and Northeastern Railways, as the loggers traveled north, back into the woods. The flour sacks contained the entirety of the loggers' worldly possessions, except for their winter clothing, which they wore upon their backs.

George McAdams puffed on a hickory pipe and sent sweet clouds of tobacco smoke into the air, before placing the pipe on the white pine surface of the primitive table in front of him. McAdams and Maki sat on wooden benches and considered metal cups filled with hot coffee. The men maintained a familiar and easy silence while the cooking crew worked steadily in the background.

"The first Saturday in August," McAdams finally said.

"How's that?" Andrew Maki asked, puzzled by the reference.

"Wendy and me. We're getting married then," the Canadian added.

Maki's mouth broke into a broad smile. "You old dog. I knew you were hooked, but I never realized she'd land you so soon."

McAdams smiled and lowered his head in embarrassment. "I'm not getting any younger. Fifty-three next November. It's time I had a family."

"I'd say. You're an old man, my friend. But nonetheless, I am happy for you."

McAdams sipped coffee, nearly spitting the liquid onto the floor when it scorched the inside of his mouth.

"Damn, that's hot."

Maki nodded and spat another wad of tobacco into the spittoon.

"What about you? Any prospects?" McAdams asked.

Andrew Maki hesitated. He liked his boss. Trusted him beyond words. He was beholden to the Canadian in too many ways: for his job; for the loan to buy his property. *Do I want him to know? Should I tell him about Heidi?*

Maki held his tongue. He was uncertain as to what course his blossoming romance with the Widow Genelli would take. There was a good chance that the dates they'd shared – the odd film at the silent movie houses in Aurora and Virginia; the quiet walks through snowy streets; the innocent visits she had allowed to take place in the living quarters above Olson's Café she shared with her son and her father – would all disappear with the advent of summer.

There were eight single men on the Mesabi Iron Range for every available woman, a circumstance that had provoked married Finnish women to rally around the Finnish Temperance Society with a vengeance, in hopes of warding off the untoward advances of drunken out-of-work miners and loggers that they endured on a constant basis. It was a vicious cycle. The lack of female companionship compelled visits to the bottle for comfort. The use of the bottle for comfort thwarted any possibility of attracting the few single women available.

Andrew Maki knew he was fortunate to spend time with the Widow Genelli, given the number of potential suitors, including men of means, business owners of greater wealth than Andrew Maki would ever accumulate, who stood ready to knock on Heidi Genelli's door.

"You're awfully quiet," George McAdams noted.

A dark-haired, narrow-faced logger stomped in from the cold. The wooden door to the mess hall slammed behind the man as he approached the table where McAdams and Maki sat.

"What brings you in out of the woods, Kinkkonen?" Maki asked as Olli Kinkkonen walked hesitantly towards his boss.

"We've got a problem with one of the teamsters," the slender logger advised in Finnish. "Uho Rutilan says he can't get the skidder sledge any closer to where we're cutting. I say he can. It's foolish to require us to drag logs by hand when he can get in close with the sled."

Maki frowned.

"You know Mr. McAdams?" Maki asked Kinkkonen in English.

Olli Kinkkonen shook his head in the negative and did not offer his gloved hand to the camp owner.

McAdams didn't extend his hand but offered a smile and a greeting: "Pleased to meet you, Mr. Kinkkonen."

Olli Kinkkonen nodded.

"Seems there's a problem with one of the skidders. Fellow I've had to come down hard on before. I need to take care of this myself," Andrew Maki advised.

"Go ahead. I'll just go over the books with the clerk and be on my way. Can you arrange for a sleigh to take me to Brimson? I'm catching the train to Two Harbors from there in an hour. Wendy will be waiting in Two Harbors for me with my motorcar."

Maki grinned. "Kinkkonen can take you. He knows how to manage a team."

"That will suffice."

Andrew Maki spoke in hushed tones to Kinkkonen. The man departed to ready the sleigh and team. Andrew Maki stared hard at his boss, a wide grin apparent on Maki's face.

"What's on your mind, Mr. Maki?" McAdams asked.

"Wendy is meeting you with your automobile?"

"That's right."

"She drives?"

"This is the twentieth century," the big Canadian said through an extraordinary smile.

Chapter 25

On April 5, 1917, President Woodrow Wilson introduced to Congress the Army Bill, America's first compulsory military conscription act since the Civil War. The following day, the United States declared war on Germany and its allies. Along with the draft, which was eventually passed into law on May 18, 1917, calling for the registration of healthy adult males for service by June 5, 1917, Congress passed a host of laws meant to crack down on "slackers," those Americans who, for a variety of reasons, were vocal in their opposition to the Great War. The most egregious of these erosions of constitutional rights was found in the Espionage Act, a statute that made it a federal crime, a felony, to utter or promote any position that hindered the draft or the war effort. Religious leaders who preached from the pulpit against the Great War, farmers from the Great Plains who protested that they could not afford to send sons off the farm to fight, housewives who wrote letters condemning the draft to the editors of local newspapers: all of these dissenters found themselves rounded up by authorities and convicted of espionage in United States District Courts around the country. Most of these political prisoners received one-year sentences, which, because of federal budgetary constraints, were served in local county jails or workhouses and not in federal prisons.

Prominent immigrants formed organizations akin to the American Liberty League across the country. These groups supported the new conscription law with vigorous patriotism. The president's call to arms had been long anticipated and welcomed by many new citizens as a means of proving their loyalty and dedication to their adopted country. Bond rallies and fundraisers began to spring up across the nation. Britain and France were making a terrible mess of it, the argument went. "They need our boys to strike a killing blow against the

Germans" was the mantra recited as the solution to the stalemate along the Western Front.

Amidst all the hoopla and enthusiasm for conflict, daily life in Northeastern Minnesota continued unaffected. As winter turned to spring, as the snow pack covering the forests began to melt, water released by the warming sun trickled towards the swamps, bogs, and marshes that fed the area's numerous creeks and streams. Gathering power in unity, the melt merged with smaller watercourses to form rivers: the Cloquet (once known as the Rapid), the Whiteface, the Savanna, the Paleface, and the Beaver, before reaching the ultimate watercourse draining the landscape – the St. Louis River. As the banks of these creeks, streams, and rivers lost their winter cloaks, as slumbering vegetation was exposed to the sun, new grass and leaves erupting with the lengthening of every day, water levels rose. Ponds and lakes, including those created by man to hold back the flood for commercial gain, quickly filled. Finally, in the second week of May, when all of the ice was off the surface of Wolf Lake, when the melt restrained by the log dam on the lake, rose to a level that threatened the neatly stacked piles of tamarack and cedar lining the shores of the artificial reservoir, it was time for the men working McAdams's Wolf Lake Camp to begin the log drive to Island Lake.

"Keep 'er straight in the channel," Tim Laitila advised from his perch on the bow of the Wanigan.

Olli Kinkkonen manned the sweep oar at the rear of the boat, changing the course of the flat-bottomed raft upon command to avoid the vicious rocks demarcating the plethora of rapids that bedeviled the voyage from Wolf Lake to Island Lake. An identical oar rested in its pivot at the front of the vessel, unmanned and unnecessary until the Wanigan reached calmer waters.

"That's it," Laitila shouted over the din of the roaring water.

The creek leading out of Wolf Lake was swollen. The few trees remaining along the stream's banks, primarily balsams and sugar maples, were surrounded by frothy water that reached halfway up the trunks of the trees. In ordinary times, the creeks and rivers draining the Cloquet River Valley boasted dark water, the color of camp cook Iner Halvorson's homemade root beer. Diluted by rain and melting snow, the water in the rivulet leading from Wolf Lake to the West Branch of the Cloquet River was light brown, the color of coffee mixed with cream. Here and there, errant cedar and tamarack logs, released prematurely from the lake, raced past the Wanigan. Laitila, Kinkkonen, and Halvorson rode the surging melt of the creek in the flat-bottomed houseboat. They sought the calm of a pool located below the Wolf Lake Dam, where the Wanigan would tie up and await the release of the harvest and the arrival of Andrew Maki and his six-man crew. The crew working the logs would negotiate the raging stream in two wooden prams (square nosed rowboats with flat bottoms and wide gunwales) before eventually joining up with the Wanigan for the night.

The clerk, Ingmar Benson, had remained in camp until the departure of the pig men. Benson had distributed the final reckoning of debits and credits to the employees of Wolf Lake Camp not making the trip. Andrew Maki released thirty men for the summer. Each furloughed logger was given a time check, a negotiable note written against McAdams Wolf Lake Camp's bank account. Deductions were made from the men's pay prior to the issuance of the notes, for clothing, tobacco, stamps, or other articles purchased during the logging season at the camp store. The time checks were redeemable at McAdams's office, located on the second floor of the Palladio Building in downtown Duluth, or at a variety of restaurants, saloons, shops, and brothels located throughout Northeastern Minnesota.

The Wanigan roared past stunted trees. The water released from Wolf Lake catapulted the boat forward. Olli Kinkkonen had manned rafts on the Upper Cloquet during prior log drives. A steady hand with a keen eye for submerged dangers, Kinkkonen possessed the ability to discern minute changes in the river's current well in advance of a raft striking a sunken log or a hidden boulder. Due to the urgency of the water released from Wolf Lake, any hesitation, any momentary grounding of the flat-bottomed craft on an obstacle would cause the boat to capsize, an important consideration since, of the three men on the Wanigan, only Tim Laitila could swim. In fact, of the ten men working the drive, Tim Laitila and Andrew Maki were the only swimmers.

"Take care on the left," Laitila shouted in Finnish, pointing to a rooster tail of water splaying against the gray spring sky.

"Got it," Kinkkonen responded, pivoting the nose of the boat away from a partially submerged rock with a deft refinement of the sweep oar's blade.

In low water, the rapids and ledges underlying the riverbed would be impassable. Due to spring runoff, modest spring rains, and the additional volume of water artificially released from Wolf Lake, shoals and rocks of the watercourse normally exposed to view lurked beneath the surface. The shallow-drafted Wanigan passed over these hazards with impunity, so long as Kinkkonen maintained his watch.

The Wanigan came to rest in a small pool of charcoal water. Tim Laitila used a hemp rope to secure the vessel to a cedar stump. This remnant of an ancient tree was anchored to the sandy soil by a web of sun-whitened roots. Iner Halvorson puttered about in the crude wooden cabin of the boat, the roof and walls of the twenty-foot-long structure sealed with tarpaper nailed over pine planking. Single-pane windows interrupted the boat cabin's boxy appearance, and allowed those inside the cabin to view the landscape. A small barrel stove, its steel chamber and pipe affixed to the interior walls of the cabin by a primitive system of wires and screws, puffed white smoke into the close atmosphere hanging over the Cloquet River Valley. Halvorson busied himself storing bacon, ham, canned goods (a recent innovation in camp staples), potatoes, and other supplies in the space reserved for his use at the rear of the cabin. A crude table, the table's legs, benches, supports, and eating surface crafted out of white pine, occupied space beneath a window. Three tiers of bunk beds of pine planking and spiked to the floor and ceiling adorned one wall. Two tiers of identical beds lined the opposite wall. There were ten sleeping platforms in total, one for each man making the journey down the river. The houseboat did not move at night. The vessel carried no illumination beyond kerosene lanterns, making it impossible to discern submerged dangers even under the most favorable of nighttime conditions, a fact which compelled the boat to remain idle from dusk until dawn.

Back on Wolf Lake, Andrew Maki supervised his crew. Over the prior week, the pig men had moved the year's harvest across the marshy shoreline of the lake into open water by rolling the logs down a system of wooden timbers, which prevented the cedar and tamarack from becoming mired in the peaty ground. A massive raft of logs now clogged the lake from end to end.

"All set," Andrew Maki called out as the last of the harvested tamarack and cedar splashed into the lake.

The two prams used by the pig men floated amongst the logs. Tim Laitila had repaired the rowboats, which would be used as work platforms by the loggers during the drive, over the three months he'd been in camp. The Finn had used scrap cedar to replace broken ribs, and white pine to replace punctured planking before coating the hulls of the vessels with water-resistant pitch. The small boats eased their way through the confused flotilla of timber, working the assembly of logs, organizing the harvest, prodding the product towards the outlet of the lake. To accomplish the job, the pig men stood upright, their boots braced against the sides of the boats, and used twelve-foot long pikes or shorter gaffs, the business ends of the poles made of roughly-smithed iron, to urge logs towards the dam.

Andrew Maki waded into the frigid water with Alex Rutanen, their woolen trousers rolled up to their thighs, their winter Chippewas and socks hanging around their necks by the laces of the boots. The men worked in waist-deep water, the embrace of Wolf Lake so numbing, so cold, that they had coated their limbs with Vaseline prior to entering. The two men in the water worked in concert with the rest of the crew and shoved reluctant logs towards deeper water, where the current could grab the floating harvest and move it towards the lake's outlet.

"That's the last of 'em," Maki called out to Runtanen in Finnish. "We best get a move on."

Maki extended his hand. A pig man drew him into the nearest pram.

"Thanks. Keep moving the product towards the dam," Maki advised the men in the other boat.

The crew continued to work the edges of the harvest, cajoling logs towards the artificially created tug of dissipating water. As the last log slipped over the lip of the reduced dam, the boat carrying Andrew Maki nosed up to a clearing located along the lake's southern shore, where the two men who had removed the gate logs from the dam climbed aboard.

The bow of the lead pram shot downstream unimpeded. The rowboat carrying Andrew Maki followed the first boat into the turbulence, but became hung up on the submerged residue of the dam.

"Pull hard to the right," Maki shouted over the roar of the water, the lip of the rapids curling high above the angled prow of the vessel as the boat remained motionless.

The boat hesitated. The descending water level made the clearance between the boat's hull and the lake bottom precarious.

"Use your pikes," Maki urged, yelling to the pig men as the boat teetered.

Two men in Maki's boat strained at their poles. A logger in the stern of the pram steadied the boat in the current with his pike, keeping the bow of the craft pointed downstream. The loggers' poles sliced through muck that had accumulated behind the dam, until the iron tips of the pikes struck the hard sand base of the creek bed. Contact with solid ground provided leverage. The boat crept forward, pulled by the strength of the current and pushed by the efforts of the men, until, without warning, the lake bottom released its grip.

"Here we go," Maki shouted, adrenaline causing the Finn's heart to race and his blood to pump as the second boat slid over the threshold and into fast water.

Chapter 26
June, 1917

Elin Gustafsson studied a menu in a booth of the Glass Block Department Store restaurant. Wendy Heikkonen sat across the table, sipping coffee and humming a catchy tune as she waited for her friend to make a luncheon selection.

"The herring is supposed to be very fresh," Wendy interjected. "Caught by Sivertsons daily; or at least, so they claim."

Elin smiled and placed the cardboard menu on the tabletop.

"I think I'll go with the soup. I've somehow managed to catch a chill."

June. Though proclaimed a summer month on the calendar, June in Duluth, Minnesota, is generally a month of cold rain, and is usually only a precursor to summer. True summer rarely becomes established along the North Shore of Lake Superior until the end of June, just in time for Independence Day. The summer of 1917 was no exception. Cool weather had been stalled over the city for ten straight days. In the process, countless citizens, like Elin Gustafsson, found themselves battling the common cold.

"It has been an absolutely rotten month," Wendy agreed, dumping cream from a small pitcher into her coffee. "My father's vegetable garden is three weeks behind. I doubt he'll see any corn or potatoes this year."

The women were at the Glass Block to register Wendy for wedding gifts. The largest department store in Duluth, the Glass Block took up an entire city block at 128 West Superior Street, and boasted the finest china, silver, and other assorted household treasures sought by young brides.

A waitress appeared. The woman, a matronly appearing soul in a stiff eggshell uniform and matching hose, her hair completely gray, her midsection extended by too many complimentary lunches taken at the restaurant, listened patiently while the women ordered. Elin Gustafsson smiled and looked at the woman. The waitress' face reminded Elin of etchings from *The Legend of Sleepy Hollow*, in that the waitress' chin was prominent, her eyes were sunken, and her head was altogether too small for her features. The waitress retrieved the menus and retreated to place the women's order, leaving the faint scent of inexpensive bath powder lingering over the table.

"Are you getting anxious?" Elin asked her friend, lifting a cup of black coffee to her lips.

"For the wedding, you mean?"

Elin nodded.

"Anxious isn't the word. I'm petrified. Not that George and I won't do fine together, once we get used to each other's company. It's just that..."

Wendy's words trailed off, as if she were reluctant to finish the thought.

"What?"

Wendy batted her eyes and pondered the completion of her statement. She ran a hand through a strand of hair that had fallen loose from a decorative hairpin. The gilded surface of the butterfly holding her lovely, silky hair in place caught the electric light and shone brightly as the woman patted the errant lock back into place.

"I'm hopeful I can measure up to George's experience."

Elin smiled. "You mean in terms of amore, don't you?"

Wendy Heikkonen nodded and drew another mouthful of tea.

"You'll be fine. You've already been through the worst, with ... what was his name again?"

Wendy's face flushed.

"Barett Edgewater."

"Ah, yes. That creep. Well, if you could survive an introduction to the world of love with that cretin, you will likely be pleasantly surprised by the abilities of a man as experienced as George McAdams."

Wendy studied her hands, noting that her skin shone like that of a newborn, the result of a daily regime of oils and lotions to forestall the march of time.

"You don't seem convinced," Elin added.

A moment passed between them.

"It's just that... well, George is a wonderful man. Kind. Obviously industrious. Patient. When I told him I wasn't a virgin but that I wanted to wait until our wedding night, he didn't complain. Didn't protest. He simply patted my wrist, withdrew from an embrace, and respected my wishes."

"Something's troubling you about a man willing to abide by your wishes?"

Wendy swallowed hard.

"Well, George is the same age as my father."

Elin Gustafsson laughed.

"That's apparent."

"I know. It didn't bother me at first. George is so vital, so strong. You'd never know that he was over fifty."

"Do you love him?"

"You know I do."

"Have you met anyone else, anyone who compares more favorably than Mr. McAdams, in your eyes?"

Wendy shook her head in the negative.

"Well, then, I don't understand your concern. Life is what it is. Pastor Sarvela says that one can never truly know which circumstances we encounter are those intended by God, and which are merely attributes of chance. The trick is to accept both acts of God and the random ups and downs of life, and to bear the bad with the good. If you love George, and you trust that he loves you, his age shouldn't be a factor. As I said, there are creeps and charlatans behind every bush in this town, a fact that is especially true when you are a beautiful young woman of intellect and grace. I'd advise that you follow your heart and ignore your doubts."

The waitress arrived with food. Elin Gustafsson's throat caught as she tasted her soup. The hot liquid provoked a coughing spasm.

"You OK?" Wendy Heikkonen asked in a concerned tone.

Elin nodded and attempted a smile, but continued to cough. She reached hurriedly for a tumbler of water, tilted the glass, and swallowed.

"Piece of beef went down the wrong way," she explained, taking a deep draw of air once her throat was clear.

"It always scares me when a child does that," Wendy observed, stabbing at a small filet of pan-fried herring on the white porcelain plate in front of her.

The women continued to eat, their attention caught up in the hustle and bustle of patrons, universally women much older than themselves, coming and going from the café.

"What about you and Horace?" Wendy Heikkonen asked as a busboy cleared the table next to them.

Elin spooned soup into her mouth in an effort to delay her response. Wendy stopped eating and waited. Elin Gustafsson fixed her steel-blue eyes on her companion before answering.

"Things are going well," she affirmed, using her considerable powers of suggestion to sound convincing.

"Are you excited about the wedding?"

The betrothal of Elin to Horace was scheduled for September, a month after the marriage of Wendy and George. The women had allowed a full month between the ceremonies to ensure that the McAdamses would be able to relish a long honeymoon before Wendy served as the Matron of Honor in Elin's wedding. Elin would fill the same role in Wendy's wedding in August. Upon Wendy and George's return from British Columbia, Elin and Horace would be married in Bethany Lutheran Church on West Third Street, the Swedish Lutheran Church where Horace's parents were members. Pastor Sarvela, Laina Gustafsson's close friend and confidant, would not officiate but had been invited, with the permission of the Swedish pastor, to give the sermon, a task that Sarvela readily accepted.

Wendy Heikkonen and George McAdams were to be married in the First Presbyterian Church on East Second Street. George's Scottish heritage dictated that Wendy yield to his wishes and forego a wedding in the Lutheran Church. She made no complaint at her future husband's insistence in this regard. Her father, Henri, was a pragmatist, and did not object to Wendy's religious capitulation. Wendy's mother, Anna, initially claimed that she would not attend a wedding in "a pagan chapel", but fell into busy preparations for the ceremony and wedding dance nonetheless.

Elin considered her answer, chewing stringy beef with exaggeration as she thought.

"I'm ready to be married," Elin finally disclosed.

"I hope so. Your wedding is in less than four months. But do you love Horace?"

Elin Gustafsson smiled. Wendy had asked the question before. Elin had always changed the subject and cleverly avoided making a commitment one way or another. There was no reason to dodge the issue any longer.

"I respect him."

"There's a world of difference between romantic love and respect," Wendy offered.

"I know that," Elin remarked, the moment becoming strained between the women.

Wendy exhaled for effect.

"So you're marrying a man you do not love? Is there someone else occupying your heart, someone, say, that left you without so much as a goodbye?"

Wendy had access to news about Andrew Maki through her husband. She had shared bits and pieces of Andrew's story with Elin Gustafsson since Maki's departure from Duluth, but Elin appeared uninterested.

"That's not the case."

"Isn't it? Aren't you carrying a torch for a certain immigrant Finn, now living in the wilderness? Isn't that why you're incapable of loving Horace Ellison? Because you remain in love with someone else?"

Elin's demeanor evinced anger.

"Wendy, I said that is not the case. When I say something, would you at least give me the courtesy of listening? Anders, or Andrew as I guess he calls himself these days, no longer occupies my thoughts. That's as clearly and plainly as I can express my feelings on the matter."

Wendy made no further challenge to her friend and the discussion turned to less threatening topics. Their meals finished, the women paid their respective bills, stood up, lifted shopping bags full of clothing items and toiletries from the floor, and walked up the stairs to the Superior Street exit.

Outside, the sun was shining. Trolleys, automobiles, carriages, and horse-drawn wagons clogged Superior Street. Pedestrians, mostly businessmen returning to their offices after lunch, paced quickly along the sidewalks on both sides of the busy thoroughfare. A ship's whistle sounded from out in the harbor, indicating either the departure or arrival of a vessel. A flock of rock doves, gray, white, and black variations of the same theme, took flight above the sandstone and brick buildings.

Wendy and Elin walked east. Fellows that recognized the women tipped their hats before resuming their hurried strides. A faint wind touched the edges of Elin Gustafsson's fine hair as she matched her companion stride for stride.

"I'm sorry I upset you," Wendy finally remarked as they stopped at the corner of Lake and Superior, and waited for traffic on the viaduct leading to Finntown to clear.

Elin batted her eyes. The sun, not tears, was interfering with her ability to see.

"You're forgiven. Not everything in life is perfect, Miss Heikkonen. Perhaps I thought I had the perfect life once, back when Anders and I lived together in Houghton, far away from my father, far away from the constrictions of my place in this town. But it didn't last. Couldn't last. We came from different worlds, Anders and I. Love isn't enough to overcome the obstacles we faced."

The women crossed Superior Street and began to walk uphill. Duluth Central High School loomed above them, casting its shadow over them from several blocks away.

"But surely you must feel something for Horace."

Elin Gustafsson smiled as she thought of her fiancé's fumbling attempts to bed her in his automobile and on the couch of his apartment at the Munger Terrace, a picturesque complex constructed of yellow sandstone brick, overlooking Cascade Park and downtown Duluth. She had resisted Horace's every effort in that regard, though she had ensured that he was, in a most primitive sense, satisfied.

No, there is no love. There is no deep emotional bond between us, she thought, unwilling to divulge her neutrality on the subject to Wendy Heikkonen. *There is only necessity. And convenience. I will trade time with Horace for the freedom his wealth will allow. I will promise to honor and obey him. And I will do what a wife must do. But there will be no love in our union. There will be no love,* she repeated to herself as the women stopped in front of the Gustafsson Mansion.

Chapter 27

Andrew Maki was concealing a letter from Heidi Genelli in the front pocket of his blue wool work shirt. Maki and the other members of his crew worked non-stop as the Wanigan inched its way down the swollen Cloquet River. Logs meandered off course and hung up in the infrequent trees, creating hardship. The crew, with the exception of the cook, sweated and toiled under the growing power of the sun. As the days grew longer, the atmosphere became humid and insects became plenteous. The men clambered over floating logs on cork-soled shoes and used long pikes and short gaffs to draw wayward cedar and tamarack timbers into the current, where the logs rejoined the flotilla bound for Island Lake. The pig men faced the constant danger of slipping from the flotsam and drowning, a danger that lessened in the calm waters of the meandering savanna-like portions of the river between Indian Lake and Alden Lake.

The river slowed. Although the work of the crew became less hectic, the lessened current attracted mosquitoes from fetid marshes bordering the river. Hordes of newly hatched flying vermin sought the exposed skin of the loggers. The men meticulously covered their flesh with wool clothing and draped netting from their Stetson and Knox hats to protect their faces and necks but the insects would not to be denied. Despite their best efforts to mitigate the swarming pests, the pig men were forced to slap and swat their way through the exhausting days on the water.

The mosquitoes were only the beginning. The loggers knew that once summer had fully arrived, as the month of June progressed, blackflies, deerflies, and horseflies would hatch. While the smaller blackflies sought out exposed flesh, most notably at the men's ankles, and attacked with stealthy vengeance, the larger deer- and horseflies preferred to land in the men's hair, where they extracted huge chunks of skin from the loggers' scalps. The welts left behind itched and pestered the men for days. Insect repellents were non-existent. The only defenses to these assaults were wool clothing, ineffective mosquito netting, and stoic indifference.

Night brought an early bombardment of mosquitoes that dissipated with evening's chill. Supper, the fourth (and last) meal of the day, was prepared. The men drank hot coffee – the traditional drink of the Finns – ate their meal aboard the Wanigan, and attended to their personal needs. No consumption of alcohol was allowed. Hangovers in the morning from drunken binges the preceding night made for slow reactions, and slow reactions tempted catastrophe.

The water remained cold, barely rising above sixty degrees by the first week in June. The men did not bathe in the river. They washed their hands and faces with harsh, homemade soap before each meal. The Finns working at Wolf Lake were used to taking a sauna every Sunday, both as a hygienic and as a spiritual respite before beginning a new workweek. Such cleanliness was unheard of during a log drive when perspiration inundated the loggers' clothing. Woolen long underwear remained the uniform of choice. Union suits added a layer of protection against insect bites, but the men's undergarments quickly became impregnated with body odor, making the cabin of the Wanigan nearly uninhabitable at mealtime. After supper, generally a ham or bacon soup or stew accompanied by Finnish rye bread, smoked meat being the norm as no refrigeration was available, the men settled in around the dining table for games of poker or cribbage, or took to their bunks. When the weather permitted, the more adventurous loggers unrolled their woolen Hudson Bay blankets on the modest foredeck, located outside the cabin, and slept beneath the stars. Occasionally Tim Laitila would play a Finnish lullaby or a familiar American Negro spiritual on his mouth organ, though the blacksmith, like the others, was usually so exhausted by the end of the day that he only had enough energy left for a single tune.

The Wanigan was tucked against the riverbank above Island Lake. The houseboat had negotiated the rapids below Big

Alden Lake. The prams worked upstream. Few logs had been lost. Historically, the loss from log drives was in the neighborhood of ten percent, and this drive was no exception. The water level of the Cloquet River had steadily declined. There were more and more exposed boulders and rocks to contend with as the pig men worked their way downstream. Within the week, the Wanigan would be through the worst of the rapids. Once on Island Lake, the crew would be called upon to gather the logs and move them across open water to the western shore of the reservoir.

Andrew Maki sat on a log in the quiet of the floodplain forest, his rump extended over a fallen maple, his pants bunched around his ankles, the letter in his hand. Mosquitoes swarmed his exposed skin, landed, and drew blood from his buttocks as he re-read the last message he'd received from Heidi Genelli before breaking camp.

Dear Andrew:

I miss our talks. Joey has been asking about you. He is excited about visiting your farm. I told him what a wondrous and secluded place it is that you are building on the shores of Papoose Lake. I am very glad that you took me out there before the thaw. I shall always cherish the memory of the sleigh gliding over the icy ground, the horses' hooves thumping the frozen earth, the snow gently waltzing down. It was one of those rare moments we humans only experience in brief intervals as we toil through life, as we are challenged, as the Gospel says, by the Great Ordeal.

You asked if I am getting over the loss of Joseph. I'd like to tell you that the pain is less, but that would be untruthful. The loss of my husband still hurts. I don't know if it will ever hurt less. But as to your other question, whether you and I should continue seeing each other, the answer to that, despite the lingering feelings I have for Joseph, is an unqualified "yes".

When we are together, you make me smile. When we are together, you make me forget, for a brief instant, my loss. And Joey is fast becoming attached to you. He looks up to you as he looked up to his father. I think it's your having been a boxer, combined with his abilities in that direction that seals the connection. Not that I approve, mind you. But I needn't tell you how I feel on that score.

202

You, of all people, understand that the life of a boxer is not a life of fulfillment.

So, in answer to your two questions, "no, I am not over Joseph" and "yes, I dearly want to spend time together".

I hope this letter finds you safe. Take care during your trip downriver. I wish you weren't going, but I understand that it is your job. Write me as soon as you can.

Affectionately,
Heidi Genelli.
April 10th, 1917

Maki wiped himself with a piece of newspaper carried in his trouser pocket for that purpose. He dropped the soiled paper to the ground. The newsprint alighted on his scat. Maki's eyes adjusted to failing light. Off in the distance, a coyote howled. The Finn drew his woolen trousers to his waist and slipped canvas suspenders over his broad shoulders. Lighting a farmer's match on one of the snaps of his shirt, Maki placed flame against the cigarette hanging from his mouth and inhaled. He had rolled several cigarettes during the day and tucked them into his shirt pocket to savor after supper. The camp boss folded the letter, pausing to hold the parchment to his nose before replacing it in his shirt pocket.

When the message had first arrived it had reeked of the scent of Heidi Genelli's perfume. Now, having endured a month of confinement in the pocket of Maki's work shirt, the letter smelled only of Andrew Maki. Despite the loss of feminine odor, Maki recalled the fragrance of Heidi's perfume. That fragrance contained memories, snippets of interlude that had taken place between the widow and the logger late at night in her parlor, while her son and father slumbered heavily in adjacent bedrooms.

She was plain-faced and average looking, not at all like Elin Gustafsson in terms of physical appeal. Nevertheless, while Heidi Genelli was not beautiful, the overall impression of Heidi's face, figure, and demeanor was attractive. She was sensual in an understated manner. Andrew Maki considered the woman and her offer to continue seeing him as he walked deliberately through the tangled undergrowth lining the receding waters of the Cloquet River.

Paul Pederson, the only Norwegian in the crew and a pug-faced brute who possessed a kindly disposition and steady nerves, stood on the deck of the boat, his body framed by light leaking from the cabin of the Wanigan. Pederson's face had been disfigured in a saloon fight in downtown Eveleth. A logger from another camp had sliced Pederson's face with a homemade hunting knife, separating the left side of Pederson's bulbous proboscis from the rest of his face.

Pederson leaned against the tar-papered exterior wall of the Wanigan's cabin and drew smoke from a cigarette as he followed Maki's progress through the woods.

"Hey, Boss," Pederson called out in a booming voice.

The Norwegian flicked ash from the end of his cigarette into the water surrounding the boat. The river, having returned to its original asphalt hue, slid past the battered hull of the vessel with patterned determination.

"Quite a night, eh, Paul?" Maki replied as he climbed aboard the Wanigan.

The sounds of a lively card game were audible from inside the Wanigan's cabin. Mosquitoes were notably absent. There was a deep chill in the air, despite the fact it was June. It was not unusual for the lower reaches of the Cloquet River to experience early summer frosts, a reality that made farming the area an iffy proposition.

"It's cooling down," Pederson added.

Andrew Maki stood next to the Norwegian. The end of Maki's cigarette flared in the plummeting darkness, the glow of the ember mimicked by thousands of lightning bugs dancing above the water.

A period of silence ensued. Maki studied the rapid progression of night. Ebony enveloped the land. Pederson drew two hand-rolled cigarettes from his pocket and offered one to his boss. Maki tossed his cigarette into the water, accepted the gift, placed the offering between his lips, and struck a match.

"So, what's your take on the war?" Maki asked his companion.

Pederson shifted his weight and stretched his legs. He was a considerable man, at least a full head taller than Andrew Maki. Pederson's hands were overly large. Pederson's skin was covered in painless nodules for which the Iron Range doctor he'd seen had offered no explanation.

"Seems like we've been drawn into someone else's affair," Pederson observed quietly. "Seems like if the Fords and Rockefellers smell money, they'll send the sons of common and ignorant men to fight the sons of other common and ignorant men."

Maki filled his lungs with smoke, held his breath a moment, and then exhaled. Bats flitted above the slowly moving river in search of insects, the slight bodies of the flying rodents presenting blurry silhouettes as they flew by.

"I'm not too keen on this war myself," Andrew Maki said. "Seems to me you're right. Seems to me it's a rare thing for a wealthy man's son to answer the call to fight. Oh, there may be a few rich boys, like the boys from Cornell with Captain Tinkham who volunteered to go to France. But by and large, I think you're right. I think it'll be the likes of me and you who fight this war."

Stars appeared above the men with startling rapidity, as if someone had opened a package of glitter and dumped it over the Earth.

"Shooting star," Paul Pederson noted, pointing to a white blaze shooting across the black curtain.

The cabin door squeaked. Yellow lantern light bathed the deck of the vessel. Iner Halvorson stepped outside.

"Who's winning?" Pederson asked, his cigarette bouncing in his tightly clenched lips as he spoke.

"Not me," the cook replied, standing at the edge of the boat, unbuttoning his dungarees to urinate. The sound of piss hitting water echoed in the night.

"Make sure those card cheats don't get too far into your paycheck," Andrew Maki cautioned with a hint of humor.

205

Halvorson nodded his head, buttoned his pants, and retreated. The cabin door slammed behind the cook.

"I'm worried about the war," Maki confided as he stood in the cold on the wooden deck of the boat. The camp boss tossed the residue of his cigarette into the air.

Psst.

The dying ember landed in the river.

"You took second papers, didn't you?" Maki asked Pederson.

"Yep."

"I'll get mine when we get back. McAdams's wedding is the first week in August. I'm planning to spend the week before the wedding in Duluth tying up some loose ends with the company. I'll apply for citizenship then."

Paul Pederson nodded but didn't reply.

"You think I should do that, what with the war and everything? Take my papers, I mean," Maki asked.

The Norwegian nodded again. "I wouldn't let the war come between you and getting your citizenship. Who knows what can happen? Already the government is passing crazy laws against opening your mouth and complaining about the war. I'd rather be a citizen in these times, with limited rights, than an immigrant with no rights," Pederson advised.

Maki poised a hand over his face as a mosquito landed on his cheek. The Finn slapped at the insect but missed. The bug returned. Maki ignored the insect's renewed assault and tilted his Stetson back on his head.

"Maybe you're right. No sense taking a chance. I'll apply for my papers as soon as we get off this flat-bottomed scow."

Chapter 28

As he worked a stubborn tangle of cedar and tamarack poles hung up behind a thicket of sugar maples lining the north bank of the Cloquet River, Tim Laitila thought about his wife, Mara. She was a slender blonde beauty he had married six years earlier when she was working as a housekeeper in Pihlaja's Boarding House in Virginia, Minnesota.

Using an eight-foot gaff, the pig man labored under an unrelenting sun. Horseflies bombarded his head, seeking his neck and face. Sweat leaked from his armpits and from beneath his fedora and slid down his skin. He prodded the stubborn logjam with the iron tip of the gaff. In frustration, he kicked at the immobile lumber with his cork-soled shoes. His unorthodox maneuver ended the impasse. The logs floated free and joined the rest of the flotilla in the steady current.

Mara's delicate face, her square, dimpled jaw, her nearly white hair and tentative blue-green eyes remained on Laitila's mind as he danced across passing timbers before arriving on solid ground. Tim Laitila lifted his hat, a battered Knox Casual, from his head, and wiped perspiration with a soiled handkerchief. The horseflies noted an opportunity and assaulted the logger's scalp. Laitila swatted them off with his hat and began to walk downriver, intent upon finding lunch, all the while considering the vision of his wife.

She was back in Virginia, caring for the twin girls that she had birthed the year before. It had been a hard pregnancy, her third since their marriage and the first one that had gone to term. Two stillborn boys had been delivered prior to the birth of the twins. Both labors with the boys had been premature. She had been barely into the fifth month with each, and the infants had not taken so much as a breath after their respective deliveries. She had been relegated to bed rest for much of her pregnancy with Susan and Margaret. Having the luxury of being employed by her father in the family business, her job was not in jeopardy because of her condition, and was waiting for her after the twins were born. The bed rest had arrested early bleeding and, ultimately, the girls, now eleven months old, had grown into chubby little cherubs of health. Mara had not yet returned to work, her strength having been tested by the birth process, but she was steadily improving her physical capacity by daily walks of considerable distance. She would return to working for her father in the family boarding house shortly, likely after the log drive was over and Tim was back at home. The girls would accompany her to work where their grandmother, Elsa Pihlaja, would tend to them while Mara made beds, cleaned rooms, and scoured the community washrooms on each of the three floors of the boarding house.

Laitila considered this portrait of his twenty-five-year-old wife, captured by his memory, as he followed a meandering deer trail along the riverbank. The noise of Iner Halvorson digging busily through the food wanigan, a wooden crate with shoulder straps used by the cook to carry lunch to the crew as they worked, greeted Tim Laitila's ears as the logger negotiated the uneven terrain. The sun blazed down. The scrub ash and sugar maples lining the banks of the river provided little shade as Laitila broke free of the underbrush and shouted out a greeting to the cook: "Iner," the blacksmith said, "what's for lunch?"

The cook nodded towards the wooden wanigan resting on dry dirt. Bacon sandwiches, freshly baked raisin bars, Finnish hard tack with honey, and hot coffee, redundant given the day's blistering heat, sat in the open box, awaiting the remainder of the crew. Olli Kinkkonen, Paul Pederson, and Andrew Maki sat on deadfall, sandwiches in one hand, tin coffee cups in the other, chewing contentedly on bacon and pickle sandwiches as they scrutinized Laitila's approach.

"How's the food?" Laitila asked Maki, stopping to wipe the sweat from his chin with his sleeve before bending over to pick up a sandwich and a coffee cup.

"Iner's the best," Kinkkonen interjected, speaking Finnish. "He can make pig flank taste like top sirloin."

Pederson's head turned towards the conversation. Though he was Norwegian, he'd worked long enough with Finns to be able to comprehend most of the Finnish words used in casual conversation. Still, there was effort involved in trying to decipher the foreign language.

"I'd say Iner is the best damn cook I've ever run across," Pederson acknowledged in broken Finnish.

"Where are the others?" Laitila asked, noting that five of the crew remained unaccounted for.

"They're working a big jam downstream. One hell of a mess," Andrew Maki observed. "They should be here shortly. Damn beavers dropped an aspen tree nearly all the way across the river."

"Beaver," Tim Laitila said derisively. "What the hell good are they?"

Laitila filled a tin plate with food, sat heavily on the ground, and leaned his tired back against an old white pine stump. The blacksmith removed his abused and ever-present Finnish Bible from his shirt pocket and read a passage from First Corinthians as unofficial grace before his meal. The other men didn't acknowledge the prayer, continuing to eat in relative silence, the noise of crunching pickles and slurping coffee the only interruptions of the forest's near absolute solitude. Other crewmembers arrived. Their advent did not increase the volume of the discourse. The men were tired. The drive was taxing. Tomorrow they would be facing a three-mile journey across the open water of Island Lake. But before they confronted the stiff westerly wind and resultant whitecaps on the lake, there was the series of three rapids leading into the lake to consider.

The Cloquet River descends most rapidly, falling more than thirteen feet per mile, in the stretch of water between Katherine Lake, its source, and Indian Lake, a small flowage lake near where the McAdams crew had begun its journey. As the river flows southwest, towards Island Lake, the terrain is less severe and the pitch decreases to slightly more than three feet per mile. Though the river boasts numerous shoals and rapids capable of testing watercraft in low water, in high water, only the series of three rapids immediately above the river's entrance into Island Lake presents appreciable danger. In particular, the last step into the lake can be, if the water is low, catastrophic and unmanageable, even in a modern-day kayak. In low water, a fifteen-foot dead drop over jagged basalt constitutes the last barrier into the lake .

"What's the water level look like?" Laitila asked Micah Wargin, one of the men who had been working on the logjam downstream.

"Getting pretty low. Lots of rocks and boulders exposed in the first set of rapids."

"How far ahead?" Laitila queried.

"Few hundred yards. There's a pretty good trail along the north bank that ends up making a portage around the rapids," Wargin continued.

"Why don't you and Kinkkonen scout it out?" Andrew Maki said to Tim Laitila between sips of hot coffee.

"Let's take a look," Olli Kinkkonen said, pulling his battered eight square cap, the brim small and edged in frayed fabric, onto his head as he stood up and tossed cold coffee into the brush.

Laitila wolfed down a last bite of sandwich, regained his feet, and brought Iner his dirty cup. The cook looked at the logger with narrow eyes, as if to chastise Laitila for not rinsing the coffee cup out in the stream, but said nothing.

Kinkkonen and Laitila walked a winding path cut alongside the log-clogged river. From bank to bank, bobbing logs of cedar and tamarack moved slowly downstream in the grip of the river, as if drawn by some unseen magnet. A bull moose snorted from behind a distant line of stunted tamarack, likely wading the mire of a backwater pond in search of water lilies. Laitila and Kinkkonen never slowed their pace and they never saw the animal.

"There she be," Kinkkonen announced, pointing to a series of significant rapids. Kinkkonen was familiar with the landscape from other log drives on the Cloquet, and had successfully run the rapids into Island Lake on two prior occasions.

The men studied the pattern of water racing over stone. The drop was not significant, maybe ten feet over one hundred yards, but due to the diminished water level, there were countless exposed and nearly exposed rocks and boulders littering the channel.

"Can it be run?" Laitila asked his companion.

Kinkkonen wrinkled his dark facial skin, pulled off his cap, reminiscent in style of those worn for driving open motor cars, and studied the river while he squinted against the sun. There was episodic silence as the Finn considered the various avenues open to the Wanigan.

"There. On the left of the main channel. If we avoid making too great a turn around that boulder there, we can pass through and stay dry."

"You sure?" Laitila asked, skepticism edging his query.

The boulder Kinkkonen referenced was positioned so as to require a sharp right-hand maneuver, followed by a precise left, to avoid being caught sideways in the current and broken apart on the rocks. To Tim Laitila, the path appeared iffy at best.

"I've done it before," Olli Kinkkonen said matter-of-factly. "Let's take a look at the other two."

The second series of riffles was less onerous. There was a clear path, even to the uninitiated eye of Tim Laitila, through the exposed stone ledges and rocks, with little threat of floundering the eight-foot-wide vessel. Enough water still poured down the funnel formed by the narrowing of the riverbanks to assure safe passage over the concealed danger.

The loggers spent considerable time viewing the river's final plunge into Island Lake. The water level of the Cloquet had not dropped sufficiently to expose the entirety of the fifteen-foot cascade. However, after an extended stretch of calm, an easy drift for the houseboat following the second rapids, the roar of the ultimate approach into the lake was audible as the two men emerged from a dense alder thicket and onto an out-cropping of smooth volcanic rock, which overlooked the merger of lake and river.

"Shit," Tim Laitila muttered, staring at the narrow tongue of black water gushing into the placid lake.

Olli Kinkkonen cocked his head and walked to the water's edge. His eyes strained to measure the distance between two large stone incisors jutting from beneath the frothing, swirling water, which, if they caught the exposed hull of the Wanigan, would surely rip the boat in two.

"It can't be done," Laitila said quietly, almost to himself. "There's not enough water."

Olli Kinkkonen shook his head in the negative.

"There's enough water, all right," the Finn whispered quietly. "The question is: 'Is there enough space?'"

Chapter 29

The inside of the First Presbyterian Church in Duluth was cool against the blistering heat of early summer. Wendy Heikkonen and her mother, Anna, sat in the dim light of the sanctuary, refreshed by the damp chill retained in the red sandstone church that stood imperiously above downtown Duluth. There had been much consternation and argument between the pair as they discussed Wendy's upcoming betrothal to George McAdams, not the least of which concerned Wendy's conversion to the Scottish faith.

Reverend Allan Jeffries, the assistant pastor of the large Presbyterian congregation, waited patiently for the bride-to-be and her mother in his office. He was, by nature and training, an extremely contemplative man, a man who could, if necessary, assess his own internal demons during hours of silent meditation. Jeffries sat behind his modest pine desk in an unimposing fir swivel chair, his hands on his lap, his eyes closed, pondering.

"Mother, I don't understand you. You say you like George. You tell me you are happy for me. Yet you insist upon pulling these little tantrums whenever we must close ranks and decide crucial elements of the service, the reception, or anything else of significance related to the wedding," Wendy bemoaned in a careful whisper.

The altar was stark and bare of adornment, in keeping with the Presbyterian faith. A simple wooden cross adorned the wall behind the altar. Anna Heikkonen focused her fawn-colored eyes on the cross and maintained silence.

"Mother?"

A large sigh escaped the older woman's lips. In reality, Anna was only forty-seven. The weight of motherhood, of mentoring Wendy, the oldest child of the three she had carried to term as the wife of Henri Heikkonen, played a part in adding unnatural age to Anna's face as she sat in the uneven light that illuminated the emptiness of the sacristy. The mother turned her eyes, but not her head, towards her daughter.

"I respect your choice of husband, even though he is old enough to be your father," Anna began in Finnish, "even though he is old enough to be courting me, should I need such attention. What I have difficulty accepting is that you are so ready to toss aside generations of our faith, to be wed in a church that has absolutely no connection to your beginnings, your history. That is something that, quite frankly, I find more than a mere annoyance. I find it startling, to say the least."

Wendy Heikkonen took her mother's narrow wrist in her hand and placed it against her breast. The young woman's heart thudded noticeably against the structure of her chest.

"We've been over this. George's family has been Presbyterian, been elders in the church, for generations. There is history there as well, history that George has asked me to respect and accept. I love him so much, Mother, that I am willing to follow his lead. After all, isn't that what it tells us in the Gospel, 'and a woman shall leave her mother'?"

Anna focused hard eyes on the face of her oldest child.

"I know of no Biblical verse that demands that you also leave your faith."

Wendy's face reddened. The possibility of recrimination dissipated as quickly as it had materialized. The young woman held her tongue and allowed her mother's words to vaporize without consequence.

The moment passed. Something lightened in Anna Heikkonen's heart. Whether it was due to a faint recollection of her own disobedience to her parents when she had fled Finland in pursuit of Henri Heikkonen, the only beau she had ever known, traveling alone across the Atlantic in desperate dedication to the love she felt for him, or due to a sudden twisting and unbinding of her Lutheran conventions, she could not discern. Whatever the cause, there was, within Anna's soul, the sudden release of burden and the ability to, if not accept, then at least become conciliatory over her daughter's resolve.

"This is what you want to do?" Anna finally asked, her eyes riveted on the stone floor as she spoke.

Wendy shook her head and whispered, "It is."

"Then I will not stand in your way."

Wendy threw her arms around her mother's neck and kissed her significantly on the cheek. The older woman remained stoic. She did not acknowledge the embrace. Wendy withdrew, patted the pleats of her summer dress, and smiled.

"Are you ready to meet Pastor Jeffries?"

Her mother managed a false smile. "I believe I am."

"Good. George should be joining us shortly. He can catch up with us in the pastor's study," Wendy advised as she stood up and began to leave the pew.

Anna Heikkonen hesitated.

"Mother?"

The older woman emitted a weak smile as she rose to follow her daughter.

"Coming, Wendla. I'm coming."

Several blocks west of the church on Second Street, in front of the St. Louis Courthouse, a crowd had formed along the sidewalk and across the front lawn of the building. A significant gathering of men, women, and young children, predominantly Finns, with a smattering of other nationalities, stood at the bottom of the courthouse steps, milling about in excited anticipation. Banners fluttered in the dry summer breeze, proclaiming opposition to the Army Act and the required registration of citizens for compulsory military service. The war in Europe was stalemated. Despite daily headlines in the *Duluth News Tribune* and its evening progeny, *The Duluth Herald*, proclaiming repeated Allied success along the Western, Balkan, Eastern, and Middle Eastern Fronts, Americans were not deceived. Most citizens realized that the War would not end before American blood had been spilled.

Already, American volunteers, like the college boys from Cornell or the young Americans who had enlisted through the Canadian Expeditionary Force, the Italian and French Ambulance Services or other foreign units, were in the thick of it, fighting and dying on European battlefields. The

Great War, as Oscar Larson and Victor Gran so aptly observed, could not be won without a massive influx of new soldiers. The demoralizing trench warfare in vogue along the Western Front demanded a surge of fresh troops, of fresh fodder for the opposing guns, before significant strides could be made, before the Boche could be pushed out of France. That weight, the head of such a hammer, could only be supplied by the United States.

"We demand that Congress repeal the Army Act," a speaker shouted through a megaphone. He was identified as an official in the IWW by a large campaign-style button on the lapel of his cheap business suit, likely a mail order garment purchased from Sears and Roebuck or Montgomery Wards. "American youth should not be sacrificed on the altar of English greed."

"Here, here," the crowd shouted in Finnish with enthusiasm, despite the sweltering heat of the day.

"The American worker, farmer, and citizen has no fight with Germany, no cause to support this global conflict commenced by false kings on false pretenses," the speaker continued in English.

"You tell 'em, brother," a voice called out, in English heavily accented by its Finnish heritage.

A uniform hum of concern began within the ranks of the crowd as four police officers arrived with a contingent of young men intent upon entering the courthouse to register for the draft.

"Don't go in, comrades," the speaker shouted.

"Don't buckle under to tyranny. This war is not your fight. Your country is not at risk. Don't sign away your life to fight for British colonial interests," the protesters added in unison, reading from prepared cards that the IWW had distributed before the rally.

"Clear the sidewalk," Tim McIntyre, the policeman leading the draft registrants towards the courthouse, shouted at the crowd. "You're engaging in civil disobedience in violation of Federal Law," he added, referring to the restrictive language of the recently passed Espionage Act.

"Stand fast, brothers and sisters," the speaker with the megaphone urged. "There's nothing they can do to us."

McIntyre gave a slight nod of his head. Fulton Andrews, the police officer bringing up the rear of the group, waved a hand in the air. A mechanical siren wailed from somewhere down the hill.

"You need to disperse and disperse now," McIntyre advised the crowd as he halted a few feet away from the demonstrators, "or there will be consequences you hadn't bargained for."

Again the man with the megaphone urged the crowd to stand its ground. A cordon of Duluth Police and St. Louis County Sheriff's Deputies and auxiliary officers appeared from below the crest of the hill, steadily marching in rank up the avenue towards the courthouse. The officers carried wooden batons, three-foot-long pieces of oak painted black, the weapons thickened at the business end, the leather lanyards of the clubs wrapped tightly in their hands, as they advanced.

Behind this moving wall of officers, two gasoline pumper trucks alternately idled and crawled towards the demonstration. Firefighters outfitted in full gear rode the running boards of the trucks, ready to alight and charge the fire hoses of the units.

"Stand fast, people; stand fast. You are the voice of working men and women in this country, the voice of reason," the megaphone challenged. "They dare not attack their neighbors, their fellow citizens, for exercising the rights guaranteed us by the United States Constitution. The Freedom of Speech. The Freedom of Assembly. Stand fast..."

If the man with the megaphone had more to say, he was unable to continue. His message was cut short by the unanticipated arrival of two police officers that had circled in behind the St. Louis County Courthouse before tackling the leader of the demonstration to the lawn without warning.

The crowd pressed towards the tumbling, struggling officers and the labor leader. The police marching along the avenue broke into double time, surged through the crowd, and formed a human barrier between the demonstrators and the struggling men. A nightstick rose against the hot sun. A blow struck the thick base of the speaker's skull. The IWW leader fell back to the ground and lay still. The crowd surged; here and there, a rugged dockworker or unemployed logger threw a punch along the line of policemen, only to be bludgeoned into submission by a phalanx of cudgels. The women in the assembly retreated, drawing their children into the center of the mob for protection.

On the street, the firemen unrolled canvas hoses and charged nozzles.

"Let 'er rip," Captain Roberts, the police officer in charge of dispersing the demonstration, called out from behind the line of policemen.

Water burst from the hoses and pummeled the protesters. Cries of anguish erupted from the stricken men, women, and children as the cannonade seared exposed skin, driving many demonstrators to the ground.

"Take 'em now, boys," Roberts commanded, raising his right arm against the summer sky as a signal for the armed men to advance. The captain stood indignantly aloof from the melee, his right hand resting on a holster holding a .38 revolver.

The police moved with decisiveness, securing as trophies those protesters brought to the ground by the fire hoses. The unrelenting demeanor of the uniformed officers drove the demonstrators who were still on their feet away from the courthouse. Shouts and screams of "oppressor" and "tyrant" were raised as individual demonstrators attempted to resist arrest. Those who had fallen were largely in handcuffs or under the watchful eye of the officers within minutes after Captain Roberts had given the order to advance.

Officer Andrews led the draft registrants up a stone staircase and into the courthouse, while his partner, Tim McIntyre, assisted other officers in rounding up protesters and herding them into the back of an open freight wagon, which served as a paddy wagon. Two Belgian geldings stood impatiently under the hot sun, sweat rolling off their golden flanks as prisoners were led to the wagon and hoisted onto the platform by burly officers. McIntyre led a middle-aged Finn, the man's legs bowed from hard labor as a logger, towards the wagon. No handcuffs secured the compliant prisoner. The man shuffled his small feet obediently, without hesitation, as the big Irish cop ushered him along.

"Hold on there, officer," McIntyre heard a voice call out as the cop and the prisoner came to a stop.

McIntyre doffed his policeman's cap and released his grip on the Finn as he turned to face the person addressing him. Perspiration had soiled the underarms of McIntyre's uniform shirt. Beads of moisture rolled off the cop's thick reddish-blond hair and fell to the hot cement sidewalk as the Irishman considered the man approaching him.

"Mr. McAdams?" McIntyre asked.

The Canadian smiled broadly. The two men shook hands beneath the sweltering sun.

"What can I do for you?" the cop inquired.

"Seems you've latched onto my future father-in-law," McAdams revealed, pointing a finger towards the subdued personage of Henri Heikkonen, who was waiting to board the paddy wagon.

McIntyre turned to face the Finn.

"That true? Your daughter is Wendy?"

Duluth, despite its rapid growth and burgeoning size, remained, for all practical purposes, a small town. The gossip pages of the *Tribune* and *Herald* were all abuzz with the news of bachelor-entrepreneur George McAdams's impending wedding to Wendy Heikkonen, a woman completely unknown to the readers of the society pages.

Henri Heikkonen sheepishly nodded in the affirmative.

"Cat got your tongue man? Are you or are you not the father of the woman Mr. McAdams is going to marry?" the cop insisted, hints of anger coloring his inquiry.

"I am."

The Irishman wiped his forehead with a white handkerchief and replaced his uniform cap on his head.

"I'd like you to do me a favor, Officer McIntyre," George McAdams said, his eyes level with those of the cop.

The men were of equal height and towered over Henri Heikkonen.

"How's that?"

"Release Henri to my custody. I'll post whatever bail you require," the Canadian replied.

"Bail can only be set by a judge or a justice of the peace," the cop answered.

McAdams pulled out his billfold, which was made of brown calfskin, the initials "GAM" – George Astrid McAdams – stenciled into the evenly worn leather, and removed two twenty-dollar bills.

"For a misdemeanor disturbing the peace, forty dollars seems sufficient," McAdams said, folding the currency and placing it gently in the front pocket of McIntyre's uniform shirt.

"You'll make sure he's kept under your watch until I have a chance to talk to Captain Roberts about the matter?" the officer asked, nervousness clear in his diction.

"I will keep him under my watch until I hear from you," McAdams agreed. "Call me at home later this evening. Here's my card; the second number is my home telephone," the Canadian advised, slipping a business card into the same pocket as the cash.

"Shouldn't be a problem, so long as you keep him off the streets."

"Henri, you hear that? Officer McIntyre is releasing you to my custody. But you must refrain from being out in public until he's cleared this with his superiors, understand?"

The Finn shifted his weight in apparent conflict. Nothing was said for a moment. Henri Heikkonen nodded his head ever so slightly and replied, "I understand."

"Good. Come along, Henri; I'm supposed to meet your daughter and your wife at First Presbyterian to discuss the details of our wedding with Pastor Jeffries. You might as well tag along, give me some moral support in the face of that gang of Heikkonen femininity," McAdams quipped as he turned to walk east towards the church.

"Get along now, Mr. Heikkonen," Tim McIntyre urged. "And don't be letting me see you at any more of these

IWW demonstrations. The next time, I won't be so forgiving."

Henri Heikkonen followed the big Canadian down the street in silence. The Finn moved heavily, without mirth. Tim McIntyre watched the two men depart and patted his shirt pocket, as if to ensure the money had not been withdrawn, before wading back into the milling crowd to assist his fellow officers.

Chapter 30

Andrew Maki stood at the bow of the Wanigan as Olli Kinkkonen eased the vessel around a tight corner in the Cloquet River. White water loomed ahead. They had negotiated the first of the rapids leading into Island Lake without serious incident. A few of the crew's personal items had broken free inside the cabin and had been tossed about as the craft made its run through the trough of boulders and ledges lining the first chute, but nothing significant had been lost. No one had been injured. It was June 10th, 1917, and the Wanigan, newly christened *Miss Wolf Lake* by Tim Laitila, who had painted the name on the outside walls of the cabin with spare whitewash he'd found stored under the kitchen cupboard on the boat, was edging towards the second plunge. Behind the vessel, a sea of timber floated in constrained obedience, coaxed by the pig men into tight conformation in readiness for the drive into the lake.

The water in the river had dropped precipitously. More hazards became exposed with each passing day. Maki studied the jagged gray shoulders of the emerging glacial till, accented by smooth shelves of volcanic foundation, glimmers of quartz in the rock glinting in the sunlight, as his eyes looked west, hopeful of rain. An inch or two would give them sufficient cushion when descending the last cascade. Clouds were assembling on the horizon, off at a distance towards the Duluth, Winnipeg, and Pacific railroad station at Taft. Whether the clouds contained rain or not, and whether the rain would find the Cloquet River Valley, was an open issue.

With the depth of the water declining and the summer sun shining, the cramps and aches afflicting the men, caused by wading in frigid snow melt, sometimes to their armpits to retrieve logs, had passed. The men had no further need to slather their legs and thighs with lard or Vaseline to insulate

222

their skin from the cold. Now the water was bearable, almost pleasant, as they worked, as they came to the end of the drive.

To the north, the clanging and banging of a logging locomotive, likely traversing a Duluth and Northeastern spur, the narrow gauge ties set directly on the undulating ground without benefit of ballast for support, could be discerned, as the Wanigan slipped through the last calm pool on its way towards the second rapids.

"Let's tie it up just above the whitewater for breakfast," Maki advised, calling out to Kinkkonen in Finnish as the stern man swept the great oar in a gentle arc to avoid a wayward cedar log floating in the channel.

Kinkkonen nodded and pulled hard on the sweep, turning the nose of the Wanigan towards a clearing in the underbrush that would serve as a landing.

Maki contemplated the oarsman as Kinkkonen stood hatless under the open sky. The natural canopy of the once-magnificent white pine forest, which had lined this portion of the river, was absent, rendering the horizon open and reducing the claustrophobic feeling natural to tightly drawn woodlands. Fragile fingers of storm clouds, probes of approaching bad weather, extended tenuously from the west into the sky immediately above the river. The tendrils of the storm had not yet reached the apex of the sun as Maki watched Olli Kinkkonen work.

Although there was an ethnic tie between the men, there was no corresponding equity in their thinking. Kinkkonen was an avowed member of the IWW, a Syndicalist of the first order, prone to quietly mumbled diatribes of dissatisfaction against his employer, against capitalism in general. Maki steered clear of engaging Kinkkonen in lengthy political discussions. While Andrew Maki maintained loyalties to the labor union movement due to his prior connections with the mines, George McAdams's benevolent treatment and ready acceptance of his abilities had caused Maki to develop a casual appreciation for the management side of things. McAdams had placed Maki in a position of authority over the other loggers at Wolf Lake Camp, despite Maki's dearth of supervisory experience.

Though Maki had worked for a brief time as a straw boss for Quincy Mining, Tim Laitila would have been a more logical choice as camp boss, given that Laitila had more expertise coordinating men. But McAdams had been firm with Maki when they had discussed the position. More than any facet of Maki's personality, McAdams valued the Finn's unabashed loyalty, an attribute deeply rooted in the man and one not simply learned by rote. Maintaining loyalty to McAdams assured Maki of a number of favors from the wealthy Canadian, not the least of which was the loan allowing the Finn to purchase his farm at Papoose Lake. In addition, two teams of Percherons were to be loaned out from Wolf Lake to Maki so that he and his closest neighbor, Erik Tuckanen, could pull stumps in preparation for planting hay, rye, and oats on their respective farms. Rental of a team of well-trained draft horses could run five dollars a week if one leased horses on the open market. McAdams wasn't charging Maki or Tuckanen a dime. It was this sort of considerate kindness that had compelled Andrew Maki to move away from the radical views of fellow Finns like Olli Kinkkonen, when it came to issues of master and servant.

The Wanigan turned towards shore. Maki leaped from the deck and secured the boat to an adjacent white pine stump with a stout rope. Iner Halvorson busied himself over the small wood stove in the brightly white-washed interior of the boat's kitchen, pancakes sizzling, odors of bacon grease, freshly baked bread, and hot coffee wafting out the open door of the boat cabin.

The peaks of Tim Laitila and Paul Pederson's hats became visible above the spindly aspen trees lining the south bank of the river, as the men approached the landing for second breakfast. The loggers had grabbed hard tack, slices of cold moose steak, and apples when they had left at the crack of dawn to begin their day on the water. Tired, wet, and hungry, the crew slowly made its way downstream to the Wanigan for second breakfast, the first hot meal of the day. Dinner would be carried to them by the cook in the small wooden wanigan strapped to his shoulders. The boat would be through the rapids and likely some distance away by dinnertime. The men would be fighting the second rapids, prying logs from behind rocks and boulders, dead tired and uninterested in negotiating the woods in search of their dinner. Iner Halvorson would bring the noonday meal to the crew.

"Hello," Maki said as Tim Laitila materialized out of the dense foliage.

"Mr. Maki," Pederson said, touching the brim of his dirty Stetson with an equally dirty palm.

"Food's nearly done," Kinkkonen added from his position on a home-made bench that had been removed from the Wanigan's cabin and placed on the foredeck of the boat, so as to take in the scenery.

Olli Kinkkonen spoke Finnish through a thick wad of chewing tobacco tucked inside his lower lip. His cap was on his head, the brim slightly off center and tipped up. A day's length of stubble had appeared overnight across the lower portion of Kinkkonen's face, casting a dark shadow on his dark skin. Kinkkonen whittled a piece of willow with a stubby hunting knife drawn from a sheath attached to his belt. He wore suspenders, as did the other men, in addition to a belt, the need for this redundancy being lost upon Kinkkonen's companions.

"Looks like rain," Laitila announced as he arrived next to Pederson and removed his hat and rearranged his hair.

"We're going to need it," Maki said, his eyes searching the approaching mantle of gray clouds. "The more the better."

"I'm not working in lightning," Pederson advised, looking straight at his boss. "I've already been hit once, trimming timber," he added. "Not an experience I want to repeat."

Maki smiled. "I won't send you out if there's lightening, Paul. I don't want you fried up like a sausage in a pan," the camp boss added with obvious lightness.

Laitila smiled.

"Knew a man once, in the Alpena mine, Buster Thompson," Laitila offered. "He was hit by lightening only the once, but it hit him in the arse, burned off every damn hair he had on his backside. Bald as a baby he was after that little lightning bolt came to visit."

225

The men laughed. Kinkkonen's mirth was limited to a reserved chuckle.

"Breakfast's on," Iner announced, poking his head out through the open doorway.

By mid-afternoon, the thunderhead had opened up. A squall settled in over the valley. Sheets of silver rain pummeled the tarpaper roof of the Wanigan in an unearthly drumbeat as the ten-man crew sat inside, safely out of the weather. Lightning danced and thunder crashed above them. Iner Halvorson placed pots and pans in strategic locations throughout the small cabin to catch rainwater trickling and dripping through assorted fissures and cracks in the imperfect membrane covering the roof of the structure. Men lounged in their bunks. Laitila dutifully studied the New Testament, his Bible propped on his chest as he reclined on his back in bed. Paul Pederson and Andrew Maki played a subdued game of cribbage as they sipped coffee and ate freshly baked hard rolls slathered in honey. The smell of men, wet, sweat-encrusted, and due for a good sauna bath, was strong in the limited space of the cabin, but the crew was used to the odor and refrained from voicing objection.

The deluge did not last. A half-inch of rain fell upon the Cloquet River system in the two hours that the storm stalled over the valley. Then the clouds were gone, replaced by the penetrating brilliance of a June sun erupting from behind the wall of departing weather.

The crew scurried to work. There were logs to retrieve and a boat to make ready.

"How you gonna tackle 'er?" Andrew Maki asked, standing next to Olli Kinkkonen as the men eyed the second rapids, a long flat cascade of rocks, boulders, and barely visible slivers of sedimentary stone laid out before the Wanigan, as the vessel drifted slowly above the precipice.

A flock of redheaded mergansers rose from a pool at the end of the rough water and raced back upstream, passing close to the boat as they flew, their spear-like bills breaking the air, their awkward wings pumping furiously to maintain lift.

Kinkkonen squinted as he looked directly into the sun hanging in the western sky.

"We'll take it on the left. See there, between that shelf and the line of riffles? There's more than enough water there to run 'er. If we scrape bottom, she won't get hung up, just bounce off. There's enough weight in the water there to push 'er free."

Maki studied the decline in the landscape. He was skeptical. The rainfall hadn't added much to the flow. Still, Kinkkonen had made drives down the Cloquet in years past and brought boats through without ruin. The camp boss drew heavily on his cigarette and nodded.

Because of the storm delay, portions of the log raft preceded the Wanigan down the chute. Wayward logs jammed the river from bank to bank. The prams, two men per boat, worked the edges of the flotsam, breaking up the logjam. Six men manned the Wanigan, one man on each gunwale, Tim Laitila in the bow, Maki and Kinkkonen at the stern sweep oar, and the cook inside the cabin, securing the contents of the kitchen for a ride down the cascade. The loggers held long pikes at the ready for use in keeping the vessel away from floating logs and vicious rocks. Kinkkonen gripped the handle of the sweep with both hands, though once the flat-bottomed craft entered the grip of the river's downward plunge, the fifteen-foot-long oar would become unwieldy in the close quarters of the rapids.

"Here we go," Tim Laitila shouted over the din of the roaring water, as the prow of the Wanigan dipped momentarily beneath the surging current. Water washed over Laitila's cork-soled shoes. The vessel's pace accelerated. The two sidemen kneeled along the gunwales, their pikes at the ready. Kinkkonen stood on a wide wooden step affixed to the stern of the boat, so that he could see over the flat roof of the cabin. The Finn swept the water with the crude hand-made blade of the oak oar and drove the Wanigan hard to the right. The hull scraped bottom, but the boat did not flounder. Spray washed over Tim Laitila as the blacksmith struggled to maintain his balance.

"Here's the tricky part," Kinkkonen called out in Finnish. A plume of white water, reminiscent of the fanned tail of a peacock, sent a shower of water into the air ahead of the boat. There appeared to be no room to squeeze the eight-foot-wide vessel between the obstacles that were creating the disturbance. Kinkkonen bent heavily into the oar, using it like a lever against a shelf of stone on the right-hand side, careful not to splinter the device under the weight of the pivot. The maneuver sent the boat straight through the funnel.

The Wanigan slammed out of the last flurry and into the calm below the rapids. Cedar and tamarack logs shot past the drifting vessel like torpedoes. The prams bounced through the passage without incident, joining the larger boat in the pool below the falls.

"That was some boatmanship," Maki proclaimed as Olli Kinkkonen lit a smoke and stepped down from his perch.

The cook opened the door to the cabin and stepped out, intent on disputing the camp boss's observation.

"Who the hell is piloting this tub of shit?" Iner Halvorson shouted. "You busted up half my plates on that last run," he bemoaned.

"Be thankful you're not swimming in the Cloquet River," Tim Laitila said, pounding the cook on the back. "Kinkkonen did one hell of a job back there."

"Some job," Iner muttered, retreating into his lair. "If he keeps this up, you'll be eating your food directly off the table," the cook muttered as he slammed the door.

Laitila smiled and leaned his pike against the front wall of the cabin. He reached inside his wool shirt, touched the leather binding of his Finnish Bible, and withdrew the book. Turning to Isaiah 33:17, Laitila read the passage aloud:

But there the Lord in majesty will be for us a place of broad rivers and streams, where no galley with oars can go, nor stately ship can pass. For the Lord is our judge, the Lord is our ruler, the Lord is our king; he will save us.

Kinkkonen blew a billow of white tobacco smoke into the still air, the mosquitoes absent, the flies momentarily thwarted by the passing storm, as he considered a response to Laitila's epistle. Andrew Maki left the stern, intent upon giving the other men their duties regarding the retrieval of the disorderly log raft. The camp boss did not hear Olli Kinkkonen's dismissal of the Biblical reference: "God didn't save us back there. This old Finlander did."

Kinkkonen's agnostic observation was audible despite the background noise of the rapids. The other men on the boat didn't respond to Kinkkonen's mild arrogance.

Morning. Gray descended upon the Cloquet River Valley. The sky was weighed down by expectant weather. A light drizzle coated the physical world and in complimentary griseous shades cloaked the loggers working the flotilla of cedar and tamarack above the last drop into Island Lake. Olli Kinkkonen worked the aft oar, coordinating his strokes through the placid water with those of Tim Laitila, working the bow sweep. Andrew Maki and Micah Wargin floated past the rocky bank of the south shoreline in one of the rowboats. Paul Pederson danced across floating logs, his cork shoes gripping the scaly bark of the flotsam, assisting Maki and Wargin in their efforts to retrieve timber that was hung up on the shoreline. Four other pig men worked the north side of the watercourse in the second pram. A pair of silvery and white kingfishers flitted through the dreary sky, chattering warnings to other forest creatures that men were making their way to the lake. Mist rose from the warm water as the chill of evening departed. Through the rising steam, the maples and ash lining the riverbanks appeared as shadows against the amorphous sky.

"Bring 'em in, boys," Maki urged the other crew as the boats drifted steadily downstream. "We'll need them as tight as possible for the last run."

The Wanigan bobbed in the reduced current. Yesterday's rain had not increased the flow of the river to any substantial degree. The camp boss was concerned that the Wanigan might have to be abandoned above the final drop. Maki knew that if the boat could not negotiate the plummet into Island Lake, the only course left would be to tie the craft

229

to the shoreline above the falls, escort the logs to the Duluth and Northeastern landing across Island Lake in the prams, load the logs, and then return upstream with a crew to carve a road through the swamp, tag alder, and brush. They would then have to drag the Wanigan over the crude trail, rolling it on logs to the nearest rail spur located three miles to the north. Such an effort would mean at least a week of work and a minimum of four men besides himself. It would mean waiting at least two days at the landing while extra provisions were brought in by rail. The food larder was nearly empty. Men would not work without food. The delay would add to the expense, costs that George McAdams had not anticipated. Leaving the Wanigan above the lake was a choice that Andrew Maki did not want to have to make, unless there was no possibility of safely passing through the last cascade.

A cool breeze began to blow. The zephyr moved across the broad expanse of open water to the west, propelled by winds out of Canada, from the most northerly reaches of Manitoba, causing the wet and tired loggers to shiver uncontrollably as they worked the logs. Teeth chattered. Hands and fingers turned numb as the temperature of the air dropped into the high forties with the advance of the cold front. The men struggled to organize the floating mass of timber for the final drop into Island Lake, despite the hardships created by the weather. Wind began to whip the wide channel of the Cloquet River. Whitecaps danced across the water. The birds and animals of the depleted forest took refuge against the increasing wind. Rain began.

"Maybe we should take a break," Maki said as the two prams came together in the middle of the floating harvest.

"Better to get it done with; get through the last rapids and into the lake. There's a nice pool, calm water, just to the other side of the last drop. We can put together the log raft there for the final push to the landing when the weather breaks," Paul Pederson urged.

Maki's eyes scanned the water. There was no horizon apparent, the land to the west having been obliterated by the storm. Sheets of precipitation descended. The men's clothing was soaked through. Still, the wool captured the majority of their body heat and prevented hypothermia. The camp boss looked into the faces of the men gathered around him in the two small open boats, rocking on the disturbed surface of the water. A small-mouthed bass leaped into the air in defiance of the storm, in search of insects. The ripples caused by the fish disappeared as soon as the bass returned to the depths.

"What do the rest of you think?"

"Push on," Tim Laitila urged.

The other men muttered agreement.

Andrew Maki tilted his face so as to see look into their eyes.

"Let's push on," the camp boss said quietly.

Miss Wolf Lake wagged lazily in the turbulent current, the bow of the vessel secured to a generational red cedar leaning over the water, the stern of the boat moving back and forth, back and forth, straining against the hemp rope tethering the craft to land.

Andrew Maki, Tim Laitila, and Olli Kinkkonen stood on the gabbroitic escarpment, overlooking the final pitch of the Upper Cloquet River. The scene had not changed appreciably from the earlier scouting expedition. Despite a near-constant summer rain, now warmer and less onerous due to a shift in the wind, the level of the river had not risen significantly. The full fifteen-foot shelf of the falls was not disclosed. There was sufficient water present to disguise the danger, though the limited aperture through which the boat would have to pass was well known to Olli Kinkkonen.

"I don't see how it can be done," Andrew Maki advised, pointing to the narrow funnel of water spitting and spewing between the two rocky cornices defining the river's final descent. "There's barely enough space to slide the bow through between those spires. And that's if you hit the approach perfectly, with no deviation."

Olli Kinkkonen spat tobacco, the wad of chew exposed as dark matter between the Finn's tongue and the interior of his right cheek, towards the water. The mess of phlegm and tobacco fell short of its target, splattering against rocks a few feet from the swirling water.

"It can be done," Kinkkonen advised, his cap resting evenly on his black hair, his clothing beaded with droplets of fine rain. "Just takes a little skill is all."

Laitila nodded his head in agreement. "I agree. Olli knows what he's doing. I'd be willing to go with, to man a pike on one side. Pederson's willing to go as well. That gives you as many men as you need, Andrew."

"If anyone is going to try to ride that son of a bitch through there, it'll be me. I'm not about to let a father of two young girls risk his neck to save George McAdams a couple hundred dollars," Maki observed.

"You think I want to miss this ride? You've gotta be crazy. You can take Pederson's place if you want, but I'm going with," Laitila insisted.

Maki's face tensed as his eyes studied the boiling, careening water spilling over the rock ledge that underlay the course of the river. Common sense bade him to refuse to give permission to Laitila, a man who had much to lose and little to gain by tempting fate. But Laitila was insistent. He could be, as Maki knew from their days together at the Alpena Mine, a very stubborn man, a difficult man, when his path was thwarted. Though Laitila had been Maki's boss at the mine, there had been no second-guessing, no insubordination based upon their prior working relationship, by the blacksmith since the day Maki convinced George McAdams that Laitila would make an acceptable camp blacksmith for the Wolf Lake operation. Despite the reality that Maki had only once, as a straw boss in the Quincy Mine in Houghton, held a prior position of authority over other men, and Laitila had more experience in that regard, Tim Laitila had never raised his experience as a challenge to Maki's authority. Until that moment, as the three Finns stood poised above the cascade, measuring it, calculating it, Laitila had been the most compliant and obedient of the employees under Maki's charge.

To begin to question Laitila's motives now, to deny him the right to seek this challenge, would be wrong, Maki thought.

"The three of us, then," Andrew Maki finally said, his eyes riveted upon the dangerous gorge below them. "Only the three of us will run this."

The other pig men positioned themselves below the falls in the prams. Logs floated towards the narrow chute of water demarcating the end of river and the beginning of lake. The timbers bobbed innocently in the increasing current above the ledge and then, with sudden viciousness, disappeared over the crest of the plunge, re-emerging moments later in the calm pool at the foot of the falls, where the crew organized the logs for the final raft across Island Lake.

"Ready?" Laitila asked, his hands resting upon the rope that secured the boat to the cedar tree. He stood knee-deep in water, ready to loosen the tether.

"Might as well give it a whirl," Maki said through a nervous smile, his hands gripped tightly around a pike as he stood next to the Wanigan's cabin on the port side. The men had fastened loops of rope to the exterior walls of the cabin with twenty-penny spikes. Maki looped the rope around his right wrist and pulled the noose snug, securing himself to the boat for the turbulent ride down the chute.

"Ready," Kinkkonen agreed, his feet planted firmly on the step, his legs spread apart for balance as he held tightly to the rear sweep.

Laitila untied the rope, threw the loose end onto the deck of the Wanigan, and eased the boat away from the shore. Bronze water lapped at Tim Laitila's waist. He pulled his feet from the river's grasp and crawled onto the deck of the boat as the Wanigan began to drift downstream.

Laitila took his position along the starboard gunwale and placed his left hand through the loop of rope anchored to the Wanigan, pike in his right, ready to assist Kinkkonen should the oarsman require aid navigating the plummet. The pace quickened. Kinkkonen steered the craft with broad sweeps of the oar. Boulders and rocks emerged from the black water. The helmsman's movements became constrained. Laitila and Maki used their pikes to fend off the rocks, bracing the iron business ends of the poles against the sharp teeth of the riverbed.

Kinkkonen's approach was perfect. The bow of the Wanigan squeezed between the twin spires that demarcated the waterfall. The bow tipped. Pans, dishes, and foodstuffs crashed from cupboards inside the Wanigan's cabin, the cook's efforts to secure the items defeated by the suddenness of gravity.

"Here we go," Laitila shouted over the roar of descending water.

The vessel's prow teetered precariously in mid-air until the weight of the river shoved the Wanigan forward, over the precipice, down the passage to the lake. The course was set. There was no ability to correct the path that Olli Kinkkonen had selected. Unbeknownst to the Finns on board *Miss Wolf Lake*, the water was an inch too shallow for the houseboat to clear the cascade. As the bow plunged downward and the men grasped the lashings with all their strength, the hull struck a rock ledge, snapping the cross timbers holding the boat together. The boat split, not slowly, as one would anticipate given the former solidity of the craft, but instantly, without warning. The port side of the Wanigan was beached solidly on the basalt shelf. The hull began to disintegrate.

"She's breaking up," Kinkkonen shouted.

The helmsman released the oar. Laitila struggled to free his left arm from its restraint. A shifting of the vessel on the ledge pinched the rope between two rafters, making it impossible for the carpenter to loosen the rope. Andrew Maki used his hunting knife to sever the rope on his wrist and struggled to maintain his balance as the deck of the boat broke apart beneath his feet. Water cascaded over the stern of the stricken vessel, sent high into the air by the force of an entire river. Spray doused the three men as they struggled to escape.

A pram in the lower pool raced towards the stricken Wanigan. Paul Pederson and Iner Halvorson pulled hard on the oars. The little boat skimmed across the gray water. Renewed summer rain pummeled the occupants of the pram as the men sought to lend assistance.

"I can't get my hand out of the rope," Laitila screamed, the cabin wall buckling, water lapping at his waist as the structure began to slide beneath the turbulence.

Andrew Maki's eyes widened. There was no way for Maki to reach Laitila.

"Use your knife," Maki urged, his own hunting knife back in its sheath.

Tim Laitila reached for the handle of his knife. The boat slid precipitously on underlying rocks, immersing the carpenter in water up to his chest. Laitila drew his knife from its sheath. His fingers grasped the carved bone handle of the dagger as he tried to slice through the rope. A cedar log slammed into the stern of the Wanigan. The violence took Tim Laitila by surprise. The Finn dropped the knife into the water.

Chapter 31
August, 1917

Bells rang out. Rice flew through the air. The bridal couple moved gracefully from the dim light of the church sanctuary, out into the brilliance of an August sun. Wendy McAdams strode delicately alongside her dashing husband, down the red sandstone steps of First Presbyterian Church and across a cement sidewalk, before waiting to be lifted by George McAdams into an open, horse-drawn wedding carriage standing idle on Second Street. A team of identical black Morgans, blinders forcing the horses to gaze uniformly to the east, stood patiently at the curb, reins slack and resting comfortably in the coachman's gloved hands.

George McAdams reached over, planted a significant kiss on the lips of his new wife, adjusted his top hat and swept the woman into the carriage through the open wooden door, before claiming a place next to his wife on the forward-facing bench seat in the rear of the buggy. The black leather seat crackled as the big Canadian dispersed his weight over the cushion.

The best man and maid of honor, Andrew Maki and Elin Gustafsson, stood beneath a sweltering sun, waiting to enter the carriage. Maki's black tuxedo retained his body heat, rendering him extremely uncomfortable. The light green muslin dress worn by Elin and the other bridesmaids was airy and light, allowing the slight breeze to touch bare skin through the porous fabric. It was an awkward circumstance, Maki standing beside his former lover on a public street in front of a throng of well wishers, made more awkward by the physical discomfort of Andrew Maki's formal attire.

There had been a moment, while they awaited the ceremony in the dark antechambers of the church, when Elin Gustafsson and Andrew Maki had been left alone. It was the first such circumstance in over three years. In the interim since he had left Duluth, Maki had lost his job at the mine, met and fallen in love with Heidi Genelli, acquired the Papoose Lake property, made significant progress in clearing the land and erecting buildings, and watched helplessly as one of his best friends, a man under his charge, had drowned needlessly in the roaring waters of the Cloquet River. The moment of confrontation had been filled with inexplicable dread.

Paul Pederson's pike had located the battered body of Tim Laitila in the calm pool below the waterfall. The Norwegian had probed the inky waters of Island Lake in the fatal minutes after the Wanigan had slid off the rocky shoulder of the cascade, until the iron hook at the end of Pederson's spear snagged the dead man's clothing. It was painfully obvious, once Tim Laitila was brought to the surface, that the blacksmith's skull had been crushed between the hull of the floundering boat and the craggy shoal forming the narrow chute of transition from river to lake. The entire right side of Laitila's face had been mashed into gelatin by the weight of the descending Wanigan, trapping the Finn beneath black water.

Maki and Kinkkonen had been lucky. Both men had managed to leap from the dispersing craft onto level basalt, where they were rescued. But the Wanigan itself, supplies, personal belongings, cook stove, pots, pans, utensils, and all the rest, had slipped rapidly into twenty-five feet of cold, inhospitable water.

The funeral had been an awful experience. Andrew Maki, his ribs bandaged, a gash on his forehead sutured with nine black stitches of cat gut, sat in the first pew of the Finnish Evangelical Lutheran in Virginia as a pallbearer, along with Tim Laitila's two older brothers and three fellow Finns from the Iron Range. Mara Laitila, her parents, Matti and Elsa Pihlaja, and the twins, Susan and Margaret, who turned a year old the day after their father died, sat in a narrow oak pew with other family immediately behind the pall bearers. The moments of silent reflection spent at the small Finnish cemetery to the west of town had been brutal on Andrew Maki's nerves.

I knew better, the Finn thought over and over as he watched Mara Laitila wail, her hand placed upon the smooth maple surface of her husband's coffin, held over the gaping mouth of the ground by a lattice of two by fours,. *We should never have tried to run that falls.*

Money. It had all been about the money. His better judgment had been obliterated by a desire to save George McAdams a few dollars, to save the toil and labor of carting the Wanigan through the woods above the last plunge to the Duluth and Northeastern spur, in a pitiful attempt to ingratiate himself to his boss.

There was no need, Maki had thought standing in the soft mist that fell over the mourners in the open cemetery field the day of Tim Laitila's burial. *George never pushed me, never forced me to pinch pennies. I can't blame this on him. It was me. It was me.*

Mara, her daughters huddled to her skirt, her parents bowed in silent grief, had trudged away from the place of Tim's final rest. She had left Tim Laitila's Finnish Bible, the one book that he had owned, resting on top of the lacquered surface of the coffin, the pages damp and clinging together, the message of the pastor's sermon and the words of the book both lost, lost to the reality of the sudden absence of a beloved man.

Tim Laitila's death steeled Andrew Maki in ways that the camp boss could not have anticipated. Upon his arrival in Duluth two weeks after the funeral, he took his second papers and became an American citizen. He scribbled a hurried note to Heidi Genelli, explaining, as best he could, his new mindset, his new-found compunction to cleanse his soul, his burnished spirit, by seeking risk:

Dear Mrs. Genelli:

Doubtlessly you will have heard about the tragedy involving my friend and co-worker, Tim Laitila. There is no question in my mind that I am, unfortunately, solely, legally, and morally, responsible for this event. I was greedy. I thought that running the last rapids of the Cloquet into Island Lake, where the logs were to be loaded for transport to the city of Cloquet, would save Mr. McAdams significant monies and endear me to him, ensuring future employment. I am afraid my folly-filled haste not only cost a man his life; I fear that McAdams has likely lost all faith and trust in my ability to make sound decisions.

I know that you are anticipating I will be asking your father for your hand sometime in the near future. That is what I had fully intended to do prior to the occurrence of Tim's death. But now my faith in institutions governed by the Almighty has been sorely shaken. The words spoken at Tim's funeral, the Scripture quoted by the man of God from the pulpit on that afternoon, have done little to assuage my guilt or provide me with providential understanding. There seems to be so little meaning, so little beauty in this life. I am, at this juncture, I must confess, a lost man.

Please understand when I write to tell you that, given the circumstances, I must take some time to consider the gravity of what I have done to Mara Laitila and her family. I fear that she, as a woman of thirty with two small children, no husband, and only the meager severance provided by George McAdams ($500.00 out of the goodness of his great heart), will never be consoled nor compensated for the loss that I have caused her. This fear weighs upon me like a rock, a great and heavy stone that threatens to immerse me in self-pity and the bottle. I have been drinking far too much. The Finnish Temperance women would be after me as a target for conversion to sobriety if they knew the depth of my reliance upon vodka as an aid to sleep. I must remove myself from this life, at least for a time, to consider it all. My work. My farm. Us.

It is only after great consideration that I have decided to enlist in the United States Marine Corps and offer my miserable body up to the War, in hopes that staring death in the face on the field of battle will bring me answers, or, if not answers, at least peace. My friend Olli Kinkkonen (whom you have not met) believes that I am crazy for offering myself up to a war that has nothing to do with me. He is enraged that the Allies have taken up the side of the Czar in the Russian equation, and has taken to calling me a "church Finn" and a Republican. You know me better than that. I bear no sympathy for bosses and capitalists. My church going is

239

rudimentary, at best. Kinkkonen denigrates me without foundation. And yet, despite all his leftist diatribes, I respect him as a man of conviction.

I will not ask you to wait for me. You are under no obligation to withdraw from society and the company of men. You are a young, vibrant, attractive, and engaging woman who deserves to remain vigilant for love. Should I make it back to Minnesota and should you still be a single woman willing to consider my meager proposal, I will ask you to be my wife. But that question cannot be posed until I determine the course my life is destined to take. And that determination now requires that I make penance to Tim Laitila and his family by fighting for the country that he loved.

Yours,

Andrew Maki

*June 25*th*, 1917*

PS

Paul Pederson has agreed to live on the farm while I am away. The farmhouse, barn, and sauna buildings have been completed and the fields are ready to be cleared of stumps. Mr. McAdams has agreed to forego collecting on the note until I return.

There was no response to Maki's letter. Andrew Maki did not know what to make of Heidi Genelli's silence. He understood her well enough to recognize that the lack of response could be taken in a number of ways, some of which he did not want to consider.

The reunion of the two lovers in the dimly lighted passageway of First Presbyterian Church had been an occasion of strained civility. No great revelations were unfurled by either participant. Andrew Maki simply inquired as to Elin Gustafsson's health and the health of her father. Elin imparted her condolences regarding the death of Tim Laitila. There was a brief moment, as she delivered this expression of concern, when Maki believed he saw a glimmer, a recognition in her eyes of what they had once shared. However, this aspect disappeared behind Elin's newfound façade, a burgeoning impunity that she had constructed around herself as a result of her mother's death and Andrew's unexplained abandonment of their relationship.

"Hello," she had said as they stood awkwardly in the hallway, each waiting to use the water closets labeled "Gentlemen" and "Ladies".

"Miss Gustafsson," he had responded with politeness.

"You look very prosperous and distinguished in that tuxedo," Elin replied, her gloved hand placing a tress of her auburn hair behind her left ear. "The years have been kind to you."

"And to you as well," he responded, shifting nervously on the balls of his feet, rented shoes pinching his toes.

He wanted to ask about her relationship with Horace Ellison and her impending betrothal, the ceremony only a month away, as reported by the *News Tribune* society editor. The wedding, an event for which he had not received an invitation and for which he did not anticipate receiving one, was to be the gala event of early autumn in Duluth, the merger of two prominent Duluth families and their progeny. Maki held his tongue, keeping a multitude of questions, personal and inappropriate to their new relationship, locked in his mind.

"They make a lovely couple," Elin said, shifting her slip, the fabric of her gown swooshing as it moved. "Wendy is very much in love," she added.

"George is exceedingly enraptured by her," Andrew observed. "I believe he is truly, unequivocally, happy in his life."

Elin nodded dramatically, falsity clear in the movement.

She has changed, Andrew Maki observed. *The young woman that I spent nights entangled with in the sweaty, close atmosphere of that little cottage on a bluff above Hancock, Michigan, has vanished. Innocence has been lost. Guile and cunning have replaced honesty and virtue. Why? Why has she seen fit to reject all that made her appealing and beautiful?*

One of the ushers had exited the men's washroom. Maki nodded to Elin and entered the lavatory, closing the heavy oak door behind him without another word.

241

They sat next to each other in the open carriage as the horses' hooves clambered against the hard paving bricks of Second Street. The carriage headed east towards Northland Country Club, where a gala reception and wedding dance would be held. Across the narrow open space between the rear bench seats, the bride and groom snuggled intimately, in stark contrast to the obvious distance maintained between the best man and the maid of honor. A line of Tin Lizzies and other motorized vehicles, their metal skins freshly washed and gleaming beneath the high sun, followed the carriage in slow procession. Three vehicles behind the wedding party, Horace Ellison drove his parents in their convertible Bentley, the vehicle's gasoline engine purring elegantly, the driver's face drawn in a scowl as he stared out the thick plate glass windshield and considered the situation.

"Don't be dismayed," his mother urged, patting Horace on the shoulder from the rear seat. "Elin isn't about to run off with that Finnlander at this stage of the game. She knows what she wants and it's wealth, and power, and prestige, the stability of a good home and a prosperous husband. I doubt there's any danger of her second-guessing her decision and bolting for the wilderness with a dairy farmer, if that's what Mr. Maki intends to be."

Eustace Ellison nodded in agreement.

"Son, you're taking this little reunion too seriously. There's no connection between the two of them that remains from their past. It's gone, burned away by the love Elin feels for you."

If they only knew, Horace thought as he steered the Bentley around a pothole in the pavement, where bricks had exploded from summer heat, leaving the tar under-layment of the street exposed. *Elin has made it plain that she does not love me. There is no fever in her for me, none at all. This union is one of convenience for her and nothing more.*

The Bentley stopped as the vehicles in front of it slowed to allow a delivery truck to pass through on the avenue ahead.

I am a fool for going through with this. To marry someone who blatantly confides that she does not, and will likely never, feel passion for me as I feel passion for her, is stupidity. Still, her eyes draw me. Her body summons me. I am helpless to retreat in the face of her beauty. I am, in all respects, a doomed man.

The caravan meandered through East Duluth, until it climbed the dirt road leading to Northland Country Club. The Craftsman-style building spread out low along the crown of a small rise, the larger weight of Duluth's hills rising behind the clubhouse like the foothills of a mountain range. There were no mountains further west beyond the bluffs and the gravel surface of Skyline Drive threading through the hills. There was only brush and farms and sparkling rivers, interspaced with swamps and marshland covering miles and miles of denuded land, land absent of its canopy of pines. The bald prominence of the hillside, towering above the golf course and clubhouse, the bare gabbro coal-like in color beneath the exhaustingly bright sun, rose above the rolling, perfect green lawn of the retreat, as if to insulate the men and women of means and privilege from the riff-raff working the forests, farms, and mines to the north.

"Son, you haven't said a word," Eustace Ellison remarked as the motorcar skidded to a halt on the graveled surface of the country club parking lot. "Your mother and I are worried about you."

Horace opened the driver's door and then opened the rear passenger door for his mother. He offered his hand to the woman and she accepted it, using it as a pivot to allow her to exit the automobile.

"I'm fine, father," Horace replied, smiling effortlessly, concealing his ultimate emotions. "Elin is faithful. I have no doubts about that," he lied.

"That's good, son," Eustace Ellison replied, exiting the car on his own. "The last thing we need is self-doubt creeping into your wedding plans."

You mean 'merger', don't you? Horace mused silently. You and Karl Gustafsson have been salivating over this merger of families, the brokerage of Finnish blood, or, in my case, half-Finnish blood, for three years. You selfish, self-important bombast. Don't you think I know the motivation, the financial considerations behind Elin and I becoming a family? Do you think I am some stupid,

243

uneducated dolt you can manipulate at will? I'll do this thing, not because you will it, Old Man, but because I desire it. My yearning for this woman is not about wealth or prestige or the solidification of commercial interests. It is about desire, something I doubt you know anything about.

All this young Horace Ellison thought, ever mindful to conceal his disgust of his father behind a broad, exaggerated smile.

The photographer snapped portraits of the wedding party standing on the covered porch of the elegant clubhouse, roses and daffodils arranged artificially around the group against the reality of departing summer. When the last explosion of light had flashed from the light bar, when the last shutter had clicked, Horace Ellison advanced up the staircase leading to the porch, to reclaim what was his.

Chapter 32

James Olson of the Morgan Park neighborhood of Duluth refused to register with Selective Service on the date appointed by Congress: June 5, 1917. This act of civil disobedience, like others punishable under the Espionage Act, was prosecuted by the United States District Attorney for the District of Minnesota, Mr. M. Jaques. Olson was promptly arrested on June 17, 1917, and confined to the Duluth City Jail, located at 132 East Superior Street, a location that, in 1920, would play a significant role in the mob-lynching of three black circus works wrongly accused of raping a white woman.

The day before Olson's arrest, June 16th, 1917, General John L. "Black Jack" Pershing, leader of the American Expeditionary Force, the American Army that would ultimately be deployed along the Western Front in the Great War, landed in England. Within the year, the Russian Empire would collapse in the face of the Bolshevik Revolution and Finland would declare its independence. Red and White brigades would fight for control of the disintegrating Empire. The Allies would lend support to the Russian Whites, loyal to the Czar, in the form of men and munitions. But in Finland, the Whites, forces of democracy opposing the Marxist Red Finns, would receive the benefit of German support. Evaluating this complex geo-political morass from across the safety of the Atlantic, the Knights of Kaleva remained firm in their resolve.

Formed as a Finnish response to secret fraternal organizations, such as the Masons and the Roman Catholic Knights of Columbus, the Knights of Kaleva in Duluth counted amongst its founders and sustaining members the same men who had been instrumental in founding the American Loyalty League. Lawyers Victor Gran, Oscar Larson, and Karl Gustafsson were, along with Finnish business owners like Dove Clothing proprietor, Alex

Kyyhkynen, influential in formulating the political conservatism, "the church Finn philosophy", so to speak, that sustained the Knights of Kaleva through the Great War.

There was, behind this fraternal organization, a fundamental pride in the re-discovery of Finnish culture, based upon the collection of old Finnish folk tales into the epic *Kalevala*, a work founded upon heroism, mysticism, and magic:

> At that old Vainamoinen
> sings and practices his craft
> he sang a spruce topped with flowers
> topped with flowers and leaved with gold;
> the top he pushed heavenward
> through the clouds he lifted it
> spread the foliage skyward
> across heaven scattered it.
> He sings, practices his craft-
>   sang the moon to gleam
> on the gold-topped spruce, he sang
> the Great Bear on to its boughs.

Victor Gran sat heavily in his chair. The windows to his law office were open, allowing the even dispensation of September air throughout the room. Gran was engaged in a discussion of ponderous weight with his friend and fellow Finn, Karl Gustafsson.

"There is a need for 70,000 new recruits to the Army, for the Expeditionary Force," Gran observed. "Though the *News Tribune* and the *New York Times* claim enlistments are exceeding expectations, I doubt the veracity of those claims," the lawyer added.

"How so?" Gustafsson asked, his fingers wrapped around the base of a snifter of ten-year-old brandy, the liquor supplied courtesy of his host.

"There is wide-spread ignorance amongst our own people as to why the recruits are needed," Gran explained between sips of liquor. "The local paper is recounting acts of individual disloyalty on a daily basis. Look at this Olson character. He's openly belligerent in his refusal to register. This on the heels of two Boche being arrested in an attempt to deliver a bomb to J.P. Morgan's office on Wall Street. Ironic, isn't it, that a fellow from a neighborhood sponsored, erected, and funded by J.P. Morgan would resist registration, even as the benefactor of that neighborhood is being targeted by terrorists for destruction?"

"I see your point," Gustafsson replied. "Reminds me of back in '08, during the Miner's Strike, when they tried to bomb Tom Nichols' home in Aurora. He was a captain at the Mohawk Mine, if I recall. Damn Syndicalist instigators were to blame then, and they're likely to blame now. So what do you propose we do?"

"First, we cannot, as attorneys, agree to represent any of our fellow Finns with respect to their arrests for civil disobedience. We cannot."

Gustafsson didn't respond immediately. He was thinking of George McAdams and the Canadian's request that he represent George's father-in-law Henri Heikkonen, with respect to Henri's upcoming trial for rioting and disturbing the peace, which stemmed from the June draft rally in front of the St. Louis County Courthouse. The forty dollars McAdams had paid to Officer McIntyre hadn't been sufficient to forestall the pressing of charges by the St. Louis County Attorney's Office against the disabled logger. There would be a trial. The topic of Karl Gustafsson's representing the Finnish demonstrator had come up at McAdams's wedding.

Other topics, most notably McAdams's insistence, despite Karl Gustafsson's protestations to the contrary, in selecting Andrew Maki as McAdams's best man had been bandied about in the men's smoking lounge of Northland Country Club, while the wedding dance progressed in the adjacent social hall.

"Why in thunder did you pick Maki, of all people, George, knowing how I feel about the man?" Gustafsson had bellowed, his voice emboldened by good vodka and the closed door of the lounge.

247

"Karl, I know your history with Andrew. I know how you and Eustace chased the lad out of town."

"Lad! That's rich. He was a thirty-year-old man having his way with my young daughter," Karl Gustafsson had continued. "You haven't any children, McAdams. Once you do, especially if you have daughters, then you'll understand. What he did, taking my little girl to Houghton, ruining her good name – why, there's simply no excuse for that sort of churlish behavior."

Following the attorney's initial explosion the men had conducted their conversation in muted tones. The sounds of an orchestra playing contemporary dance tunes bled through the lathe and plaster walls of the country club, into the smoking lounge. The celebratory voices of men and women were audible despite the cacophony of music. McAdams lit his pipe and puffed great clouds of sweet tobacco smoke into the close air of the room.

"It's long past, what happened between Maki and Elin," McAdams finally observed. "She's set with young Ellison. Maki is himself smitten with a lady from Aurora, a fine Finnish woman who has had her own tragedy. There's no cause to dredge up what took place in the past, my friend," the Canadian added, pouring clear vodka into a tumbler of ice for his companion.

Gustafsson had signaled with a hand that his glass was adequately filled. The lawyer placed the cool edge of the tumbler to his lips and drank the liquor in one swallow.

"Perhaps you're right. Perhaps it is time to let go of the thing."

McAdams slapped the Finn on the back.

"What say we join the party?"

Gustafsson had smiled.

"I thought you wanted to talk about your interest in the *Blue Heron*," the Finnish lawyer had advised, referring to a derelict "outside" tug, a powerful work vessel of over one hundred and twenty-five feet sitting in dry dock at the McDougall-Duluth Shipyard in Riverside, next to Morgan Park on the St. Louis River.

"We can visit about that another time," McAdams replied, anxious to be a good host to his wedding guests.

"There's room for a man like you in Duluth, you know," Karl Gustafsson had acknowledged, opening the door so that the groom could exit. "You've got spunk."

"Spunk, I have plenty of," George McAdams had replied with a wink. "It's capital that I need."

Karl Gustafsson and Victor Gran continued their conversation as they walked up Fourth Avenue West, towards the St. Louis County Courthouse. From time to time, the men reached for the brims of their McKibbon bowlers to secure the hats against vagrant gusts of wind.

"I don't know if I can put McAdams off," Karl Gustafsson lamented as the men trudged up the hill against the stiff Northwestern wind. "You know I just helped him out with the *Blue Heron*; put him onto Juda Tylla. Tylla financed the purchase and refurbishing of the boat as a lumber tug through his bank," Gustafsson continued. "McAdams is someone I'd like to cultivate."

Gran looked straight ahead as the men reached the pavement demarcating the plateau of First Street. His eyes focused deliberately upon the men's path up the hill.

"I see your point. Perhaps an exception can be made for you to represent this unfortunate Mr. Heikkonen in this one instance. If that accommodation were made, would you have a problem foreswearing undertaking any further criminal cases involving slackers?"

Gustafsson breathed heavily and felt the familiar onset of angina pain, a condition he had kept to himself since its diagnosis earlier that summer. The inadvertent clutching of his chest caused his companion to stop their advance up the hill.

"Something wrong?"

"A little queasy is all. It will pass with a momentary pause," Gustafsson said cautiously, his big jowls quivering with nervous fear.

"You don't look well," Gran replied. "Why don't you take a seat," he added, pointing to a park bench.

249

The men sat down. Gustafsson took short, cleansing breaths as he waited for the pain to abate. His heart rate decreased. The pain began to retreat.

"There something seriously wrong?" Victor Gran asked.

Gran's companion looked away in shame.

"A little heart condition. Angina pectoris. Nothing serious. The doctor says I simply need to rest when I feel an onset of symptoms."

A period of time passed as the men watched other lawyers, clerks, women out shopping, and businessmen negotiate the adjacent sidewalk.

"I can abide by your request," Gustafsson finally acknowledged.

"How's that?"

"I'll get a dismissal of the charge against Heikkonen. Chief of Detectives Lahti owes me a small favor or two. Once that's accomplished, I won't take any more cases involving protestors."

"The Knights of Kaleva would appreciate that," Gran said quietly, "as does the American Loyalty League," the lawyer added. "How are your daughter and Horace doing?"

Karl Gustafsson's dark features brightened.

"Elin and Horace are doing fine. Your generous wedding gift was much appreciated. They used the money they received to buy a house out in Lakeside. Nice little two bedroom bungalow on 45th Avenue, just off the trolley line."

"And Sofia?"

"Sofia? What can I say? She is the light of my life," Karl Gustafsson admitted.

"You ready to go?" Victor Gran asked, picking up his leather satchel, rising from the bench with grace in defiance of his age.

"I'm fine. I need to talk to Judge Cant about a motion I'm thinking of bringing in a case," Gustafsson said as he forced his bulky torso from the wooden bench. "Then I'll take a walk over to the police station and have a chat with the Lahti about the unfortunate incident involving Mr. Heikkonen."

The attorneys climbed the concrete stairs leading to the courthouse. Before the pair entered the building, its exterior a solid fortress of gray stone standing formidably against the autumn sky, Victor Gran stopped his companion by placing his right hand on the man's shoulder.

"More platitudes about the Knights?" Gustafsson quipped as the smaller man held him back.

"It just came to me. Have you heard the news about Elin's former beau, Anders Alhomaki, who now goes by the name of Andrew Maki?"

Karl Gustafsson frowned:

"I'm not sure I want to hear this."

"Yes you do. He's departed. Gone. May never come back."

"Departed?"

"Word on the street has it that he took his citizenship papers, left McAdams's outfit, and joined the Marine Corps. He's apparently headed to France."

Karl Gustafsson's mouth turned into a broad smile.

"Now that, my friend, is good news."

Chapter 33
October, 1917

Olli Kinkkonen rolled over in bed and stared at the pink backside of Sadie Salmela as the whore sprawled prodigiously across dirty sheets. There was a chill about the shabby room. Sadie was behind on her account with the Duluth Steam Cooperative, the central heating plant that supplied heat to the core of Downtown Duluth. The plant sat a few blocks away from Sadie's brothel, burning coal to produce steam that was distributed throughout the business district via huge underground pipes. Occasionally, when the chill became too much, when the other whores complained too loudly and the customers were shivering as they disrobed, Sadie would fire up the woodstoves located throughout the tenement. But with wood heat came the danger of fire, fire that could sear through the decaying, old frame building like a blowtorch. The woodstoves were a last resort. The stove in Sadie's room was not burning. It sat dormant in a corner of the space, as Kinkkonen's eyes adjusted to the accelerating light of morning.

Olli Kinkkonen sat up, dug beneath the edges of the narrow maple bed and withdrew his skivvies. His woolen long johns were stained and dirty from working the docks. Kinkkonen had returned to stevedoring. The work was tedious and taxing. The loads he carried were heavy and his pay, two dollars a day, no better than Kinkkonen had earned working the Wanigan. Unlike logging, there was a complete absence of freedom in working the docks. Hour after hour, six days a week, Kinkkonen showed up at the steamship wharves located along the rusty waters of St. Louis Bay, looking for work. The jobs came steady and would last until ice-up at Sault St. Marie. Once the locks on the St. Mary's River, which flowed between Lake Superior and Lake Huron, froze solid, the ships

252

would stop and Olli Kinkkonen would be without work for the remainder of the year. In the winter, he would have to make a decision: return to the woods or draw on his savings, cash he had secreted in his shoe. Like many working-class Finns, Kinkkonen did not trust banks. He kept his life savings, a little over three hundred dollars, in his shoe, within easy reach.

There was no chance Olli Kinkkonen would be rehired by George McAdams. His connection to the Canadian had been severed by Andrew Maki's departure for the war. There was also the nasty business of the death of Tim Laitila. Though McAdams had never accused Kinkkonen of dereliction of duty or complacency regarding the tragedy that claimed the blacksmith, the rumor on the street was that Mara Laitila was contemplating bringing a civil lawsuit against McAdams. The five hundred dollars that George McAdams had gifted the widow seemed generous, an act of Christian kindness, but most observers looked upon the charity as an indicator of McAdams's responsibility. Though no papers had been filed, the mere hint of a lawsuit meant that Kinkkonen was not likely to be re-employed at Wolf Lake Camp.

The Finn stood up and pulled the legs of his underwear over the varicosely white skin of his shins and thighs. Kinkkonen was a spindly specimen, with coarse dark body hair and tendonous extremities. No more than five-foot-eight, Kinkkonen was a sliver of a man, but his chest was large for a person of his size, built up by hard labor. He pulled the dirty union suit on over his spidery legs and calmly watched the sleeping woman's massive left leg kick a scratchy wool blanket away from her sagging body.

She's not what I would call comely, not like Elsie Laine, Kinkkonen thought as he dressed in the frigid room. The reference was to a laundress he was seeing. Elsie Laine worked at the Model Laundry, located at 126 E 1st Street, a block away from Kinkkonen's room. *Elsie is shy, not at all ready to commit herself to things physical between us. But her eyes. Those stark blue eyes. Her soft, nearly white, blond hair. And that figure. A wisp of a girl, that one. Just barely a woman. But so lovely. Ever so lovely.*

253

The dockworker sighed as he compared the snoring prostitute splayed across the soiled linens in front of him with the idealized version of the washerwoman retained by his mind. He picked up his work jacket, the plaid wool clean and fresh from Elsie's handiwork at the laundry, pulled out a five - dollar bill, deposited the currency on a dusty end table next to the bed, and walked out of Sadie Salmela's place.

Sunday morning. There was a bustle of activity along the streets of Finntown. Nattily dressed couples conversed in reverent tones as they advanced towards the various houses of worship located throughout downtown Duluth. Most Finns were bound for the Finnish Evangelical Lutheran Church to hear Pastor Sarvela preach. A few uppity Suomi would catch streetcars and journey west, to Bethlehem Lutheran in the West End, the Swedish church where Elin and Horace Ellison had been married a month earlier.

Olli Kinkkonen had no compunction to listen to religion. He was an ardent atheist. His faith was the IWW. His doctrine was that of higher pay, safer conditions, and shorter work hours. He'd taken to attending as many anti-war and pro-labor demonstrations around the city as his work schedule allowed. He wasn't a leader in the labor movement, but his face was well known to conservative Finns, to the men active in the Knights of Kaleva and the Lincoln Liberty League (the Duluth American Liberty League having joined the National Lincoln Liberty League organization in October of 1917), and to the Duluth Police. Kinkkonen had no arrest blotter, no convictions for vagrancy, disorderly conduct, anti-Americanism, or rioting. But his face was known.

He had followed recent cases, the matter involving Duluth steelworker James Olson of Morgan Park, and a similar incident regarding Dominic Silver, an Italian immigrant who, as the secretary of the Hibbing chapter of the IWW, had been detained on charges of treason under the Espionage Act, for handing out leaflets that urged fellow immigrants to refuse registration in the draft. Kinkkonen himself had not applied for citizenship and had not registered for the draft. Eventually, once he applied for his second papers, his failure to comply with the Army Act would be discovered by the local draft board, and he would be called upon to publicly register for compulsory military service.

Kinkkonen had shared a beer with Andrew Maki the day Maki left for the War. Maki was to report for United States Marine Corps Basic Training at Parris Island, South Carolina. Prior to Maki's enlistment, a debate had raged between the Army, which had primary authority over basic training policy and which urged a full year of training for recruits being sent to fight in Europe, and Congress, which wanted the men trained quickly, ready for deployment on the Western Front in a month's time.

Congress won out. A shortened training regimen was adopted. Andrew Maki was to complete basic training in three months' time and ship out, ready for combat the moment he landed in France. Maki would spend eight weeks at Parris Island, another month in Quantico, Virginia, for advanced infantry training, and then board a transport ship for Europe.

Despite the immediacy of Maki's departure, there had been an initial cloud interfering with the men's conversation as they sipped beer in Alan Lehto's Stag Tavern on St. Croix Avenue in Finntown.

"I hear Elin Gustafsson's wedding is tomorrow," Kinkkonen had said as the two Finns sat on stools, waiting for the bartender to bring them mugs of Fitger's draft.

Maki would have preferred People's Lager, his beer of choice, but Lehto's didn't carry it. The Finn stared at the ceiling as he waited for his beer and didn't acknowledge the information conveyed by his drinking partner.

"You deaf or somethin'?" Kinkkonen had asked in Finnish.

Maki smiled and turned towards his companion.

"No, I heard you. It's just not something I want to talk about," Andrew Maki confided.

"Wound goes too deep?"

"I'm leaving for the war. I should've made more of an effort to let Heidi know why I'm going. And I didn't say anything to the kid."

The bartender placed two heavy mugs of foaming draught beer on the water-stained lacquer of the oak bar in front of the men. Olli Kinkkonen handed the man twenty cents to cover the beers.

"He's not your kid."

Maki had sipped beer.

"I know. But he's a great boy. Smart. Strong-willed. Quick with his hands."

"Sounds like someone else I know."

"Maybe."

Maki left other thoughts unsaid. Things had been hanging between the men since the death of Tim Laitila. Andrew had never questioned Kinkkonen's piloting of the Wanigan on that fateful day, never hurled blame at the other man for beaching the craft on the rocks of the Cloquet River. There was no point in attempting to divert public scrutiny away from himself and onto the pilot. It had been Maki's decision, against his better judgment, to try to bring the houseboat into Island Lake. It had been a foolish, ill-planned misadventure that had cost a friend his life. Kinkkonen, to Maki's way of thinking, bore no responsibility for the act.

"You're plenty smart, Maki. With one exception: this enlistment idea. Setting yourself up to be a patsy for rich men who started this war, who are profiting from blood being spilled by working men. That, my friend, is the height of pig-headedness."

Kinkkonen slurped foam and watched his companion out of the corner of his eye. Crimson flamed Maki's face. The emotion dissipated. Serenity returned.

"You won't drag me into a debate over your IWW ideals," Maki replied evenly. "Save your rhetoric for parades and demonstrations."

Kinkkonen leaned back from the bar and laughed derisively.

"You used to be as supportive of workers' causes as I am. What happened to you, Maki? One season working for a benevolent master get to you, tricked you into believing that every businessman is like your friend, George McAdams?

256

You know that's not the case. The George McAdamses of this world are few and far between."

Maki made no answer.

"And even McAdams, if push comes to shove, I'll wager would toss off his employees like dead weight from a sinking ship. He's no different, when you peel away his egalitarian sensibilities, from Eustace Ellison, J. P. Morgan, or James Hill."

Maki faced his accuser.

"I don't think so. George is a good Christian man with a big heart. Look at what he's done for me. Gave me a job. Placed me in a position of authority over forty men. Then backed my decisions, including one that I wish I'd never made, one that cost a man his life, without hesitation. George McAdams is a good man. An honest man. There's no comparison between McAdams and the others you named."

Olli Kinkkonen shook his head in disbelief.

"You'll take that silly notion to your grave, over there, fighting a war that can't be won, in a conflict that makes no sense. You read the papers, don't you? You see how, day after day, biased reporters cheer on the Allied effort, making claims about success after success on the battlefield. And yet, look at the map. The Boche remain entrenched in French territory. Nothing the Allies have done has budged the enemy one inch. Assault after assault has been thwarted," Kinkkonen had said, taking a breath. "Men die in piles, in bunches under the fire of machine guns and tanks. Do you really think that men like George McAdams care one plugged nickel whether you live or die? It's the George McAdamses of this world who are the generals and politicians. You don't see their sons on the front lines, do you? You don't see young Horace Ellison joining up to fight for his country. He'll remain here, enjoying the charms of his new wife, making Ellison babies and drinking imported scotch, while you dodge bullets and try not to inhale poison gas."

Maki's lips pursed. He was on the verge of saying something that he would regret to his friend. Instead, Maki simply drained his beer.

"My train leaves in an hour," Andrew Maki observed casually as he stood up. "I best be on my way."

Kinkkonen finished his beer and stood as well.

"I'll walk you to Union Station," the dockworker offered.

"I'd like some time alone," Maki advised, his dark eyes mirrored in those of the other Finn.

Kinkkonen took mild offense at the brush-off, but gave no indication of his upset.

"Suit yourself," Kinkkonen replied plainly.

Maki detected the other man's anger.

"I mean no disrespect, Olli," Andrew Maki added, lifting his battered Duluth Pack from the tavern's hardwood floor and sliding a leather strap over his right shoulder. "I just need time to sort some things through."

Kinkkonen's face brightened.

"Heidi Genelli?"

"That would be one of the things."

"Elin Ellison?"

"That would be another."

"The wisdom of your good friend, Olli Kinkkonen?"

"That too," Maki admitted as he began to walk west, towards the rail yard.

The men had laughed as they exited the bar. A light early snow drifted in off Lake Superior. There was no force, no significance behind the flurry. There was, however, an element of fragile beauty in the white flakes that descended from the pewter sky.

Olli Kinkkonen caught a westbound trolley later in the day. The Finn was intent upon attending a rally scheduled for 7:00pm at the Work People's College in West Duluth. Minnesota Governor Burnquist's consistent lobbying of federal authorities for a crackdown on dissident labor organizations, most particularly the IWW and the Western Federation of Miners, had eventuated the arrest of 166 IWW leaders. The matter was set for trial during the spring of 1918 in Chicago. The crimes charged against the labor leaders, most notably Fred Jaakkola, Charles Jacobson, Leo Laukki, William

Tanner and Frank Westerlund, all so-called "Red Finns", included violations of the newly enacted Espionage Act by opposing the military draft, by urging the overthrow of the United States government, and by advocating violence to achieve labor reform. Elizabeth Gurley Flynn, one of the IWW organizers instrumental in the General Strike of 1916, was in town, slated to make one of her impassioned speeches. Serious discussions on raising bail money for the prisoners would follow her address. Kinkkonen, like many men and women represented by the IWW, was ready to contribute a small amount of his savings to free the IWW leaders from custody, because he believed those leaders, those accused in the "Case of the 166", had been wrongly arrested.

A New York Irishwoman comes to urge Minnesota Finns to embrace Socialism and rise up against the masters, Kinkkonen mused, adjusting his cap on his narrow head as he sat quietly on a wooden bench in the trolley car.

The trolley bounced over joints in the slick steel rails and over the distressed paving bricks of Superior Street on its journey west. Kinkkonen's mind wandered as he sat on a hard oak seat, his eyes squeezed shut in opposition to the late afternoon sunlight that shone through the dirty windows of the trolley.

Olli Kinkkonen had come to the United States, as Anders Alhomaki had, back in 1908. He had left his mother and father behind in Finland. Most of his other relatives had died during the famines that had decimated rural Finland during the late 1880s and 1890s. There was a brother, a somewhat distant and reclusive fellow, about whose whereabouts Olli Kinkkonen had no information. There were rumors the brother was in the States. Beyond the rumors, Olli had no idea if the man was dead or alive.

When Olli Kinkkonen arrived in Minnesota with five dollars in his pocket, he had immediately set off from Duluth's Union Station intent upon finding work. Work was what he found, and work was what his life had consisted of since his arrival in America. His life in Minnesota evolved into day after day of hard, exhausting, mentally unfulfilling

259

physical work at the behest of others. He owned no property. He'd saved the three hundred dollars in his left shoe. The clothes on his back and the Chippewas on his feet, as ragged and shabby as they appeared, were his own. Beyond what he carried with him on the trolley, his possessions included a potato sack stored beneath his bed at Talonen's Boarding House, containing a few books written in Finnish, a hunting knife, an extra pair of winter Chippewas, a pair of dress shoes, and one tattered old black wool suit, his funeral suit. He was thirty-six years old, single, marginally educated, and, despite his affection for Elsie Laine, unlikely to settle down any time soon.

Am I any better off here than in Finland? Kinkkonen asked himself as the trolley bounced over a breach in the rail, rousing him from light sleep.

Kinkkonen was, despite his lack of formal education, a consistent reader of the various Finnish-language newspapers published in and around Duluth. He was thus fully aware that the Finns had declared their independence from the Russian empire and were in the process of building a new nation.

Was Sylvester Tolonen's lot here in Minnesota an improvement from his life in Finland? Olli asked himself as he watched West Duluth rush past the speeding trolley.

Sylvester Tolonen was an iron miner whom Kinkkonen had befriended upon Kinkkonen's arrival in Duluth. Their brief connection had made a lasting impression upon Olli Kinkkonen. Within weeks of meeting Tolonen, Kinkkonen had read an account in *Siirtolainen* (The Immigrant), a Finnish newspaper published in Kaleva, Michigan, that Sylvester Tolonen had died in a mining accident while working underground at the Pioneer Mine in Ely. A steel drill bit had dropped into an ore shaft, falling several hundred feet before striking Sylvester Tolonen in the head, killing him instantly. Sylvester Tolonen left behind a widow and five young children. Workers' compensation was unknown in the mining industry at the time. Tolonen's children and his widow were left to fend for themselves, to feed and clothe themselves in the dead of a brutal Minnesota winter. The story of Sylvester Tolonen's death, coming so early in Olli Kinkkonen's life in America, hung around Kinkkonen's neck like a millstone.

What the hell was I thinking? Kinkkonen asked himself as he tried to push the image of Sylvester Tolonen's face from his mind. *Sylvester's death should have been enough to convince me to go back home.*

Olli Kinkkonen sighed. The Finn arched his back against the firm wooden bench, the October sun warming the interior of the trolley as the car rattled on.

Chapter 34

Elin Ellison regretted her decision to marry Horace Ellison the moment their vows were spoken and the couple retreated down the aisle of Bethlehem Swedish Lutheran Church.

This was the least responsible, most foolish mistake of my life, the woman had thought, feigning a smile at the pews of well-wishers as she and Horace paraded past family, friends, and acquaintances. *There was no reason for me to rush into marriage. What was I thinking?*

Her intentions regarding the young businessman had formed slowly, after more than a year of contemplation. Elin knew that she and Andrew Maki, a man bound for the Great War on a tramp steamer somewhere in the North Atlantic, were over. They were part of a history that could not be reclaimed. The veil of darkness that had descended over her after her mother's death and Andrew's migration to the Iron Range to work the Alpena Mine hadn't lifted during the intervening years. Her relationship with Horace Ellison, culminating in Elin's final, complete submission to Horace's desires on their wedding night, had merely filled in space, had only occupied time.

That's a poor excuse for a marriage, she thought to herself as she hung clothing on hangers in a huge walk-in closet, adjacent to the bedroom she now shared with a man she did not love. *I was born to live a life of passion and depth. I have doomed myself to days, weeks, and years, of ordinariness. How did I let this happen? How?*

It was nearly Christmas. Although Horace was working for his father, Eustace, and making a handsome salary, Elin found herself in charge of the modest home Horace had purchased for them in the Lakeside suburb of Duluth, out east, at the end of the streetcar line. The home, a newly built, two-bedroom Craftsman-style cottage with a covered front porch facing Superior Street, was her responsibility. In fact, care of the structure, with its narrow fir siding painted a subtle yellow, its windows and trim painted a complimentary white, and its cedar shake green roof, was now her sole avocation. She no longer taught at the Duluth Normal School. Her duties were rooted in the home. Cooking. Cleaning. Laundry. Rudimentary tasks that did not, in any respect, sit well with Elin Ellison.

Their bedroom was at the top of the stairs on the second floor. The room was, despite Elin's internal dreariness, open and airy. Light poured in from the east, from the rising sun, through a bank of tall windows stretching from the oak hardwood floor to the white plaster ceiling. As Elin stored newly laundered clothing on hangers and in dresser drawers, the furniture throughout the home uniformly constructed of dark oak and done in the Mission Style, her eyes were drawn to a steamship, an ore carrier, chugging north along the rocky Minnesota coast of Lake Superior. The boat sat low in the gray winter swells, obviously loaded with iron ore bound down-lake, for Gary, Indiana, or Cleveland, Ohio, or some other steel town.

The nautical scene caused her to ponder where Andrew Maki might be on his journey. Whether the Marine was already in a muddy trench, rifle at the ready, his face kissing the dank French soil as bullets and shells flew by. Or whether he had already fallen in battle, his eyes rigidly open and fixed upon the Parisian sky rising above the killing fields, the No Man's Land stretching between the trench lines of the opposing armies.

Why didn't I try harder to find him before he left? Elin asked, fighting a random tear as she carefully sorted her silk under-things on the thick quilt covering her marriage bed.

Elin Ellison had, at the behest of her husband, taken a leave of absence from her teaching position. The intent of the break was to conceive a child, to bring into the world Eustace Ellison's legacy.

It's not that I'm such a modern woman that I have no maternal instincts, Elin thought as she wiped the tear away, exited her bedroom, and descended the wide oak stairs leading to the home's main floor. *I want to bear a child. I want, at some point, to be a mother. And I am getting on in years. After thirty, having one's first child is said to be risky,* she considered. Elin stopped at a cupboard in the kitchen and filled a china cup, the chinaware's porcelain surface covered by intricate blue flowers, with steaming black coffee. *I do so want to be a mother. I want to have a little girl and name her Laina.*

Elin Ellison sat lightly on a maple kitchen chair and sipped coffee. The woman's eyes followed the ore boat's passage through a big picture window overlooking Lake Superior.

She knew that Andrew Maki had finished his training because Wendy McAdams had shown her a letter Andrew had sent to George McAdams the day Andrew left Quantico, Virginia, the day Andrew Maki shipped out.

Elin knew from the letter that Andrew was one of the oldest recruits in the 6th Machine Guns. Most of the other trainees were adults only in chronological terms. The boys in the 6th being sent to war had not lived life, had not experienced much beyond youthful escapades. At the ripe old age of thirty-six, Andrew Maki announced in the letter to George McAdams that he had finished first in his regiment in physical preparedness. There was boastfulness, an uneasy pride in Andrew's writing that did not reflect the person Elin Ellison had once lived with, had once taken into her arms and loved.

It must be the death of Tim Laitila, Elin surmised, finishing the last of her coffee, rising from her chair and depositing the cup in the kitchen sink. Her hands opened white porcelain taps at the sink, allowing warm water, pumped directly from Lake Superior without filtration into a gas hot water heater, to run over the dishes collected in the sink. She added dish soap and worked the soap into lather.

The loss of a close friend, she considered further, *is akin to the loss of a family member. It causes one to break with the past, to seek solace in risk and adventure. Why else would Andrew, a man with little interest in nationalism, volunteer for a conflict where the antagonists have nothing to do with America or Americans?*

Elin's fingers rubbed a dishrag over the plates, utensils, and cups immersed in the soapy water. Once clean, she carefully removed each item from the basin, rinsed the dishes in water running freely from the tap, and placed them in a drying rack.

A child doesn't mean the end of my freedom, Elin asserted, returning to her own situation. *Marrying Horace isn't the end of my individual life,* she added, wiping her hands on a towel. *I'll use this time to reacquaint myself with my love of the written word; perhaps take a part-time position working for Tyomies, writing stories for our people,* she postulated, referring to the Finnish language newspaper that had moved from Upper Peninsula Michigan to Superior, Wisconsin. *Marriage and children do not mean the end of a woman's ability to think,* Elin Ellison concluded as she drained dishwater from the iron sink.

Horace Ellison had, after his wedding to Elin, and coincidental with the merger of the American Liberty League into the Lincoln Loyalty League in October of 1917, become active in assisting his father, Eustace Ellison, and Eustace's compatriots, Victor Gran, Oscar Larson, and Karl Gustafsson, in galvanizing other young men Horace's age and social standing to begin speaking out against the slackers, draft dodgers, and anti-Americanist sympathizers causing disturbances throughout Duluth's immigrant working class. These young zealots adopted a system of covert persuasion against the peace advocates and trade unionists opposing America's intervention in the Great War. Horace's involvement with these "Knights of Liberty" was something that the young tycoon kept from his pretty new wife.

No need to trouble Elin with the details of duties and responsibilities I owe my country, Horace had rationalized. *The less she knows, given her bleeding heart and unreasoned fondness for the working class, the better.*

The Knights were hard at work nearly every evening, planning, discussing, coming to an accord as to which labor leaders, immigrants, slackers, and Socialists deserved "special attention" from the group. The young men meeting in the smoke-filled Fireside Room of the Kitchi Gammi Club on East

Superior Street considered themselves true patriots, despite the fact that nary a one had volunteered to serve their country in battle. It was no accident that all the members of the Knights had managed to obtain deferments from the draft through means of privilege.

Elin Ellison knew nothing of her husband's newfound interest in conservative politics as she finished her daily chores around the house. Shortly after noon, she reclined wearily on a well-polished Mission rocker in the living room, fatigued by the boredom of domesticity and not from physical exertion, yesterday's issue of the *Duluth Herald* in hand. The newspaper indicated that a well-known labor leader, the fiery Syndicalist and Socialist, Elizabeth Gurley Flynn, was in town to speak at the behest of local officials of the IWW. A rally was being held that evening at the Work People's College, the place Elin had first encountered Andrew Maki nearly six years before.

Elin knew that, in addition to Flynn's well-known support of workers' causes, she was also an ardent feminist and suffragette. While Laina Gustafsson had not been enthused by the young New York orator's political views, Flynn's tone being too Socialistic for Laina's tastes, Elin's mother had evinced a begrudging admiration for Gurley Flynn's opinions regarding birth control, women's suffrage, and equal pay for women.

It's only one o'clock, Elin thought. *Plenty of time to take a trolley to Superior, make application for a position with Tyomies, and then to make the rally in West Duluth.*

Elin Ellison set her copy of the *Herald* down on an adjacent coffee table and scrawled a note in pencil to her husband on a pad of paper, indicating that she had been summoned away to deal with "a friend's personal issues". She then threw her wool coat, the collar decorated in black lamb's wool, around her ample body as she rushed out the door, intent upon hearing what it was that Mrs. Flynn had to say.

266

Chapter 35

The social hall of the Work People's College was filled to capacity. Folding chairs had been set up across the hardwood dance floor, filling every inch of the space with seating. The crowd consisted of predominantly immigrant men: Slavs, Italians, Greeks, Finns, Scots, Irish, with a smattering of Norwegians, Swedes, and the occasional Jew, the faces distinctly white, the hubbub of noise a messy chorus of foreign languages and poorly spoken English. All sat excitedly on the hard chairs, waiting for the rally to begin.

Elin Ellison recognized Matti Peltoma and, in her finely polished, expensive dress shoes, thirty-dollar winter coat, and her fifteen-dollar skirt and blouse, stepped uneasily towards the man.

"Mr. Peltoma, is that seat taken?" she asked shyly, her voice catching as she spoke.

"Miss Gustafsson," Peltoma remarked. "It's open. Please, sit down."

The man next to Peltoma, a thin wisp of a laboring man displaying battered hands, nodded to the woman as if he knew her from somewhere.

"I believe, Mr. Peltoma," the worker observed in Finnish, "that it's now Mrs. Ellison; Mrs. Horace Ellison." The man took a short breath and studied the newly arrived woman. "Am I correct?"

Elin smiled nervously.

"That's right," she agreed, switching the conversation to English. "Do I know you, sir?"

The skinny man extended his calloused right hand.

"Olli Kinkkonen. We met a long time ago. I'm a friend of Andrew Maki."

Elin's face did not acknowledge the prior connection.

"Ah yes, I should have recognized you, Mr. Kinkkonen. Where was it we first met?"

"It was right here, about five or six years ago," Peltoma interceded as Elin Ellison sat next to him. "The Suffragette Dance."

Elin smiled at the reference. The gesture was meant to conceal her continued lack of recognition.

"This is Elsie Laine, a friend of mine," Kinkkonen continued in English, pointing a blade of a finger at the woman seated to his left.

Elin Gustafsson smiled. "Pleased to make your acquaintance," she offered.

"Elsie's English isn't so good," Kinkkonen added.

Elin repeated the greeting in Finnish.

The slight girl nodded, but remained non-committal. Elin turned her attention to the stage.

The meeting at the newspaper had gone well. *Tyomies* had an immediate opening for a freelance reporter. The woman who normally covered political rallies and events had taken ill, chicken pox it was said, and there was no one to cover the event at the Work People's College. Elin's qualifications were impeccable. She was degreed in English from a well-known institution, and had connections, through her mother, to elements sympathetic with the workers' cause. Still, the paper's assistant editor, Tiko Aluni, eyed with unease Elin's dress, her formal manner, her Philistine demeanor during the first few moments of meeting her.

"You're married to Horace Ellison, aren't you?" Aluni had asked in Finnish.

Elin had fought the urge to smile.

In a manner of speaking, she thought. But there was no reason to begin a discourse with a stranger, and a man at that, about the failings of her union with Horace Ellison.

"That's correct. We were married just recently, in September."

"Seems a bit unusual that a woman married to someone who has no love for working men and women would wish to write for a progressive – indeed, a Socialist journal."

"I find politics fascinating. I am not my husband. Nor am I my father."

"Ah, yes, Karl Gustafsson. Prominent attorney and Knight of Kaleva. Can't get much more Republican and Church Finn than Karl Gustafsson."

Elin fidgeted in the pine chair she was occupying in the dingy office of the newspaper. The sound of a banging printing press in the production room next to the office interfered with her ability to think clearly.

"Noisy," she observed.

"Very," Aluni agreed, tapping his hands against an ink-stained blotter nominally protecting the surface of his oak desk.

"My father is a Roosevelt man," Elin said, nearly shouting the words over the noisy linotype machine. "A Bull Mooser."

"I see."

"But you must have heard of my mother, Laina."

Aluni had arrived in Superior shortly after the death of Laina Gustafsson and joined the small staff of *Tyomies* at the Head of the Lakes. Still, he had heard of the efforts that Laina Gustafsson had made on behalf of the disenfranchised and less fortunate.

"Laina Gustafsson is somewhat of a legend around here," the man announced, his voice sounding loud due to the sudden silence coming from the adjacent production room.

"Rightly so," Elin added proudly.

"Now I understand," Aluni had said approvingly.

Elin had been given the assignment and the promise of further work. She was to telephone Aluni each morning to assess the events and news that he wanted covered. Her articles and opinion pieces would be printed, provided the work she did on the Elizabeth Gurley Flynn story was acceptable.

Geno Antolelli, an Italian worker at the United States Steel Plant in Morgan Park and the President of the local chapter of the IWW, took to the stage at exactly 7:00pm. A small group of dignitaries, IWW officials and prominent local Socialists, followed Antolelli onto the stage. Walking with dignity behind the Italian and in front of the other men, Elizabeth Flynn's appearance brought the audience to its feet.

"Good evening, gentlemen," Antolelli began in broken English. "And, I daresay, ladies," he added apologetically, noting Elin Ellison and Elsie Laine seated in the second row of the crowd. "Tonight, we are pleased to have with us Mrs. Elizabeth Gurley Flynn. Mrs. Flynn, as you all well know, needs no introduction. She is, as proclaimed by our beloved brother, Joe Hill, fellow miner, fellow Wobblie, fellow immigrant..."

"And a Swede," someone, obviously proud of his Swedish heritage and its connection to Joe Hill, shouted out from the floor.

"And a Swede," Antolelli added to much laughter. "We know her here in Minnesota for her support of the Strike of 1916. We know her as 'The Rebel Girl'. In fact, in her honor, I have asked the ushers to pass out copies of the *IWW Songbook* to each aisle. There are not enough for everyone, so you'll have to share with a neighbor. Let's welcome Mrs. Flynn to Duluth by singing the song that her friend Joe Hill wrote about her."

Men scurried up and down the aisles, handing out leaflets to those seated in the rows of folding chairs and to those standing throughout the hall. One of the IWW officials claimed the bench in front of an upright piano located immediately in front of the stage and began pounding out chords. Antolelli's voice, a high, beautiful tenor, its only fault a thick accent, began the song:

> *There are women of many descriptions*
> *In this queer world everyone knows*
> *Some are living in beautiful mansions*
> *And are wearing the finest of clothes*
> *There are blue- blooded queens and princesses*
> *Who have charms made of diamonds and pearl*
> *But the only and thorough-bred lady*
> *Is the Rebel Girl.*
>
> *That's the Rebel Girl*

That's the Rebel Girl
To the working class she's a precious pearl
She brings courage, pride, and joy
To this fighting Rebel Boy
We've had girls before
But we need some more
In the Industrial Workers of the World
For it's great to fight for freedom
With a Rebel Girl.

"I give you Mrs. Elizabeth Gurley Flynn," Geno Antolelli shouted above the thunderous applause at the conclusion of the second verse of the song.

Mrs. Flynn, her plain face freshly scrubbed after her long train ride, her dark hair cut short off her shoulders, wearing a plain blue dress with a starched white collar, walked across the platform, embraced the Italian, and stood patiently in front of the podium waiting for the crowd's cheers and appreciation to subside.

"Thank you, workers of Duluth," she began in a clear, concise voice the instant the clapping stopped. "Thank you for that warm and appreciative welcome. I come before you today, bringing the best wishes and support of the International Workers of the World," she began, applause once again interrupting her speech.

"It is a fitting tribute, not to me, for I am nothing more than a speechmaker and organizer, but to our murdered brother," she stopped, placing much emphasis upon the word "murder", her New York accent heavily infecting her speech, and waited for the tumult to die down.

"Yes, murder. Joe Hill was, over the objections of President Wilson, over the objections of most thinking men and women, murdered, plain and simple, by the thugs and robbers who own the factories, mines, and means of production in this country. I did not come here today to mourn Joe Hill. It has been over two years since his execution by firing squad at the hands of the State of Utah. I mourn my dear friend, a wonderful musician and organizer, every day

271

that I breathe. But I did not come here to eulogize or mourn Joe Hill."

The woman's eyes looked across the seated crowd as she took a drink of cold water from a glass tumbler on a table next to the podium. Elin Ellison's hand shook with eager anticipation as she took notes on a secretary's tablet, carefully keeping her Finnish words even on the lines as she wrote with a finely sharpened wooden pencil.

I am watching history, the Finnish woman thought. *No, I am living it.*

"So, here we are, as I have said, nearly three years after the death of Joe Hill. President Wilson, a man who promised to save Joe Hill, the same man who promised not to drag us into the Great War raging in Europe, has been unable to accomplish either promise. And why, I ask you, is this? He is an honorable man. But his hands are tied. Tied by the forces of capitalism that want us to fight this war, to send young men, men like those here in this audience, men who immigrated to this country, like my family did from Ireland, to avoid fighting another disastrous, murderous war over European boundaries, over European sensitivities."

The woman looked hard at the crowd.

"So now we are sending our men to die. For what? For the Rockefellers, the Fords, and the Morgans. Yes, that's right; J.P. Morgan. The very fellow that your new Model Town right next door, Morgan Park, is named for can be blamed, ladies and gentlemen, as can all the other fat cats and bully boys, for dragging America into someone else's war. And why, you ask? Why would patriotic American Captains of Industry send our fathers, our husbands, our brothers, and yes, our lovers, off to die in France? It is for greed. The almighty dollar. Profit."

Elin's fingers began to cramp.

"She's a powerful speaker," Olli Kinkkonen murmured, his eyes watching the pencil churn furiously across the tablet resting on Elin Ellison's lap. "I'm not sure you can capture that in words," he whispered in Finnish.

Elin smiled. Her eyes noted that the laborer's face seemed tired and appeared troubled. She did not know the man. She made no inquiry.

"I'll do the best I can," she whispered in response, her eyes returning to the stage.

"But I am not here today to talk of the war. I am here to urge you all to continue your struggle against the bosses, against the folks that write your paychecks. I want to impress upon you the urgency, the need, for you to shout from the rooftops that the time has come in America for the eight-hour work day."

A huge cheer went up.

"The time has come in America for the five-day work week, so that husbands can spend time with their wives, so that fathers can spend time with their children, and so that working women can be mothers and wives when they are not toiling at the sewing machines and textile mills of the masters."

The crowd took to its feet.

"The time has come for workers' compensation reform so that workers killed or injured on the job are not put out of their homes, so that their children do not go hungry, so that their possessions are not stolen by the banks and financial institutions."

"You tell them, sister," a big Slovenian, his face craggy with age shouted as he stood above the center of the crowd on his chair.

"The time has come for Congress to stand up and be counted, for the unconstitutional laws, the Espionage Act, for the Sedition Act, to be repealed, and for our rights to protest and dissent to be restored to us."

Fists rose in the air until every man and woman in attendance, with the exception of Elin Ellison, who was busily capturing the event in words, had joined the gesture of solidarity.

"That is why you must unite, workers of Duluth, workers of Minnesota, workers of the World. This is what we are fighting for. And this is the task that I lay at your feet. To dissent. To protest. To complain. To lay down your bodies when the police come, when the National Guard is called out, to strike when necessary, to picket when appropriate, and to boycott when the situation demands."

Geno Antolelli joined the woman at the podium and raised his hand to silence the rapturous throng.

"Let us sing 'The Rebel Girl' again, in honor of Mrs. Flynn; in honor of the International Workers of the World."

The house on Superior Street emitted the soft glow of yellow electric light. A decaying Maxwell roadster that had seen better days, its body pocketed with rust, its gasoline motor wheezing from abuse, pulled in front of Elin Ellison's home.

"Thanks for the lift, Mr. Peltoma," the reporter said, as she opened the door against a bitter December wind surging out of the northwest.

"Are you sure you don't want to join us for a nightcap?" Matti Peltoma asked through a smile. "I'd like to hear your thoughts on Mrs. Flynn's speech," the Finn added, trying to conceal his personal interest in the beautiful woman. "I'm sure that Miss Laine and Mr. Kinkkonen would welcome the company."

Elsie Laine sat in the rear seat of the automobile behind the driver. She had been quiet throughout the trip from West Duluth, having made no conversation with Elin as the two women sat next to each other in the car. Olli Kinkkonen occupied the front passenger seat. His eyes studied Elin Gustafsson's face from behind the thick plate glass of the window.

"I'm sure that Mrs. Ellison has other obligations," Olli Kinkkonen said, his left hand pointing to the front of the Ellison home.

Horace Ellison stood on the cold cement stoop of the house, his eyes squinting in the direction of the motorcar, hands on his hips, dressed only in trousers, suspenders, bare feet, and a ribbed t-shirt.

"I think it's best I said goodnight," Elin added quickly, closing the door. "I had a marvelous time. I think you'll enjoy the article. It should be out in a couple of days. Thank you

274

again for the lift," she said, as she turned towards her waiting husband.

Chapter 36
December, 1917

The USS *Dekalb* plowed through the rough seas of the Bay of Biscay, off the shore of Western France. The converted passenger ship (originally a German vessel bearing the name *Printz Eitel Freidric*), was just over five hundred feet in length, fifty-five feet in beam, and was, as of December 26th, 1917, transporting the 77th (C) and the 81st (D) Companies of the 6th Machine Gun Battalion, 4th Brigade of Marines, 2nd Division of the American Expeditionary Force from Newport News, Virginia, to St. Nazaire, France. Below deck, out of the inclement winter weather, Private Andrew Maki, a machine gunner with the 77th, huddled with his fellow recruits, intent upon retaining whatever meal he had last eaten despite the constant pitching and bucking of the dawdling ship.

Maki had reported to Parris Island, South Carolina, in early October and completed eight weeks of rigorous basic training in the company of men far younger than himself. He was, at thirty-six years old, as recorded in his letter to George McAdams, the oldest recruit in his unit. Maki had been insulated from the taunts and badgering of his drill sergeant by the dull ache that tormented his soul, the incredible emptiness that had filled him following the death of Tim Laitila, a Christian man with a family and wife, a believer whose visions of heaven had been fulfilled far too quickly, in Andrew Maki's estimation. Day after day, in the autumnal weather that settled over Parris Island, making it a damp, cold, forlorn environ, Maki did the drills, performed his training tasks, without complaint. As boot camp progressed, as the sergeants became confident in the abilities of the recruits, Maki and the other soldiers were brought to the rifle range to train with .303 caliber British-made Enfields. Having grown up with firearms, and having developed no bad habits from the experience, Maki's aim was true. His rounds struck the heart of the target, regardless of the distance. He was, on the strength of his performance with the Enfield, selected to be a machine gunner. Upon completion of his training in South Carolina, he was assigned to the 6th Machine Gun Battalion, a separate Marine unit being deployed alongside the 5th and 6th Marine Regiments in France.

The .30 caliber Lewis gun was the light, accurate, and reliable weapon assigned to the gunners for their training at Quantico, Virginia, where the 6th Machine Gun Battalion spent an additional four weeks in preparation before being transported by rail to Newport News and boarding a troop ship bound for France. On December 11th, that ship, re-named *USS Dekalb* by the United States Navy (after the Bavarian General who assisted the Americans against the British and perished due to wounds received during the final stages of the War of Independence), made the short voyage from Virginia to New York City to join a Trans-Atlantic convoy.

Andrew Maki began his second sojourn across the Atlantic, the reverse of the trek that had brought him to his adoptive homeland, when *Dekalb* waddled past the Statute of Liberty on December 14, 1917.

It interests me, Andrew Maki had thought as the massive flotilla of transports, destroyers, cruisers, and destroyer escorts churned away from New York City, *that the ship bringing me to Europe to fight Germans was made in Germany and is named after a German aristocrat.*

This realization had prompted a slight chuckle from the Finn, a gesture that was lost upon the young men standing at the railing alongside Maki, as the seventeen-year-old vessel's twin stacks spewed black smoke across the silver maritime sky stretching out behind the New York City skyline.

The *Dekalb's* convoy had encountered no opposition from the Germans until the fleet entered the Sea of Biscay, the watery basin lying northeast of Spain and west of the coast of France. In those turbulent waters, a German U-boat had sent a number of torpedoes speeding towards the vulnerable transport. None of the missiles hit the *Dekalb*. Rumors that the destroyer *Jenkins* had sunk the offending Boche vessel remained just that: rumors.

Maki and his mates grew uneasy as the convoy approached St. Nazaire. Reports of renewed German reliance upon poison gas as an offensive battle weapon, coupled with unconfirmed tales of thousands of Allied troops being asphyxiated in combat, dying wretched, tortured deaths from inhaling mustard gas, chlorine, or, the worst of the agents, phosgene combined with chlorine (nick-named "the white star" by the French), unsettled the resolve of the green recruits, although the mood of the new Marines was more one of apprehension than panic.

The troops were ordered to assemble on the foredeck of the ship as the *Dekalb* entered St. Nazaire harbor on December 28th, 1917, the escort ships remaining behind the transports to patrol the coastal waters as a deterrent to U-boats. Andrew Maki wondered at the warmth of the air despite the season, and marveled at the hustle and bustle of a port dedicated to receiving and dispensing millions of American fighting men bound for the trenches of the Western Front. The Finn's eyes studied the cranes, wharves, and piers of the harbor, carefully taking in the totality of the unloading operation spread out along the waterfront before him. There was, at the moment the *Dekalb* slid slowly into its berth alongside Pier No. 3, a reminiscence, a recalling of the past, which came to fruition within Andrew Maki's mind. Standing at rigid attention, his broad-brimmed campaign hat having been replaced by the narrow sliver of an overseas cap, the Finn's memory replayed the scene of Elin Gustafsson's hurried walk across the tortured wooden slats of a similar waterfront pier in Duluth the day the two of them had left Minnesota for Houghton, Michigan, aboard the *Christopher Columbus*.

"A long time ago," the Finn mumbled.

"Pipe down," Ernst Gruber, Maki's platoon sergeant shouted, in a voice loud enough for Major Edward Ball Cole, the commander of the battalion, to hear. The major stood at the head of his troops, imperiously rigid as the ship snuggled against the pier.

"Yes, platoon sergeant," Maki responded, sweat beading beneath his cap in anxious appreciation of his faux pas.

Gruber nodded tersely and returned his gaze to the front of the formation. Naval officers and sailors, resplendent in their dress whites, had arranged themselves along the upper decks of the vessel, overlooking the troops. The Marines were dressed in campaign clothing, canvas rucksacks hanging from their backs, canteens filled and in place on their belts, their boots newly polished. While the ship was secured to land, the assembly of green fighting men remained as mute and motionless as a tin army standing parade on a child's bedroom floor. The Marines were weaponless. Their Lewis guns remained packed in crates below and would follow the men ashore.

I should write to Heidi Genelli, Andrew Maki thought absently, changing the intentions of his idle recollection as he covertly watched white puffs of scarce cloud pass against the azure blue sky hanging high above the French harbor. *Whenever I have a few minutes tonight, I will write her, explain myself to her*, the Finn mused.

But the truth of the thing was that Andrew Maki was at a loss as to how to explain his actions, his sudden urge to fight another man's war, his need to feel fear, to dodge bullets in a foreign country, to meet death and defeat it, as if, by defining his own mortality, he could somehow obtain a modicum of repentance for his part in the death of Tim Laitila.

If I cannot explain it to myself, the Finn thought as the order to move out was shouted by Gruber and the other sergeants, *how can I ever begin to explain it to her?*

Chapter 37

January, 1918. The Vosges Mountains in Northeastern France. Andrew Maki watched carefully as a French officer instructed Maki's platoon on how to operate, disassemble, clean, and reassemble the 8mm Hotchkiss gun that was now in their charge. Elsewhere in France, the .30 caliber Lewis guns that the 6th Machine Gun Battalion had trained on in the States were being retrofitted on French and American biplanes. The lightweight Lewis was a perfect gun for observation planes and bombers, planes that did not need their guns synchronized to fire through their propellers. It had been a surprise to the entire 6th Battalion, including its commanding officer, Major Cole, that the gun they had trained on, the Lewis, was no longer theirs to use. It fell upon the French, the manufacturers of the Hotchkiss gun, to instruct the 6th Machine Gun Battalion regarding the heavier, less reliable Hotchkiss.

The units of the 6th that arrived in St. Nazaire harbor on December 28th, 1917, marched to an adjacent rail yard and were loaded into boxcars for the journey west. Forty American Marines and their equipment were crammed into boxcars meant for a similar number of physically smaller French soldiers. Maki and his fellow Marines made the cramped journey from the seacoast to the town of Damblain in the foothills of the Vosges without complaint, despite the close quarters. When Maki's unit disembarked in Damblain, it was joined by elements of the 5th Marine Regiment. Portions of the 5th Regiment had been in France since July 3, 1917, the Marine Corps having insisted to General Pershing, the Army commander in charge of the American Expeditionary Force, that Marines be amongst the first troops to land in Europe after the declaration of war on April 6, 1917. It was a newly reconstituted 6th Machine Gun Battalion that set out to learn the intricacies of the stubborn French weapon in the rolling hills of Alsace-Lorraine, while encamped next to the 5th Regiment.

"Maki, aim that gun," Sergeant Gruber shouted as the Finn sat behind a Hotchkiss, the heavy frame of the weapon resting on a steel tripod set upon frozen French soil. "Don't simply rip off rounds towards the target. Hit the damn target," the non-commissioned officer implored.

Gruber stood behind Andrew Maki and Maki's gunnery mate, Private Eb Winslow, watching the performance of his men. Though the sergeant's stocky five-foot-five frame was incapable of towering over anyone, his bulldog face and heavy jowls, set above a thick, muscular neck, accented by his ruddy complexion, cast a large shadow over his charges despite his lack of physical size.

"Yes, Sergeant Gruber," Maki replied, carefully enunciating the words, conveying the required level of respect for his direct superior.

"Winslow, are you that Goddamned stupid?" Gruber yelled out, grabbing a tangled cartridge belt the lanky North Carolinian was attempting to feed into the machine gun and straightening it before the weapon jammed. "Keep the damn belt even. Feed it carefully, or you and the Finlander will be digging German bullets out of your flesh. That is, if you're still lucky enough to be alive."

Not much bothered Eb Winslow. His Southern demeanor precluded internal excitement:

"Yes, Sergeant Gruber. Will do, Sergeant Gruber," Winslow repeated, the words flowing like a child repeating a nursery rhyme heard every night before bed.

"You mocking me, Marine?" Gruber stormed, a faint smile suppressed between his lips as the North Carolinian straightened the belt and Maki's rounds began to hit a disabled British tank set across a leveled wheat field.

The immobile vehicle sat five hundred yards away. Bullets from the Hotchkiss began to strike the tender metal skin of the light tank with regularity. Other gunners had also found their range, hitting disabled trucks, horse wagons, and a variety of other objects set out across the dormant field as targets.

Gruber ambled on, shouting similar admonitions at other soldiers, his gloved hands clasped tightly behind his back, his helmet askew on his round head, as he walked up and down the line, providing criticism, and, where appropriate, hints of encouragement.

"Damn cold," Maki lamented, wiggling his frozen fingers inside the thin wool of his Marine Corps-issue wool gloves. "Must be ten below zero."

"Fifteen, I heard this morning," Winslow added, lugging another belt of ammunition from a wooden crate behind the firing line.

The gunner's assistant fed a new belt into the gun. Maki slid the bolt back, locking the first round into the firing chamber.

"You must be used to this shit," the North Carolinian drawled, his eyes focused across the field, the sun shining brightly off the dusting of new snow that had fallen across the foothills over night.

"You never get used to the cold," Andrew Maki replied, squeezing the index finger of his left hand, holding the barrel of the weapon steady on a mock pillbox set out across the flats at 800 yards.

Rat-a-tat-tat.

The Hotchkiss spit rounds through the delicate mountain air; air made more ethereal under the influence of cold.

"I thought you were a lumberjack," Winslow stated plainly, his soft brown eyes studying the face of his companion as the Finn concentrated on the target.

"One season. The woods in Minnesota do get awfully cold this time of year."

Maki eased off the trigger and allowed the barrel of the machine gun time to cool. Overheating was a persistent problem with the Hotchkiss, something that the French had learned after four years of combat refinement of the weapon. An overheated gun was a dangerous gun for the operator and his crew. The Hotchkiss needed consistent relief from action to prevent jamming or premature firing due to overheating.

Either malady, if experienced during a German offensive, would likely mean a dead machine gun crew.

"How cold?" Winslow asked, his hands tucked inside the waist of his fatigue trousers, underneath his storm coat.

"Forty to fifty below."

"You're shittin' me."

"Nope. It's the gospel truth."

The North Carolinian whistled. "Then fifteen below should feel like summer."

"Fifteen below feels like fifteen below."

Camp life involved drudgery and routine. Every day the men of the 6th trained in various aspects of modern warfare. Sessions were held to acquaint the Americans with the reality of life at the Front: weeks of day-to-day boredom, punctuated with moments of sheer madness. Trench warfare meant not only holding the Allied salient, it included leaving the austere protection of the trenches, advancing across open ground between the two lines ("No Man's Land"), cutting through enemy barbwire, and attacking the Germans in their protected positions, in their trenches. And, of course, the Germans too possessed the deadly new technology of the machine gun.

A direct copy of the original Maxim Gun, the first true machine gun developed by Hiram S. Maxim in 1884, the Machinengewehr (MG08) was a heavy, nearly indestructible weapon deployed in every unit of the German Army. Due to its size and weight, even when attached to a bipod rather than its traditional sledge mount, the MG08 was a ponderous unit. But as a defensive weapon, the gun had no equal. Firing a 7.92mm round at 250 rounds per minute, the gun had an effective range of over two thousand yards. The French and the British Commonwealth troops along the Western Front had learned a healthy respect, based upon thousands of comrades left dead in No Man's Land, for the accuracy of the German gun. Despite this knowledge, the steady and keen understanding of every soldier in the alliance was that, at some point in time, they would be called upon to leave the confines of their trenches and confront the MG08 on open ground.

Maki and his cohorts in the 6th were unlikely to lead any advances across No Man's Land. The Hotchkiss, though lighter than its German counterpart, was not an offensive weapon. Its weight and size limited the ability of the Americans to carry and set the gun up for use while under fire. Gunners and their mates would, of course, advance at some point towards the enemy lines, because the machine guns were necessary to lay down a blanket of fire for further advances. But the gunners would not be leading the charge.

Nighttime in camp. Hot food and tight canvas tents warmed the tired Marines as they confronted the cold.

"You know, the food's not half bad," Andrew Maki related from his cot, wool bedroll drawn around him, his clothing neatly tucked under the foot of the blanket, his polished boots standing in orderly array in front of his pack on the ground beneath the cot.

"Eat all you can now," Winslow advised. "When we hit the trenches, I hear it's canned sardines, salmon, or, once in a great while, cold corned beef."

"I've eaten worse things than cold corned beef," Maki advised. "Ever tried Lutefisk?"

"Can't say as I have."

"Codfish preserved in lye. Swedes love the stuff. You soak it and then bake it. Turns into a mess of ..." Maki struggled for the English term he needed to describe the fish... "quivering goo. Not very appetizing at all."

"At least it's hot food."

"If you don't like what they serve up at the Front, you can always break into your reserve ration or your emergency ration," Maki said.

The Finn's reference was to the two types of personal rations issued to American Marines on the Western Front. More complete, but cumbersome and bulky, the reserve ration consisted of a can of corned beef, hard tack, sugar, coffee, and salt, containing in excess of 3,000 calories. The entire meal was pressure sealed in a one-pound tin can, which the Marines carried in their backpacks. There was little chance a reserve meal would follow its owner out of the trench, given its weight and size. Any additional, unnecessary burden to a soldier about to enter No Man's Land decreased his agility and speed and increased the likelihood that he'd end up a casualty.

The emergency ration was more compact and portable. Each soldier was provided with three cakes, consisting of beef powder and cooked wheat, as well as three chocolate bars. The meal, known as an "Armour" ration, was self-contained in a round can not much larger than a tobacco tin, making it easily carried in a shirt or trouser pocket. But an Armour ration was, due to its taste and dryness, a soldier's meal of last resort.

"I'll pass and try the corned beef," Winslow agreed, turning his head in search of sleep.

Andrew Maki wrote by candlelight. He'd rigged a remnant of fence wire into a candleholder. He wrapped the contraption around the cedar pole holding the tent above their heads. Lights-out was long past but, given the extreme cold of the evening, it was unlikely that any sentries would be wandering into Maki's section of the encampment.

The Finn's left hand struggled to move his stubby pencil, a thick black piece of wood and graphite he'd liberated from the paymaster's desk, against a sheet of expensive stationery he'd obtained in similar fashion.

France
*January 30*th*, 1918*

Dear Mrs. Genelli:
You are doubtlessly wondering what has happened to Andrew Maki since his last letter to you. You are likely questioning why, after becoming acquainted, after spending many blissful days together, after becoming involved with a young boy who has lost his father, Mr. Maki would suddenly and inexplicably vanish. I wish that I could explain my behavior to you in simple terms. I cannot. All I can do is attempt to convey my situation and allow you to judge whether my conduct has been honorable or not.
I have already conveyed the circumstances of the tragedy that befell my good friend, Timothy Laitila. Though you and I have

285

never spoken since Tim's death, I am confident that, due to the swift way gossip travels amongst the Finns, you have been provided with the details of the story. Please accept my apologies for not personally discussing the event of Mr. Laitila's passing with you. There are no good reasons I avoided you after his death. There is no virtue in hiding from you and Joey once the truth of the tragedy was brought to light. If you think me a coward for such avoidance, I cannot disagree with your assessment in that regard.

The best that I can say is that I was solely and totally responsible for my friend's untimely death. I was the man in charge of Wolf Lake Camp. I was the man who decided, against my own better judgment, to attempt the passing of the last falls on the Cloquet River. I am the man who killed Timothy Laitila, left his wife a widow and his daughters without a father. The reality of my failings in this regard is what has compelled my silence. It is also what has compelled me to join the United States Marine Corps.

I am not at liberty to reveal where I am at present, other than to say that I am in Europe, in the country of France, making ready to go to the Front. I cannot tell you which Front or when that will happen, as the censors would likely obliterate any such disclosures from this letter before you receive it. I can tell you that I am safe, that I am with the 77th (C) Company of the 6th Machine Gun Battalion, assigned to the 5th Regiment, 4th Brigade, 2nd Division of the American Expeditionary Force. If you decide, upon due consideration of this letter of apology, to write me, please include all of that information in the address. Your letter will, if addressed in that fashion, eventually reach me wherever I may be.

As to the specific reasons I enlisted rather than waiting to be drafted, I cannot tell you much, other than I determined that, after Mr. Laitila's death, I felt that I had dishonored myself, my friends, and my heritage by my conduct. I allowed a desire to succeed in my employment, the desire to advance my lot in life, to override common sense and the loyalty due to those under my charge. Please understand that my decision to enlist and enter this war was not something done on the spur of the moment. I do, however, sincerely apologize for remaining out of contact with you from the beginning of July until now. I am heartily sorry if my silence, which you must have taken as neglect, was hurtful in any way.

Silence on my part was demanded. It was imperative for my soul that I look inward and determine a course of action. I hope you understand that my intent was not, in any fashion, to impinge the respect and admiration I have for you. I hope that, in time, you will forgive my pigheadedness and allow me to, if nothing else, remain your friend.

The night grows long. Everyone else in my tent is asleep. The candle melts. I must bid you, as the French say, "adieu". I would appreciate a reply if, in your heart, there is sufficient forgiveness to allow that. If not, I will understand.

Very Truly Yours,
Andrew Maki.

With a heavy sigh, the soldier folded the parchment and placed it in a matching envelope. His hands quivered in the cold as he affixed postage stamps to the parcel and placed it carefully inside the top flap of his packsack on the frozen ground next to his cot.

I'll mail it tomorrow, he thought. *It's Sunday. After services I'll have some free time. I'll mail it then.*

The countryside remained silent as Andrew Maki cupped his weathered hands around the flickering light of the candle and extinguished the flame, plunging the tent into darkness.

Chapter 38

Christmas dinner at the home of Karl and Sophia Gustafsson, December 25th, 1917. Helen Lammi, the household cook, prepared a traditional Finnish feast for the family gathering. The table in the dining room of the Gustafsson Mansion was set for four adults.

"Pass the *kaalikaaryleet*," Horace Ellison asked, politely pointing to the cabbage rolls on a silver tray next to his stepmother-in-law.

Sofia Gustafsson moved awkwardly to lift the dish and hand it to her husband, Karl, who in turn, passed the food to his son-in-law. Around the room, platters and bowls filled with *graavi lohi* (salted salmon), *Karjalan piirakat* (Karelian rice patties), *mustikkapiirakka* (blueberry pie), and *pulla* (coffee bread) waited to be consumed by the diners. A huge venison roast, marinated for hours in red wine and served smothered in onions and scallions, sat in the center of the massive dining table, slices of meat cooling in the winter air of the room.

"What's the news of the day?" Karl asked his daughter, cognizant that her position as a freelance writer for *Tyomies* put her "in the know".

"There's growing anxiety amongst steel mill owners and factory managers that there may be, under the auspices of the AFL and the IWW, a massive general strike after the New Year," Elin related, her words mildly distorted by the meat she was chewing.

"Rubbish," Horace Ellison admonished. "We've heard that sort of Red propaganda for the past four months. They'll never strike. The pay is too good; the work, too steady. It's a bluff."

Elin's face reddened at her husband's cavalier rebuke. "That's the information I've been provided. Comes from some fairly reliable sources. The American Federation of Labor is bound and determined to get an eight-hour day out of

Congress while the war is on," Elin related, calm returning to her face.

A platter of mashed potatoes steamed in front of Horace's place setting. The starchy mass gave off a cloud of vapor that settled at just the right altitude to create an obstruction at eye level.

"Well, I don't buy it," Horace Ellison said with authority. "I'd wager ten dollars that labor can't pull it off. Folks want to work and aren't willing to risk good jobs on the chance of an ideal."

Karl Gustafsson nodded his head.

"Well put, Horace. I tend to agree," the attorney said with approval.

Asserting subtle control over the conversation, in an attempt to settle the obvious discomfort brewing between his daughter and her husband, Karl Gustafsson switched topics.

"And the war?" he asked his daughter.

"Nothing is happening in France. The Western Front is silent. There has been fighting along the Italian Front, but to what extent, I cannot say," the woman said, before lifting a cup of coffee to her lips and taking a small sip. "Svinhufvud's declaration of Finnish independence the 6th of December, on the other hand, seems to have set off a civil war. The news is sketchy but, by most reports, the Reds seem to have the upper hand."

"Germany sends aid to the Whites, does she not?" Karl Gustafsson asked.

"That's true," his daughter responded.

"I'd speculate that the Allies are happy to see the Boche units bound for Finland rather than France or Italy," Karl Gustafsson added.

"It's unlikely the assistance will mean much, in the end. I suspect a worker's revolution will bring Finland back into Lenin's hand before the decade is out," Elin postulated.

Horace Ellison's eyes displayed displeasure at the boldness of his wife's prognostication.

"I daresay, Mrs. Ellison, that you are unsophisticated in forecasting world politics," Horace murmured with rancor.

"I daresay that it would be best that you not advance propositions that are unsupported by intellectual integrity."

"Am I too bold a woman for you to stomach, a mere four months after our wedding?" Elin hissed, placing her fork heavily on the white linen tablecloth.

Sofia Gustafsson swallowed audibly. Although upset by the brewing discord between the Ellisons, Sofia maintained silence. Elin glanced at the woman. Sofia's eyes appeared tired. The woman's movements belied her age. An aura of change, something noticeable only to another woman, hung over the young mistress of the Gustafsson mansion. Elin returned her attention to her husband.

"Reverend Sarvela's sermon was a bit much last night, if you ask me," Karl Gustafsson said, in obvious discomfort, to alter the path of the conversation.

Horace Ellison's focus locked upon his wife's pretty face. There was upset, pure unadulterated anger, seething beneath his outward calm.

"Karl, I appreciate your attempting to change the subject, but I would like to respond to my wife's charge."

The attorney sighed. "I think it's best we avoid further political discourse tonight. It's Christmas, Horace. Let's leave the war to the soldiers and the politicians and simply enjoy each other's company."

The young businessman's face suddenly cleared of animosity.

"I quite agree. Could you pass the venison?"

After dinner, the men retired to Karl's study for a smoke, while the women remained in the dining room. Karl lighted his pipe, sweet tobacco smoke filling the dry air, as his son-in-law drew heavily on an expensive domestic cigar.

"What's going on between you two?" Karl Gustafsson asked Horace Ellison as the men sat in front of a fire raging in the stone fireplace, which was the focal point of the study. The men occupied two overstuffed chairs constructed in an out-of-date Federalist style as they talked.

The younger man considered the question. "I think I bit off more than I can chew."

Karl Gustafsson smiled wearily.

"My daughter, as I so plainly related to you when you asked me for her hand, can be a difficult woman."

Horace Ellison blew a cloud of rancid cigar smoke into the warm air.

"Yes, you did forewarn me on that score," the younger man agreed.

"She's like her mother: a brilliant, stubborn woman with modern ideas. You knew that when you married her."

"I did."

"And?"

"I thought I could change her."

The attorney's massive frame surged with laughter.

"Oh that's rich. Change her? No, my boy, that's not something I would wager you'll ever be able to accomplish. I thought I had laid it all that out for you. I told you she was a progressive, perhaps even a Socialist. I told you she valued her freedom and her intellect. I warned you that you would never, as the Germans would say, reduce her to being a 'haus frau'. These things were made abundantly plain to you. And still, despite my cautions, you persisted."

Horace Ellison stared at the undulating flames of the fire. "I misgauged her resolve."

Karl Gustafsson nodded.

"What do you intend to do?"

"It's not that I am unhappy. We get along well enough, when I allow her space and privacy to do whatever she wills."

"Then give her that. To do otherwise, to rein her in with restrictions, will only make matters worse. Trust me, son, when I tell you that the best course is to exercise subtle restraint and patience."

Horace Ellison drew another mouthful of smoke and exhaled.

"I'm not sure I'm up to it."

Karl Gustafsson's massive right hand reached through the smoggy air and grasped his son-in-law's shoulder in a firm grip.

"At this point, my young friend, what other choice do you have?"

The women retired to the parlor to sip after-dinner cordials from imported crystal. There was rigidity between them as they attempted small talk, conversation without meaning or import.

"How is your work at the newspaper?" Sofia asked, as she sat on a satin-covered davenport in the small room. "It must be exciting to attend all those meetings and speeches, to hear firsthand what is going on in the world."

Elin Gustafsson shook her head slightly. "Actually, it's rather boring. I often find myself daydreaming and not paying strict attention to the matter at hand. Most of the men and women who speak at these functions repeat the same old tired IWW or AFL dogma. There's very little that's new and intriguing. But I do enjoy hearing the rare unusual person, such as Mrs. Flynn. Listening to someone of her standing was incredible."

"I read the piece. It was wonderful."

Elin's eyes took in the slender form of her stepmother, a woman nearly identical in age. There was a new fullness, a subdued filling-out, to Sofia that was more apparent under the parlor lighting. The woman's fatigue was also more readily visible as she sat in close proximity to the reporter.

"You look tired," Elin observed.

"I have been."

"Have you seen your doctor?"

There was a gap in conversation as her stepmother sipped liqueur. Sofia Gustafsson cleared her throat and answered, "I have."

"Anything serious?"

Depends upon how you define "serious", the former maid thought. There was another break in the dialogue.

"Not so serious. Manageable."

Recognition stole across Elin Gustafsson's face.

"You're pregnant, aren't you?" Elin asked, her hands beginning to tremble as she spoke.

Elin Gustafsson placed her glass on an adjacent end table and stared bitterly into the eyes of the other woman.

"You are, aren't you?" she repeated.

A long delay, followed by a whispered response: "Yes."

Elin puffed her cheeks in rage and stood up from her chair with a rapidity that startled Sofia Gustafsson.

"Elin..." the woman began as her stepdaughter lunged out of the room.

Elin Ellison burst into her father's study without announcing her entrance.

"Elin," Karl Gustafsson said as he noted his daughter's hasty arrival. "Where's Sofia?"

The young woman strode to her father and stood before him. Her body cast a shadow across a wall of books standing opposite the fire. She placed her hands firmly on her hips as she glared at the men.

"Father," she mumbled in Finnish, her voice choking with emotion, "how could you?"

Karl Gustafsson stood up and extended a hand to steady his daughter. She batted the gesture away with a flip of her wrist.

"What's this all about?" Horace Ellison asked in a startled tone. "What do you mean by barging in and addressing your father in that manner?'

"This is none of your affair," Elin Gustafsson blurted out, her eyes locked on those of her father, who was much taller than she. "This is a matter between father and me," she continued, switching to English.

"Sofia told you?" the lawyer asked, his normal demeanor humbled by his daughter's assault.

The woman drew a heavy breath and raged on: "She did not. I guessed at her condition. She did not tell me. What's worse, my own father concealed the fact that he had impregnated his former servant girl with his seed. What? You thought I might 'make a scene', Father? Well, I guess you were right, now, weren't you?" Elin shouted, stamping her feet against the Oriental rug covering the oak flooring.

"Calm down, Elin," the lawyer implored, his voice beginning to regain authority. "This wasn't meant to cause you harm."

"Not meant to cause me harm? What about Mother? What do you think this would do to her, knowing that you conceived a child with a woman Mother threw out of the house?"

"That's quite enough, young lady," Karl Gustafsson bellowed, his voice striking out at his daughter like a hammer. "I understand that you're upset. It's Christmas. We can let things simmer for a day or two, and then sit down and discuss the situation like mature adults."

Elin pivoted on the balls of her feet and stormed away.

"Come back here," the attorney admonished.

"Elin, turn around and respect your father's command at once," Horace Ellison chimed in, rising to his feet to stand next to his father-in-law, the men's backs to the fire, the heat of the conflagration warming their buttocks.

Elin Ellison stomped out of the room. Unwilling to respond, she retrieved her winter coat, scarf, and boots before slamming the front door of the mansion as she left.

Chapter 39

A crowd gathered around the two men. The combatants were stripped to their waists, their torsos bare to the sixty-degree weather as they warily circled each other, their hands balled into fists and held in classic boxing fashion. Clarence Callahan, a meaty Irish kid from St. Paul, Minnesota, the champion of the 66th Company, 5th Marine Regiment, 4th Brigade, his skin pink in the defuse morning sun, his red hair shorn and laying nattily against his scalp, towered over his opponent. Jerome Pettis, an illiterate farm boy from Bell, Mississippi, was the favorite of the 6th Machine Gun Battalion. The impending struggle, an effort by the Marines to ease the boredom of training in the shadow of the Vosges Mountains, was the culmination of months of weekly contests leading to the championship. Pettis, a lean, angular lad standing five-foot-eight, his abdomen rippling with muscle, his arms sinewy and long, appeared over-matched against the six-foot-tall Irishman. The Mississippian's eyes, however, were fixed and dedicated to his task, as the men moved slowly around the makeshift ring, a cord of rope attached to hand-hewn aspen stanchions driven into the rain-softened French earth.

"Hit the bastard," a soldier from the 66th shouted as the two pugilists shifted about the ring.

"Stop playing with him, Callahan, and deck the little bugger," another man cried out.

Andrew Maki sat on a three-legged milking stool, an artifact liberated by his unit from an abandoned French farmhouse, and studied his charge.

"Steady, Pettis," the Finn shouted over the noise of the crowd. "Make him come to you."

The second in the opposing corner, another St. Paulite, Sergeant Louis Cukela, urged similar caution: "Easy,

295

Callahan. Don't rush. He's yours for the taking, lad. Patience is the key," counseled Cukela, a Croatian immigrant.

Outside the crude prize ring stood a crowd of perhaps two hundred men, including an animated group of Army muleskinners who had just completed a quarter-mile caisson race using teams of rangy, dog-tired mules indentured by the American government to pull field guns and supply wagons. The soldiers' feet sank ankle-deep in black mud, the rain of more than a week having left its mark throughout the Marine encampment. Shouts and jeers erupted from the spectators as the combatants faced off. The crowd's demand for fisticuffs had no apparent impact upon the Southerner, but seemed to rattle the Irishman into action.

Callahan lunged forward, bringing a wild haymaker from his side that aimed his mitt straight at the jaw of his opponent. Pettis danced away from the blow and landed a combination in the ribs of the bigger man.

"Patience," Cukela observed, his high-pitched voice recognizable above the din of the crowd. "No need to bring the fight to him."

Maki smiled. He knew Cukela, had shared a bottle of fine burgundy, a beverage purloined from the same farmhouse as the milking stool, some weeks back, as the men planned the championship bout. The men shared a history. Cukela's older brother, Stanley, had worked with Andrew in the Pioneer iron ore mine in Ely, Minnesota, and had helped Andrew Maki get a job in the copper mines of Northern Michigan when Andrew and Elin Gustafsson fled Duluth in 1912. But whereas Stanley was a prankster and full of the devil, a great drinking buddy and the life of the party, Louis Cukela was all business. Even draining the bottle of wine had not cracked the sergeant's serious demeanor. He was, first and foremost, a career soldier. A Marine.

"Keep your feet moving," Maki admonished, noting that Pettis had slowed his retreat, as if to ready an assault.

Maki understood that the only salvation for the smaller man was to avoid, at all costs, opening himself up to the Irishman's left hook or an uppercut. If Pettis maintained speed and distance, darting in and out, landing multiple left jabs and the occasional strong right to the body, in all likelihood before the fifth and final round, an opportunity to land a stiff right to Callahan's jaw would present itself.

The first three-minute round, the time kept by Captain Euclid of the 17th (A) Company, whose champion had already been dispatched by Callahan in a one-minute debacle of a slugfest, expired without either man landing a significant blow. The second round was identical and brought a chorus of "boos" from the spectators. They had come to see a battle, a centrifuge of fists. Instead, they were being treated to an exhibition of boxing, an art form that did not suit their impatience.

Round four. Callahan began to listen to voices other than his trainer's. He stepped up his efforts to land convincing blows. Nearly all of his lefts missed the mark. The speed of the little Southerner, his lean white body darting out of danger, a retaliation of jabs and body strikes neatly delivered, began to upset the soldier from St. Paul. Callahan's hands dropped. His feet began to catch on the furrows that the men had worn in the mucky soil. Callahan himself knew he was tiring, that the small pillow of flab, all that was left of a once significant gut after the rigors of infantry training, was taking its toll.

Screw Cukela, the Irishman thought. *I'll never last another round. Need to make my move now.*

A minute left in the fourth. Callahan inhaled deeply and launched himself at the smaller man. Pettis was surprised. A hard left hook landed against the Mississippian's left cheek. The force of the blow rocked the machine gunner's head. Blood and spit flew through the moist air. Crimson flowed from Pettis' mouth.

"Stay away from him," Maki called out. "Make him work."

Pettis shook his head as if to resituate his brain in its rightful resting place. He nodded to his second and danced away from Callahan's follow-up, a wild roundhouse meant to end the matter.

Now, Pettis thought. *He's open. I need to take him now.*

Though not nearly as large a man, Pettis realized the advantage of speed, combined with leverage. His first punch, a sharp left to the ribs, lifted the Irishman off the congealed ground and into the air as if kicked by a mule. A combination to the face followed, stunning the bigger man. Callahan stumbled. His face betrayed confusion.

Nighty night, the Southerner mused, as he planted a strong right on the pinnacle of Callahan's jaw.

"I owe you a five-spot," Sergeant Louis Cukela said, walking across the muddy prize ring towards Andrew Maki.

Maki extended his right hand, shook the sergeant's hand in a strong grip, and accepted the five-dollar wager from Cukela with his left hand.

Callahan's friends assisted the big Irishman off the ground and into a stool in his corner. Callahan's eyes were glazed over. Blood poured out of Callahan's nostrils. Pettis' lightning jab had done its dirty work. There was no question of who was the better-trained fighter.

"Where'd you learn so much about boxing, Marine?" Cukela asked Pettis as the lean Southern boy, a lad of no more than nineteen, stood next to Maki so that the Finn could mend a cut over the boxer's left eye.

"Ask the Finn, sergeant."

"Maki?"

Andrew Maki smiled. "I boxed in Finland."

"Must have taken note of what you were taught, by the way your man schooled our big lug," Cukela said, without smiling.

"Private Pettis is a fast learner," Maki noted.

Cukela nodded and shook the boxer's hand.

"Congratulations, boy. That was one hell of a fine exhibition of fisticuffs, wherever you learned it."

"Thanks."

The sergeant nodded to Maki and turned about, intent upon leading his men back to their sector of the encampment.

May 31st, 1918. Pettis' pugilistic exploits were relived and retold over the evenings following the fight but, due to the certainty of looming combat, were eventually relegated to history. The 6th Machine Gun Battalion was rushed, along with the rest of the 2nd Division, 4th Brigade, 5th Regiment, to defensive positions in the French province of Marnes, located to the west and north of the Vosges. The Marines of the 5th Regiment, along with the Marines of the 6th Regiment and the 6th Machine Gun Battalion, were assigned to defend the main road at Chateau-Thierry.

At the end of May, German forces mounted a massive attack, the last major German offensive in the war. The German Army's destination was the city of Paris, a mere fifty miles away. At Chateau-Thierry the enemy reached the zenith of its effort. The forward-most prong of the German attack extended onto a piece of forested ground near Chateau-Thierry, known as Belleau Wood.

Having taken Belleau Wood, the Germans advanced no further. Newly arrived American units of the 2nd Division were rushed into a gap in the French lines located at Chateau-Thierry. The Americans were given the mission of holding the road to Paris, to prevent the German Army from obtaining a clear and direct path to the French capital. The 2nd Division, along with French Colonial elements, Moroccan soldiers, held this line, stalling the enemy offensive short of its goal. It was in this battle, the defensive battle for Chateau-Thierry and the subsequent Allied drive to re-take Belleau Wood, where Andrew Maki would come to understand the nature of war.

Chapter 40

June, 1918. William Burnside studied the man standing in front of him on the other side of a painted pine desk. Burnside's small eyes appeared as mere sequins against the broad scope of his gelatinous face. The other man, his head bowed in respect, five o'clock shadow emerging even though it was only early afternoon, stood at the head of a line of men applying for work with Western Labor, a day labor company owned by brothel and tenement king Eino Laine. Laine supplied men, mostly immigrant men, to companies located along the various piers and docks in Duluth and Superior, paying two dollars for a ten- to twelve-hour workday. Laine charged the companies three. The companies paid the premium to avoid having to manage, hire, and fire the mass of men needed on the docks.

"Name?" Burnside asked as the thin, dark complected man stood in front of the desk.

"Wirta. Olli Wirta."

The response carried a thick Finnish accent. Burnside checked the name against a list of "undesirables", known union organizers or blacklisted Socialists. The name did not appear.

"Ain't you Kinkkonen?" asked a tall, strong-shouldered man standing behind Burnside, the other man's long torso leaning against the rustic raw wood wall of the warehouse office.

Wirta hesitated. Matti Peltoma, the next man in line for work, spoke up: "No, that's another guy. This here's Wirta. I worked with him last summer on the coal dock."

Burnside considered the face of the job applicant.

"Bears some resemblance to Kinkkonen, as I recollect," Burnside remarked, shifting his large body on the small oak chair. "As I hear it, Kinkkonen's IWW."

"Wirta. I am Olli Wirta," the man repeated.

300

A tense moment passed.

"Two bucks a day. Sign here. You start tomorrow. Dock No. 3, over in Superior. A load of new tires. A couple of good days. Then come back. We'll have more."

Kinkkonen scrawled his alias across the ledger and stepped away.

"Next."

"Goddamn it, that was close," Kinkkonen muttered to Peltoma, as the two men stood outside the Western Labor shack on Railroad Street, near the Duluth waterfront.

Peltoma lit a cigarette, a commercially rolled brand, and blew smoke into the warm summer air. Rippled clouds passed overhead, propelled by southern winds assuring that there would be hot, dry days ahead.

"Thanks for the help back there," Kinkkonen added, rolling his own tobacco in paper before tucking the unfiltered end of the cigarette into his mouth.

Peltoma nodded. "Sons of bitches, ain't they? The owners and their lackeys, like Burnside and old Bud there. They are just plain assholes," Peltoma said, as he walked alongside Kinkkonen towards Finntown.

"Read in *The Truth* where the English and the Japanese are invading Russia, trying to help the Whites beat back Lenin. Want to re-install the Czar on the throne," Peltoma asserted in an attempt to change the subject.

"You read English?" Kinkkonen asked, blowing a perfect smoke ring with relish as the men moved slowly over the gravel shoulder of the roadway.

"Well enough to know the Czar's goose is cooked," Peltoma replied in Finnish.

The men continued to walk. Kinkkonen's mind raced. Thoughts collided. English words battled Finnish for supremacy as he attempted to sort out what it was he wanted to say.

"The draft board's been after me to register," he finally said in a whisper.

"You haven't registered yet? You're jeopardizing your chances for citizenship," Peltoma admonished as he threw the butt of his smoke into a ditch that was partially filled with standing water.

"I know," Olli Kinkkonen continued.

"I thought you were taking the citizenship oath. There's no way you will become a citizen if you're avoiding the draft."

Olli Kinkkonen tilted his thin face and pulled a final drag on his cigarette, before dropping the butt to the ground. Kinkkonen stopped to crush the smoldering ember beneath the abused sole of a well-traveled work boot.

"I know that too," the dockworker replied in Finnish.

Near Beaver Bay, Minnesota, along the rugged coastline of Lake Superior's North Shore, the *Blue Heron* worked a raft of birch and aspen logs being hauled across the big lake to a pulp mill in Ashland, Wisconsin, along the lake's South Shore. The gathering of logs behind the vessel extended nearly a thousand yards behind the boat. Iron chain, the links rusted from constant immersion in water, held the perimeter of the raft together and confined the logs. A calm sea, the absolute stillness of the lake's surface, was required to tow the logs the fifty or so miles across Lake Superior. Such weather, even in summer, was a rare thing on the lake.

George McAdams stood with Captain Ian Lord in the pilot house of the retrofitted tug, as the vessel pulled away from the shoreline and headed east for Ashland, across a placid plane of crystal water. His flowing white beard accented the captain's stout stature, the fibers unstained and pristine, reminiscent of postcard depictions of St. Nicholas.

"Great day to make our maiden voyage," Lord observed as he nudged the throttle, requesting more steam for the single screw propelling the boat.

"Calm as piss on a plate," McAdams agreed.

The *Blue Heron's* purchase had been orchestrated through Juda Tylla, the president of the Finnish-American Bank, and had required that McAdams leverage all of his American assets including Wolf Lake Camp and the contract he held against Andrew Maki's farmstead. McAdams was making a calculated gamble that harvesting pulpwood for papermaking could profitably replace the harvesting of pine, tamarack, and cedar stands by his logging crews. Huge tracts of aspen and birch had sprung up behind the protective phalanx of the remnants of the Sawtooth Mountains along the North Shore, replacing the evacuated conifers. McAdams had obtained attractive terms from the mining companies that held most of the tracts to log the softwoods for pulp. But there was no easy means of getting the timber from the North Shore to local paper mills. Shipment by rail to Cloquet or Duluth would be too expensive and require numerous transfers from one logging line to another. The simple solution, in McAdams's mind, had been to move the wood via water.

McAdams Industries was booming. George's brother Adrian, newly installed as the president of the holding company under which all the brothers' various business operations were collected, ran the day-to-day affairs of the holding company from corporate headquarters in Port Arthur, Ontario. George had selected his younger brother as president to relieve himself of the burgeoning stress and frustration that accompanied the rapid expansion of their empire, an expansion accomplished with borrowed money based upon a speculative and uncertain wartime economy. McAdams Industries, like many other boom-or-bust operations of the early 20th Century, was constructed, in a very real sense, on the illusion of safe and easy credit, backed by the value of raw land, land essential for the extractive commerce of Northeastern Minnesota.

George McAdams sipped hot tea as the *Blue Heron's* single stack displaced black coal smoke in response to Captain Lord's demand for speed. The vessel's pace increased to five knots.

"That's as fast as I dare push it," Lord said, his voice deep and resonant within the close quarters of the small bridge.

"You're the boss, Captain Lord. I'm just along for the ride."

"And a risky ride it is, at that," Lord replied, the texture of his voice changing slightly as he spoke, as if he wanted to recall the words.

McAdams noted the uneasiness in the captain's phrasing, but didn't object.

"You're right. Towing sticks across a pond as big as this one is a crazy notion indeed. But, if worst comes to worst and this old tub goes down... well, that's what Lloyd's of London is paid a premium for."

Insurance. A piece of paper written in London and forwarded through the mail to Port Arthur at the behest of Ignatius Steward, the insurance broker used by Adrian McAdams to procure insurance coverage for all of the assets of the McAdams empire. The premium to insure the *Blue Heron* was likely steep. George hadn't seen the bill. That was Adrian's job, to worry about and scurry around paying bills. George's new role, as executive vice president, was to envision the future, to facilitate bold and new means of making money.

Bills. Wendy is spending enough on the new house. I don't need to worry about what it cost to insure this boat, George McAdams thought as he finished his tea.

The house. Wendy McAdams was pregnant. She was a country girl. Her father Henri Heikkonen had once owned a "Finnish rock farm" along the northern shores of Pike Lake, located fifteen miles north of downtown Duluth. Henri had lost the farm when his potato crop died of blight. The note for the seeds was called. The bank had foreclosed on the land, taking back not only the soil, but the log barn, cabin, and outbuildings. The land sat empty for five years. No one wanted to attempt to farm the suspect soil. No buyers came forward to purchase the parcel from the bank, until George McAdams stepped in and bought the hundred-acre spread two days before his wedding. The old buildings were leveled to ensure a fresh start. Now Wendy and George McAdams were engaged in the construction of a new house, a palatial mansion that, when completed, would outshine the Markell Country Estate and its oval horse racing track.

"You look preoccupied, Mr. McAdams," Captain Lord observed as the propeller of the old steamer churned and rattled beneath the boat.

"Just thinking about my wife. We're building a new house in the country. She's likely spending money faster than I'm making it," the businessman said with a pensive smile.

"Isn't that the way of the world?" the captain observed, his comment occasioning the big Canadian to laugh.

"So it is," George McAdams agreed as he turned his gaze towards the east, shielded his eyes from the bright morning sun that was climbing over the sparkling plain of blue-black water, and set his vision on the outline of the Wisconsin shore.

Chapter 41

June 9th, 1918. Andrew Maki withdrew a wrinkled piece of parchment from inside his khaki shirt as he sat in a shallow trench in a reserve line of the American position. The Hotchkiss gun, unlimbered and pointed in the direction of the Germans, stood ready. The gun's tender, Private Eb Winslow, slept at the bottom of the machine gun emplacement, his bare head resting heavily on his rucksack, his steel pot carelessly cast to one side, his body curled around an Enfield rifle that had been issued to him as a precaution should the Hotchkiss jam. Winslow snored loudly. The soldier's snoring was the only sound audible in the quiet sector of the reserve line. Dawn ascended. To the left of the defensive line, gossamer fingers of magenta, orange, and purple foretold the advent of a new day.

A thunder of Allied guns just a short distance behind the Marines erupted and disturbed the quiet. The cannonade pounded German positions hidden in the thick forest ahead, in the forest known as Belleau Wood.

Most Marines of the 5th Regiment had seen their first blood while defending the roadway against a German offensive on June 6th, during an assault on the village of Bouresches. The 6th Machine Gun Battalion remained unblooded, held in reserve, its machine guns delayed in transit somewhere between the Vosges Mountains and the Western Front. The guns finally arrived on June 4th, after which Major Cole, the commanding officer of the 6th Machine Guns, personally inspected the construction of all forty-eight defensive gun pits of the Battalion before turning over command of the individual placements to his non-commissioned officers. Winslow and Maki's site had passed upon first inspection.

On the cusp of his first engagement, beset by nervous anticipation of confronting the unknown, Andrew Maki reclined against the heavy dirt bank of the machine gun pit, his steel pot tilted forward to block out the rising sun, a .45 Colt hanging in its holster, and read for what seemed like the twentieth time the letter he'd retrieved from his blouse:

April 3, 1918
Aurora, Minnesota

Dear Mr. Maki:

It was with much apprehension that I received your recent letter. I was heartened to learn that, at least as of the time of your writing, you remained safe and unaffected by combat. It is my understanding, from reading newspaper accounts of the war, that the Germans are once again set upon taking Paris and that American men, like yourself, will be called upon to stop them.

I can't imagine what it must be like to sit in anticipation of facing death at the hands of another human being, for no reason other than duty. I cannot understand the motivations that drove you to leave home and enlist in the Marines. I know you have explained, now on two occasions in two separate letters, why it is that you felt compelled to join up. Not having known Mr. Laitila, not having been privy to your friendship with him, it is difficult for me to comprehend that such an accident, though certainly tragic, should in any way be responsible for your sudden departure. There is nothing, so far as I have been able to determine from discussing the incident with friends, family, and, on one occasion when I saw him in Duluth, Mr. McAdams, about Mr. Laitila's death that wasn't simply and succinctly an accident.

However, having considered the matter, and though I cannot understand your heart in this regard, I have determined that you know what it is that you must do to cleanse yourself, if such cleansing be possible, of the stain you feel from the accident. I only hope and pray (yes, I pray for you, Mr. Maki, every single night, as does Joey) that you return to Minnesota safely and with renewed purpose and vitality.

As to where we stand, I remain convinced that you are an honorable man. Whether there is the depth of affection between us to command something beyond friendship, I will leave to Providence. Please be assured that I have not, since your leaving, taken up with any other gentlemen. I intend to keep my heart open with the intent upon renewing our bond, wherever that may lead. I am a patient woman.

I had the opportunity to see Mr. Pederson in the café last week and inquire about your farm. He says all is well. The deep snows (another ten inches fell yesterday) have not impeded his ability to come and go, and have not impacted the buildings. The fields are apparently ready for planting once the snow has gone. You could not, in my estimation, have selected a finer man for the job of caretaker. You may be assured that your property is in good hands.

Joey has been asking about his "Uncle Andrew". I have told him as much about where you are and why you are there as a ten-year-old is capable of comprehending. He looks forward to the day when you will resume teaching him how to box, though I daresay, I am somewhat hesitant on that score.

I will close with a beautiful poem that recently appeared in the Duluth newspaper. It was written by a soldier such as yourself. I believe there is value in the sentiments it conveys:

Release
There is a healing magic in the night,
The breeze blows cleaner than it did by day,
Forgot the fever of fuller light,
And sorrow sinks insensibly away
As if some saint a cool white hand did lay
Upon the brow, and calm the restless brain.
The moon looks down with pale unpassioned ray-
Sufficient for the hour is its pain.
Be still and feel the night that hides away earth's stain.
Be still and send your soul into the all,
The vasty distance where the stars shine blue,
No longer antlike on the earth to crawl.
Released from time and sense of great or small,
Float on the pinions of the Night-Queen's wings;
Soar till the swift inevitable fall
Will drag you back into all the world's small things;
Yet for an hour be one with all escaped things.
Colwyn Phillips

Kindest Regards,
Mrs. Heidi Genelli
Aurora, Minnesota.

Andrew Maki nodded, fighting back tears of relief, as he carefully folded the letter, brought it to his nose, and inhaled. A faint residue of Heidi's perfume permeated the expensive linen paper that she had used to pen her message. The scent triggered emotions deep within the Marine's psyche, emotions ill suited for the battlefield. There was no chance, no ability within Andrew Maki to ignore his feelings. He let them come, let them sweep over him like a soft summer rain falling on the calm waters of Papoose Lake.

"Time to get ready to move out," Maki heard Winslow advise, the gun-tender rising from the bottom of the gun emplacement at the sound of Sergeant Gruber walking the line, urging the men to be at the ready to advance.

Winslow gathered up his rifle and placed his helmet firmly on his head as he sat up, his eyes riveted on the wide-open wheat field that stretched beyond the front lines of the Marines' position. At the far side of the open ground, shells from Allied guns burst through the congested forest, where the Germans were dug in. Trees fell in the distance, toppled by shrapnel. Smoke wafted over the ground, enveloping the landscape in disorder. Here and there, rifle shots rang out, sniper fire from the German side determined to pick off any American or French Moroccan soldier foolish enough to peek over the protective rim of their positions.

The barrage stopped. Gruber was at Maki's side, pointing to the woods. "Step lively lads," the sergeant urged. "When I give the signal, pick up the Hotchkiss and follow the infantry across that ground," Gruber ordered, pointing to the farm field.

Maki's eyes studied the craggy face of the stout man.

"We'll take casualties for sure," Maki whispered, fear clear in his voice.

"No time to think about it, Maki," Gruber responded without emotion. "We've a job to do. Our boys will be taking heat all the way across the field. We'll lay down what fire we can from here and, when it's time, we'll follow them into that damned forest. They need us. So buck up, Old Man," Gruber replied, using his nickname for Maki, the oldest soldier in his command. "We're assigned to lay down fire and support the 6th Regiment. Some of their guns are fouled up. It's what we've been called to do, Maki, and we'll damn well do it."

Maki's eyes scanned the shoulders of the American line, fixing on the right wing, where the 6th Regiment was dug in.

"It would be easier if we had the Lewis," Winslow observed, readying gun belts for the Hotchkiss, to provide a wall of fire to cover the Allied advance.

"We'll do our job with what we have," Gruber responded, standing up from a crouch before moving off to alert the next emplacement under his control.

Minutes went by. A loud clamor arose as the men of the 5th and 6th Regiments joined French Moroccan troops exiting the shallow depths of their temporary trenches to attack. The gunners and their tenders opened fire on the woods, raking distant trees and underbrush with calculated fire. The barrage continued for a few minutes. The signal came from Gruber to cease-fire. An unholy pall installed itself over the land. Bright sunlight filtered through the haze of departing gunpowder smoke and illuminated the details of the flat killing field, which spread out for, what seemed to Andrew Maki, an incalculable distance.

Chapter 42

"Let's move out!" Sergeant Gruber screamed, the cataclysmic roar of combat swirling around his men.

The sergeant waved his arm in the acrid air. Clouds of sulfurized smoke distorted the light of the pulsating sun. Maki and Winslow stood up and labored out of their pit, the Hotchkiss slung between them, Maki carrying the butt of the weapon, Winslow the barrel. Other Marines scurried across the exposed farm field, the soil pock-marked with shell craters, the landscape littered with the moaning, writhing bodies of fallen Americans and interrupted by the serenely silent corpses of the dead. Members of the 6th Regiment wandered back through the haze, their backs exposed to enemy fire from Belleau Wood, to escort the machine gunners to shallow positions already clawed from the forest soil by the infantry, in an effort to protect the Hotchkiss teams when they arrived to set up their guns.

"Move it, you sorry excuses for Marines," Sergeant Fred Stockham, a non-commissioned officer with the 96th Company, 6th Regiment, screamed out over the clatter. "You're not doing yourselves any good by dawdling across open ground," the sergeant added, shoving gunners and tenders forward as they passed by.

"Son of a bitch," Maki muttered as the sergeant gave him a significant push in the direction of the Wood.

"Keep it to yourself, Marine," Stockham warned. "It's my job to see to it you make it across this shitty piece of France in one piece. And I don't really give a good Goddamn how I do it."

Maki and Winslow stumbled forward. Bullets whizzed past their heads. Mortar fire and grenades sent clods of moist dirt into the air at unpredictable intervals around them. Men moved like ghosts through air heavy with gunpowder. The south edge of the Wood appeared

311

intermittently through the haze as a black line beneath the clouds of smoke. The Marines slogged on, though men of their number fell by the dozen under the unrelenting predation of German rifles and machine guns.

"Move faster," Winslow shouted as they passed the halfway mark in the wheat field. The gun-tender tripped over the torso of a former Marine torn apart by a grenade.

"I'm moving as fast as I can," Maki replied, his boots slipping on congealed blood and bodily ooze as he struggled to keep up with the taller man.

Shells erupted as the sun ascended. A thunderous ovation of fire from German 105s began somewhere behind the tree line. Explosions rocked the battlefield, tossing men, equipment, and supplies into the air like children's toys thrown in the midst of a tantrum. Earth showered the men as they worked to cross the open ground, totally exposed to German infantry, machine gun pits, and snipers hidden within the thick forest.

One of the other machine gun teams from the 6th, the men's faces invisible behind the dust and grime of the bombardment, made the Wood, only to have both men cut down by enemy fire. The gunner and tender were defenseless, burdened as they were by the heavy gun and ammunition belts. The discharge of German Mausers greeted the men as they stepped from the field into the trees. The two Americans collapsed, their Hotchkiss gun falling with them. No words, no cries were emitted as they died.

"Johnson and Smith just bought it," Maki yelled to Winslow as the gun team moved through wheat stubble and interrupted dirt, the deaths of their comrades prodding them to renewed agility.

"Double-time it," Sergeant Stockham commanded. "Take cover as soon as you make the tree line."

A bullet glanced off Winslow's helmet with a sharp "ping", exposing steel.

"Shit, that was close," the Marine muttered, collapsing into a shallow foxhole, which had been dug in the moist earth of the forest by the 6th Regiment for use by the gunners.

"What's that?" Maki asked, oblivious to the close call.

"The Goddamn Boche shot my helmet," Winslow said, removing the steel pot to show his companion the mark.

"Put that on your head, you idiot," Maki said, "or the next one won't cause just a dent."

Enemy gunfire continued. The two men worked quickly, their eyes wide, their hearts racing, as they set up the Hotchkiss, fed the belt into the weapon, and waited.

Their position was less than one hundred yards into the trees. All around them, the 5th and 6th Regiments had dug in.

Whether there was a need to retake Belleau Wood is a debate that still rages to this day. Having successfully turned back the German offensive at Chateau-Thierry, historians dispute whether the French desire to retake the Wood was fueled by tactical considerations, or whether that desire was artificially enhanced by the American commander, General James Hoarboard's need to show what the American Marines were capable of. The square mile of forbidding forest that became the site of the first significant American offensive in the Great War was not strategically important. The Allies could simply have cut the Germans off from their supplies and starved the enemy out of the forest. That is not what took place. What took place within Belleau Wood was the bloodiest battle ever experienced by the United States Marine Corps, until the battle for Tarawa in the Second World War.

More Marines arrived. The infantry dug in around the machine gun positions, reinforcing the forward line of the American advance into the forest. Wet heat, the force of the sun combined with a smothered atmosphere, cloaked the countryside. Scattered firing. The occasional explosion of a hand grenade. The big guns ceased their roar. The Wood became quiet.

Sergeant Gruber arrived and stood exposed, completely oblivious of danger.

"Well done, Maki. We made it across with only a few casualties. Bitter earth, that farm field was. Other units

313

suffered a lot worse than we did. But we're here, Old Man, and the damn Huns are not going to move us now, are they?"

For the first time in days, Maki noted that Gruber had a smile, though it was more a weary smirk, on his dirty face. The sergeant adjusted his helmet, drew a cigarette, and lit the tobacco, remaining fully exposed to the enemy.

A sniper snapped off a round. The bullet whizzed by Gruber and slapped into the trunk of a defoliated oak standing behind the machine gun placement.

Nonchalantly, Gruber slid his body into the pit with the other men.

"That was close," Winslow observed, his eyes fixed on Gruber.

"No, that," Gruber said, pointing to the silver scar on Winslow's helmet, "was close."

"What's the word, Sarge?" Maki asked, his teeth chattering from nerves, nerves that had not calmed from his race against death across the wheat field.

"We're sitting tight until tomorrow morning. We've got some units strung out too deep, too far into the German defensive lines to ensure their safety. Those will fall back a bit; artillery will open up. Then we'll hit those bastards with everything we've got," Gruber said confidently.

"A question, Sarge," Maki said.

"Shoot."

"Your last name, it's German?'

"That's right."

Maki pondered how to broach a thought that had been nagging him.

"Out with it, Old Man," the sergeant said, pulling smoke into his lungs with vigor as he crouched on his haunches next to the soldiers.

"What is it about this war that compels you to fight your own countrymen?"

Gruber hesitated, stubbing out his cigarette in the wet soil.

"My father immigrated from Bavaria fifty years ago. He's long since passed on. The relatives I have back in the Old Country, I don't know them. I'm American. America was called to fight this war because we're allies of the French. I'm a Marine. My duty is to go where my country tells me to go," Gruber advised. "You start to think too much, Old Man, and you'll just get yourself in a tizzy. Leave politics for the rich. You and me, we're here because it's what poor men do. We fight, and sometimes," Gruber paused for effect, "we die. But not today."

The sergeant stood up, picked up his Browning Automatic Rifle, a light machine gun newly introduced into the war, and left Maki and Winslow to consider what tomorrow would bring.

Chapter 43

Horace Ellison was certain that he had venereal disease. In the nine months that he'd been married to Elin Gustafsson, the deterioration of their relationship had been marked by arguments regarding many things:

The failure of the Senate to pass the Woman's Suffrage Act on May 19, 1918. The passage of the Anti-Syndicalist Act, a law aimed at snuffing out radical labor groups, such as the IWW, or any group seeking to bring about "governmental, social, industrial, or economic change" in the United States. Woodrow Wilson's failure to adhere to his sworn promise of neutrality with regard to the Great War. A.C. Townley of the Non-partisan League's appearance on May 12, 1918 before the Minnesota State Senate to challenge comments made by Judge McGhee, the Judge having advocated the position of Governor Burnquist that any criticism of the Governor's handling of slackers within the state was an act of disloyalty. Nearly daily squabbles over money. Elin's constant absence from the Ellison home, due to her job reporting for *Tyomies*. Her lack of emotion or affection for her husband.

And now, after the appearance of the discharge, the painful urination, and the sores, Horace Ellison was convinced that he'd contracted venereal disease from Beatrice Oddin, one of the "good time girls" he escorted around town from time to time.

Doc Graham handled Horace Ellison's genitalia beneath the harsh light of the examination room. The businessman sat on a wooden examination table, his drawers dropped around his ankles, his eyes closed in embarrassment.

"No question about it," Graham concluded, standing upright in front of the younger man. "Worst case of gonorrhea I've seen in quite a while."

The doctor went to a nearby washbasin, turned on the hot water spigot, and washed his hands with strong soap.

"You're married, aren't you, Horace?"

The businessman gulped warm air. "Yes."

"I take it you didn't get this condition from your wife."

An absence of comment.

"Well?"

"I don't think so."

"You're going to have to tell her."

"That's impossible."

"Let me ask you this. Do you have relations with your wife?"

Hesitancy.

"Occasionally."

"How occasionally?"

"Every other week, except when she's having her monthly."

"Then you must tell her. Gonorrhea can cause serious complications in females if untreated, including sterility and a host of other maladies. I can treat you with colloidal silver. That should do the trick, but if you've had relations with your wife since you contracted the disease, she's at risk. She needs treatment as well."

"Colloidal silver?"

"Combination of silver and albumin, suspended in liquid. It's an unstable mixture, prone to sensitivity to light. You need to keep it in a cool, dark place."

Horace Ellison muttered indiscernibly as he pulled up his boxer shorts and slacks, buckled his belt, and accepted a script for the medicine from Doctor Graham.

"You need to tell your wife immediately. You understand? Her health is at grave risk if she remains untreated."

"I understand," the businessman said as he left the brightly lighted room, conviction absent in his reply.

Elin Ellison sat in the cool interior of the Lyceum Theater, watching a movie. She was tired. An unsettling discomfort

317

bothered her. There was a physical component to it, an unnatural condition involving feminine hygiene. But it was more than that. Her marriage was, she knew now, a horrible mistake, a terrific error in judgment.

To wed without love, for money, for position, to escape the bondage of my father's house, his unholy connection to that parlor maid, was a foolish, impractical act of desperation, she thought, as scenes from *The Whip* rolled across the giant screen in front of her.

She sat in the first balcony of the movie house. She was the only patron for the Saturday matinee sitting in the balcony. As she studied the action taking place in the screen and listened to the rise and fall of the theater organ, Elin considered her life, the life she had chosen since the departure of Andrew Maki four years earlier. The inventory brought a steady stream of tears to her eyes.

What am I to do? Elin lamented silently. *I cannot live on the little money I make from writing. My job at the Normal School has been filled.*

Her thoughts paused as the film's plot suddenly veered in another direction.

He comes to me at night, when I am tired, she thought, refusing to think her husband's name. *I don't want to, but I am his wife. He demands that I give of myself, that I allow him inside me to satisfy his desires. He does not satisfy mine. He is so unlike Anders. His methods are so selfish and repulsive. But there is the likelihood that I'll eventually, despite my greatest reluctance, bear his child. That cannot happen. That must not happen.*

Tears poured out, wetting the folded newspaper, the latest issue of *The Truth*, on her lap. The reporter for the paper had scooped her on the A.C. Townley story. The paper had sent their reporter to St. Paul to hear the famous politician lambaste the Governor. She had not been privy to the speech. Though she'd missed a golden opportunity to set herself above other reporters working for Finnish newspapers, the tears did not fall because of her journalistic failings.

Divorce is out of the question. He'll never grant me one, and I have no basis upon which to prevail without evidence that he's been sleeping around. I know he is. I'm not stupid. I can smell it on his clothing when I take his underwear from the hamper to do laundry. I know my own odors. He is sleeping with someone else. A mistress? Unlikely. He's not that clever. A whore? Perhaps. That's more his style. Impersonal, uncluttered. Pay the tab, then walk away. A fee for services, like getting a haircut. But I have no proof. Without proof, there's little I can do.

The movie ended. Elin rose from the soft, cushioned seat and exited the theater. Outside, the weather had turned nasty. Wind pulsed in from the west, escorting the reality of a thunderstorm. Black clouds seemed to scrape the peaks of the hills surrounding Duluth as the storm boiled through the St. Louis River Valley. Whitecaps rolled away from the piers and docks of the harbor, slamming into the confining contours of Park Point as the waves tried to run out into Lake Superior. Dockworkers scurried along the concrete wharves, tightening lines securing bobbing vessels.

Elin walked absently. She had no current reporting assignment. She had no place to be. Horace was gone, having said he needed to attend to some business in West Duluth. She'd telephoned a friend about having lunch. Wendy McAdams wasn't in.

She made a far better bargain than I, Elin thought as she hurried east, towards the nearest streetcar stop, her black pumps pounding the cement sidewalk, her chiffon summer dress and blouse rustling as she moved. *George is devoted to her. Would do anything for her. There's a depth of connection, a bond between them that, given the differences in their backgrounds, should not be.*

This last thought hung in Elin Ellison's mind as she stepped onto the trolley, deposited her token in the glass receptacle, and found a seat near the rear of the car. Her mind turned over and over, as one's stomach does when something is troubling it, as when a bit of food lodges disagreeably.

Like it was with Anders and I, the woman thought, her eyes watching dollops of silver rain descend. *Like it was with Anders and I.*

319

David Stevens ran his right hand through his red hair. The rich young man, heir to the fortune of MacDavitt Stevens, owner of numerous businesses connected to the logging industry, including Cloquet Tie and Post, slid his fingers through waxy hair tonic holding the wavy crimson fibers in place. David hadn't worked a day in his young, spoiled life. He was a gadabout, a dandy, a man who had never sweated an ounce of perspiration. Stevens wiped the excess hair oil on a rag hanging from the pool table in front of him and studied the arrangement of balls on green felt.

"You seem down this afternoon, old boy," Stevens commented, his eyes steady on the cue ball as he lined up a shot. "I haven't seen you take a drink in years. Somethin' wrong?"

Horace Ellison drained a rye and water as he stood next to the bar, a few feet from the gaming table, in Olcott's West Duluth Tavern. The young tycoon shook his head in the negative before swallowing the liquor, feeling the rye burn his throat on its way down.

"Can't I take a drink if I want one?" Ellison muttered.

"Not saying you can't. But somethin's up," Stevens persisted, stroking the cue stick with precision, the white ball striking the seven perfectly, propelling the colored ball into the nearest pocket before coming to rest, ready for another shot. "You haven't been pie-eyed in years," Stevens continued. "You know I'll keep whatever you tell me in confidence," the redhead said as he picked up his glass of Fitger's draft and blew foam off the beer.

"I'll have another," Ellison bellowed at the bartender, a small, dark-skinned Croatian standing a full head shorter than the businessman.

"No need to holler," the Slav protested, the words coated with accent.

"Just give me the damn drink, Bohunk," Horace Ellison chided, derision clear in his use of the less-than-flattering ethnic slur.

The barkeep frowned, considered the two men playing pool, but did not challenge the insult.

"Probably a Bolshevik," David Stevens added, beneath his breath, as he lined up another shot. The cue ball ran straight, knocking the four into the side pocket. "So what the hell is eatin' you?" the redhead repeated, standing to loosen the tightness in his hips before taking another shot.

Horace Ellison chewed the wet end of a fat Cuban as he contemplated whether he wanted his best friend to know the predicament in which Ellison now found himself.

"It seems I've caught myself a case of the clap," Horace admitted, his voice low in deference to the three other men sitting in a distant booth, sipping their drinks.

Stevens stood up and frowned. "That's a pisser."

Ellison cocked his head in mild annoyance. "That supposed to be funny?"

David Stevens forced a smile.

"Didn't intend it as such. But now that you mention it, it was rather clever of me, wasn't it?" the smaller man said, sliding the cue stick through his hands, sending the eight ball into the far left corner pocket.

"I fail to see the humor in my situation," Ellison lamented, crossing the beer- and chewing-tobacco-stained plank flooring of the bar to claim an empty booth.

Stevens joined Ellison in the booth. Gaslight flickered.

"You seen a doctor?"

"Doc Graham."

"Gave you the cure?"

"He did."

Two men stood up from the far booth and exited the building, leaving only one other patron in the place.

"There's more?"

"He wants me to tell Elin."

"And?"

"She's already skittish. If she finds out, I think she'll file for divorce."

Stevens inhaled a significant breath and considered his beer before responding.

"You haven't even been married a year."

"Ain't that the shits?" Horace Ellison observed, staring at the painting behind the bar: a nude of a young woman holding a lyre in her hands as she walked through a vibrant green pasture.

"You've got to tell her," David Stevens counseled.

"I'm tired of people telling me what I have to do," Ellison advised, the tone of his voice becoming threatening. "I guess I'll do what I damn well think I need to do."

Stevens shook his head, tipped his beer glass, and swallowed the last bit of amber from the bottom of the mug.

"You're the boss, Horace. I just hope you know what you're doing," Stevens advised, covering his crimson hair with a brand new bowler, a hat that looked out of place on his youthful head as he took his leave.

The bar became quiet, except for the clinking of glassware as the barkeep washed dirty dishes in the sink behind the bar. Ellison stared at the naked woman adorning the wall, above the plethora of liquor bottles on the back bar.

Women, Horace Ellison lamented. *The Book of Genesis was right.*

Chapter 44

Bouresches, France. The Marines of the 5th Regiment and the gunners of the 6th Machine Gun Battalion awaited the arrival of the 23rd Infantry, an Army unit, and contingents of the 6th Marine Regiment that had been called up. The Germans mounted a counter-offensive.

The 5th Regiment was tired. Andrew Maki and Eb Winslow had been spared the bloodiest of the fighting, due to their temporary attachment to the 6th Regiment. The two men scurried towards Bouresches, along with the rest of their adopted regiment, under the cover of darkness.

"This damn gun weighs three times as much as the Lewis," Winslow lamented as he struggled over shell-torn ground towards the front, the barrel of the machine gun heavy on his shoulder, the weight of an ammunition box throwing him out of balance as he moved.

"Pipe down," Gunnery Sergeant Fred Stockham hissed. "You want to give away our position to the Germans?"

"Sorry, sergeant," Winslow said, contrition clear in his voice.

Andrew Maki plodded along, the great burden of the magazine end of the Hotchkiss pressing upon his shoulder. The toes of his leather boots, battered and worn from the constant maneuvers and movements of his adopted unit, caught unexpected ridges and furrows in the soft French soil. He was hungry. They hadn't had a hot meal in three days. The German counter-offensive had cut off the supply train from the front, necessitating the use of the trench and emergency rations carried by each individual Marine. These had been eaten cold due to the prohibition against starting fires. The last bit of Maki's Armour ration, concentrated cakes of dried beef powder and cooked wheat, had been digested. He had one chocolate bar left in his pack. The emptiness of his stomach made itself known through loud and uncommon bowel sounds, as the men trudged along behind their comrades from the 6th Regiment, towards the front lines.

Between the lines of the two American regiments, there was open ground to be crossed under the cover of darkness. The men of the 6th Regiment came to the end of their cover and enjoyed a moment's respite before scrambling across the exposed field.

"The other side of that," Sergeant Stockham whispered as his men, including the gunners from the 77th, gathered around, "is where the 5th Regiment is dug in."

Andrew Maki and Eb Winslow knelt on the cool ground and studied the forbidding landscape sprawled out before them, as the sergeant explained their duty.

"We're to cross that field and relieve the 5th so it can push on into the wood to roust out the Germans, who've retaken much of what we had gained," Stockham explained.

The Marines remained silent as they studied the grim reality of their task. Men would die if the Germans figured out that there was a relief column on its way to the front. The snipers located in the wood across from the American defensive position would pick them off like ducks on the flat surface of a pond as they tried to gain the tree line. German heavy guns would drop rounds on them, adjusting the trajectory of the cannons to land 105s and 77s in the opening beyond the American trenches. The success of the 6th Regiment's effort would be based upon stealth. If the Germans were aware they were coming, the advance would fail.

"We move out at midnight," Stockham noted, pulling a timepiece from his shirt pocket and studying it under the soft light of a candle. "It's twenty-three fifteen. Forty-five minutes. Get some rest, but keep alert," he admonished, leaving the congregation of soldiers, his body merging with the shadows as he departed for a final briefing with the officers of the 6th Regiment.

Maki and Winslow found thick oaks, the trunks still intact, the limbs and leaves long since destroyed, and sat down, their backs supported by the lifeless trees. Winslow cradled his rifle in his lap. The weapon had yet to be fired in battle. The Hotchkiss rested on their packs, its mechanism clean and ready for combat. Andrew Maki adjusted his spine against the harsh wood and closed his eyes, aware that all around him, men were doing the same despite Sergeant Stockham's admonition to remain alert.

A vision of Heidi Genelli. Her lean form, her round face, and fragile hair. Her kind manner and feminine voice, the vowels and consonants softly edged. Maki touched the right breast pocket of his field shirt, his fingers dirty from days without washing, the fabric similarly stained. He felt the crinkled parchment of Heidi's letter, the only one that he had received at the front, and found solace in the open possibility that she cared for him. Nothing definitive had passed between them. There had been no promises, no plans advanced which bound them to each other. Still, the soldier believed that she loved him, as he loved her.

There was a sudden shift in the wind. A steady hot breeze blew in from the north, from where the Germans hunkered down in their section of Belleau Wood. The change in the wind caused Maki to consider his enemy.

Do the Boche sit in their trenches, waiting for us, knowing of our weight and strength, new soldiers in an old war, here to push them back, to defeat them?

The Finn adjusted his buttocks on the ground and shifted his holster.

Do they know that they are destined to lose? Do their girls back home, the ones who send them letters, the ones who send their love, realize that their men will die?

Maki's eyes fluttered open. There was movement behind his position. Troops were moving towards the edge of the forest.

"Time to go," Sergeant Stockham urged as he walked briskly down the line of Marines huddled behind the last oaks marking the edge of the field. "Let's step lightly, gentlemen, and keep our wits about us. No dallying. No looking back. If we're lucky, the Germans are asleep and we'll cross this bugger without being noticed."

Rifles and equipment rattled as the Marines stood up and reclaimed their weapons.

"Form ranks," Stockham ordered.

The men quickly found their positions.

"Forward at the double time," the sergeant bellowed.

"I don't like the looks of this," Winslow said under his breath, as he and Maki left the protection of the oaks and began to trot across the disrupted surface of the field.

"Not much we can do about it now," Andrew Maki advised. "Just step quickly, and we'll make it."

Minutes into their journey, the Marines crossed the halfway mark of their trek. There was no sign, no evidence that the enemy knew the relief column was on its way.

Psssst.

A flare shot up into the moonless night sky and burst into showers of light. The marker hissed like an angry snake as it descended, its decline slowed by a parachute so that the entirety of the field was illuminated.

"They're onto us, boys," Stockham shouted. "Make for the trees."

Thunder erupted from somewhere behind the forest's dark horizon. Artillery shells began to plunge towards earth, the horrific screams of their trajectories clear in the evening air. Explosions rocked the open ground. Maki and Winslow were better than halfway across when the barrage began. There was no purpose in turning back. The men broke into a trot, their progress complicated by the burden of the Hotchkiss.

"Move your damn legs," Winslow shouted above the din.

"I'm moving as fast as I can," Maki replied, his voice shaking, his mouth parched, his eyes wide as he took in the carnage of men being tossed whole into the air, only to return to the earth as dissected corpses.

"There, to the left. Let's make for that opening in the trees," Winslow shouted, nodding in the direction of a space in the Wood.

The gunner and tender pounded their boots against the firm ground, maneuvering around the dead and the dying as they struggled to make it across the killing field.

Whoosh.

Andrew Maki detected something ominous, something particularly striking in the latest round of artillery fire from the enemy gun emplacements.

"What the hell is that?" Winslow asked, pointing up into the sky at the unusual shell burst.

There was a moment of eerie quiet. The Americans' forward progress ground to a halt as the Marines stood in awestruck wonder.

"Gas!" Sergeant Stockham screamed. "Mask up!"

The Marines fumbled en masse for their M2 gas masks, French masks supplied to the Americans before they had arrived at the front. Maki and Winslow dropped the Hotchkiss to the dirt and dug into their canvas pouches for their protective masks.

"Move faster, damn it," Stockham shouted, his mask already in place, his voice muffled by the covering.

Gas shells burst all around them. In addition, the Germans continued to drop explosive munitions in clusters around the chemicals, killing or wounding hundreds of Marines as they stood exposed on the flat ground, trying to mask up against the deadly combination of chlorine and phosgene. The impact of the two asphyxiating agents was deadly if a soldier inhaled large quantities of the mixture before fitting his mask.

Andrew Maki had his mask in place and fully tightened when the gas cloud settled over him. Eb Winslow struggled to free his gas mask from its canvas sack, the straps of the unit having become tangled.

A 77-round thudded to earth. Maki dove to his right, away from the concussion. Winslow disappeared in gas vapors, his mask held in both hands, the acrid stench of poison settling over him as he vanished.

Kaboom.

Another artillery shell exploded.

"I'm hit," Winslow cried out from somewhere inside the white shroud of gas.

Maki scrambled to his feet.

"Stay put, soldier. I'll handle it," Sergeant Stockham bellowed, appearing from behind Maki fully masked, a .45 held at the ready. "We can't afford to lose a gunner."

Stockham waded into the descending smog, the atmosphere thick with gunpowder and toxin. His eyes scanned the uneven terrain, searching for the fallen gun-tender. He found Winslow sprawled across damaged earth. Winslow's mask was missing. His hands were clasped tightly to a vicious wound in his right thigh. Blood surged through the tightness of Winslow's fingers, staining his knickers, flowing onto the soft dirt where it pooled beneath the fallen man.

"I'm hit," the Marine whispered as he noted Stockham's considerable form hovering over him like a savior.

"Where's your mask?" the sergeant asked quietly, a lull in the artillery allowing him to speak normally.

"I lost it after I got hit," Winslow muttered, floating near unconsciousness.

"Take mine," Stockham offered, removing the protective gear and placing it over the mouth and nose of the fallen soldier.

Phosgene wafted in the air. Fred W. Stockham held the mask in place on the wounded soldier as the poison sought the sergeant's nose, his mouth, his lungs.

I'm a dead man, Stockham thought as the gas began to irritate his throat. *I'm a dead man.*

The shelling intensified. Rounds dropped around the exposed Marines like hailstones in a storm. Andrew Maki cowered in a shell hole, his uniform covered with dirt sprayed over him by the constant explosions. There was the leg of a man in the pit with him. The man's boot was still on his leg. The appendage looked as if someone had sliced it off at the thigh with a cleaver, separating it neatly, bloodlessly, from its owner. A finger also lay in the earth near Maki's head. An index finger. Left hand. The wedding band was still attached.

"I'm hit," Winslow repeated.

"I'm coming," the Finn replied.

"Stay put," Stockham advised, his words cut short by coughing.

Andrew Maki pulled his body out of the depression, hoisted the Hotchkiss over his shoulder, and lumbered in the direction of the sergeant's voice. Smoke and gas vapor hung over the landscape like a surreal fog. Rounds continued to pummel the earth and explode with deafening regularity. Isolated rifle fire, the attempts of German snipers to pick off advancing Marines before they made the wood, added emphasis to the deadly nature of the exercise.

"Where are you?" Maki called out, stumbling over corpses and gas-affected comrades, struggling to breathe as he dragged his body across the uneven terrain.

"Stay put soldier," Stockham advised, his lungs filling with fluid, his voice failing under the effects of the gas.

The Finn staggered into the shell hole containing his partner and the sergeant. Maki's eyes squinted to see through the fog-distorted lenses of his mask. Winslow's leg wound was tightly wrapped with a cloth bandage. The tender was out cold, his eyes closed behind the mask held firmly in place by the hands of Sergeant Stockham.

"I told you to keep down," Stockham whispered, a low gurgling apparent behind his words.

"Let me help you," Maki said, placing his hands over those of the stricken man, strapping the gas mask in place on Winslow's face.

"Thanks," the sergeant said, his breathing shallow, his face contorted from the effort.

"That was one hell of a thing you did for Winslow," Andrew Maki advised, his words echoing within the mask as he spoke.

Whummmp.

An artillery shell landed a few meters from their position. The shell exploded and showered the three men with debris. A man screamed out in pain from the vicinity where the round struck.

"He would have done the same for me."

I doubt that, Maki thought to himself. *Eb's a good man, but I doubt he'd give up his life for someone he didn't know.*

Maki smiled behind the mask. "The medical officers will be here shortly."

Stockham struggled to speak. "Take him first."

"Medics!" Maki shouted through the mouthpiece of his gas mask. "Over here. Two men down."

Figures appeared. Two medics, conjured whole from the departing smoke, knelt down next to Maki and placed their stretcher on disrupted earth.

"No mask?" one of the men asked the Finn, nodding towards the sergeant as they slid the stretcher under Winslow's broken body.

"He gave it up, saved this man's life," Maki advised.

"Here it is," the other medic announced, reaching into the darkness, grasping Winslow's mask, shaking the dirt free of the device and handing it to Stockham.

Fred Stockham shook his head, sat up, and uneasily regained his footing.

"Sarge, you need to stay down," Maki advised, reaching up to pull the man below the rim of the hole.

"We're in retreat," Stockham whispered. "Best see to my men."

"Sergeant," the first medic called out as Stockham began to stumble through the darkness, "you need medical attention."

"Too late," the sergeant replied, steadying his gait as he went in search of his Marines.

Chapter 45

June 25th, 1918. The 7th Infantry, United States Army 2nd Division, replaced the 5th and 6th Regiments and the 6th Machine Gun Battalion of the United States Marines, 4th Brigade, in the Belleau Wood after a last-ditch German counter-offensive, under cover of an artillery and gas bombardment, failed. However, the 7th did not take the Wood, and was, in fact, in danger of losing the gains made by the Marines. The 1st and 3rd Battalions of the 5th Regiment, and the 6th Machine Gun Battalion were ordered back into the Wood, to reclaim what the Army had lost.

Andrew Maki lugged his Hotchkiss along a tortured path leading to the front line of the American advance into the Wood. A fourteen-hour bombardment by French and American heavy guns had reduced the forest to splinters. The trees in Belleau Wood were empty of leaves. Most were also empty of branches. Smoke hung low over the destroyed foliage, lingering like early morning fog on a country pond. Hunting chateaux and assorted farm buildings within the Wood had been reduced to rubble. The Marines marched back into the fray, to the jeers and derision of the withdrawing soldiers of the 7th Infantry. Catcalls between the units threatened to erupt into fisticuffs. Officers on both sides of the road put an end to the name-calling, as the Marines moved slowly, doggedly, back into battle.

"Take up a position behind that wall," Sergeant Gruber advised, turning his head in the direction of Andrew Maki and Bill Walker, the new man assigned as Maki's gun-tender.

Walker was a short, round ball of flabby flesh that moved slowly but had a keen eye and a quick mind. When Winslow had been carted back to the field hospital, his leg wound secure, his life ensured by the actions of Sergeant

Stockham, Walker was Maki's choice to take Winslow's spot. Gruber didn't object, noting that a gunner needed to have confidence in his tender. Walker's gunner had been killed in the counter-attack launched against the Marines holding the Wood at the far edge of the field where Winslow had been hit. Maki needed a tender. He knew Walker from Quantico and trusted him. It had been an easy decision.

"Load 'er up, Bill," Maki said quietly, the tripod of the Hotchkiss secured on a flat spot behind the rock wall that served as their protection.

The stones of the wall, gray, yellow, and brown, were pockmarked from bullet and shrapnel strikes occasioned during the awful, bloody, seesaw battle between the Americans and the Germans for the one square mile of forest. The wall was mortar-less, held together by gravity. It was substantial and timeless, an artifact constructed by several generations of French farmers. It was all that stood between Andrew Maki and an enemy bullet.

A shout arose from behind Maki's position. A wave of Marine infantry advanced, their helmets cocked across their heads, their rifles gleaming beneath the rising morning sun, their clustered rush skirting the wall, moving at a blistering pace over damaged ground, their faces steeled against fear. These men were now veterans, like Maki, of seeing comrades fall. They were capable of valor, of incredible physical feats, despite withering enemy fire. The Wood, whether the Germans realized it or not, would be cleansed of the enemy by the end of the day.

"Move out," Gruber advised as he approached the wall. "We're to get to the front of the attack, find protected ground and hunker down, setting up a wall of fire to cover the infantry."

Maki and Walker stood up, cradled their gun, and eased the cumbersome weapon onto their shoulders. Walker didn't carry a rifle. He stooped to pick up a box of shells, two bandoliers of ammunition draped across his wide body, before the men moved out at the double quick.

Rifle fire erupted from the last corner of Belleau Wood occupied by the enemy. Marines staggered when hit, collapsing to the soft forest ground amidst shattered bark and branches littering the earth. Hand grenades exploded, tossing bodies into the air, sending clouds of leaves and debris upward in miniature whirlwinds of percussive force.

"There, behind that line of boulders," Gruber shouted, pointing to a protected enclave near the front of the American advance. "Set up here. Rip into those bastards. Show them they can't mess with the Marines," the sergeant commanded, chambering a round into his BAR with a flourish as he gained the rocks and took up a position to provide cover, while the gunner and tender established the Hotchkiss.

Rat-a-tat-tat.

Gruber's Browning sent the Germans closest to the machine gun nest scrambling for cover. Within seconds, the heavy gun was unlimbered and chattering at the enemy, raking the exposed position of the Germans with fatal efficiency.

"Nice work, Maki," Gruber shouted as he knelt next to the Hotchkiss and admired the gunner's aim. "You've got the bastards pinned down good. I'll see how the others are doing," Gruber said, scrambling to the rear of the rocks, keeping his profile low as he retreated.

The Hotchkiss grew hot from use. A round jammed in the chamber, bending the cartridge, wedging the action open.

"Shit," Maki muttered, trying to pull the jammed round out with his bare hand, burning his fingers in the process.

"Watch it," Walker shouted, pulling his .45 from its holster as two German soldiers darted towards the gun.

Crack. Crack.

Marines advancing behind the gun cut down the Germans before Walker could pop off a round. The stout private reached into the chamber of the Hotchkiss, his fingers immune to the heat from years of working as a baker, and withdrew the damaged cartridge.

"Nice work," Maki said, nodding as Walker admired the bent round. "Here they come."

A platoon of German soldiers rose as one from behind a scanty log wall that served as the enemy breastworks.

Maki leveled the heavy gun at the approaching men.
Rat-a-tat-tat.

Seven enemy soldiers threw up their arms and danced as if on strings when the heavy rounds of the machine gun hit them. The remaining attackers abandoned their attempt and ran off.

"Nice burst," Walker said through a grimy smile. "Good thing you had your lid on," the private said, pointing to Maki's helmet.

A crease interrupted the flat green paint of the helmet. The round had struck the steel pot and glanced off, doing no harm.

"Must have been the prayers I said last night," Andrew Maki replied nervously, cognizant of how close he'd come to death.

Men of the 5th Regiment flowed around the gun position. Maki laid down a thunderous fire. The remaining Germans behind the log wall fled, leaving equipment, rifles, and ammunition in their haste to escape the advancing Marines.

A sergeant strode out of the gun smoke and into the morning light filtering through the haze. He was carrying a light carbine and admonishing his men to make haste.

"The boys of the 6th Machine Gun have them on the run, lads. Step lively now, the advantage is ours," the non-commissioned officer shouted, urging his men to throw themselves at the departing Germans without concern.

The sergeant stopped at the Hotchkiss, tilted his pot to reveal his face, and smiled.

"That you, Maki?"

"Sergeant Cukela?"

"In the flesh."

"You're stepping lively, sergeant. God speed to you and your boys," Maki said through a broad smile. "But don't do anything foolish. Cousin Stanley is waiting safe in his easy chair for you back home."

Cukela winked before moving out after his men.
Crack.

A shot, fired from a well-positioned German sniper who had chosen to remain, to fight to the death, rang out.

The sergeant hit the ground. Maki looked at the man, searching for signs of a wound. There was no blood, no evidence that Cukela had been hit.

"Sniper," Cukela shouted, "on the left, in that grove of aspen."

Two Marines lobbed grenades towards the hidden enemy.

Kaboom. Kaboom.

Dirt, leaves, and wood exploded into the air.

"Got him, Sarge," one of the men shouted.

"I don't feel so good," Maki observed in Finnish, the words spoken so softly that Walker and Cukela were unable to hear what Maki said. Sticky warmth spread beneath the gunner's tunic on the right side of his chest.

"Maki's been hit," Walker cried out, cradling the Finn as he collapsed to the ground.

Cukela bent to examine the stricken man.

"Lung shot," the sergeant advised. "We need a medic. We need a medic now."

Chapter 46

The deadline for draft registration was September 12th, 1918. Proclamations of patriotism appeared in the area newspapers, urging the young men of Northeastern Minnesota to do their duty and register for service. Opposition to slackers and war protesters grew to a fevered pitch. Arrests mounted. Protests were quashed. Violence erupted.

In California, Thomas Mooney, an anarchist who had killed innocents with a bomb detonated in protest of the war, a man scheduled to hang for his crime, waited to hear whether the California Supreme Court would overturn his conviction.

Mennonites who had fled to Manitoba from the Dakotas to avoid military service in the Great War were denied asylum by the Canadian Government.

The draft board in Grand Rapids, Minnesota, called upon the proper legal authorities to punish all "loungers and loafers". "Either work or fight," local newspapers proclaimed.

Men and women in Virginia, Minnesota, who objected to the door-to-door solicitation of war bonds by their neighbors, were arrested and jailed under the Federal Espionage Act for voicing complaints critical of the United States Government.

Walter Pasewalk, Secretary of the Minneapolis branch of the IWW, was arrested on charges of sedition and brought to trial in Federal Court in Omaha, Nebraska.

A Federal Grand Jury in Mankato, Minnesota, indicted newspaper publisher Albert Steinhauser of the *New Ulm Post* for printing articles and editorials "disloyal" to the United States.

The Duluth-Superior Traction Company, the owner of the Incline Railway, denied that John Wick, a Finn who had appeared before the draft board to renounce his application for citizenship, was an employee of the company.

John Sacker, a thirty-eight-year-old laborer, was arrested and removed from his job at the McDougall-Duluth Shipyards in Riverside, on allegations that he was pro-German and that he had failed to register for the draft.

Dr. John Steinback of Virginia, Minnesota, was held by authorities on suspicion of making seditious references.

Lumber mills in Northwestern Ontario, Canada, just across the border from Minnesota, erupted in violence due to "Bolsheviki intrigue and unrest."

Explosions at a United States Post Office in Chicago killed four citizens and wounded scores of others. One of those arrested for the crime was said to have ties to the IWW.

In Owen, Wisconsin, one man was killed and six others wounded in a pitched gun battle between the Krueger Brothers and nearly one hundred members of the Wisconsin Home Guard. The Guard was at the Krueger place, assisting local law enforcement in their attempt to arrest the Kruegers for draft dodging. The two brothers escaped in the melee.

These were but a few of the incidents that took place between factions opposing American intervention in the Great War, and those displaying their American Patriotism on their sleeves in the waning days of the armed conflict in Europe.

Olli Kinkkonen sat at a small, round table in the Metropolitan Café across from Elsie Laine, spooning hot pea soup, the green broth filled with chunks of stale ham and soggy potatoes, into his wide mouth. His eyes strayed over the tiny woman seated on the other side of the table, but did not linger impolitely. His mind was preoccupied, unable to give the woman his complete attention.

"You seem distant tonight, Olli," Elsie Laine remarked. "Is something bothering you?" she asked.

The dockworker smiled. His hand reached across the tabletop, the pine surface distressed and spotted with grease, and patted the dainty wrist of his companion.

"I have a lot on my mind," he revealed. "But nothing as important as spending time with you."

His words, spoken in Finnish, did not carry conviction.

"Are you certain you don't want to talk about it?"

Kinkkonen did not want to discuss his personal turmoil with the woman. They were friends, it was true, but his internal disturbance was not something appropriate for public discussion.

"I'm certain," he said, forcing his mouth into a wider smile for appearances.

Elsie Laine sighed and returned to eating her pot roast.

I'm scheduled to take my oath of citizenship in less than a week, the Finnish laborer thought, scraping the bottom of his bowl for the last bit of soup. *And I'm supposed to be at the draft board the day after taking the oath. They'll send me to France. Well, I left Finland to avoid being killed in some rich man's fight. I'll be damned if I'm going to go to war to support the Rockefellers and the Fords.*

Kinkkonen turned the quandary over and over in his mind as he sat watching Elsie nibble her food. His eyes followed the slight curve of her bosom, the narrow waist of her form, taking in her small figure and her bright eyes under the dim light in the dowdy café. Olli's right hand drew a cup of hot coffee to his lips. He sipped gently, avoiding any noise, as he watched Elsie Laine.

"You have a brother who works at a steel mill in Ashtabula, Ohio, don't you?" he finally asked, the inquiry bearing no apparent regard to their prior conversation.

"I do. Samuel. Why?"

Kinkkonen stretched his arms above his head. He was wearing his best dress shirt, a heavily starched white linen affair. He had been careful to avoid shirts with stains around the collar or in the armpits. A narrow black tie hung loosely around his small neck. Kinkkonen dropped his arms to his sides and grinned sheepishly.

"I've been thinking about moving, maybe going east, finding some steadier work."

The woman's eyes widened. Theirs was not an exclusive arrangement. She had other beaus, casual relationships that involved a dinner, a play, a film. Still, it was obvious from the glistening of Elsie Laine's eyes that her emotional bond to the Finn was significant, that she hoped it would evolve into something serious.

"In Ohio?" she asked.

"It's just a notion I've had," Olli Kinkkonen said, downplaying his interest in the idea in response to the woman's reaction. "You say his name is Sam?"

Elsie nodded as she wiped her mouth with a white linen napkin.

The dockworker removed a small pad of paper and a thick stub of pencil from his pants pocket. He wrote the name "Sam Laine" and the words "Ashtabula, Ohio" in careful English on the paper, before returning the notebook to its former hiding place.

"Shall we take a walk?" Kinkkonen asked, counting out enough money to cover the tab and a small tip.

"That would be nice," the woman replied, her concern having abated.

Chapter 47

The *Blue Heron* crashed through waves the height of small buildings in deep water off the North Shore of Lake Superior. Captain Ian Lord studied the Lake rolling and pitching in front of the struggling tug. The vessel's single screw was hard-pressed to make progress against the early autumn weather. The pulsing drive of the brass propeller fought troughs of steely water, encouraged by gusts of wind from the west, from the prairie provinces of Canada.

The boat crawled forward, seemingly inch-by-inch, seeking the protection of Knife Island just off Sugarloaf Cove, the boat's destination. To attain the lee shore of the island, Lord planned to swing *Blue Heron* around the jagged reefs and sharp rocks ringing the atoll, a tricky maneuver requiring that the vessel's starboard side be exposed to the howling wind. The boat, built in 1874 in Detroit as an "outside" tug, a tug used outside the harbors and narrow channels of Great Lakes ports to carry supplies and to tow log rafts, was powered by a fore and aft compound-type engine, rated at six hundred horse power. The *Blue Heron* was returning from a successful run to Marquette, Michigan, having delivered a raft of 500,000 board feet of aspen to a mill there, losing nary a log in the crossing. In addition to Captain Lord, a crew of ten and five passengers pitched and rocked aboard the *Blue Heron* as the tug neared the point of decision.

"It's now or never," Ian Lord muttered to himself, careful to keep his pessimism out of the hearing of his first mate, Alan Farmington, an ugly man whose face bore the scars of countless drunken brawls, fights won and lost in taverns, brothels, and cheap hotels from Duluth to Green Bay to Detroit. "If we don't get out of this gale, this old wooden tub will be bashed to bits," Lord observed, pulling nervously on his white beard with his right hand, a sense of restrained urgency beneath his words.

"Sure we can swing 'er, Cap'n?" Farmington asked, a pug of chew expanding his cheek to Popeye proportions.

Lord stared through the thick paned glass windows of the tug's pilothouse, clouds hanging only a few feet above the prominence of the boat as it plunged and rose with the waves.

"If I've got us on the right line, we'll be home free after we make the turn."

Lord glanced at the magnetic compass. His eyes studied the throbbing needle. Something about the directional indicator didn't sit right.

"That compass look right to you, Farmington?"

The mate glared at the device through bloodshot eyes, the red obliterating all natural color of the man's irises.

"Looks fine to me, Cap'n."

"We should be just off the shoals, far enough away from Knife Island to make the turn," the captain theorized, still puzzled by the compass readings.

Lord pushed the throttle lever to full. The tug's boiler clanked and sputtered. A surge of power slammed the bow of the boat through a monstrous wave. Without hesitation, Captain Ian Lord threw the wheel hard left, forcing the boat's single brass rudder against the frothing water. Slowly, with agonizing stubbornness, the boat began to swing to port, towards the protection of the island.

"She's making the turn, Cap'n," Farmington shouted above the noise of the over-worked engine. "She's a tough old sea dog, she is."

The *Blue Heron's* rudder became unresponsive as the vessel fought the raging surf along the shallow reefs and rocks lining the edge of Knife Island. The boat had made its turn fifty yards before the channel. Instead of riding the calm waters of the island's lee side, the vessel and crew found themselves trapped in vicious waves cresting over rocky shoals.

"Christ," Lord cried out in a voice devoid of calm. "The damn iron in the rocks must have thrown the compass off. We're in too close."

The captain threw the boat's screw in reverse. As the drive shaft to the propeller changed directions, precious seconds were lost, seconds when the surf pounded the exposed stern of the boat, driving it like a hammer pounding a nail towards the shoreline of Knife Island. The propeller churned and splashed ineffectively in limited water. There was not enough depth for the propeller blades to grab hold and defeat the storm.

"Shit," Lord muttered, holding his breath as the boat became suspended between two breakers crashing over the volcanic rock of the atoll. "Shit."

The tug *Edna G* was summoned from Two Harbors, a short distance from Knife Island in good weather, to the assistance of the *Blue Heron*. Dock workers waiting at the pier in Sugarloaf Cove watched helplessly as the lights of the *Blue Heron* bobbed and twisted in the grip of the storm before become stationary, the result of the big wooden boat floundering on the hidden shoulders of Knife Island. A quick-thinking employee of McAdams Timber working the pier dialed the local operator and got a call through to the Duluth and Iron Range Railroad's office in Two Harbors. The on-duty supervisor alerted the crew of the *Edna G*. Within minutes, the sturdy wooden tug was fired up and on its way, battling four-foot seas and a steady forty-mile-an-hour gale up the lake.

No lives were lost, but shortly after all of the crew and passengers were safely aboard the *Edna G*, a mammoth cascade of black water surged across the shallows, rolled the stricken tug on its side, and sent it over the rock shelf to the bottom of Lake Superior.

What the hell am I going to tell Mr. McAdams? Captain Ian Lord wondered silently, shuddering beneath a wool blanket in the wet heat of the pilothouse of the rescue tug.

Captain Blare Potts, the skipper of the *Edna G*, noted the furrowed brow, the anguished look that encompassed the face of his fellow boatman. Potts leaned over and placed a weathered hand on the stricken sailor's shoulder.

"I expect it'll be fine, Captain Lord," Potts advised sympathetically. "I expect the insurance will cover anything

Mr. McAdams lost. These things happen. No shame in losing an old tub like that to a storm like this. No shame at all."

Lord looked into the meaty palms of his hands. Intent on keeping his own counsel until it was time to tell Mr. McAdams the bad news, Ian Lord closed his eyes and tried to empty his mind of thought.

Chapter 48

Fingers of clear water stretched to the northwest, towards the seaport of Oulu on the Gulf of Bothnia, nearly one hundred miles away. Wood smoke smelling strongly of pitch pine rolled off the stone chimney that protruded above the roofline of the sauna. A little boy shivered in thigh-deep snow, his skin pink and bare against the icy cold, his nakedness a common thing to the others standing near him.

"Come back now, child," a blonde-haired woman said gently. She possessed a pretty face, oblong breasts and scant hair over her private regions. The wind out of Lapland cooled her skin as she began to walk back towards the sauna building standing on the edge of the frozen lake.

"Yes, son, it's time to come in out of the cold and warm up," a man added, his coarse, dark hair freely distributed over his body in nearly every location except his prematurely bald head.

The boy, a lad of no more than eight or nine, smiled.

"Can I have some more pulla?" the boy asked in Finnish, referring to the coffee bread traditionally served in Finnish saunas.

"Yes, you may," the woman responded, her buttocks quivering in unison as she walked gingerly through the deep snow in bare feet. "There's at least one piece left for a good little boy."

The treetops of the pines bent and swayed. A blue sub-arctic sky soared above the rolling hills and myriad lakes of Central Finland, a land of plains, deep woods, and gently stooped hillocks. The woman and her husband entered the log building that housed the iron stove and the hot rocks. The boy felt the needle grip of the snow beginning to burn his shins and ankles. It was time to go back in. It was time for pulla.

In the dream, the faces of Andrew Maki's parents were sometimes replaced with his own face as that of the father and Elin Ellison's as that of the mother. When these shifts of fantasy occurred, usually when the infection from his lung wound caused his fever to escalate, Andrew's face, the face of the young boy in the dream, vanished, replaced by shadow. His brother Urho was never in the dreams. Never. It was as if Urho had never been born. In his moments of lucidity, Andrew wondered why that was. He bore no malice towards his older brother, not even for the beatings and rages he'd endured from Urho as a child, whenever his parents had gone away from the farm to the Poulanka town hall for Socialist meetings, or to a friend's neighboring farm for an evening of vodka and cards. For whatever reason, Urho had not, at least in Andrew's imagination, risen to calculated existence.

The dream was always the same. The feel of the cold. Winter. Deep snow. A blizzard in the air. It was as if Andrew's mind was attempting to use visions of his past to chill his body, to defeat the fever raging within.

The 4th Division's lines had moved once Belleau Wood was secured, after nearly thirty days of bitter, deadly contest, during which over six thousand members of the Marine units in the forest died in combat or from their wounds. The dead included Major Cole, the commander of the 6th Machine Gun Battalion, and Sergeant Stockham, who expired two days after giving up his gas mask to Eb Winslow, saving Winslow from the same fate. The Marines were shifted to the west, to Soissons. There, the last German attempt to capture Paris was turned back, sending the enemy packing, clearing the way for the Allied advance on the Rhine. Ten miles from Soissons in a United States Army Field Hospital, Andrew Maki battled fever and delirium due to his chest wound, the bullet having been removed, the bullet's point of entry having been sutured.

It was at Soissons that Sergeant Louis Cukela single-handedly destroyed two German Machinengewehr 08 positions, killing a handful of Germans in a bayonet charge, and capturing four enemy soldiers. Cukela, the unassuming Croatian immigrant from Minnesota who had served his country in the regular Army before re-enlisting to fight in the Great War as a Marine, was being heralded as a hero.

In the dream, as the faces of the man and the woman shifted, so too did the locale of the vision. Papoose Lake replaced the Finnish landscape. The little log sauna that Andrew Maki had cobbled along the shoreline of the lake bordering his Minnesota farm replaced the more refined dovetailed building of his past. And at times, when his mind began to clear, the face of the woman, of Elin Ellison, altered, as if by the wave of a conjurer's wand, into the plainly honest reflection of Heidi Genelli.

"How's the patient today?" Captain Harry Smith, a medical doctor assigned to the ambulance unit, asked Andrew Maki during the doctor's morning rounds.

Maki's journey from the Front to the field hospital at Meaux, on the road from Chateau-Thierry to Paris, was mostly a blur of images, which flashed in and out of the Marine's memory like the newly invented neon signs which were appearing along the streets of Maki's adopted hometown, back in Minnesota.

After being shot, Andrew had collapsed in the arms of Sergeant Cukela. Two stretcher-bearers had arrived within minutes to whisk the stricken Marine to the rear, to a dressing station. There, in the bombed-out basement of an old Catholic chapel, the wound was bandaged, a shot of morphine sulfate was administered and an impervious cellophane covering was applied to allow Maki's lung air to remain inside his chest. There had been no time to thoroughly clean and debride the entry wound, the German bullet having bounced around in the Finn's torso, barely missing his spine, before becoming lodged in a rib. German artillery fire had zeroed in on the old church, causing the evacuation of the injured to the rear.

Orange and gold light had just appeared above the eastern horizon when Maki began the jostling, bouncing fifteen-mile journey from Belleau Wood to Meaux by ambulance. As the sun warmed the ground, blanketing the landscape in the steamy stickiness of summer, the stench of dead flesh – human and horse – rose to greet the noses of the departing soldiers. The corpses of German men and boys littered the once-vibrant farm fields, their flesh gnawed and chomped off piece by piece by hordes of migrating rats. Clouds of flies filled the air and feasted on the dead. As the Allied ambulances skirted the battlefields, the flies followed the convoys, seeking the bandages of the wounded, burrowing deep inside the tattered flesh of the casualties to lay their eggs.

This plague of insects was not all destructive. The maggots that emerged from the eggs left behind by the flies proved miraculously effective at defeating the toxic gases which caused gangrene, although masses of maggots squirming within patients' open sores were not generally seen as beneficial by the majority of battlefield surgeons.

There had been no leaves left on any of the trees lining the dirt roadway to Meaux. There had been no flowers, no houses, no barns, no crops in the fields. For four years, the French and the Germans fought bitterly to control the rolling French countryside, north of Paris. The land through which Andrew Maki departed the War was wasted, ruined beyond any measure of human comprehension.

Shortly before noon on the day of Maki's ambulance ride, the sounds of German Mercedes engines had droned through the sky. A squadron of German Giant biplanes, on its way to bomb Paris, roared overhead. The ambulances pulled off the road. The bombers continued on, indifferent to the ambulances. The noise of the magnificently engineered Giants flying low across devastated farmland was the last memory Maki had of the bucking, pitching trip from the Front to the field hospital in Meaux.

A steady, hot breeze migrated through the white canvas tent. The temporary hospital ward where Maki was being treated held twenty wounded. Odors of disease, filth, and blood mingled with the smell of antiseptic inside the canvas. There were only surgical cases in the tent occupied by Maki. Victims of other maladies – venereal disease and the Spanish Flu (a virulent strain of influenza roaring through soldiers on both sides of the conflict) – and gas victims were cared for separately. There were no female nurses at the field hospitals. The women served further to the rear, in the evacuation and surgical hospitals located in the northern suburbs of City of Paris.

"How are you?" Dr. Smith asked again, his voice etched with considerable patience.

"Better," Maki mumbled, his chest feeling heavy, the result of an abscess that had formed around the entry wound, the sore finally on the mend after days of excruciating surgical debridement.

"The wound is coming along nicely," Dr. Smith observed, lifting the cotton gown covering Maki's torso to observe the inflamed tissue. "I'd say another week and you'll be stable enough to make the trip home."

Visions of choking smoke, calamitous battle, and men falling like harvested cornstalks emerged from Maki's memory as he listened to the broad-shouldered doctor.

His accent is somehow familiar, Maki thought.

The doctor's eyes studied the patient's wound. His mouth turned upward in a distinct smile as he leaned in close, as if to share a secret with his patient: "Yes, I'm from the Midwest, Mr. Maki."

"Where?" the Marine whispered with effort.

"Iowa."

"Never been there."

Smith continued to smile as he delicately excised necrotic tissue from the patient's chest. The skin was beginning to knit together. The lung had already repaired itself.

"You're doing quite well," the doctor continued. "Never been to Iowa? Pretty state. Rolling hills. Farms as far as the eyes can see. Black, fertile soil. And pigs. Lots of pigs."

Maki tried to smile.

"Your accent. You're Swedish?"

Maki frowned. "Finnish," the patient whispered defiantly.

"Ah. A world of difference. Well, Private, I'll check in with you towards the end of the day. But I'd say another day or two, and you'll be on your way to the evacuation hospital."

Andrew Maki weighed the news. The specter of Tim Laitila's body, bloated and swollen in death crept into his

348

thoughts. The Finn closed his eyes, his pain dulled by morphine. The narcotic played havoc with reality, made it difficult for the Marine to concentrate on the doctor's revelation. A sense of unfinished business, the need to experience additional fear under enemy fire, to reconcile himself with mortality; his, that of Tim Laitila's, that of those he loved, percolated behind the veil of his medicated stupor. Maki opened his eyes.

"Can't you send me back to my unit?" Maki asked weakly, the plea of his petition clear despite his infirmity.

"You'll not be going back to the Front. Your time here is done," Dr. Smith replied. "I'll not have your blood on my hands. You're going home," the officer said curtly, but with sympathy.

The reality of the message startled the Finn. His eyes grew wide as he processed the information being conveyed by the physician.

"That's right, man. You're going home."

Tears welled in the logger's eyes. Unexpectedly, his chest suddenly felt lighter, as if the elephant that knelt there had arisen and returned to the jungle.

"When?"

"As I said, probably in a week or so. They'll process you through an evacuation hospital outside Paris, put you on a ship. You'll be in New York by the first week in September."

"Praise God," Maki mouthed, the reference more an accidental reflex than an affirmation of religious faith.

"After what you've seen, maintaining any belief in the Creator is a miracle," the Iowan observed, as he rebandaged the gunshot wound and covered the Finn with a cotton sheet.

Chapter 49

September 15th, 1918. Heidi Genelli pulled a hairbrush through her snarled blond hair. Her cheeks were rosy red. She had been crying. Her tears had not been shed in sadness but in joy.

Mrs. Heidi Genelli
Aurora, Minnesota

August 15th, 1918
New York, New York

Dear Mrs. Genelli:

It is with much happiness that I report to you that I am back in the United States. The circumstances of my sudden departure from the battlefields of Northern France are not, at this juncture, important. What is important is that I have survived my baptism of fire with only minor residual consequences.

There is much that I wish to say to you. Having had many weeks of convalescence to ponder things over while under the expert watch of kind doctors and nurses, I believe that I owe you more than a mere apology for my disrespectful conduct. It is clear that there is more in my heart for you than simple affection. I dare not write the word in this letter for fear that you will laugh at my infantile emotions. I will, however, broach such topics with you in person the first time I am able to see you, which, according to the doctors, should be around the middle of September.

Enough of that. How is the little prizefighter? I expect he has grown like a weed in the year since I have been away. I do so wish to spend time with him, with your permission, and educate him in the ways of settling conflicts without resorting to fists. There is much I have seen in the war that replicates the unreasoned fights of little children. There must, as President Wilson asserts, be a better way to resolve differences between nations. *Whether that is a League of Nations, as he proposes, or some other mechanism, I am not schooled enough to say.*

But I ramble. I have missed you. I have missed our walks together along the sidewalks of little Aurora. I have missed taking you to my farm on Papoose Lake in my paltry attempt to show you the future. I have missed your yellow hair, blue eyes, and slightly crooked smile. There is a word I wish to whisper to you in the quiet of the night, a word I dare not write on this page. Please forgive me for these last few lines. I cannot help myself. I will explain my feelings to you as soon as you will allow me to do so.

     Fondly,
     Andrew

The letter had arrived unexpectedly. She had torn open the tattered envelope, the paper dirty and crumpled from its journey across the country, and read each and every word with heart-rending deliberation.

Love, she had concluded. *He is expressing that he loves me.*

The impact of this realization forced Heidi Genelli to sit down at her kitchen table with the letter and consider what Andrew Maki's declaration of affection meant to her.

But do I love him? she had asked herself as she sipped warm coffee, diluted with heavy cream and sweetened with brown sugar. *Do I want to walk into those waters again, having almost drowned once, after the death of Joseph?*

The morning sky had sat high and blue above the tiny mining town of Aurora the day the letter arrived. Heidi Genelli had walked down the narrow staircase from the apartment she shared with her son and father, found her father beginning the day's work in the restaurant, and told him she needed to take a walk. Her father had seen the letter in her hand and suspected the worst. He nodded his acquiescence, giving her the permission she sought to absent herself from work for a time.

Walking the concrete sidewalk that bordered the wide, newly paved street in front of Olson's Café, Heidi Genelli took deep breaths of morning air, autumn apparent in the atmosphere. Iron ore dust from the nearby mines gave the air a reddish hue. Heidi's blue eyes teared. Her face became tight. There was an uncertainty in her gait as she considered the contents of Andrew Maki's letter.

Love, the tall, narrow-hipped Finnish woman thought. *What is love? Mutual admiration? Respect? The ability to talk about things that are important? Torrid sexual desire?*

This last thought embarrassed Heidi Genelli as it surfaced, causing her to blush. There was no one out and about on the street to see her face flash red and then abate.

Andrew is a kind man. An honest man. A faithful man. Shouldn't that be enough? Shouldn't I be able to overlook his history, his scandalous relationship with Elin Gustafsson?

Andrew Maki had bared his soul to her, told her about his relationship with Elin. The details had been spared, but the gist of the connection had been made obvious.

They lived together in sin. As husband and wife without benefit of the sacrament.

Heidi Genelli had converted to Catholicism when she married Joseph. Her father's conversion soon followed. She, Joey, and Jerome were regular attendees at Sunday services at Holy Rosary in Aurora. Heidi Genelli was a serious believer. This was one area in which she and Andrew Maki differed, though there had been no arguments or quarrels between them involving religion. Their discussion had been intelligent and adult. She was a Christian. He was uncertain as to the quality of his belief.

Perhaps it is my task to make him see the beauty of the Lord, Heidi had thought as her path brought her back to the front door of Olson's Café. *Perhaps, after all he has been through, after all he has seen, God is calling me to help him find Grace.*

The woman stood up and studied her hair, her make-up, and her dress, a long shift she'd purchased by mail order through the Sears and Roebuck catalog. Heidi Genelli smiled. Her slender fingers, the nails absent of polish but cleaned and filed to perfection, touched the worn script of the envelope resting on her dressing table. With much thought, she fingered her wedding band as she studied the envelope. Nodding, she removed the ring and placed it carefully in her jewelry box. She massaged the envelope on her dressing table. She did not pick up the document. Instead, her fingers wrapped around a train ticket, a ticket for a Duluth, Missabe and Northern passenger train leaving from Virginia and bound for Duluth. She nodded at the oval mirror and came to the realization that her reflection contained the answer to her question. It was in considering her own image that Heidi Genelli came to understand that she did indeed love Andrew Maki.

Chapter 50

Olli Kinkkonen and Matti Peltoma waited at Duluth's Union Depot for the train from Chicago. They had received a telegram from Andrew Maki, asking them to be there when he arrived. Kinkkonen had arranged with Charles Talonen for a bed to be made available for the returning veteran at Talonen's boarding house in Finntown. It was expected that Maki would stay the night and then catch the train to the Iron Range, making his way eventually to his farm on Papoose Lake. Kinkkonen and Peltoma knew nothing of their friend's intentions with respect to Heidi Genelli. So far as they were aware, Maki's connection to the widow had been severed when Andrew Maki left for the war. To their understanding, Andrew was coming back to the life of a bachelor farmer. A war hero, yes, but one destined to lead a quiet, solitary existence, like so many other single Finnish men in their middle years.

"He's been wounded, you know," Kinkkonen said, as the two Finns sat on a hard, wooden bench in the cavernous lobby of the train depot.

"Shot in the chest, as I heard it," Peltoma advised, his hands resting on his lap, his dark brown beard, the fibers flecked with gray, trimmed for the occasion. A Dobbs Daily dress hat rested on Peltoma's bald head. Wisps of brown hair, the color identical to that of Peltoma's beard, escaped from beneath the edges of the hat.

Kinkkonen's head was bare. His eight-quarter cap, the brim snapped to the cap, the light gray wool of the headgear soiled from constant use, rested in his fingers, the joints gnarled from premature arthritis. His long black hair was slick with tonic. His suit was rumpled and distressed, in need of replacement. His black shoes, newly polished and looking smart, rested against the tile surface of the Depot floor. Kinkkonen's left foot was cramped. His entire life savings, over four hundred dollars now, were crammed into the bottom of the shoe.

Another man, a large man, approached the two Finns on the bench. The man was decked out in an expensive worsted wool suit – brown tweed – and a matching Homburg. The man's fiery red hair cascaded down from beneath the fabric of the hat, nearly reaching his shoulders. His skin was pink, like that of a new baby's bottom. His jowls, their expanse covered in a stiff red beard and muttonchops, jiggled as he walked.

"Mr. McAdams," Olli Kinkkonen called out, rising to his feet as the Canadian approached. "Nice to see you."

George McAdams stopped at the bench and extended his hand to the Finn. Kinkkonen accepted the gesture and shook the larger man's hand. Peltoma stood as well and repeated the familiarity.

"I take it you're waiting for our returning hero," McAdams said loudly, his voice echoing in the near-empty space.

They were thirty minutes early. There were few patrons in the depot. McAdams dug into his vest pocket and withdrew a watch.

"Only eight o'clock," he observed. "Still a half-hour until Maki gets in."

The men nodded.

"I'll spring for coffee at the St. Louis," the Canadian entrepreneur offered. "It's only a block away."

"Sweet rolls, too?" Kinkkonen added, a look of mischief about his face.

McAdams chuckled.

"Sweet rolls, too."

The men departed the building. Outside, an Indian summer sun ascended over Lake Superior. Yellow light, clearly autumnal and a harbinger of the change of seasons along the North Shore, filtered through the dingy city atmosphere, through air contaminated with coal dust and wood smoke.

McAdams strolled with the Finns, restraining his broad gait, matching their pace. As he walked, his mind became lost in personal concerns, concerns wholly unrelated to the return of Andrew Maki.

There were problems brewing with McAdams Brothers Industries, Inc., the corporate label that was the umbrella for George and Adrian McAdams's American holdings. The loss of the *Blue Heron*, an investment of more than a hundred thousand dollars, should not have, in the normal course of business, caused alarm. Adrian's failure to secure maritime insurance on the vessel, after having been directly advised to do so by his brother, created the difficulty. The tug had been financed through Juda Tylla's Finnish-American Bank. The bank had sold the mortgage on the boat to Amalgamated Investments, a holding company owned by Eustace Ellison.

Ellison had not only acquired the mortgage on the vessel, he had also obtained mortgage notes on Wolf Lake Camp and the North Shore aspen tracts being logged by the McAdams brothers. The money loaned to McAdams by the bank against these properties had been used to build George and Wendy McAdams's seasonal mansion on Pike Lake. Due to cash flow problems, additional security had also been given by McAdams Brothers Industries to secure operational funds for their logging business. All of these securities were acquired by Eustace Ellison and provided the tycoon with a significant measure of control over George McAdams's financial well-being. Ellison's newly acquired financial position also included the land contract covering Andrew Maki's Papoose Lake property.

That stupid son of a bitch, George McAdams thought as the three men walked into the restaurant of the St. Louis Hotel. *I put Adrian in charge of a few minor details – paying taxes, procuring insurance. What does he do? He spends his time fishing, hunting, and carousing. He ignores the necessities of business, but relishes in the profits my hard work brings home. I hope to God that this is the end of his failings, that he's learned his lesson. Come the end of the year, I'll evaluate our arrangement. If he's been negligent in any other way, I'll sever our relationship, even if it means going to court.*

"Pardon me, Mr. McAdams," Kinkkonen interrupted as the men were shown a table, "but you seem preoccupied. Anything wrong?"

McAdams put on his best poker face.

"Nothing a good cup of coffee and a hot caramel roll won't cure."

The Union Pacific steam locomotive chugged over sleek steel rails and solidly anchored, creosoted ties, sending clouds of thick coal smoke billowing into the polluted air. The three men stood on the loading platform, behind the cautious form of a conductor, and watched the mighty engine ease to a graceful stop. White steam blew from the locomotive's brake lines, concealing the engine, coal tender, and passenger cars from the crowd of people gathered on the platform to meet friends and loved ones.

Men in expensive suits traveling to Duluth from the Twin Cities of Minneapolis and St. Paul on business; husbands, wives, and their children arriving for a visit; single folks of all ages coming to the Twin Ports of Duluth and Superior for a variety of reasons: all these folks stepped off the train and onto the wooden walkway leading to the Union Depot.

"There he is," Matti Peltoma bellowed out in Finnish.

"What'd he say?" George McAdams asked Olli Kinkkonen.

Kinkkonen smiled.

"He says he can see Maki," Kinkkonen replied.

Peltoma nodded.

"Sorry about that," Peltoma apologized in English. "He's coming down the steps right now. There, in the uniform."

Andrew Maki descended the steps from the third passenger car of the train. The Marine's face was partially concealed by the wide brim of a campaign hat. His drab khaki uniform hung loose from his diminished frame as he gingerly stepped onto the platform.

"Maki," Kinkkonen called out, advancing with his companions towards the veteran.

The Marine smiled and tilted his head.

My God, look at him, George McAdams noted to himself as he stopped in front of Andrew Maki. *He's lost at least twenty pounds.*

Peltoma moved between McAdams and Kinkkonen and wrapped an arm around the skeletal shoulders of his friend.

"Good to see you," Peltoma said in Finnish through a wide grin. "Welcome home."

Maki's stern demeanor broke under the emotion of the moment. Uncharacteristic tears escaped and fell onto the dusty wooden landing.

"It's good to be home," the veteran whispered. "It's Goddamned good to be home."

Chapter 51

Andrew Maki tossed his canvas duffel bag onto the wooden floor beneath a bunk in an upstairs room of Talonen's Boarding House. Olli Kinkkonen stood in the doorway of the room. There were six beds, three bunks of two mattresses each, occupying the confines of the small room. Kinkkonen's room was down the hall.

"What's your plan for the rest of the day?" Olli Kinkkonen asked his friend.

Maki sat heavily on the wool blanket and cotton sheets that covered the bunk's insignificant mattress.

"Remember Mrs. Genelli?"

Kinkkonen's eyes widened with interest.

"The waitress from Aurora? The widow?"

"That's the one."

"What about her?" the dockworker asked, continuing their conversation in Finnish.

Maki worked the brass buttons of his tunic. The fasteners of the wool uniform were stubborn. His breathing was still affected by the wound he'd received at Belleau Wood. He found he did not have the stamina he'd once had.

"Maki, what about the widow?" Kinkkonen asked impatiently.

The soldier finished unfastening his blouse, removed the garment, and hung it over the pine headboard of the lower bunk.

"What do you think of her?"

"Well, that's a hell of a question, seeing as how I only met her one time, out at Wolf Lake. But I found her right enough. Nice smile. Pretty figure. Smart woman. Why?"

Asking the man what his opinion was, based upon such scanty evidence, seemed somehow reckless.

I shouldn't have asked the question, the veteran thought as he slipped his uniform trousers off his legs.

359

The soldier struggled to breathe. Stress impacted his residual condition in ways that made it seem like he was about to suffocate.

"Something wrong?"

Maki nodded in the negative.

"I'll be fine. It'll pass."

"You asked what I thought about Mrs. Genelli. I answered, straight as I could," Kinkkonen added, now speaking in English with an accent. "Why?"

Maki dug into his duffel for a pair of trousers and a sweater.

"I think I've fallen in love with her," the Marine confided, slipping the legs of the pants over his feet, drawing the black wool trousers to his waist. "I think I'm going to ask her to marry me."

Kinkkonen's eyes flickered. "Marry you? Are you crazy? You barely know the woman."

"Not true. I've spent considerable time with her. I admire her. I am fond of her son. I think it could work."

Maki drew a heavy wool sweater over his head. It was a hand-knit garment he'd purchased in England before his trip home. The Marine stood up and patted the pleats of his trousers.

"How do I look?"

"Like a man about to make a grave error," Kinkkonen replied in Finnish.

Maki's face glowered.

"That's none of your concern. I told you how I feel. There's nothing more to be said on that score."

Andrew's anger dissipated. He approached his friend, reached out, and patted Kinkkonen on the shoulder.

"Let's talk about you. Peltoma says you refused your second papers?"

The two men began to walk down the hallway towards the stairs.

"That's right. I went with five other men. All of us returned our applications for citizenship on the day we were to take the oath."

Maki stopped in the passageway. It was too early for the gas lamps to be lighted. The hall was dark. The only illumination came from high windows at the far end of the narrow space. Dust motes floated in the sunlight at the end of the passage as the two men considered each other.

"It's my turn to ask why."

Kinkkonen thumbed the pockets of his dress pants and looked at his shoes.

"In Russia, the workers having finally taken charge, the Bolsheviks are on the right track. The Czar is finished. But there are rumors America will intervene to restore the Czar to power. I won't be a party to that."

Kinkkonen drew a breath.

"The other reason I won't serve is that I've seen what's happened to men like you, men who've been broken fighting on behalf of the masters, the bosses, in a war that makes no sense. They can't require me to register for the draft if I'm not a citizen."

"But they'll lock you up, or, worse yet, send you back to Finland as an undesirable," Maki replied, ignoring Kinkkonen's critique of the veteran's condition.

Kinkkonen resumed walking.

"I know that. I've got a plan."

Maki followed.

"How's that?"

"I'm telling everyone I'm going back to Finland. But I'm not. I'm going to Ohio, to work in a steel mill. They'll never catch on. I'll use the name 'Wirta', like I've done here to avoid the blacklists."

The men came to the landing at the bottom of the stairs. Charles Talonen sat in his favorite overstuffed chair, reading a magazine.

"Hello, Mr. Maki," the landlord bellowed. "I'd get up and shake your hand but you know me. Takes a crane to move me once I get settled in," the man noted in Finnish. "All of us in Finntown are mighty proud of the service you rendered over there, fighting the Huns."

"Thanks," Maki replied in their language.

"I hear you were wounded. Chest wound. That had to be hell," the fat man continued, placing the magazine, a copy of *National Geographic*, on his plentiful lap. "How was it – combat, I mean? I can't imagine the brutality, the horror."

Andrew Maki winced. He was not willing to talk about what he'd seen on the battlefield. Those memories were secreted in his mind, behind a wall of stern denial.

"It cannot be described," was Maki's only reply.

The fat man nodded, and returned to reading a story about cannibals in New Guinea.

The Finns walked slowly along the wooden sidewalk towards the harbor entrance, intent upon killing time until Mrs. Genelli's train arrived from Virginia. Maki labored to keep up. His stride was confined; his ability to breathe, constrained. Olli Kinkkonen slowed his pace.

"You're really going to Ohio?" Maki asked.

The dockworker smiled.

"The IWW is fighting with the AFL to take control of the workers there. I'd like to help the Wobblies out, if I can. I don't see compromise, the use of politics, as the solution to the working man's problems. I'm not a leader, mind you; just a follower. But I figure it can't hurt to lend a hand, see if we can't even things up a bit. The five-day week. The eight-hour day. Decent pay for hard work. These things aren't that outrageous to ask for. Don't you agree?"

The men came to the concrete breakwater beneath the Aerial Bridge. Maki and Kinkkonen stood watching deep blue waves tipped in white roll between the cement piers, under the bridge and into the harbor. White gulls soared above the water, their flight patterns graceful against the high blue sky. No clouds floated above the lake. No weather, beyond a meager south wind, a warm wind, made its presence known. Lovers held hands as they walked along the waterfront, and couples with children sat on blankets, eating picnic lunches while they too watched the waves and the birds. There was a dissonance to the scene, an incompatibility with what Andrew Maki had witnessed in the devastated woods of Northern France, which unnerved the soldier and caused him pause.

"You look tired," Olli Kinkkonen said, his eyes avoiding the face of his friend.

"I am."

A fishing boat appeared, its single stack pulsing black smoke as it rode the lake, towards the calmer waters of St. Louis Bay. Maki's eyes fixed on the boat as a way of redirecting his attention.

"I can't talk you out of this foolish plan?" Andrew Maki finally said, as the trawler bobbed in the channel between the piers, waiting for the bridge basket to shift to one side and so allow the vessel to enter the harbor.

Kinkkonen sighed. "I'm afraid not."

Chapter 52

Horace Ellison studied the newspaper article from the front page of the *New York Times* he'd been provided by David Stevens. The newsprint was yellowing. The article was nine months' old, bearing the date of January 15th, 1918. Ellison was reading the article at the insistence of Stevens because that afternoon, the afternoon of September 17th, 1918, Olli Kinkkonen, a Finn known to some of Ellison's acquaintances (most notably William Burnside and Peder "Bud" Nordquist), and five other immigrants had appeared before a local draft board and refused induction, based upon the fact that they had renounced their applications for citizenship.

"Something needs to be done," David Stevens had implored. "The Knights need to be called together to deal with these slackers."

Horace Ellison had agreed. That evening, the Knights of Liberty would meet in one of the upper dining rooms of the Kitchi Gammi Club, and, over a well-prepared meal of roast beef, mashed potatoes, and sweet apple pie, accompanied by ample snorts of good scotch, the Knights would discuss the punishment to be meted out to the slackers.

It did not concern Ellison that he and his cohorts had themselves escaped induction to fight the war in Europe. Their respective exemptions from service were of no interest to Horace Ellison, as he read the article in front of him at the kitchen table in the late afternoon sunlight. The windows of the room overlooked the rolling lawn of the backyard, which pitched towards the shimmering silver water of Lake Superior.

The newspaper account Ellison was scrutinizing recounted the story of Otto Wangerin and Joseph F. Arver, two Minnesotans who failed to register for the draft. The two draft dodgers had been convicted and sentenced to one year in prison before a United States District Court Judge in St. Paul.

The case was ultimately argued on appeal before the United States Supreme Court. The defense had alleged that the Selective Service System itself violated the Constitution's prohibitions against involuntary servitude and the provisions establishing a well-regulated citizen militia. The *Times* article recounted the Supreme Court's rejection of those arguments. The convictions had been sustained in a decision written by Chief Justice White on January 7, 1918.

These bastards, Horace Ellison thought as he sipped a small coffee cup filled with coffee and a shot of expensive brandy. *These Duluth slackers have found a loophole. If they remain non-citizens, refuse their second papers, they aren't eligible for the draft. Meanwhile, thousands of our boys are dying, over in France. It's time someone taught these ungrateful bastards a lesson.*

Horace pushed the *Times* article aside and looked out the window. His eyes fixed on the leafless elms and the hardy oaks, the oaks' brown leaves still stubbornly hanging from their gray limbs, as he thought about the nationalities of the slackers.

"I'm only half-Finn, thank God," Ellison mumbled, referring to his mother's ethnicity, raising the cup of coffee and brandy to his lips as he watched a blue jay flit from barren tree to barren tree. "I don't understand why they just won't do as they're told. There's going to be hell to pay for this insolence. Of that, there can be no denying."

The front door opened. Elin Ellison walked into the foyer of the home, her arms laden with two paper sacks filled with groceries.

"Hello, dear," Horace said with false sincerity, rising from his chair in the kitchen to meet his wife. "Need some help?"

"I'm fine. Why aren't you at work?" she asked, annoyance clear behind the question as she kicked low pumps off her feet and brushed past Horace with nary a glance on her way to the pantry.

The businessman's eyes flared at his wife's gall, which soured his mood.

"It's none of your Goddamned business," he muttered, following her into the kitchen. "I did what needed doing, then

365

took the rest of the afternoon off to golf nine at the Club," he advised, referring to Northland Country Club, the swanky local enclave of the rich.

"Golfing again? When do you find time to work?" his wife retorted.

Horace stood behind his wife as she hurriedly unloaded staples and placed them on the shelves of the pantry. Without a word, Elin whirled around, walked past her husband, opened the electric refrigerator, the cooling mechanism exposed and situated on top of the unit, and placed two quart bottles of Arrowhead Creamery whole milk on the unit's lower shelf.

As Elin attempted to leave her husband's side, his right hand darted out, grabbed her sleeve, and drew her into his body.

"I guess I can take a day off to go golfing if I damn well want to," Horace whispered, liquor clear and obvious on his breath. "What's got your dander up, darling?" he asked, bending over in an attempt to place his lips on those of his wife.

"Get off," Elin commanded, pushing her husband away, her open wool coat swaying from the effort. "I'm not interested."

Horace reached out and grabbed his wife's left ear lobe, twisting the flesh, and with it, a sterling silver ear fob.

"I guess you'll do as I say, now, won't you?" he muttered, menace clear and present in his demeanor.

He left her humbled on their bedspread. He had not raped her, but he had also not been kind. Horace had made it plain what he was expecting and she, though uninterested in the process, complied. Her clothing was strewn in disarray about their bedroom. No words had been spoken, no niceties observed as he had emptied himself of desire for another week. She lie there, her white skin exposed to the cool air, her breathing calm and unexcited, listening as he donned his clothing, left by way of the front door, started up the Buick, and drove off.

This is my life, Elin Ellison said to herself, tears welling but unable to descend due to the attitude of her body, prone as it was on the down bedspread. *This is what I have done to myself.*

She waited for what seemed like an hour – in reality, little more than minutes – before she raised her naked self from the bed and walked into the adjacent master bath. Her hands fumbled with the white porcelain knobs of the faucet on the big claw foot tub. Steam rose in the cold air as scalding water struck chilled porcelain.

He forgot to put away his overnight kit again, Elin thought, her gaze focusing upon a ditty bag that rested on a chest of drawers, across the room from the sink.

The zipper to the bag was open. She strode across the pink and black ceramic tiles, picked up the bag and threw it, in dramatic fashion, against the clouded mirror above the pedestal sink. A straight razor, a bottle of cologne, bars of soap, a shoe shine towel, a washrag, and three medicine bottles struck the mirror. The mirror broke but did not fall. Cracks spread across the reflective glass like the webbing of a spider. The medicine bottles shattered when they fell to the tile. She recognized the contents of two of the bottles: heartburn remedy and aspirin. The third bottle contained an unfamiliar liquid, which spilled onto the floor.

"What's this?" Elin Ellison asked in a quiet voice as she gingerly walked barefoot over the tile, avoiding broken pieces of colored glass as she moved, and bent down to inspect the spilled medicine. She knelt, her breasts hanging freely from her torso, and picked up a piece of green glass.

"Colloidal silver," Elin Ellison mumbled as she read a paper pharmacy label affixed to a shard of emerald. "That son of a bitch."

Chapter 53

Heidi Genelli fidgeted as the train from Virginia pulled into the DM&N Depot in Proctor. Her fingers arranged unruly strands of thick blond hair. Her lean form appeared boy-like in her new gauze dress. A sweater, the dark green wool distressed from wear, covered her upper torso. Heidi stood up, adjusted the pillbox hat on her head, and walked past other passengers, slumped in their seats, apparently unaware that the train had arrived at its final destination.

As Heidi Genelli moved, she occasionally ducked her head to look out the small windows lining the interior walls of the passenger car. Her eyes searched for a glimpse of the man who had written to her, inferring the one word that she thought, after the death of her husband Joseph, she would never find again in connection with an adult relationship.

Love, she mused silently, turning the word over and over in her mind as she stopped in the aisle. An elderly gentleman, his ears large, his stature small, assisted a frail, ancient woman out of her seat and into the aisle. *Will we still be in love when we are their age?* Heidi asked herself as she watched the old couple shuffle towards an exit.

The air felt crisp on Heidi Genelli's pale face when she emerged from the railroad car. Her blue eyes scrutinized the small crowd gathered on the wooden platform. Men of every stature and description, their clothing a cross-section of ethnicity and economic status, wearing hats of varied construction, stood smoking, talking, or in stony silence, some holding the hands of their women, others searching the departing passengers for the people they were waiting to greet.

"Mrs. Genelli," a male voice called out.

Her eyes darted from figure to figure. Her eyes locked on the profile of a man. He was wearing his best clothes, the same rumpled, out-dated suit that he'd worn while courting Elin Gustafsson. Heidi Genelli did not know this, of course, and nor would she have cared. There appeared, in the most distant corner of her heart, a flutter, an emotive glee that she had not experienced in years.

"Mr. Maki," she answered, with a slight wave of her gloved right hand.

The woman regally descended the steel steps of the passenger car and stepped onto the wooden slats of the landing, with the assistance of a short-statured railroad conductor.

"Thank you, sir," Heidi said, as the conductor left her to attend to another passenger.

Andrew Maki stepped around the old couple standing in front of Heidi, the two aging lovers engaged in a warm embrace with family members in the middle of the loading platform. Maki came to an abrupt, almost ceremonial stop, in front of Heidi Genelli.

"You are looking well," Maki said, his eyes obvious in their intensity, "very well indeed."

Heidi felt Andrew's eyes inspect her body. The subtle gesture did not alarm her Victorian sensibilities. Andrew Maki's deliberate inventory was forgiven, forgiven because he had inferred the most cherished of words between two human beings.

He appears so tired, so utterly spent, she thought.

Heidi Genelli stood in the sun, oblivious to the sounds and smells of the railroad town swirling around her, and considered a response.

If we're to mean anything to each other, I must be honest. In all things, even this.

"Andrew," she whispered, placing her arm around his neck, "you look tired."

Their eyes, his as dark as ink, hers, as blue as the sky soaring above the coal haze that smothered the Village of Proctor, met as they embraced publicly for the first time. Andrew Maki pulled Heidi Genelli's rail-like form into his body.

"I am. There is something that war leaves inside you, a weariness," he said plainly, in Finnish, "that never seems to abate. But let's not discuss how I am. Let's talk about how you and Joey are faring."

Andrew turned, picked up Heidi's overnight bag from the platform, and gently prompted the woman to walk by his side.

"We've been fine. Father's slowed down considerably," Heidi volunteered. "Something to do with his heart. The doctors aren't sure what it is. But he's sluggish, hasn't been able to do everything that needs doing around the café."

"I hope it's not serious."

"Not so far as the doctors are concerned. They haven't limited him. He's to do whatever he feels capable of doing."

Maki nodded, and continued to guide Heidi Genelli towards the Incline terminal.

"And Joey; how's my favorite boxer?"

The woman smiled. "Anxious to see you. Since I told him you were coming home, all he's been able to talk about is 'Mr. Maki, the war hero.'"

Andrew grinned slightly and steadied his focus.

"There are men who are heroes," he replied in a near whisper. "I'm not one of them."

Heidi Genelli studied Andrew Maki's profile and matched him stride for stride. As they moved smartly, she slipped the gloved fingers of her left hand into his right palm.

"You sell yourself short. You were wounded in battle. You faced things that many men are unwilling to face," she responded. "To those of us here at home, you are indeed a hero."

They passed Boundary Avenue, the demarcation line between Proctor and Duluth, and entered the Bayview Heights neighborhood of Duluth. Children ran past the couple. Dogs barked in fierce defense, chained to trees or to the front porches of working class bungalows, which were painted bright yellow, white, or pale shades of green and blue. Men and women reclined in painted wicker furniture on the covered front porches of the modest homes, and waved to the passing couple.

370

Andrew Maki mulled the woman's comment over in his mind. He was no self-promoter. He had no interest in tooting his own horn, in terms of his recent experiences in the Great War. He had, when all was said and done, been away for less than a year. He had been wounded and removed from action after being in combat for a little over a month. His mind kept wandering back to the other men, those men who had not been so lucky.

Despite the gayness of his homecoming and the sweet interplay of life around the couple as they strolled, in the concealed crevices of Andrew Maki's memory, bits and pieces of Maki's time in Northern France played over and over again. These visions were projected like the herky-jerky frames of a silent movie. Andrew Maki could not banish these horrific thoughts. He could only stall them momentarily, hold them at bay, until the projector in his mind was startled into action by some comment, some odor, some scene from real life. Heidi Genelli innocently activated these unpleasant scenes despite Maki's metaphysical efforts to avoid reliving them.

Sergeant Cukela leaned over him. Two soldiers assigned to medical duty were hurriedly opening their canvas stretcher to carry him to the nearest dressing station. Sergeant Gruber, his face blackened from gunpowder, his eyes fierce, appeared. William Walker, Maki's replacement tender, remained with the Hotchkiss, just a few feet from where Maki lay bleeding.

"What's wrong with Maki?" Gruber asked.

"Shot in the chest. Lung shot. Having a hell of a time keeping his breath," Cukela interjected.

"Too bad. He's a good man," Gruber observed as he crouched next to the wounded Marine.

"Pretty good fight trainer as well," Cukela said, through a weak smile.

Gruber nodded. "I can take it from here, sergeant. Your men need you at the front."

Cukela placed a filthy palm on Maki's bare left wrist.

"Take care, Marine. Sergeant Gruber will see that you get patched up," Cukela said, moving out behind a line of dirt protecting the group from enemy snipers.

371

Gruber removed his steel pot and knelt next to Maki. The Finn floated in and out of consciousness.

"Will he make it?" Gruber asked the litter-bearer closest to him.

"Dunno," the medic responded in a deadpan voice. "Maybe. Maybe not."

"Well, see to it that he gets attention right away. I can't afford to lose another gunner," the sergeant said, as he stood up, intent upon placing his helmet on his head.

Crack.

The sound of the Mauser round shattering bone had awakened Maki. His eyes fluttered open just in time to see Gruber's head explode.

Sergeant Gruber made no sound. There was no final expression of faith or angst or loss. There was nothing. Nothing. Nothing.

"I didn't face so much," Andrew Maki whispered, melancholy clear in his voice as the couple entered the Bayview Terminal for the West Duluth Incline.

Heidi Genelli sensed regret and shame working upon the psyche of her companion. This suspicion caused Heidi Genelli to stand quietly behind Andrew Maki as the veteran paid a cashier for their ride down the hill.

Chapter 54

The Finn held the woman's forearm in a loose embrace as they walked along the sidewalk on Superior Street. They strolled past the Lyceum. Their attention diverted to a small demonstration that was occurring in front of the Spalding Hotel, across the street. An intimate crowd of two or three dozen protesters, painted signs carrying messages against the Great War, against the Espionage Act, against the draft, marched in a small circle in front of the hotel.

"I believe that's Mrs. Ellison," Andrew Maki observed as the couple slowed their pace to watch the demonstration.

The veteran stared hard at the short woman in the elegant dress and blue wool coat.

"Indeed," he whispered, his heart palpitating, his palms becoming sweaty.

Maki released his grip on Heidi's hand.

"Mind if I say hello?" Andrew asked quietly.

Heidi Genelli studied the man's face. His countenance was a clean slate. His eyes betrayed no untoward intent.

"If you must, I shan't stop you," she whispered.

The edge to her voice, Andrew thought as he glanced from the woman across the street to the woman he was with. *Heidi is not comfortable with this.*

"I'll only be a moment," he advised, stepping out into traffic before Heidi Genelli could protest.

The tall woman placed her hands on her hips, but did not announce her displeasure.

"Governor Burnquist supports tyranny," the protesters chanted in unison, carrying their signs, moving in shuffling steps on a pre-determined path. "Vote the Socialist Workers' Party," they continued. "Vote the Governor out."

Andrew Maki dodged a trolley headed west, darted around a delivery wagon and draft team standing patiently in front of the hotel, and stepped up onto the cement curb. He placed himself in such a fashion so as to become immediately visible to Elin on her next pass in front of the hotel entrance.

Elin Ellison was oblivious to the newcomer in the crowd of hecklers standing around the protesters, as she moved robotically in step with her fellow Socialists.

"Send a message to Burnquist," the group chanted, their voices uneven and staggered. "Vote Socialist this November."

"Give it up and go back to Finland, you bunch of Reds," a derisive voice called out. "We don't need your kind here, especially when honest men are dying over in France, and you slackers are here, dodging the draft."

"You Finns are gonna get what's coming to you," said another tall man, his face covered in stubble, his eyes squinting in the late afternoon sun. "You've been playing with fire; now you're gonna get burned. Hang the draft dodgers is what I say."

The taunts left the protesters unmoved. Their dedication and discipline were remarkable. They simply ignored the insults and continued to deliver their pre-determined message.

Elin's gaze was locked on the spine of the man walking in front of her. As she rounded the corner of the protest circle, her face lifted, as if drawn by an unfathomable force, and their eyes met.

Andrew Maki smiled.

"Oh my," the woman blurted out. "Anders?"

Elin Ellison stepped out of the moving stream of men and women to stand in front of Andrew Maki.

"It's Andrew now, remember?"

"Andrew," she said quietly.

There was unsolicited affection in the way she said his name.

"Andrew Maki," she repeated with the same tenderness.

"I see you haven't changed much," Maki observed, removing his new Stetson Chatham so that he could see her better. His hands fidgeted with the felt hat. His fingers moved back and forth along the hat's brim as he stared into the woman's hazel eyes. "You're looking well," he added.

She leaned her sign against the stone exterior of the hotel and smiled.

"I hear you were in France. Wounded, I'm told. It must have been a frightening experience."

His expression darkened.

"It wasn't what I expected," was all he said.

"Are you still pained by your wounds?"

"Wound. One bullet. In the chest. I had a skilled doctor, a fellow from Iowa. I'm fine. A little twinge now and again. But I'm fine."

He could not help but inventory her face: the indigo eyes, the fine auburn hair, the hollow cheeks. She wore no make-up, and yet her physical beauty evoked radiance. She fairly glowed under his scrutiny.

"So you're a Socialist now?"

She smiled broadly. "I'm actually working as a reporter for *Tyomies*. I was sent to cover the demonstration and just fell into it. The Governor is staying here tonight, attending a major Republican fundraiser for his re-election campaign. They just happened to have an extra sign for me to hold," she said, with a slight laugh.

Andrew glanced across the street. Heidi Genelli was sitting patiently on a wooden trolley stop bench. His eyes fell upon the tall widow and lingered, as if comparing options.

"You with someone?" Elin asked.

There was a brief moment of hesitancy.

"Yes. Mrs. Genelli, a widow from Aurora," he said, nodding his head in his companion's direction.

"Ah, yes. Very lovely woman, I've been told. Has a little boy. Well..." Elin said, the sentence trailing off without resolution.

"It's nice to see you, Mrs. Ellison," Andrew Maki said, a sense of angst imbedded in his pronunciation of her married surname. "How are you getting along, other than the reporting?"

"Tolerably well," she replied, the expression lacking sincerity.

"You don't sound too convincing," he observed, their pattern of speech returning to the familiar.

Elin Ellison sighed and looked across the street at the widow. The other woman looked into the depths of her purse, withdrew a linen handkerchief, and dabbed the corner of an eye.

"I think we've upset your friend," Elin observed.

Andrew looked back at Heidi Genelli.

"I think you're right. I best be on my way."

If I ask him to stay, he just might, Elin Ellison thought, her eyes still riveted on the blade-like form of Heidi Genelli, sitting across the street. *If I unburden my soul, explain my plight to Anders, he will likely give her up, perhaps even consider taking me back.*

Thoughts of betrayal and deception swirled in Elin Ellison's mind as she retracted her gaze and looked into the eyes of her former lover.

He has been hurt enough, she concluded. *I have no right to tamper with his happiness. I have made my decisions. I have walked my own path, with full knowledge of what I was giving up. He deserves to be able to do the same.*

"I must get back to my friends," Elin said quietly, placing a bare hand to the Finn's whiskerless face. "It was lovely to see you, Anders. I hope our paths cross again. Give my best to Mrs. Genelli and her little boy."

"I will. But the next time you see us, I hope that it will be 'Mrs. Maki. Mrs. Andrew Maki'," he revealed as Elin turned to rejoin the milling group of protesters.

The news of his intentions towards the widow startled Elin, causing her to falter slightly as she walked away.

"Are you all right?" he called out.

"I'm fine. Just caught my shoe," Elin replied, her hands trembling as she reached for the wooden handle of her sign.

Crossing Superior Street, Andrew's mind was in a tizzy. A Stutz Roadster nearly hit Maki as he moved through congested traffic. The driver cursed. The Finn did not reply.

"That took a while," Heidi Genelli observed as Andrew Maki returned to her side and sat next to her on the wooden surface of the trolley stop bench.

"We had a lot of catching up to do."

The woman's long face turned towards the man. Her eyes studied his demeanor.

"Are you sure that's all that happened?"

Andrew was taken aback by Heidi's bluntness. It was a trait he'd come to admire in Elin during their years together, but an attribute he had not expected to discover in Mrs. Genelli.

"What do you mean?"

"Isn't it obvious why I'd ask such a question? You've always been open and honest about what Mrs. Ellison meant to you. Don't you think I fear that those feelings remain? Don't you think I have the right, given my situation, to ask whether you yearn for something more with her?"

Andrew grasped the woman's hand.

"I will always have a fondness in my heart for Elin. But she and I, we live different lives in different worlds. My letter to you was an honest expression of my feelings."

The woman nodded and patted his hand. They rose from the bench and began to walk east on the sidewalk, intent upon finding a café where they could order a meal and continue their discussion in private. As they strolled the cement walkway, they passed in front of Bagley's Jewelry Store. Andrew Maki stopped beneath the canvas awning that shaded the store's entryway.

"We need to go in here," Andrew advised.

"Why?"

Maki did not answer. He simply opened the door and urged the woman across the threshold. Once inside, Andrew moved quickly towards a glass display case with purposeful strides. Heidi Genelli lagged behind, uncertain of the reason for their visit.

A clerk behind the counter addressed Maki in familiar terms: "Mr. Maki. Nice to have a war hero in the store again."

"Mr. Emerson, I've told you before that I'm no hero. Just a man who chose to do his country's bidding. Do you have it?"

"Ah, yes. It's been cleaned. It's a rare thing, I'll have to say. You have excellent taste. Not usually found in the male of the species, I might add," Emerson said.

The salesclerk was a short, round man with many wrinkles on his pale face, a face neatly covered with a well-trimmed brown beard, the hairs coarse and thick like those of a bear.

"All we need do now is size it to the lady's ring finger."

Heidi Genelli stood apart from the men, shifting her weight nervously on the heels of her narrow dress shoes. The clerk handed Andrew the ring, a platinum engagement band boasting a small chip of diamond centered between two fiery blue opals. Maki turned slowly towards the woman, and, oblivious to the other patrons in the store, extended the ring in his left hand as he knelt to one knee on the marble floor.

"The diamond represents your heart, bright and pure," Andrew Maki whispered. "And the opals... well, they represent your eyes, blue and full of fire."

The woman's face reddened. Her breath became quick and shallow. The reaction was involuntary and obvious.

"Mrs. Genelli, would you do me the honor of becoming my wife?" Andrew Maki asked in Finnish.

Heidi Genelli's heart raced. Her eyes moistened. There was a long, painful pause, a silence that drew the attention of the other customers and employees to the slender man kneeling on the floor in front of the statuesque woman.

The woman's left hand curled and uncurled against the gauze fabric of her dress. Her eyes blinked, batting away tears. There was hesitancy in her movements, a steady deliberation regarding her future.

"Yes, I will marry you," Heidi Genelli finally whispered, as she allowed Andrew Maki to slide the platinum band onto her ring finger.

Chapter 55

Wednesday, September 18, 1918. Olli Kinkkonen and Matti Peltoma worked feverishly. It was close to six o'clock, nearly quitting time. They were loading the last of three open trucks with rubber automobile tires bound for Ford dealerships located in Northwestern Wisconsin and Northeastern Minnesota. The men were working in Superior, under the auspices of Western Labor, making two dollars a day for their efforts. They worked alone. Other crews had been dispatched by Theo Laine, the son of Finnish businessman Eino Laine, to other locations throughout Duluth and Superior.

The air cooled as the sun settled behind the hills standing above the city of Duluth. Kinkkonen and Peltoma worked in long-sleeved flannel shirts. Peltoma's green shirt was nearly new. Kinkkonen's blue shirt was distressed, more a rag than a garment. There was talk of going out for a beer in Superior before taking the trolley over the Interstate Bridge to Duluth. Mostly, though, the men worked silently, their motions and efforts coordinated without words, as they moved a wooden cart filled with tires from the pier, where hundreds of tires had been off-loaded from a steamship, to the waiting trucks.

Three men approached. The sound of boots striking gravel drew Olli Kinkkonen's attention. Kinkkonen recognized two of the men as they walked towards the pier with deliberation.

This doesn't look good, Olli Kinkkonen thought.

Olli nudged Matti.

"Wonder what they want," Olli Kinkkonen said.

Olli Kinkkonen stood up, stretching as tall as his meager frame would allow, and shook out a kink in his right hand.

"They're here to sack me," Kinkkonen replied quietly.

"What?"

379

"I've heard talk. There are some folks who are upset that I renounced my papers. Some say I'm a slacker, a coward," Kinkkonen continued in Finnish.

Theo Laine stopped in front of the two workers. The young man, at nineteen really not much more than a boy, was small, with untidy blond hair, slotted blue eyes, and a somewhat distorted jaw. William Burnside and Peder "Bud" Nordquist stood a step behind their boss.

"You Kinkkonen?" Laine asked in English, his eyes riveted on the taller man's face.

"Wirta. Olli Wirta," Kinkkonen replied.

Burnside stared hard at the dockworker from his position behind Theo Laine.

"Bullshit."

The young boss turned quickly and barked at his employee. "There's no call for cussing, William," Laine admonished sternly.

Theo Laine returned his attention to the two laborers and scrutinized Kinkkonen.

"Mr. Burnside says you're a man known as Olli Kinkkonen. Same man who, along with five others, tore up their citizenship papers and refused to join up with the Army. Read about it in today's *Paivalehti*. Paper had much to say about men who won't fight for their country. Said the rest of us Finns should 'brand the slackers with shame'."

Kinkkonen was startled. He had not read the article.

"Wirta," Kinkkonen insisted, his voice steady, no evidence of nerves present. "I am Olli Wirta," he added in Finnish.

"Don't speak Suomi. For Chris sake, you're in America. Speak American," Laine rebuked.

"English," Peltoma said, correcting his boss. "You mean English."

"Stay out of this," Burnside hissed, his form towering over the other men. "This is none of your concern."

"No, no. That's quite all right, Mr. Burnside. I relish being corrected by uneducated immigrant slackers," Laine continued.

"I'm no slacker," Peltoma asserted. "I'm registered. I've taken citizenship."

"And your friend?" Laine asked. "What about your friend?"

Silence imposed itself on the group. Dusk hung over the St. Louis River basin. Kinkkonen's mouth became dry. His eyes shifted.

"Burnside says you're Kinkkonen. You say you're Wirta. It is a dilemma," Laine said. "Tell you what, my fine immigrant friend. Show me something in writing, some legal document, like a birth certificate, or your immigration papers, that confirms you are who you say you are."

Olli Kinkkonen shuffled his battered leather work boots. His hands pushed heavily against his dungarees, massaging the muscles of his thighs.

"I have no need of such documents," Kinkkonen responded defiantly in Finnish.

Laine's eyes stared hard at the belligerent dockworker. "Then I guess you'll have to work elsewhere. Burnside, pay him his wages and then sack him. Draft-dodgers are not welcome in my father's employ," Theo Laine said dismissively, turning on his heels to leave.

William Burnside withdrew a small tablet of paper from his suit coat and licked the end of a stubby pencil as he thumbed through the tablet. Peder Nordquist stood behind the bigger man, watching the two Finns carefully, his Nordic features defused with shadow caused by the descent of the sun.

"You have no right to treat a man this way," Peltoma shouted as Laine withdrew in even steps towards a waiting motorcar. "Olli has worked hard for you, done all he was asked," Peltoma added in Finnish.

Laine turned and smiled brightly.

"Watch yourself, sir. Or you too will be looking for a job. And for God's sake, speak American," the young man added stubbornly, climbing into the rear passenger's door of a waiting Paige touring car.

"Here's what's due you, Kinkkonen," Burnside advised, drawing ten dollars in coins from a money pouch that he removed from the inside pocket of his suit coat. "If you know what's good for you, you'll think about relocating, if you get my drift," the big man said menacingly. "There's talk of taking care of you slackers, like Collinsville took care of that Hun, Bobby Prager."

The reference to the lynching of Robert Prager earlier that year was not lost upon Kinkkonen. A Socialist and union man from the coal-mining country of Illinois, Robert Prager had been dragged from the Collinsville jail, paraded in front of crowds, beaten, humiliated, and, ultimately, hanged from a tree outside of town, because of his German heritage and leftist leanings.

Olli Kinkkonen stared stubbornly at his accusers before turning to seek assistance from his friend. Matti Peltoma stood motionless in the background, holding a tire, his eyes downcast, an indication he had nothing more to offer in the way of support. Kinkkonen returned his gaze to Burnside and extended his right hand to accept the money.

"Like I said, Kinkkonen, you best think about making some place other than Duluth your home," William Burnside advised, tipping his black bowler as he motioned for Peder Nordquist to accompany him back to the idling automobile. The big Norwegian grunted, pointed a bony finger at the two Finns, and turned to follow his associate.

Olli Kinkkonen fidgeted the coins, his fingers tight, the muscles of his wrists contracted, as if he sought to wring the silver out of the money. As the two thugs joined Theo Laine in the Paige motorcar, Olli Kinkkonen shoved the ten dollars he had earned into the front pocket of his trousers, lifted his eight-square cap and jacket off a half-driven nail protruding from the rickety railing of the pier, and waited patiently for his friend to finish working.

Chapter 56

Elin Ellison changed trolleys at the Interstate Bridge and caught the line running down Tower Avenue, Superior's main drag. If Duluth, with its claimed population of 110,000 souls, its symphony orchestra, its museums, its natural beauty, and its arrogant belief in its own destiny, was the "San Francisco of the North", a term its citizens had given the city during its expansive heyday, then in the second decade of the 20th Century, Superior, Wisconsin, was, in many ways, like Oakland. Drab. Hard-working. Blue-collar. A rough and tumble town filled with men and women who labored and toiled in the businesses and industries owned by the rich folks living in the mansions that lined the hills and lakeshore across St. Louis Bay. Superiorites worked hard and drank harder. Per capita, the small city of twenty thousand souls, isolated by geography and broad expanses of cutover forest from the rest of the State of Wisconsin, claimed to have more bars, taverns, and brothels than any other city in America.

Whereas Duluthians prided themselves on their ability to situate a metropolis up and down the awful steeps of the hills rising above the western rim of the St. Louis River, platting streets, alleys, and avenues in a grid pattern that, given the pitch and roll of the land, made absolutely no sense, Superiorites had used the river's floodplain to lay out a clean and careful city, albeit a city lacking the gurgling streams, the interlaced woodland parks, and the scenic overlooks found in Duluth.

Tyomies editor Emil Parras stood next to a massive printing apparatus scrutinizing the editorial that Elin Ellison had just handed him. Elin had left the demonstration emotionally shaken after her encounter with Andrew Maki. She had returned to her empty house in Lakeside and, after a considerable amount of self-pity and tears over lost chances, sat down at her new Underwood portable typewriter and unleashed her frustration upon the page. It was after six o'clock in the evening. The sun had set, casting the streets outside the building at 601 Tower Avenue into darkness.

"This is good stuff, Mrs. Ellison," Emil said, nodding thoughtfully. "I guess I'd missed the blurb in the *Tribune* where the editor endorsed lynching as a viable means of dealing with war protesters."

Elin stood across the room from the banging, clanging press, which was being operated by two Finnish men in their late forties, a trial run after minor repairs.

"The exact reference from the *Tribune* is very clear, as I stated," the woman shouted over the machinery:

Page six. September 11, 1918. Maybe Montana's way with IWW agitators is better than Chicago's. Little's trial was shorter and it had no such aftermath as Haywood's."

Parras nodded as he listened to Elin read the quote.

"Let's go in the office and talk a bit about this," the editor said.

The newspaper's office was crammed with an oak desk, file cabinets, and glass-fronted barristers' bookshelves, which were stuffed to the ceiling with books, tracts, articles, and papers of all sorts. Emil Parras closed the door and took a seat on the other side of the cluttered desk while continuing to read the woman's work. Elin scrutinized the man as he read.

"I think it is utterly reprehensible and irresponsible that the largest newspaper in the Twin Ports would openly advocate lynching as a solution to the perceived problem of un-Americanism," she said quietly. "It was bad enough when the *News Tribune* endorsed what happened to Mr. Debs. This is far worse."

The woman was referring to Eugene Debs, founder of the IWW and perennial candidate for President of the United States as a Socialist, garnering in excess of a million votes during the election of 1912. Debs had recently been tried and convicted in the United States District Court in Cleveland, Ohio, of three counts of violating the Espionage Act, including the offense of "uttering language to incite, provoke, and encourage resistance to the United States and to promote the cause of the enemy." Debs was facing ten years in a federal penitentiary for the conviction, although he was free on bond, pending appeal.

"Your reliance upon other editorials and articles from recent issues of the *Trib* isn't quite as clear, such as the one regarding the Russian threat in Detroit," Parras continued, reading as he talked.

The editor reached across the water-stained surface of his desk and poured a shot of vodka into a water tumbler.

"Care for a drink?" Parras asked, pointing to another glass sitting on the far edge of the wooden surface, the sides of the tumbler smudged with inky fingerprints.

"No, thanks," Elin Ellison replied. "I feel it's important to let the readers of *Tyomies* know, to warn them, of how serious the local situation has become. My friend, Wendy, her father was arrested some time ago in a protest in front of the courthouse. The police called in the fire department and used hoses to disperse the crowd. While I don't agree that the police had the right to end a lawful protest, the police action was at least done under auspices of legal authority. No one was killed. This," she continued, pointing to her handwritten notes, "this advocating of the formation of lynch mobs to deal with folks who advance ideas and principles that you may not like... well, that's quite another matter. It is, in my view, a very dangerous atmosphere, one that the *Duluth News Tribune* is fueling for its own benefit."

"Benefit?"

"Nothing sells papers, or so I've been told, like a good lynching. Hooded spooks in the night. Men being dragged from their beds and hanged from railroad trestles without trials, without evidence. Like Frank Little. Like Bob Prager. These are the sorts of things that I expect will happen, if the *Tribune* continues its drumbeat of patriotic intolerance," the woman said, licking her dry lips as she spoke.

There was no further discussion between Parras and Ellison of the *Tribune's* articles describing the recent trial and conviction of IWW President Big Bill Haywood, a radical unionist who had escaped the death penalty in 1905, when he was acquitted of murdering a mining executive during a copper-mine strike in Montana. Haywood was now behind bars, convicted of violating the same provisions of the Espionage Act that had claimed Eugene Debs' freedom.

"I think I'll take that drink now," Elin said, pointing at the dirty glass.

Parras poured a dollop of booze into the dirty tumbler and pushed the glass towards the woman. Elin Ellison lifted the tumbler off the desk, opened her mouth, and drained the liquor in one swallow.

The editor smiled. "You're an impressive woman, Mrs. Ellison. You drink like a veteran reporter."

Elin revealed her emotions. Her views on the topic they were discussing were serious. Her intent was to impress the editor that the situation confronting the Socialists, unions, and IWW adherents was critical.

"Just listen to this," she implored, her eyes returning to her notepad. "It's from yesterday."

She read: "*September 17th. Any foreign-born in Duluth who hereafter remain un-American are distinctly undesirable as citizens or residents.*

"And this is after the paper rails, time and time again, that the largest undeclared ethnic group in Duluth's Third Draft District, the area that includes Finntown, are the 'Russians'," she spat. "You and I both know that 'Russian' is simply a euphemism for 'Finn'. The paper is using the term, and the government is using the term so that they can incite the rest of the populace to take action against persons of Finnish descent who do not want to fight this war."

Arvid Nelson, another of the bosses at *Tyomies*, knocked on the office door and let himself into the room.

"Arvid," Parras said in greeting. "I was just going over a potential editorial with Mrs. Ellison. She's good. Damn good."

Nelson removed his dirty eight-quarter cap when he noticed the woman seated across the room. The slender Swede smiled at the woman, but addressed his comments to Parras.

"Press is ready to roll. We'll be able to make tomorrow's issue."

"That's good news. Let me finish up with Mrs. Ellison, and then we can start to lay it out. It's going to be nip and tuck, but we should be able to go to press before dawn."

Nelson nodded and put his cap back in place on his short blond hair.

"Nice to see you, ma'am," he said.

"Same here, Mr. Nelson," she added too late, after the door had closed.

"Now where were we?" Parras asked.

"Just about done, I believe," Elin said. "The last point I make in the editorial is that the powers that be are irresponsible for continually referring to the Finns as 'Russians'. It's an obvious and deliberate attempt to Red-bait, especially when the paper prints articles that claim 20,000 Bolshevik sympathizers were bound for Detroit, the beginning of an attempt by the Socialists and Communists at a countrywide revolution, nipped in the bud, or so it's claimed, by federal agents. That's from a front-page article in the *Tribune* two days ago. Of course, there's no evidence to back up the claim: the newspaper simply copied wire service reports, without any attempt to verify how this supposed army of Reds was recruited and how it was going to slip into the country."

"You make a persuasive case to run your words just as they're written," Emil Parras said, thumbing the dirty edges of his printer's vest as he sat in contemplation, under the dim gaslight of the newspaper office. "I'll talk to Arvid. We may just run it as is, or I might make some modifications to it; nothing drastic, just some fine-tuning, if that's agreeable to you."

"You're the editor. Whose byline will it run under?"

Parras smiled and stood up from behind his desk.

"Why, yours, of course. You went to all the trouble to write it. It's your work. You get the credit, and, I might add, the blame, once it hits the streets. Now, if you'll pardon me, Mrs. Ellison, I need to see about putting a newspaper to bed."

Elin hesitated. She did not rise from her chair.

"Something else I can help you with?" Parras asked.

There was a moment of awkward silence.

"This is personal," the woman whispered. "I'm in need of a physician, but I don't want to see anyone in Duluth. Do you know of a doctor over here, in Superior, one who is an excellent practitioner, but also discreet?"

The editor was taken aback by the request. Other than assigning Elin Ellison work and reviewing her finished articles, he had had little personal contact with the woman. Her request seemed tinged with desperation. There was a pleading look in Elin Ellison's eyes.

"I know of someone. A very, very good man. Judson Meyers. Office is on Tower, about nine blocks from here. He's the person I'd go see if I had a delicate medical problem in need of resolution."

The editor remained standing as he opened the top drawer of his desk and pulled out a telephone directory. Parras thumbed through the book, found the doctor's telephone number and address, wrote the information on a scrap of paper, and handed the note to the woman.

"Thank you," Elin whispered hesitantly.

The editor noted the concern etched on the woman's face.

"It stays here, Mrs. Ellison. I will keep this matter within the walls of this room. No one else will know."

The woman nodded, closed her notebook, and drew her winter coat around her, buttoning the garment against the brisk fall wind that was sure to await her outside the building.

Chapter 57

George and Wendy McAdams sat across the table from Andrew Maki and Heidi Genelli in the West St. Paul Restaurant, located at 5th Avenue West and Superior Street in downtown Duluth. The West St. Paul was a seedy little joint, the kind of establishment an unemployed war hero could afford. The couples sliced through thick beef steaks with battered silverware. The meat, though an inexpensive cut, was expertly prepared. The vegetables, homemade bread, and mashed potatoes were equal to the rib eyes. Though the couples laughed and talked gaily of the impending marriage between the returning Finn and Mrs. Genelli, Andrew Maki felt an undercurrent of unrest emanating from his Canadian friend.

There was nothing in particular that was said, or any separate and distinct gesture that formed Maki's perception. It was a multitude of unspoken glances, fidgets, and facial expressions that called Maki's attention to the unspoken.

Finally, their plates clean, apple pie and homemade ice cream having been devoured for dessert, Andrew Maki leaned back from the cracked oak surface of the dining room table and confronted his friend:

"George, you seem to be preoccupied with something. Anything wrong?"

The businessman swabbed melted ice cream on the corner of his mouth with a cloth napkin.

"Not in particular."

Maki hesitated before continuing. "I have a couple of nice domestic cigars one of the officers at the New York Army Hospital gave me. Care to join me?" Maki asked, placing his soiled napkin on his empty plate and rising from his chair. "Mrs. Genelli, would you excuse us for a few moments while we take in some of that brisk Lake Superior air?"

Heidi Genelli smiled.

"You mean, some of that stinky, foul cigar smoke, don't you, Andrew?"

Wendy McAdams laughed.

"Go ahead, George. I'm enjoying my cup of coffee with the future Mrs. Maki. We haven't had the chance to spend much time together, to get to know one another. We'll be fine."

George McAdams rose from his seat and followed Andrew Maki out of the restaurant. Outside, the stars were brilliant against the black velvet night, despite the interfering glow of new electric streetlights up and down Superior Street. Traffic was minimal, since many folks were at their churches or in their homes, Wednesday evenings being reserved for religious studies and gatherings. A freight wagon drawn by two lumbering oxen clattered down the brick surface of the street, the bed of the wagon empty, loose straw falling from the platform with each plodding step of the animals. A 1910 Stanley Steamer coupe blew by the men as they stood lighting their cigars, the automobile sleek and quiet in comparison to the Fords and other internal combustion motorcars, which were becoming more and more popular due to their cheaper cost.

"Nice car," Maki mumbled over the thick stem of the cigar hanging from his mouth.

"The Stanley will be around a long time," McAdams quipped. "I'd wager a lot longer than the cheap Fords and Buicks everyone seems so taken by. Stanleys are fast, clean, and easy to maintain, everything an internal combustion automobile is not."

Maki nodded and studied the huge face of his companion.

"OK, out with it, George. I've known you long enough to detect that you have something you want to get off your chest."

The Canadian looked away from the Finn, allowing his eyes to follow the course of the distant Steamer. The gaze was clearly a subterfuge.

"George?"

A heavy sigh.

"You realize you're eight months behind on your contract for deed payments," McAdams began.

"I know. I've been a little preoccupied, being shot at, wounded, and all," the Finn replied.

"I understand."

"That what's bothering you? You think I'm not going to catch up on the note?"

Silence.

"George, you know me. You know that's not the kind of man I am. I'll pay just as soon as I find work. You've got to know that, if you know nothing else about me," Maki continued, the tone of his voice becoming more severe as emotion took hold.

McAdams leveled his light blue eyes and drew a heavy cloud of cigar smoke into his ruddy cheeks. He held the pungent vapor for a moment before releasing a pillowy bank of smoke into the night air.

"It's not that at all. I've run into some problems of my own."

"Problems?" Maki replied, a hint of incredulity in the word.

"My brother."

"Adrian?"

"You remember him?"

"We only met the once, at your wedding. But yes, I remember him. Very serious man. No sense of humor."

"That's Adrian."

"Something's wrong with him, health wise?"

McAdams forced a pained grin.

"There's nothing wrong with him, at least not in terms of his health. You heard about the ship we lost?"

"The *Blue Heron*?"

"You don't miss much."

Maki drew smoke into his mouth and adjusted his dress hat, raising the brim higher so that he could more easily see his friend.

"Well, it seems that Adrian didn't do his job. He was left in charge of obtaining insurance to cover all our assets.

391

Says he simply forgot. I can't see how that's possible. But that's what he says."

Quiet interceded. Nothing moved on Superior Street.

"The boat wasn't insured?"

"That's right. A complete loss. I had over a hundred thousand on the line, owed to Juda Tylla and his bank."

"But my little pittance of a contract payment isn't going to do much to offset that. I'm only... what, a few hundred behind?"

McAdams threw the half-consumed cigar onto the sidewalk and mashed it slowly with the heel of his dress shoe.

"It's not the amount I'm worried about," the Canadian revealed.

Maki tossed his cigar onto the uneven brick surface of the street.

"Then what is it?"

George McAdams drew a deep breath:

"That son of a bitch Horace."

A puzzled look crossed the Finn's face.

"Horace Ellison?"

"Yes, sir."

"What about Horace?"

McAdams drew his large right hand to his chin and stroked pink skin as he looked directly into his friend's brown eyes.

"The bank was pressing me on the boat mortgage. I couldn't come up with the cash. I've sunk every dime I have into building our house," McAdams revealed. I'm land-rich and money-poor. Tylla was insistent. Said I needed to pay off the boat mortgage or his investors would be screaming. We took a bath on delivering the pulpwood to Ashland. Without the *Blue Heron*, we were forced to send it by rail. Took time and money, again compounding the situation. I had no other option."

Andrew Maki stopped in front of the door to the café:

"What do you mean?"

"I had to sign off on the bank selling all the papers they had an interest in."

"Papers?"

"Contracts and mortgages."

Quiet ensued as the men studied each other.

"Eustace Ellison bought them," George McAdams finally said, the words sliding uncertainly off his tongue. "He bought the papers and assigned them to his son to administer. Horace Ellison now holds the contract for the deed to your farm on Papoose Lake and the mortgage deed to Wolf Lake Camp."

Chapter 58

Creosote: a mixture of chemicals prepared by the distillation of coal tar.

On May 15, 1916, seventeen-year-old Jesse Washington was arrested for the alleged rape and death of a white woman in Robinson, Texas. He was convicted in a four-minute trial the same day. Before the trial judge could pronounce the death penalty and transfer custody of Mr. Washington to the State of Texas, courtroom spectators grabbed the defendant and dragged him from the courthouse. In a city park, the crowd doused the troubled youth in creosote, placed a chain around his neck, and brought him to a raging bonfire that had been started in anticipation of Washington's conviction. The chain was tossed over a substantial tree branch and Washington was raised from the ground and dangled over the bonfire where, for the better part of several hours, members of the mob slowly tortured him. When Washington attempted to pull himself out of the fire by grasping the red-hot links of the iron chain, members of the crowd severed Washington's hands from his wrists with an ax before lowering him back onto the pyre. Over 15,000 Texans cheered as Jesse Washington was roasted alive. Photographs of Washington's disfigured and charred body were taken and preserved as postcards, which spectators purchased and sent to friends and relatives in other parts of the United States.

Five men. The dead of night. A knock on the front door of the Talonen Boarding House in Finntown. Waves quietly breaking in the distance as Lake Superior was stirred by a cold September wind.

"Can I help you?" Charles Talonen said in Finnish as he opened the door on the evening of September 18, 1918.

"Speak English," a gruff male voice said. The potato sack that covered the man's features hid the face of the speaker.

Two slits were cut through the burlap bag to serve as eyeholes.

"It's after midnight," Talonen said in English. "What do you want?"

The biggest of the five men shoved his way into the parlor of the boarding house. Four smaller men, nearly identical in height, spanned out behind the hulking silhouette of the leader. The man closest to the leader kept his right hand shoved deep into the pocket of his Mackinaw.

"We're here for the slacker," the leader advised, his voice modulated and without any trace of anger. "The one they call Wirta."

Talonen, a short, barrel of undulating fat, stood in front of the group in his long underwear, a dirty union suit stretched to the limit of its fabric over Talonen's enormous gut. The Finnish proprietor ran the stubby fingers of his right hand through sparse hair.

"Wirta?"

"Goes by that name, or by the name of Kinkkonen," the stranger continued, shifting his weight slightly as he spoke.

"Who are you?"

One of the smaller men piped up, "None of your damn business, Finlander. Just do as the man says."

The leader turned and gestured for his companion to be silent.

"You'll have to pardon my companion's rudeness. We need to talk to Kinkkonen about his recent decision to renounce his second papers and avoid service in the Army."

Talonen studied the man.

"If you're with the draft board, why are you wearing masks?"

Despite the cloth covering the broad face of the man standing in front of him, Talonen detected the brief intervention of a smile on the big man's face.

"It's nasty business, this calling out of slackers. We have families. We have jobs. Better to keep our identities anonymous, if you know what I mean."

Talonen pondered a response.

"He's wasting time," another masked man interrupted. "I haven't got all night."

The big man nodded and drew aside his coat to reveal the grip of a Colt pistol, tucked into the waistband of his pants.

"He's right. We don't have all night. Tell me which room is Kinkkonen's, or we'll go through every damn room in this place until we find him."

The fat man shivered.

"Third door on the left, second floor," Talonen whispered.

"That's fine. That's real fine," the leader said quietly.

Pointing to the two men closest to Talonen, the big man said, "You two stay down here with Mr. Talonen. We'll find Kinkkonen."

The three remaining men walked quickly up the worn pine treads of the stairway. Their shoes scuffed against the sand coating the stairs, sand that had migrated into the boarding house from the dunes located along the lakeshore behind the building. A single electric light bulb at the far end of the passage illuminated the hallway. Old gas fixtures remained on the walls but were not lit. The big man covered the distance to Kinkkonen's room with mighty strides. He did not stop to knock at the door. He simply turned the tarnished brass doorknob and flung the door open.

"Kinkkonen," the big man announced, his voice firm but not overly loud. "It's time to pay the piper."

Olli Kinkkonen had been dreaming. His mind was locked on an image of a little frame house in an unnamed village in Ohio. Frames of the slowly moving drama included pictures of Elsie Laine, now Elsie Kinkkonen, and their two children. A brilliantly beautiful boy and a girl. In the dream, the Finn was happy. He was content. His job at the steel mill, where he was paid a fair wage for a day's work, had made his wallet fat and his life easy. Elsie was pregnant. Their third child was due. It was a good life, the life Olli Kinkkonen dreamed that night. At the sound of a stranger's voice in his room, the images shattered like a pane of glass struck by a rock.

"Who are you?" Kinkkonen muttered in confusion, his mind slowly emerging from sleep. "What the hell are you doing in my room?" he asked in Finnish.

"Stop talking gibberish," a man's voice reprimanded. "Speak English. We're here for you. That's all you need to know."

Hands grasped Kinkkonen and pulled him from his bunk. There were at least three men in the room, though as Kinkkonen was still dazed from his brutal awakening, he could not be certain of their number.

"Get dressed," the largest of the men said, shoving a blue serge suit, a tan shirt, and a red Mackinaw at the Finn.

"Get out of my room," Kinkkonen retorted, his mind becoming clear, his anger rising.

The largest man stepped into the space between them and showed the handle of the revolver in his waistband.

"Put the clothes on or I'll leave you with a bullet in that thin little Finnish head of yours," he whispered.

The look in the stranger's eyes was one of pure animus.

He means business, Kinkkonen thought. *I best do as he says.*

"There must be some misunderstanding," the Finn mumbled as he dressed. "I'm not the man you want."

"Sure you are, slacker," one of the others said, a slight chuckle in his voice. "You're exactly the man we want."

Kinkkonen slipped on his dress shoes. The big man towered over the Finn as Kinkkonen tied the shoelaces.

"Let's go," the leader whispered, shoving Kinkkonen towards the open door.

"Where are you taking me?"

The other two men closed in behind Olli Kinkkonen, making retreat impossible.

"You'll see."

The contingent marched in order down the stairs into the dimly lighted parlor. Charles Talonen's wide body sat in a hard wooden chair, the seams of his long underwear strained to near oblivion. The proprietor watched the other men parade into the room, where they were joined by the two guards posted to keep Talonen away from the telephone.

"Who the hell are you, coming into my establishment in the dead of night, taking one of my boarders?" Charles Talonen demanded, making no attempt to stand up as he confronted the group.

The big man passed by without responding. Kinkkonen shuffled by, surrounded by strangers. The last man in the group turned as he closed the door behind him.

"We're the Knights of Liberty," the stranger disclosed. "Make sure you get it right for the newspaper."

Chapter 59

Heidi Genelli bustled about the kitchen of Olson's Café with renewed enthusiasm. Her father sat in a chair at one of the tables, dicing potatoes and carrots for stew. Joey, now grown a full three inches taller and having passed his eleventh birthday, scrubbed hard at the bits and pieces of burned food stuck to the restaurant's big wood cook stove.

A steady autumn rain fell, the first significant weather in months. But the rain did not fall to the south, in the Valleys of the St. Louis, Cloquet, and Whiteface Rivers. There, the ground was parched and tinder dry. Two summers of inadequate rain had dried up the swamps and marshes and left the spindly second-generation aspen and birch forests thirsty. The trees had prematurely lost their leaves, adding a layer of brittle fodder to an already dangerous situation.

"We surely can use the rain," Heidi observed, speaking Finnish as she pulled out a sack of flour, in the midst of making dumplings for the stew. "I hope it keeps up for days," she added as she poured flour into an earthenware bowl.

"You're right about that," Jerome Seppo, Heidi's father, said, stopping his peeling motion in midstroke to consider the storm raging outside.

Raindrops splattered against the fir siding of the café and beat a staccato rhythm against the fragile single-paned windows overlooking Aurora's main street. Thunder rolled in from the west, booming and crashing at well-spaced intervals. Lightning flashed through the thick clouds. The bolts of electricity added an uneven spectral aspect to the burgeoning daylight.

Bowls of pancake batter sat on the counter, waiting for the rush of diners who would crowd into the café after the evening shift in the mines. Strips of bacon, already cooked and covered in a frying pan, warmed on the top shelf of the wood stove. Bowls of milk and eggs cooled in the walk-in icebox at the rear of the kitchen in anticipation of being whipped into scrambled eggs to be served to impatiently hungry men. Two large pots of coffee simmered on the back burners of the stove. Thick whole milk, freshly drained from a neighborhood cow, waited in a glass pitcher on the bottom shelf of the icebox. Slabs of toasted homemade wheat bread were stacked high on platters. Joey had coated each slice of toast with thick swabs of home-churned butter. Pots of honey and maple syrup stood on each table and on the lunch counter adjacent to the kitchen. The owners of the café and the small boy worked together as a team to make ready for the day's trade.

"You seem awfully happy this morning," Jerome said Seppo remarked to Heidi Genelli as he rose from his chair to bring the diced vegetables into the kitchen. "Must have been nice to see your fellow again."

The woman smiled and wiped a line of sweat from her forehead with the edge of her apron.

"I'm just glad he's home."

Jerome placed his hands on the linoleum surface of the lunch counter and looked squarely at his daughter.

"He's OK, I mean, after being wounded and all?"

The question caught her off guard. She paused before answering.

I wish I knew the answer to that, she thought, continuing to knead dough. *We slept in the same bed Wednesday night, in a warm and clean room in the Columbia Hotel. But that was all. We slept. Not that I wanted more. That wasn't for me to decide. I would have given myself to Andrew. After he gave me the ring, after we had dinner with the McAdamses. I would have allowed him to make love to me, if that was what he wanted. But we only slept together, in the fullest and most complete sense of that term. And he dreamed. Throughout the night, he tossed and turned as if tortured. There were words. There were names. I didn't know them. They were his comrades, I assume. Men who died over there, in the War. Men who he will never forget. That is what I will face, as his wife. But I am willing to do so. I am willing to try to heal the wounds in his heart that have been opened. God has charged me with this task. Jesus will give me the tools to deal with whatever we face together. Of this, I am certain.*

Heidi Genelli wiped the mixture of flour and water from her hands on the front flap of her apron.

"Joey, please come over by Grandfather," she asked.

The boy, his dark features accentuated by gaslight, left his position at the stove and joined his mother and grandfather by the counter.

"Father, Joey, I have something to tell you."

She reached into the front pocket of her blouse, removed the ring, and slid it over her left ring finger.

Her father smiled and leaned over the barrier between them. "He didn't."

She smiled. "He did."

"What are you talking about?" Joey asked, his brown eyes riveted on the small diamond and the two opals set in the platinum band.

"Your mother is to be married," Jerome Seppo said, patting his grandson on the back. "Mr. Maki is going to be your stepfather."

The boy's eyes widened. "Is that true, Mother?"

A tear slid down the woman's left cheek and dropped onto the sparkling, clean surface of the countertop.

"It is," she whispered, drawing her son into her slight bosom with her hands.

"When?" Jerome asked.

"Next June. Once Andrew has found work and the situation with the farm is cleared up. We'll be married on the shores of Papoose Lake, by Father Martini from Holy Rosary," she said, referring to the local Catholic priest.

"He's willing to marry in the Catholic faith? Isn't he Lutheran?" Jerome Seppo asked.

Heidi Genelli released the boy. Her hand flicked away a remnant of tear in her right eye.

"He is. But he's not a strong believer. He's willing to convert."

The old man studied his daughter.

"Are you sure he's up to this, taking on a boy, a wife, new obligations, after what he faced in France, and all?"

401

The woman nodded and walked back to her work.

"I'm certain," she said, switching their conversation to English. "Andrew has the strength."

And I, she thought to herself as her hands dipped back into the cold dumpling dough, *I will provide the faith.*

Chapter 60

The victim hung from the rafters. The shed concealing the crime was located on property owned by the Cloquet Tie and Post Company, a sprawling creosote works situated upon the banks of the St. Louis River in the city of Cloquet. The shed was not on the main property of the plant, but was located a few miles north of town. The shack, where the man swayed from the oak beam, was an abandoned industrial artifact.

Little water flowed in the river. The Thompson Dam, located several miles downstream from the city of Cloquet, was starved for the want of it. The Great Northern Power Company relied upon the steady flow of the St. Louis River and its tributaries, controlled by the dams located on Island Lake, Rice Lake, Fish Lake, Boulder Lake, and Whiteface Lake, to turn the turbines at Thompson Dam, to create electricity needed to light the city of Duluth and surrounding communities. There had been no significant rain for two years. Gray boulders, newly exposed by the declining river, residue from the last great ice age, the ice age that had melted away to form Lake Superior and the inland lakes of the region, appeared when the water level plummeted. Water restrictions had been imposed. Electricity was being rationed for the first time since the dam opened.

He had been slathered with hot coal tar while his hands were bound behind his back. His answers to their interrogation had been less than satisfactory. They had felt compelled to torture him.

The five men insisted upon anonymity. The potato sacks were to remain in place throughout the ordeal. The big one, the one who seemed to be in charge, had begun the interrogation.

"We know who you are," the leader of the group had said as the motorcar carrying the six men raced through the night.

The victim's head had been covered with a sack identical to the ones worn by the men who abducted him, except that there were no holes for his eyes. The interrogation began as he sat tightly wedged between two of the men in the back seat of the automobile. He could not determine the make of the vehicle. He had no opportunity to memorize the license plate. The fear, the apprehension, made it difficult – impossible, really – for the man to think straight.

Three men sat with him in the rear seat. From the straining of the engine, from the back and forth motion of the automobile as it climbed, he believed they were headed up the bluffs overlooking Duluth. Whether they were headed west, north, or south, all possible directions given the sensations, he could not determine. The leader of the group sat closest to him, on the right, the man's bulky left arm draped around the victim's left shoulder.

"You're that slacker, Olli Kinkkonen," the big man had continued.

"Wirta, Olli Wirta," he whispered.

"You hear that, boys? Even with the Knights of Liberty breathing down his neck, he still lies. But then, you'd expect that sort of behavior from a traitor."

There was a long silence as the car reached the top of the hill and leveled off. The motor purred efficiently. The car regained speed.

"You said you were from the draft board," the captive whispered, uncertainty clear in his voice, the English words carefully formed.

"Never said we were 'from the draft board'. Said the draft board wanted a word with you," the big man corrected. "And it does. Whether there'll be anything left of you for the draft board to deal with after tonight – well, that appears to be an open question, right, boys?"

Nervous laughter broke out in the close confines of the sedan's interior.

"Bud, you got that bottle handy?" a voice from the front seat asked.

"Shut your damn mouth," a husky male voice rebuked. "No names," this new voice added.

"Sorry," the man in the front seat said. "The bottle?"

The victim listened as a bottle was passed and liquid was swallowed. The big man refused to take a drink. The car bucked and pitched over a defect in the road.

"Where'd you learn how to drive?" the husky-voiced man in the back seat asked.

"Why don't you come up here and see if you can do better?" a high-pitched, nearly feminine voice replied.

Another period of quiet ensued.

"You own any Liberty Bonds?" the big man asked.

"I have some stamps," Kinkkonen responded curtly.

"Hear that, boys, this patriot has some stamps. Boys are fighting and dying for his freedom, and all he can do is buy a few stamps."

A fist struck the victim on the right side of Kinkkonen's jaw. The Finn did not complain.

"Stubborn cuss, I'll give him that," the husky voiced man observed.

"You patriotic, Kinkkonen?" the big man asked, withdrawing his fist from the captive's jaw.

"Wirta. My name is Olli Wirta," the man whispered, unable to rub his stinging chin because his right arm was pinned to his side by the weight of the big man's body.

"Are you a citizen, Mr. Kinkkonen? I hear you took out second papers. Have you taken the oath?" the husky-voiced man asked from across the rear seat.

"We know the answer to that, don't we, Mr. Kinkkonen? Of course he's not a citizen," the big man added. "He gave that up, because he's a slacker coward. He won't fight for his country – the country that has fed, clothed, and accepted him for the better part of ten years. Isn't that right, Mr. Kinkkonen?"

They're not going to let me go, the Finn thought, realizing the seriousness of his situation. *I won't let them see my fear.*

"How is it that you gentlemen have escaped serving in the army?" Kinkkonen asked, in a voice propped up with false courage.

"The son of a bitch," the driver exclaimed.

"Turn your head around and watch where you're driving," the high-pitched voice commanded, "before you get us all killed."

"That's none of your damned business, Finlander," the big man retorted, another blow landing on the captive's jaw.

The jab snapped the victim's head back, causing the victim's mouth to bleed.

"Now you've gone and done it. He's bleeding all over my car," observed a new voice, the fifth passenger, the man seated immediately to the left of the captive.

"Will you shut up?" the big man said, clearly upset at the disclosure of the vehicle's ownership. "We'll clean the damn thing once we're done with Mr. Kinkkonen."

Done with me? I was right. I'm not getting out of this alive, the captive observed to himself. *What have I done to deserve this? I simply said I'd rather go back to Finland than fight. It is about foolish politics gone bad. Why should I serve in an unjust war?*

The journey in the automobile lasted over an hour. When the motorcar finally came to a halt, Kinkkonen was dragged from the car by two men, one whom he recognized, from the strong grip and large hands, to be the man who had struck him in the face. Kinkkonen felt blood dripping from his nose, warm and slight, as it trickled down the gap over his mouth. Beneath the burlap sack tied around his head, the captive tasted the bitter iron of his own blood. Men on either side of Kinkkonen propelled him along. His feet barely scraped the surface of the ground as they shoved him through the dark night. It was cold. The air was dry. In the distance, he heard the sound of water moving.

A river? Olli Kinkkonen asked himself. *A creek?*

A door opened. From the noise of the hinges, the captive surmised it was a heavy wooden door. Kinkkonen found himself thrust inside a darkened space. Someone lit a match. Flame sputtered and then illuminated the room in

406

kerosene light. The space was permeated with an odor, the heavy odor of oil.

Where am I? Olli Kinkkonen asked himself. *Where have they taken me?*

His coat was unbuttoned and removed. It took three men to do the job. The Finn's struggles resulted in blow after blow after blow into the side of his face and the prominence of his chin, until he yielded and allowed them to take off his outer garment. He felt his hands being tied behind his back. Crude wire dug into the skin of his wrists as the restraint was twisted. A loop of rope fell around the man's neck. The rope was thick and knotted, as if it had been subjected to hard use. The captive noted that new voices murmured in the background. Other men, men who had likely been waiting for the car from Duluth, were also in the room.

"Is it ready?' the big man asked.

"Good and hot," one of the new voices replied.

Wind buffeted the exterior of the building. From the sounds of the moaning timbers, the Finn concluded that he was in a wooden structure: a barn, or some sort of warehouse.

"Why are you doing this to me?" the captive asked in Finnish.

The big man, his left arm still maintaining a strong grip on the victim, inched closer. Though the Finn could not see the details of his assailant, due to the coverings over both their heads, he was able, by virtue of the lamp, to see the enormity of the man.

"The Knights of Liberty ask the questions. Stop speaking Finnish. It's not going to go well for you, in any event. Why antagonize us further by speaking gibberish?" asked the man who had been seated on the Finn's left in the rear of the car.

"And ask we will," the husky voice stated. "Kinkkonen, will you fight for your country? I say this because, if you will agree to fight, if you state that you will appear tomorrow in front of the draft board and register, there is still a chance that you might leave this evening with only a coat of tar to remember us by."

They mean to tar me? What have I done to be tarred and feathered? Do not the laws of this country, this land, allow me to make choices? Including the choice to return to Finland, to avoid dying, to avoid killing men that I have no personal grudge against?

"He's not going to recant," the big man said gruffly. "He's like all the other Communists. He'd rather see his country under Lenin's rule than fight to save it."

The Finn felt the rope tighten around his neck. The rope stretched under his weight. Wood creaked. Kinkkonen was unable to swallow. He thrashed wildly in an attempt to loosen the wire binding his wrists.

It is finished, Kinkkonen thought, recalling Jesus' final words from the Lutheran catechism of his youth, words he had ignored for nearly twenty years. *Jesus save me,* he pleaded, finding little solace in the prayer but sensing an ultimate need for divine assistance.

With a smooth motion, not the sudden jerk he'd expected, his body was suspended in the cool air of the room. His feet dangled above the floor. His mind raced. Hot, sticky liquid scorched his chest and stomach. The creosote was applied by brush, without his undershirt being removed.

"Christ, what are you doing this for?" he screamed out in English, his native stoicism broken by the searing heat of the tar.

"Last chance, Kinkkonen. Will you fight for your country? Do you want to go home?"

His lungs seized from the fumes. The air seemed contaminated with poison.

"Go home," he coughed, "I want to go home."

The man who had been on his left side in the car pleaded loudly, "Let him go. This has gone far enough."

"You signed an oath. You said you'd see this thing through. If you can't handle doing justice, go outside and wait," the husky voice whispered ominously, "or there may be two slackers who find God tonight."

The reference to his avoidance of the draft stung the man. The man protesting the group's actions looked at the slender form of the Finn being lifted off the ground, the creosote solidifying as it met the cool air, and turned to leave.

As he moved to leave the building, the sympathetic man wiped tar away from the victim's eyes with a clean white handkerchief, before discarding the cloth on the dirty floor.

One of the other men, a man who had waited for the car at the shed, advanced towards the victim.

"That's not the answer we wanted to hear, Mr. Kinkkonen," the newcomer said.

These voices. The big man. The husky-voiced man. This one who comes near. I know these men, Kinkkonen thought.

The victim's right hand broke free of the wire restraints. Kinkkonen's survival instincts overcame the tired metal binding. His fingers clawed the air in front of him and succeeded in grasping the edge of the newcomer's potato sack disguise. Kinkkonen's fingers closed on the rough fabric and pulled hard.

"The son of a bitch has got my hood," the man cried out as the sack flew through the close air of the shed.

Kinkkonen's eyes stared hard through the mesh bag covering his face.

Theo Laine, the victim thought, his body swaying from the rafters.

"I know you," Kinkkonen whispered, calm settling over him as he identified the man. "I know who you are."

"You fool," the big man muttered, obviously upset at the newcomer. "He's seen you. He'll go to the cops."

"I won't," the Finn whispered, the sudden knowledge of inevitability dawning upon him. "If you let me walk away from here, you won't see me again. I'll take the next boat to Finland."

"Too late, Finlander. Can't take the risk," the big man observed.

Kinkkonen's hand ripped open his shirt in an attempt to remove the creosote.

"Damn it, I told you to make sure the wire was tight," the big man had bellowed. "String him up again before he gets that hood off."

The man with the high-pitched voice offered a last plea:

"Boys, this is murder. I didn't sign up to kill anyone," he whispered.

"You too? Go outside with your pal if you can't stomach the work," the husky-voiced man commanded.

The rope drew Olli Kinkkonen's struggling body further away from the sawdust-covered floor. The Finn fought his own weight, pulling against the rope with his free hand in a futile effort to stave off the snapping of his neck.

"What you're doing is wrong. Plain wrong," advised the man who had wiped creosote from the victim's eyes with a handkerchief, as he and the man with the high-pitched voice hurried out the open door.

Chapter 61

Tar Coat Given Alien; Renounces US Rights

Complaint was made to police headquarters by the keeper of a boarding house at 237 South First Avenue East that a lodger, Olli Kinkkonen, was taken to Congdon Park earlier in the evening, questioned by members of the so-called "Knights of Liberty" and tarred and feathered. Kinkkonen was one of six aliens with First Papers who renounced his citizenship rather than face induction. Per a mysterious telephone call placed to the Duluth News Tribune *office at midnight on September 18th, Kinkkonen was found at the lodging house last night and reluctantly entered a waiting automobile when informed that the draft board wanted to see him...*

Kinkkonen allegedly admitted he was unwilling to fight for the United States and said he would return home at the earliest opportunity. He was allegedly tarred and feathered from head to foot. By midnight, he had not returned home.

(September 19th, 1918 the *Duluth News Tribune*)

Karl Gustafsson sat behind his desk at his law office, reading the *News Tribune* article detailing the disappearance of Olli Kinkkonen. Gustafsson's hands tingled. His mouth became dry. His fingers worked his telephone as he rang the operator and asked to be connected to Eustace Ellison.

"Eustace," the lawyer began, his voice becoming quiet so as to conceal the conversation from his secretary, who was located at her desk, immediately outside his office, "have you read the paper this morning?"

"The war is going well, isn't it? Kaiser's ready to fold, by all accounts."

Gustafsson tapped his free hand impatiently on the ink blotter covering his writing desk.

"That's not the article I'm referring to. Did you read the description of the taking of this Finnish man, Olli Kinkkonen?"

411

There was a slight delay. The line crackled.

"No, I missed that."

Gustafsson described the location of the story to the other man. Ellison retrieved his copy of the *News Tribune* and read the article.

"Serves the slacker right," Ellison finally said, his words carefully measured.

The lawyer let out a significant sigh.

"Eustace, we can't have folks, even well-meaning ones like those involved in this thing, kidnapping citizens and tarring and feathering them because they don't like other folks' politics."

"I don't agree," Eustace Ellison said. "So long as the man is only warned, I don't see the harm."

"The harm is that such antics rarely stop with a mere warning."

"I think you're over-reacting."

"Am I? It's a day later and Kinkkonen's still missing."

"Probably trying to take the tar off in one of those cheap saunas along St. Croix Avenue," the businessman mused.

"I don't see any humor in this. Fact is, isn't your son involved in this 'Knights of Liberty'?"

"Seems to me he is a member of the 'Knights of Loyalty'. Might be the same group."

"Well, the stupid son of a bitch is married to my daughter. I don't want her name being dragged into anything like this, you understand?" Gustafsson exploded without warning, his words shouted directly across the telephone lines at Eustace Ellison.

"Karl, there's no call to raise your voice at me. We don't even know that Horace was involved. Hell, we don't even know that the Knights were actually the ones responsible, or if the account in the paper is even true," Ellison continued calmly, refusing to raise his voice. "Might just be a stunt pulled by the Reds or the IWW, for all we know."

Gustafsson felt tightness in his chest. He reached with his free hand, opened the top drawer to his desk, retrieved a blue glass medicine bottle, uncorked the top, removed two nitroglycerine pills, and popped them into his wide mouth without water.

Damn heart, he thought. *Not even sixty years old and already falling to pieces.*

"Look, I apologize for my tone of voice, but this isn't some minor matter. If Horace is involved, I need to know. You need to know. We need to contain this thing, get to Chief of Detectives Lahti before it becomes public, if Horace is in any way connected to the disappearance of this man. Lahti's a fellow Knight of Kaleva. We can reach out to him. You also need to confront Horace and find out what, if anything, he knows."

Ellison considered the request.

"I can do that. I'll have to proceed delicately. My son..." the man paused to assess how to put his words in order. "My son and your daughter... well, I think they are having serious difficulties. I need to tread lightly with him right now. But I will, in some fashion, find out what he knows."

Gustafsson nodded while holding the telephone.

Sofia and I have noticed that Elin is starting to spend more time with us than one would expect, given her prior animosity. She seems taken with the baby, with Alexis. But, then, things change. Nothing lasts forever. Perhaps this arrangement between our families was, given her fiercely independent nature and Horace's inability to grow up, always doomed to failure.

"I've noticed the same thing," Karl Gustafsson mumbled into the telephone.

"I hope they're not headed for divorce," Eustace Ellison observed, the tone of his voice making it clear it was time to conclude the conversation.

I think it's too late for idle hopes, Karl Gustafsson thought.

"I share your concerns," the lawyer said before hanging up the telephone receiver.

Gustafsson patted his chest. The medicine had located the source of his pain and loosened up the strictures binding his heart. A thought crossed his mind: *No harm in calling Chief of Detectives Lahti to ask what, if anything, he knows about this*

Kinkkonen business, Karl Gustafsson said to himself as he rang the operator.

Chapter 62

Spanish influenza, otherwise known as "the Grippe", appeared at various military bases across the United States in September of 1918. The situation became so serious that Surgeon General Blue, fresh from a visit to the front lines in Western France, issued a national alert regarding the treatment of the disease:

> *Every case with fever should be regarded as serious and kept in bed at least until temperature becomes normal. Convalescence requires careful management to avoid serious complications, such as bronchial pneumonia, which, not infrequently, may have fatal termination... Treatment consists principally of rest in bed, fresh air, abundant food, with Dover's powder for relief of pain.*
> *(Press Release, September 15, 1918)*

The editorial written by Elin Ellison appeared unedited in the September 19th edition of *Tyomies*. It caused no great stir or consternation in Elin's home, since Horace could not read Finnish and so did not read *Tyomies*. The couple sat at their kitchen table, eating breakfast morosely. A heavy sky cloaked the sun. Mallards gathered on the placid surface of Lake Superior, paddling in place, waiting for others of their kind to join their number for the Great Migration. Traffic on the street in front of the bungalow was light. Horace loudly sipped his coffee with disregard for his wife.

"You've been out late the past two evenings," Elin observed, her eyes devoted to reading her own work in the morning issue of *Tyomies* as she spoke.

"Lots to take care of at the office."

"Until after two o'clock?" she whispered, her tone intentionally flat and without rebuke.

"Things are very busy right now," Horace added matter-of-factly, his eyes trained on the sports page of the *Duluth News Tribune*.

I'll bet you and that slut were busy, Elin thought, containing her rage. *Thank God you're seeing her. I wouldn't want to have to lie down for you more than I already do, you careless, insensitive bastard.*

"Would you pass the pulla?" Elin asked, monitoring her voice to ensure calm.

Horace Ellison passed a platter of coffee cake. The pastry was store-bought, from a bakery in Finntown – Ranta's Bakery – and was somewhat stale. Elin retrieved a slice of the sweet bread and smothered it with butter.

The woman's eyes clandestinely viewed her husband over the edge of the newsprint she held.

He doesn't even realize what he's done. By bringing home the clap, he's ended my chance to be a mother. Dr. Meyers says I'll recover, with the help of the colloidal silver, but the mechanism to deliver the ovum to the womb has been destroyed by the disease. I am barren. I am now a desert. Not that I'd want to bear Horace's seed. That's not it at all. But I am still young, on the cusp of thirty. I did so want to have a child. There may have been another, someone like Anders. Someone I have not yet even met. Now, it is impossible. I'll not bring this to Horace's attention now. It does me no good. No, I will savor it, stockpile it, hoard it, as Horace hordes his precious gold pieces in his bureau drawer. The information must be used to full advantage at the appropriate time.

Horace felt Elin staring at him, felt her eyes boring into his skin like needles.

"What is it?" he asked curtly, no love, no empathy present.

"Nothing. I was just thinking about my editorial. I could have made it more powerful, more hard-hitting. I think I tempered it too much."

Horace Ellison drew a cup to his lips and swallowed warm coffee.

"I wish you'd give up that nonsense," he advised, authority present in his voice.

"Give up what I love?" Elin replied, placing *Tyomies* on the table in front of her. "Do I ask you to give up your work, the endless hours you spend transferring stock, the days you salivate over which little company or concern you and your father can gobble up, like vultures sitting on a dead deer? No, I don't do that. I allow you to do as you please. Allow me the same courtesy, Horace. That's the least you can do."

Horace Ellison threw down the *Tribune*, stood up at the far end of the table.

"How dare you speak to me in that tone. I am the head of this household. I am the man of this house. You are the woman. I have provided for you, coddled you, humored you. And this is the thanks I get? A rebellious, spiteful bitch for a wife?"

Elin's eyes grew wide. And then, without explanation, she began to laugh.

"What's so funny?" Horace asked, irritation clear in his voice. "What about this conversation do you find funny?"

Elin waved her hand at her husband as if to command him to stop. Fits of uncontrolled mirth contorted her body as she tried to stand up from the table.

"I don't understand you, woman," Horace Ellison muttered, tossing his linen napkin onto a plate covered with the yolky remnants of poached eggs. "I'm late for a meeting."

She continued laughing as the front door to the bungalow slammed significantly shut, and as she walked to her husband's place setting to clear his dishes. Her eyes fell upon the local section of the *Tribune*, to an article that her husband had been reading at the time of his departure:

Tarred Alien Disappears: One Recants by Default
"Knights of Loyalty" Issue Circular Addressed to Those Who Renounce Citizenship.

One alien in Duluth who appeared before the third district draft board and notified them that he intended to renounce his first citizenship papers apparently reconsidered yesterday, following the announcement that Olli Kinkkonen had been tarred and feathered by the "Knights of Loyalty". Kinkkonen had taken a similar action,

regarding the renunciation of citizenship, and carried it through. The
second man did not appear yesterday to complete his evasion of
military duty.

Kinkkonen did not "show up" yesterday, according to the
keeper of his boarding house, at 237 South First Avenue East. The
tarring took place, it was stated, early Wednesday night, and up to a
late hour last night, Kinkkonen had failed to put in an appearance at
his place of residence.

Elin Ellison sat hard on the pine chair that her husband had
recently vacated.

"Oh my God," she murmured. "I know this man," she
realized. "He's the fellow who was with Anders when we first
met at the Work People's College. And he's the man who sat
next to me when I saw Mrs. Flynn give her talk at the
College," the woman continued, upset clear in her soft speech.
"Those bastards. Those damned bastards," she said, dropping
the newspaper back onto the table.

Elin Gustafsson stood up and brushed the fabric of her
housedress. Scraps of toast and bits of cooked yolk fell to the
floor. Normally fastidious in her cleanliness, Elin did not stop
to sweep up the debris. Her right hand, the fingers tingling
with nerves, stroked the unruly fibers of her auburn hair as
she struggled to determine a course of action. Elin shuffled
slowly across the tiled kitchen floor towards the living room,
where the telephone was connected. She rang up the operator
and asked to be connected with the police.

Chapter 63

Oscar Larson sat in a courtroom on the fourth floor of the new St. Louis County Courthouse, listening to Judge William A. Cant. Across the room, at the opposing counsel's table, James J. Courtney, a young trial lawyer appearing in opposition to Larson's Motion to Dismiss, sat patiently waiting for the Judge's decision.

"Mr. Larson," the judge began, "I've considered your moving papers and the arguments you have advanced here today. Normally, I'd take the matter under advisement," Cant said, removing his reading glasses and running a hand through his matted gray hair. "However, it seems to me that Mr. Courtney is right as to the law. If Wolf Lake Camp, owned by Mr. McAdams and his brother, was the employer of the decedent, Mr. Laitila, and if Mrs. Laitila, as the widow, and her children, by virtue of the loss of their father, have sustained a loss of support, companionship, and society due to Mr. Laitila's unfortunate accident and death, then it appears clear to the court that trial in this matter must be held to assess whether or not the McAdams brothers are legally responsible to Mr. Laitila's next of kin. I must rule at this time in favor of plaintiff. Trial shall commence in January, at the first call of the civil calendar."

"We will be ready for trial, your honor," Oscar Larson advised, disappointment veiled behind his magnificent courtroom presence.

James Courtney packed his briefcase and left the courtroom. Oscar Larson lingered for a bit, held up in conversation with Karl Gustafsson, who had been in the audience watching the motion proceeding while waiting to speak to Judge Cant on another matter.

"Oscar," Gustafsson said, advancing from the gallery. "A word, if you have the time."

Larson's large frame straightened from the task of loading his satchel:

"Certainly. How can I be of service?"

"Have you seen today's paper?" Karl Gustafsson asked.

"No. I came right to the courthouse from home."

"Here," the other lawyer said, thrusting a copy of the *News Tribune* into Larson's prodigious hands. "Read the article on the abduction."

"The Kinkkonen matter?"

"That's the one."

Larson studied the newsprint:

Olli Kinkkonen is still among the missing. At the boarding house at 237 South First Avenue East, his luggage still remains uncalled for but his landlord and fellow roomers state they have not seen or heard of him since a mysterious tar and feather party Wednesday night. The police have not learned of Olli's whereabouts. He's gone, that's all, is the general belief.

It is reported that the Knights of Loyalty left Kinkkonen his clothing so that he could skip town without discomfort.

"That's curious," Larson observed, handing the newspaper back to Gustafsson.

"Sometimes they call the responsible group 'Knights of Liberty'. Other times, it's 'Knights of Loyalty'," Gustafsson stated, his eyes level.

Larson leaned over the bird's eye maple counsel table and stretched his lower back.

"You think you know who is involved?" Larson asked.

Gustafsson nodded.

"Who?"

"Can't divulge that. Attorney-client privilege, you know," Karl Gustafsson fibbed, there being no professional relationship between himself and his son-in-law.

"Why are you bringing this to my attention?"

"You know Detective Lahti fairly well, don't you?"

"So do you. He's in the Knights of Kaleva."

"But he's your golfing partner."

Larson smiled. "True. I do take the odd sawbuck off the man on most days."

"Can you approach Lahti and find out what he knows, if anything, about possible suspects?"

"He's a typical Finn, Karl. Like you, like me, Lahti's tight-lipped. But I'll give it a go."

"I'd appreciate that," Gustafsson said.

The men shook hands. Karl Gustafsson picked up his valise and walked through the door leading to Judge Cant's chambers.

Joseph Peterson, co-owner of Berglund and Peterson, Co., a small construction firm located at 131 West Third Street in Duluth, stood on the roof deck of the house he was building and surveyed the surrounding landscape. The water of Pike Lake, an inland lake a short drive north on the Miller Trunk Highway, which ran between Duluth and the Mesabi Iron Range, was deep blue and calm. The air was dry. High cirrus clouds floated over the property owned by George and Wendy McAdams on the north shore of the lake, where Peterson and his crew of four men labored. Thick trunked maples and oaks dotted the ten-acre parcel, the maples bare of their scarlet crowns, the oaks still holding desperately to their brown leaves.

The mansion was framed and sheeted with white pine boards. Peterson and two men were putting the finishing touches to copper flashing installed around the two massive stone chimneys, the chimneys located at opposite ends of the structure and serving stone fireplaces inside the home: four impressive fireplaces in all. When completed, the home would boast running water, electricity from a gasoline generator, and indoor plumbing. A horse barn and paddock would house Mrs. McAdams's beloved American Standard mare and two Tennessee Walker geldings. A large garage had already been completed between the home and the barn. A two-bedroom apartment, sharing the same amenities as the main house, was located above the garage and would shelter a full-time caretaker. Peterson's eyes, blue and vibrant with excitement, the awe of watching his own creativity unfold, took it all in as he stood on the new asphalt shingles of the main building, his feet braced against the pitch of the roof.

"August," the contractor called out, watching a stout man waddle behind a fully loaded wheelbarrow full of sloshing concrete. "How goes the battle?'

August Bodin, owner of August Bodin and Sons Flat Works, a local cement and foundation firm, stopped walking and looked up at Peterson.

"The basement floor is poured and starting to set," Bodin replied, his left hand angled off his forehead to block the sun as he acknowledged the other man. "Just finishing up the floor in the sauna building."

"Plumbers are done with their work?" Joe Peterson asked.

"Done and gone," Bodin replied.

Peterson surveyed the vehicles around the construction site. The plumbing truck was indeed gone.

"This is going to be the most beautiful place on Pike Lake," Bodin observed as he sipped cold water from a metal canteen.

"Nicer than the Marshall house?" Peterson quipped, referring to the cottage of Charles Marshall, owner and president of the Lyceum Theater Company.

"No question. Nicer than the Marshall place," Bodin agreed, capping the canteen and placing it on the ground, in the shade, before resuming his labors.

"Shouldn't one of your men be doing the grunt work?" Joe Peterson teased as the cement man waddled away. "That's an awfully steep hill for an old man to attempt," the contractor observed, noting that the property sloped sharply from the promontory where the home was being built, to the shore of the lake where the sauna and boathouse buildings stood.

August Bodin made no reply as he struggled with gravity. Joe Peterson bent at the waist, pulled appropriately sized roofing nails out of his carpenter's apron, and began to secure the copper flashing around the stone base of a chimney. After a few swings of the iron hammer, the smell of burning wood wafted to his nostrils. Peterson stood up and scanned the property for the source of the odor. Two of his employees were feeding a small bonfire, located a safe distance from the rear of the house. A larger stack of brush and trees limbs created during the clearing of the property sat some distance from the smaller blaze, awaiting similar treatment.

"Boys, it's pretty dry. You got some water in case she gets out of hand?" Peterson asked.

Autumn had brought no rain to the area. Pike Lake is a spring-fed aquifer, one that relies upon groundwater to replenish its contents. A small outlet stream located on the western edge of the lake and natural evaporation had deleteriously impacted the lake's water level during the dry years of 1916 through 1918. Peterson's observation could have been made about any inland lake in Northeastern Minnesota.

"We've got four buckets of lake water and a couple of shovels ready," one of the laborers replied. "There's no wind. That's why we thought we'd get rid of this slash today."

Peterson nodded.

"Just keep 'er under control. Leave the larger pile for another day," Peterson added, returning to his task.

Last thing I need is for Mr. and Mrs. McAdams to come up for a visit and find a pile of burned lumber and two stone chimneys standing naked on their land, the contractor mused, slamming the business end of his hammer into the stubborn head of a roofing nail.

Chapter 64

The water level of Papoose Lake was also low due to the lack of rain. When Andrew Maki returned to his homestead north of Duluth, relieving Paul Pederson of his care-taking duties, the first crop of hay had been harvested and was drying in the log barn and a huge rack of cut and split maple lined the walls of the woodshed, next to the sauna. The team of draft horses on loan from Wolf Lake Camp contentedly munched dry grass behind the new split rail fence erected by the quiet Norwegian.

"You're welcome to stay on until I get married next summer," Maki suggested to Pederson as the men sat on wooden chairs that Pederson had crafted of birch and willow. The men relaxed on the covered front porch of the cabin, admiring the cabin's walls, straight and true, and the utter isolation of Andrew Maki's farm.

"If it's all the same to you, Andrew," the big Norwegian said, "it's a little lonely out here. I need a taste of the fast life," Paul Pederson added with a wink, sipping slowly from a bottle of Fitger's beer. "Plus, I've got a job with McAdams, working up in Thunder Bay in his lumber yard if I want to go."

Maki drained a beer, placed the bottle on the porch floor, reached for a bottle opener resting on a window ledge, grabbed another beer bottle from a wooden case, and pried off the cap on the second bottle.

Pop.

"Suit yourself. But I feel like I owe you a lot more than just a year's worth of room and board," the Finn observed.

Pederson pointed to the marshy edge of the lake. A bull moose, its rack shiny in the bright harvest light, its fur black and shaggy against the drab landscape, the aspen and birch leaves having fallen early, moved slowly through shoulder-high rushes and into shallow water.

"Big fellow," Pederson said.

"Hope he's still here when the season opens," Maki whispered. "The steaks alone would take me through the winter."

Pederson took a short swig of beer and turned towards his friend. "Of course, you could take him now. Who would know?" Pederson quipped.

Maki smiled.

"No, I think I'll let him fatten up a bit. He'll be back. One thing I learned from the Marines is there's no reason to hurry. Things happen when they should."

Pederson grinned, his mouth displaying broken and decaying teeth. Maki's own mouth was clear of cavities. Maki hadn't seen a dentist but once in his life, during basic training. That dentist had marveled at the pristine condition of Andrew Maki's teeth.

The moose continued to graze on water lilies. There was no wind. A pair of redheaded mergansers landed in the lake, some distance from the cabin. The fish ducks dove for prey in turn, always leaving one duck on the surface as a sentinel.

"So you're thinking of going to Canada to work?" Maki finally said, his eyes returning to his friend.

"McAdams is a good man," Pederson replied, draining his beer before continuing. "I could do worse."

"He is that," Maki agreed, holding his half-empty bottle against the sun to gauge its contents. "Despite my faults, he's been a strong friend. Without his help, I wouldn't have this place," the Finn continued, his voice dropping as he spoke.

"He helped you buy the land?" Pederson asked.

"More than that. Financed it. Loaned me the team. Gave me the job as foreman of Wolf Lake Camp when I had no business running the place. Turned the other cheek when I lost Tim Laitila in the rapids," Maki concluded, the words a mere whisper.

"You didn't lose Laitila. That was an accident," Pederson said, rising from his chair to scratch his long yellow beard with gnarled fingers as his eyes followed the retreating moose. "Bull's swimming the lake," Pederson observed, trying to steer the conversation in another direction.

Maki nodded and took a big swallow of beer.

"Accident or not, I was in charge. I'm the man responsible for his death."

Paul Pederson shook his head. "You have to stop blaming yourself. God works in mysterious ways."

"God?" Maki asked rhetorically.

Where was He when I watched men kill strangers for no reason other than that they were told to? Where was He when Gruber's head was turned into pulp, leaving a wife and three little children with no husband and no father? Where was He when Joe Genelli was blown to bits in the mine, leaving Heidi and Little Joey with no income, no future? God, if He is, surely doesn't have much contact with the day-to-day operation of His creation.

The moose waded into the far shore of Papoose Lake and emerged from the water as a distant shadow moving through a brittle landscape. The ducks took wing, their long necks and sharp bills leading them west. Pederson placed a hand on his friend's shoulder.

"I think it's time to take a sauna. The train to Two Harbors will be coming by Brimson in a couple of hours."

"Sauna," Maki said wistfully, placing his empty beer bottle on the pine floor of the porch. "I took one, the first one in over a year, in Finntown, at Erikila's," Maki continued as he stood up. "I'd relish another," the Finn announced, "then I'll give you a lift in the wagon to the train."

"Fire's going and the rocks are hot," Paul Pederson said, walking towards the small log building, located on the only solid ground along the lakeshore.

"And the lake is cold," Maki added, beginning to remove his clothing under the roof of the cabin's covered porch.

Chapter 65

Arthur Fox kept a cabin a mile north of Lester Park, above the waterfalls of the Lester River. The cottage was a one-room affair, a getaway located within the city limits of Duluth, a place for a man to contemplate nature, catch a few brook trout, and hide from his wife. Nothing had ever happened along the banks of the Lester River during Arthur Fox's sojourns there. The occasional deer, the odd raccoon, the common cottontail, and the ruffed grouse made their homes along the river. And, once, a female black bear and her cubs had made a pondering approach towards Mr. Fox as he filleted trout on a board in front of his shack. A few yells, the toss of a sharp stone against the sow's tender nose, and the bruins had departed. He kept no food in the cabin because of the bears and the raccoons. There was no lock on the door. Fox had no reason to prevent others from using the place for temporary shelter when he wasn't around.

September 30th, 1918. Someone had taken the length of slender rope that Arthur Fox kept at his cabin. The rope had been used by Fox as a clothesline to dry clothing after trips into the Lester River, angling for speckled trout. Slippery rocks and frequent unplanned dousings made for wet trousers and shirts.

"Why would anyone want that old rope?" the man asked as he inventoried the contents of his cabin after a day working his trade in downtown Duluth. "Nothing else is missing. The kerosene lamp is still here; so are the dishes and the furniture. Nothing else is gone, nothing but the rope."

Fox puzzled over the missing lanyard as he stepped outside the rustic cabin.

"That's amazing," the man whispered as he looked west.

Dusk was poised on the horizon. The sun blazed gloriously on its decline. To either side of the yellow globe, rainbows rose from the landfall. The pallets of color formed a continuous arch above the descending sun, creating a splendid halo.

"Damn, that is beautiful," the man whispered, his attention riveted on the masterpiece of nature displayed before him.

Something swayed in the shadows. Something distinctly unusual and out of place was hanging from a birch limb a short distance away from the front door of Arthur Fox's cottage.

"What the hell?" Arthur Fox muttered as he stretched out his legs and moved his leather Red Wing hiking boots through the vegetative dander covering the ground.

As the man approached the swinging object, his eyes conveyed recognition to his brain. The closer Fox got to the object, the more certain his mind became that his first inclination had been accurate.

"Christ," Arthur Fox said softly, "it's a man."

The cabin owner covered the terrain between himself and the hanging body with vigorous strides. Arriving beside the man, a horrific reality imposed itself upon the hiker.

"He's dead," Arthur Fox surmised, reinforcing his opinion by touching the body's lifeless skin with the tip of a finger, as he pondered what sort of events would compel a man to take his own life.

Chapter 66

Dangling from a tree one mile north of Lester Park, the lifeless body of a man, identified as Olli Kinkkonen, 237 South First Avenue East, was discovered at five o'clock yesterday afternoon. That the application of tar and feathers at the hands of the so-called 'Knights of Liberty' because of renouncing his citizenship, was the cause of the suicide, is the opinion of Coroner James McAuliffe.

The suicide theory comes with the opinion of the coroner that the man had not been victimized for anything other than his disloyalty as $450.00 in currency was concealed in his clothes. In one shoe, he had $300.00 in bills while in the other, he had $140.00. In his pockets there was $10.55 in silver. He also had $10.00 in war savings stamps.

The mysterious telephone call...discloses that the man was taken from his lodging house...on the night of September 18th and ordered into a waiting automobile as he was wanted by his draft board. A few days previous, Kinkkonen had renounced his citizenship to the United States, indicating he did not want to be drafted into the Army.

Arthur L. Fox discovered the body dangling from a tree. He notified the police and Chief R.D. McKercher, Captain Roberg, and Chief of Detectives Lahti accompanied by Coroner McAuliffe went to the scene, arriving shortly before six o'clock. They found Kinkkonen with feet touching the ground though bent at the knees. A close examination showed that the man had evidently committed suicide.

The body was taken to Grady and Horgan undertaking rooms, where the coroner gave further examination. Clothes were removed and it was discovered that a thick coat of tar had been applied to his chest and abdomen. A handkerchief used in removing tar was found in the man's hat.

It is believed by Coroner McAuliffe that he tried to remove the tar from his body with the handkerchief with little success. His chest bore marks of the severe rubbing despite the fact that the man *had been dead for some time. A notebook containing the name of Sam Laine, Ashtabula, Ohio, was found.*

Government investigation, as far-reaching as that conducted in Illinois recently because of lynching for alleged disloyalty, in violation of President Wilson's order, was hinted at by acting County Attorney Richard Funck. Under the statutes, those who had a hand in the affair would be taken into custody on a kidnapping charge, should they be apprehended through the investigation.
(Duluth News Tribune, October 1, 1918)

The inquiry of Chief of Detectives Lahti of the Duluth Police Department was limited to a determination of the identities of the five men who had taken Olli Kinkkonen from the Talonen Boarding House, with an eye towards charging the five with the crime of kidnapping. There was no murder investigation, Chief of Detectives Lahti and Coroner McAuliffe having convinced Chief McKercher that Olli Kinkkonen had committed suicide. The finding of suicide did not sit well with others in the Finnish-American community:

Olli Kinkkonen Did Not Commit Suicide
(Headline from The Truth, October 4, 1918.)

The St. Louis County Attorney, Warren E. Greene, and his first assistant, Mason M. Forbes, were unavailable to pursue an indictment regarding the taking of Olli Kinkkonen. Greene was serving his country as a major in the Judge Advocate General's Office in Washington, DC. Forbes was similarly indisposed. He was assigned to the Great Lakes Naval Station in Chicago as a First Lieutenant. This left the relatively inexperienced Mr. Funck and Assistant County Attorney Edward Boyle, formerly working out of the County Attorney's Iron Range office, to carry the load. Recently hired Newton Wilson was added as a new assistant but, like Funck, he was largely a neophyte in matters of trial law.

Tyomies newspaper raged out against the decision. Elin Ellison wrote that the conclusions reached by the Coroner and the Chief of Detectives made no logical common sense. The idea

430

that Olli Kinkkonen, a common laborer, someone only peripherally associated with the IWW, could be made to pay the ultimate price for stating his political views, for stating his opposition to the war, given all that her adopted country was alleged to stand for, perplexed the young Finnish woman. Her dander was up. She was determined not only to write about the injustice, but to reveal its perpetrators.

She took a streetcar to New Duluth, one of the southern-most, or, in Duluthian parlance, western-most, neighborhoods of the city. A telephone call to Duluth Police Officer William W. Bolan had preceded the trip.

Daylight claimed the valley. Rock doves rose in unison from the wooden sidewalks and bricked streets of New Duluth. The fluttering of the birds, their incessant cooing, echoed from the stone and frame buildings lining Commonwealth Avenue. Elin Gustafsson stepped from the trolley car and walked in the direction of the New Duluth police station, where Billy Bolan hung his hat as a patrolman. Bolan had been kind to Elin Ellison in the past. He had provided information on other politically charged matters that was available from no other source.

They met in the back room of a two-story boarding house, which had housed steel workers until the Model City was completed. The building was being leased by the city of Duluth for storage. Elin approached the front door of the leaning frame structure, its siding decrepit and absent of paint, the gray boards marred by water stains, the presence of nails in the siding revealed by black rings caused by weather. The windows on the first floor of the tenement were covered with white pine boards. It was seven o'clock in the morning: Elin Ellison had taken the first trolley west. She found the front door unlocked and let her self in.

The bottom of the door scraped the floorboards as Elin opened it. The interior of the building was as cold as the October morning outside. The lights were off. The gas fixtures attached to the walls were covered in cobwebs. Dust rose from the warped flooring as Elin made her way through the first room, the space piled high with lumber, barrels of chemicals, bags of salt, and other supplies procured by the

431

city. She had been in the building before, covering other stories. But this visit was different. This visit, in many ways, including her familiarity with the victim, including the ethnic heritage she shared with the man, was personal.

Her hand turned a tarnished glass knob. Another door swung open. Another cold dark space. She stood at the threshold and waited for her eyes to adjust to the lack of light.

"Mrs. Ellison," a voice called out softly from across the small room.

Elin immediately recognized the speech pattern of the man addressing her. She stepped closer. Billy Boland was seated at an old, porcelain-covered kitchen table, the white surface of the table wiped clean of dust. A blue metallic pot, presumably filled with hot coffee, sat on the table in front of the policeman. Two tin cups, dented and worn from use, sat next to the pot.

"Officer Billy Boland," the woman replied, standing hesitantly in front of the table.

Boland rose, a short, well-proportioned man with a full set of mutton-chops and mustache occupying the better part of his face, and indicated with his right arm for the woman to sit down. Elin accepted the invitation, placed her purse on the floor, and situated a writing tablet and sharpened pencil in front of her on the porcelain tabletop.

"So," the officer began, smiling easily in the presence of the beautiful woman. "Coffee?"

"I'll take a cup," she advised. "It's cold in here."

"Colder than a witch's..." Boland smiled. "Nearly forgot. Can't use that old chestnut in the presence of a lady."

"Tit," Elin said, completing the statement. "I believe the last word would be 'tit'," she added, accepting a cup of coffee from the policeman, warming her cold hands on the tin before drinking from it.

Boland's face turned red. He didn't pursue the topic further.

"So what's so urgent that we need to talk in private?" the officer asked, the details of his blue uniform becoming visible as Elin's eyes became accustomed to the room's limited light.

The woman shivered.

"Sorry it's so cold in here. The city doesn't heat it. Slated for demolition. There's talk of building a branch library on the site."

Elin smiled. "I'm fine. What do you know about the Kinkkonen matter?"

Boland's fingers tightened around the cup that rested in his chubby hands. His black eyes stared hard at the woman.

"What makes you think I know anything?"

Her smile increased.

"Officer Boland, I've seen you at the IWW rallies. I know you've been caught up in the concept of one union, one voice. Instead of the police, the firemen, the steel workers, the miners, the railroaders, the chambermaids all having their own little unions like the AFL advocates, you've been a proponent of the IWW ideal within the police department. Quietly, of course. So as not to be noticed by the folks in power. Don't want to upset the applecart, and all that."

Elin Ellison took a deep swallow of hot coffee and continued, "You know everyone in and everything about the Duluth Police Department. If you didn't, you wouldn't be much of an organizer, now, would you?"

The cop nodded.

"Whatever I tell you about the Kinkkonen matter is off the record."

"Agreed."

Her hand remained poised near the pencil, but she did not pick up the instrument.

Boland pondered the matter.

"Here's what I know. Understand that most of it is hearsay. I'm not privy to much of anything firsthand, stuck way out here in the boonies."

"Understood."

"Way I hear it is, someone prominent, someone with authority, got to Lahti and the Coroner early on, maybe even the day after the poor slob was found with his rope necktie. Not that the conclusion was going to be different. There's just nothing in terms of hard evidence to show that it's anything other than a suicide."

433

Elin Ellison bit the inside of her mouth to prevent an outburst.

"There's the man himself," she suggested.

Boland's eyebrows rose.

"You knew him?"

"Yes. I met him a number of times. I've also asked around. He was sweet on a maid, Elsie Laine. I talked to her. She's broken up about it, as you'd expect. She's convinced Kinkkonen didn't have it in him to hang himself. 'No way he'd do it' was the way she put it."

"Interesting. Rumor is that he was some sort of bigwig in the IWW; that he was working on a massive anti-draft demonstration."

Elin smiled. "Please," she admonished. "Olli Kinkkonen was a laborer. So far as I know, he was barely literate. He was a logger, a dockworker, and, on occasion, attended rallies. Other than refusing to fight and wanting to go back home to Finland, he'd never vocalized his ideals or his politics out loud, to anyone, including Miss Laine."

"Well, what I hear is that there's authority behind the request that Lahti and McAuliffe look no further than the obvious."

"Who?"

"Don't know. Someone with political savvy and the ability to get things done. Word is, might be your people are behind the request."

"My people?"

"Finns."

Elin pushed herself away from the table. Her hands met in front of her winter jacket, the buttons of the wool garment still clasped tightly against the cold. A deep sigh escaped. "Finns?"

Boland nodded.

"Here's what else I know. The handkerchief found in Kinkkonen's hat... well, I have it on good authority that it wasn't his. It was smeared with creosote, as if someone tried to wipe the tar off Kinkkonen's face, but there's scuttlebutt that the handkerchief was monogrammed."

"Monogrammed?"

"Three letters."

"Do you know what letters?"

Boland sipped cooling coffee.

Elin persisted. "What were the letters on the handkerchief?"

"Don't know," the cop replied matter-of-factly. "But they weren't the victim's. Rumor has it, whoever was involved dropped a handkerchief with his or her initials on it at the scene."

The woman blinked.

"There's nothing about a monogram in the newspaper," Elin said.

"That's because no one other than the officers on the scene saw the handkerchief."

"Saw?" she asked, noting he spoke in the past tense.

"Saw," Boland reiterated. "Seems that the handkerchief's whereabouts are no longer certain."

"No longer certain?".

"Gone. Vamoosed. Disappeared," the cop explained. "The handkerchief has mysteriously vanished from the evidence locker at headquarters."

"You're kidding, right?"

Boland smiled, stood up from the table, and collected the empty cups and the half-full pot.

"I better get back."

Elin Ellison stood as well and retrieved her unused notebook from the table. She slid the tablet into her big blue purse, the color identical to that of her coat, and looped the strap of the bag over her right shoulder.

"You can let yourself out?" Boland asked.

The woman nodded.

The policeman started to leave through the back door of the building.

"You never answered my last question," she called out as he departed.

William Boland stopped and turned to face the woman, his body halfway over the threshold, the door open to the cold morning. "How's that?"

"You're kidding about the handkerchief being stolen from police custody, aren't you? Isn't making evidence disappear a little too obvious?"

Boland grinned.

"It disappeared. But it's also been replaced. There's another handkerchief in the evidence locker right now, as we speak, one stained with creosote but lacking the distinctive monogram."

Chapter 67

Eustace Ellison sat in the rear passenger seat of his Cord Touring car, the interior of the vehicle cold and inhospitable, as the vehicle idled on the hard-packed surface of Skyline Parkway. Osprey and bald eagles floated by in migration, gliding south towards open water and abundant fish. Red-tailed hawks and lesser raptors soared high against the infinite blue ceiling of the sky as the birds readied themselves for their sojourns south. Eustace Ellison's oldest son, Everett, was behind the wheel of the motorcar. Everett's younger brother and the youngest son of Eustace and Mia Ellison, Horace Ellison, sat dejectedly next to his father on the hard leather surface of the Cord's rear bench seat. It was Sunday afternoon. There were no other cars on the Parkway.

"Let's take a walk," Eustace Ellison suggested to Horace. "Everett, you stay behind and watch the car."

Everett nodded and stared straight ahead, his eyes following the graceful plunge of a golden eagle, a rare visitor to Lake Superior from the Rockies, a raptor merely passing through on its way to warmer climes.

The men exited the Cord by separate doors.

"What the hell were you thinking?"

Eustace Ellison's fingers pulled at the stiff whiskers of his moustache, the hairs gray, white, and drooping down below his chin as he walked to the edge of the gravel road and peered over the lip of the bluff at uneven ground falling towards the lake.

"What are you talking about?" Horace asked, his voice steady despite a tremor in his limbs.

"Do I have to spell it out for you? The other night. Your wife says you were out, that you didn't come home until after two o'clock. Where the hell were you?"

Horace inhaled chilly air and pursed his lips.

"Working."

Eustace Ellison grabbed the lapels of his son's overcoat and spun Horace around.

"Bullshit. I know where you were. And it had nothing to do with Amalgamated Properties."

Horace's feigned calm cracked open like an egg struck against the side of a cast-iron frying pan.

"So now you're my baby sitter, is that it?" Horace hissed as he removed his father's hands from his lapel.

The old man stared at his son incredulously.

"Don't you ever push me away," Eustace snarled.

Horace pondered a response as his cheeks reddened.

"I'm not some little kid you can push around. I'm not one of your damn servants or employees. I'm your son; your business partner, for Chris sakes."

Eustace Ellison's eyes flashed:

"Watch your mouth. I didn't raise you common. Your mother didn't raise you to take the Lord's name in vain. You think you're so smart? You think that the education I paid for at Carlton College makes you somehow wiser than the old man? Well, I wouldn't have been so damned stupid as to leave a calling card at a murder scene, now would I?"

The son's eyes widened.

"Murder? What the hell are you talking about?"

"No wonder you and your wife are having difficulties. If you lie to her like you're lying to me, what can you expect? Marriage, like any family relationship, must be built upon absolute trust," Eustace Ellison continued. "It is a sad day when a father can no longer trust his own son."

Horace stared out across the barren tops of the meager second-growth birch and aspen, which had seeded the hillside from the bluff to the lakeshore in the three decades after the white and red pines had been taken for lumber: lumber that had made the city of Duluth prosper; lumber that had made Eustace Ellison rich.

"Quit talking in circles," Horace admonished. "Out with it."

"You want plain talk, but you won't tell the truth yourself? A hypocrite is even worse than a liar. And you, I am afraid, are both," the old man said, walking along the edge of

438

the road, a bare hand thrust deep into the pocket of his full-length black wool coat. The wind buffeted Eustace's dress hat, threatening to send it flying over the edge of the cliff as the man stalked back and forth in front of his silent son.

"The truth, you say? You want me to tell you the truth?" Horace asked.

"That would be a welcome change," Eustace said, stopping in front of Horace to consider his son's wide, hairless face.

"I was working."

The father shook his head in apparent disgust. The hand that had been concealed in his pocket emerged slowly, like that of a conjurer pulling an object out of a magic hat.

"Working?" the older man said as he handed a monogrammed handkerchief, the white linen covered in black smudges, to his son. "I doubt that to be the case," Eustace Ellison added with disdain as he retreated towards the waiting motorcar, leaving Horace Ellison to consider the extent of what his father knew.

Chapter 68

Warning! You *Slackers-Pacifists and Pro-Germans. Read what some of our most prominent citizens have said about "The Man They Left Behind", the great patriotic play which the Lyceum Players are presenting at the Lyceum this week.*
(Duluth Herald *Advertisement, September 24, 1918*)

Elin and Horace Ellison sat dutifully in their box seats in the Lyceum, watching the performance of *The Man They Left Behind*, a stage play that called upon its audience to support the war effort in France. The couple was joined in the box by Horace's parents, Eustace and Mia, and another prominent Duluth couple, Mr. and Mrs. Charles Marshall. Charles Marshall had a significant glow on his face as he watched the packed house of the elegant space leap to its collective feet at the conclusion of the performance, giving the cast and crew a rousing standing ovation.

"Quite a show, old man," Eustace Ellison said, clapping his hands together with a bit too much enthusiasm to be genuine. "Well done."

Charles Marshall smiled and joined the applause. He was proud, proud to be the owner and proprietor of the theater, proud that his fervent patriotic zeal, his utterly religious support for American intervention in the Great War, had been captured so perfectly by the actors.

"Yes, Mrs. Marshall," Mia Ellison chimed in, "a wonderful lesson to all slackers. Stand with America or find another country to love," the woman gushed.

Mrs. Marshall smiled but did not reply.

"I heartily agree," Horace added as he assisted his wife with her coat, once the standing ovation had concluded. "A marvelous piece of theater."

Elin Ellison looked hard at the profile of her husband's handsome face as she obediently slipped her arms through the sleeves of her mink coat. She was dressed in the finest of fashions from the Glass Block Department Store: a black chiffon evening dress, black pumps, a tiny bejeweled pillbox hat, and a magnificent string of natural pearls, a recent birthday present from Horace.

"I wasn't impressed," Elin observed in a voice low enough to preclude the theater proprietor from hearing her. "I thought the premise was overblown and the acting terrible."

Horace's eyes narrowed. "Keep your voice down. You'll offend Charles."

"I really don't give a damn," the woman whispered, shrugging her shoulders to align the coat. "I only came because you were so insistent. This isn't something I was hot to see."

Horace's right hand held the sleeve of her coat in a menacingly tight grip.

"Stop denigrating the play in public. We can discuss the finer points of the performance at home, in private," he insisted quietly.

Elin shook her arm in an attempt to be free of her husband's clutching hand.

"Let go of my arm," she whispered.

"I will once we're outside. Don't make a scene, darling," he said falsely. "It isn't becoming. Besides, I'm feeling a bit punk. Coming down with something, I think."

She relented. Not because of any affection or sympathy for his condition or because of any sense of loyalty or obedience due her husband, but because she caught a glimpse of George and Wendy McAdams leaving their seats on the main floor of the theater.

"Wendy," Elin shouted over the railing of the box like a giddy schoolgirl, "wait up."

The Ellison entourage met up with the McAdamses in the main lobby of the theater.

"McAdams," Charles Marshall said, extending his hand to the Canadian, "haven't seen you in ages," the theater owner added through a meaningful smile. "How's the golf game?"

"Putting is always the curse," George McAdams confessed, returning the handshake. "Ma'am," he said, addressing Mrs. Marshall, bowing slightly, his dress hat held loosely between his thick fingers. "You know my wife, Wendy."

The women acknowledged each other. All four Ellisons joined the group and extended courtesies to the Canadian and his wife. Horace's greeting was perfunctory, still colored by the memory of his first encounter with George McAdams and Andrew Maki. There was also the small matter of Eustace Ellison's purchase of McAdams's mortgages and contracts from the bank. There was nothing magnanimous in Horace Ellison's make-up. While his words were careful and deliberate, there was just the hint of gloat embedded in his voice as he made small talk.

"Nice to see you, McAdams," Eustace Ellison said. "We'd stay and chat, but we have dinner reservations at the St. Louis. "Come along," the family patriarch directed.

"I'll telephone you tomorrow," Elin whispered as she walked by Wendy McAdams, "we've got a lot to talk about."

"I'm home all day," Wendy McAdams replied, noting nervous upset in her friend's tone, extending her gloved hand to pat Elin's arm as couples separated.

"You run along," Charles Marshall said to the elder Ellison as he stood in place to converse with George McAdams. "Save us two seats and make sure the wine is expensive, seeing as how you're buying, Eustace."

Eustace Ellison waved a hand in the air in acknowledgment as his party exited the building.

"George, I hear you've constructed a palace across the lake from our little cottage," Charles Marshall said, referring to McAdams's mansion.

The Marshalls' summer place, a three-bedroom, single-story bungalow, modest in comparison to the McAdams project, sat on the south side, the more level end, of Pike Lake, in an area that had been developed as a summer playground for the elite of Duluth.

"Palace is right," Mrs. Marshall interceded. "I was up at the lake the other day, making sure our little cottage was tightened up for the winter, and I got curious. I took the motorcar over to your place and snooped a bit." The woman thrust her dainty hands into those of Wendy McAdams. "I was positively stricken with jealousy. What a marvelous summer retreat you will have once it's completed."

"Thank you," Wendy McAdams whispered. She was unwilling to enter further into the conversation and uneasy when interacting with Duluth's elite, given her working class background.

"Say, I have an idea," Charles Marshall added, slapping George McAdams on the back. "We're having a small group out to close up the cottage and celebrate the birthday of Ginny Walsh – you know the Walshes, don't you?" Marshall asked.

McAdams nodded.

"Well, then, why not come over, if you happen to be at the place? Saturday the 12th. We'll be at the cottage with the Walshes and one or two other couples. Come join us, if you're around."

"Say, that would be splendid. If you're willing, we could show off your new place, take a little tour, if that's not too pushy on my part," Mrs. Marshall said to Wendy McAdams.

"A last fling at the lake, eh?" George McAdams interjected. "What do you think, dear?" George said solicitously, knowing that close companionship with wealthy folks made his wife nervous and caused her to retreat.

"That would be lovely," Wendy McAdams managed to whisper.

Back home, Horace Ellison dressed for sleep. Covering his lean athletic torso with a cotton pajama shirt and bottoms, he crawled beneath the covers of the bed. Elin sat in front of a dressing table mirror, brushing her auburn hair, the fibers sparkling after being washed in the master bath, watching her husband's movements in the reflective glass.

"That was uncalled for," Horace muttered, his head resting on his pillow.

The woman maintained silence.

"Elin, I'm speaking to you," Horace said, his tone insistent.

"I hear you," Elin mumbled, drawing the teeth of the brush through her thick hair.

He sat up in bed and looked hard in her direction.

"This is bullshit," he said, the cuss word said plainly, without venom. "This marriage is a sham."

She continued to brush her hair without comment.

"Are you listening? I said this marriage is a joke."

Elin turned slightly on the dressing table bench so that she could see her husband.

"I believe you said it was a sham. There's a difference between something being a sham and something being a joke," she replied.

His eyes glared.

"Why won't you let me touch you?" he asked, his tone set hard in her direction.

"I have my reasons," she said quietly, refusing to indulge him in an argument.

She had been collecting soiled clothing to take to the dry cleaners. The door to Horace's clothes closet, a door that Horace routinely kept shut, had been left open a crack, just far enough for her to see his best suit lying crumpled in a ball, in a distant corner of the space.

Might as well bring the SOB's suit to the cleaners with me, she had thought, walking across the hardwood floor of their bedroom that morning, opening the door, intent upon retrieving the garment and placing it in the cloth laundry sack she was towing behind her.

"That's funny," she remarked to herself, as she bent at the waist in her housedress to retrieve the slacks to the suit. "I smell oil," she added, sniffing the air like a bloodhound as she stood in the center of the large closet.

She picked up Horace's trousers and held them to her nose.

"God, that's awful. How the hell did he get oil on his good suit pants?" she asked out loud.

Her hands dug into the front pockets of the pants. Her fingers felt linen. She retrieved an odiferous handkerchief, the article bunched, the fabric stained, and held the cloth in outstretched hands.

"That son of a bitch," she had whispered, her hand trembling as she shoved the creosote-stained handkerchief into a pocket of her dress. "That son of a bitch."

Her grooming completed, her husband having relinquished his attempt at conversation, Elin walked over to the electric light switch and pushed the button. She padded across the cold floor, found her side of the bed, and eased herself beneath the covers, careful to avoid any contact with her husband's body as she settled in. Her weight caused the mattress to sag slightly. The bedsprings creaked. Horace rolled over and faced his wife.

"I am still your husband," he whispered. "And it's been a while," he said, his hands seeking the soft skin of her flank.

"Not tonight," she replied, attempting to turn her body away. "Not tonight."

His eyes flashed anger, an expression clear and visible to her in the light that filtered in from a night lamp, illuminating the master bathroom. His hand on her side became rough, like the paw of a wild animal.

"Don't," she admonished harshly.

Inexplicably, as if scolded by his mother, Horace Ellison retreated. His fingers released her skin, and he rolled back onto his other side to face the wall.

445

Chapter 69

Probably no one will be so greatly shocked by yesterday's ghastly disclosure as the unknown men responsible for it. But that does not redeem them.

There has been enough of this business in Duluth and too much, and it ought not to have needed a tragedy like this to stop it.

(Duluth Herald editorial regarding the lynching of Olli Kinkkonen, October 1, 1918)

There are two kinds of Pacifists – maybe more, but two kinds anyhow.

One kind makes no declarations about being for the war at any stage of the game. Just sullen, continuous opposition.

The other kind yelps against the war until caught, and then says it has been for the war all along.

(The Labor World, October, 1918)

"Gutless: that's what the editors of these papers are. Spineless, cowardly men," Elin Ellison railed as she read through the newspapers stacked on her editor's desk. He was perusing her most recent submission regarding the Kinkkonen matter. Emil Parras looked up, his pale eyes straining over the wire frames of his glasses as he studied the finely featured woman on the other side of his desk.

"What was that?" Parras asked, his attention drawn to her venom.

"I can understand the reluctance, the cowardice of the Duluth papers. Their bread and butter, the grease that turns their wheels, is big money. Money from the fat cat politicians. Money from the entrenched businesses for advertisements. I understand why their approach to Mr. Kinkkonen's death is so noncommittal, so restrained. No attempt whatsoever has been made by *The Tribune* or *The Herald* to debunk the notion that Kinkkonen wandered six miles from his boarding house,

446

became depressed because he was tarred, found a rope in the middle of the woods in a cabin he likely didn't know existed, and strung himself up in suicidal despondency," Elin Ellison said, gathering a breath. "The mainstream reporters accepting that line – well, that's one thing. But for the labor newspapers, for *The Truth* and *The Labor World* to sit back and remain largely silent, to avoid controversy, to avoid causing a ruckus with the powers that be; that just doesn't sit well with me."

Parras smiled and chomped down hard on the end of an unlit stogie.

"Elin, tell me how you really feel," he teased.

She stood up and stomped her foot against the dirty wooden floor of the newspaper office.

"Damn it, Mr. Parras, are you going to run my story or not?" she asked, her voice rising in emotion as she gained her feet.

Parras considered the woman. His eyes took in her figure, her lovely face, her stern disposition.

What a spitfire, he thought. *This is a filly that will never be tamed, though I'd like to be the man to try.*

"Mr. Parras?" she asked again, disrupting his untoward thoughts.

"I'm sorry, Elin. I've gone to the board on this one. There's too much speculation in this piece. What evidence do you have that Kinkkonen was strung up by the young elite of Duluth? Where's the proof that I can wag in front of the folks who will be bound and determined to sue for libel once this is printed? Though you aren't naming names, the references are clear. Connections will be drawn. We simply can't risk it, not without evidence that your hypothesis is correct. Guessing that the 'Knights of Liberty' or 'Loyalty', or whatever the hell they call themselves, is a group of young roustabouts that intentionally lynched Kinkkonen, à la Bob Prager – well, that's a nice theory, but I'm afraid it's not one that will see print in *Tyomies*."

The editor handed the typewritten article back to the woman.

"I'm sorry," Parras added, continuing to hold the paper in the air.

"I am too," Elin Ellison replied. "I'm sorry you're unwilling to risk printing the truth," she added, ignoring the editor's outstretched hand as she opened the door to the office and walked out into the room that housed the press, slamming the door behind her.

"A firebrand," Parras mumbled, dropping the unused manuscript onto a pile of unrelated papers. "A true challenge."

She had sought interviews with Chief of Detectives Lahti, Chief McKercher, the Coroner, and others involved in the investigation into the kidnapping of Olli Kinkkonen. She got nowhere. No one in authority would discuss the case with her, on or off the record. She had managed to book time with Judge William A. Cant. Ten minutes of the jurist's time. Tomorrow.

Perhaps I can convince Judge Cant to bring pressure upon the Acting County Attorney. The Attorney in turn can push the Coroner for an inquest, an inquiry into the circumstances of Mr. Kinkkonen's death. However, I can't relate what I suspect. Those bits and pieces of information must remain hidden, like great treasure, to be used in my own way, in my own time.

Elin Ellison suspected that someone of importance, likely Eustace Ellison, had made certain entreaties, had opened certain doors, within the Duluth Police Department – particularly the door to the evidence locker – by thrusting wads of American greenbacks into the appropriate hands. Whether the money went only as far as a one-hundred-dollar-a-month evidence clerk, or climbed higher up the chain of command, she never discovered. All that she knew was that evidence had been liberated, evidence that had somehow found its way into the front pocket of her husband's dress slacks.

Still, she considered confronting the police with what she knew and what she surmised. She contemplated, despite her private musings to the contrary, visiting Chief of Detectives Lahti after seeing Judge Cant. However, other circumstances – circumstances completely unexpected – intervened.

Chapter 70

Continued dry weather and heavy winds contributed yesterday to the spread of marsh, forest, and brush fires in various parts of Northeastern Minnesota. The two most serious blazes were reported from McGregor, Aitkin County, and Prairie Lake, Itasca County. Other fires touched Larsmont, Lake County, and property just to the northeast edge of the city of Duluth.

Ironton and Moose Lake Home Guards were ordered out today to assist Aitkin Guardsmen and forest rangers in fighting a big fire, which had surrounded the village of McGregor on three sides.
(Duluth News Tribune, October 2, 1918)

Dr. E. Fisher, Director of Public Health, reported yesterday that no cases of Spanish Influenza ...have been reported in Duluth.
(Duluth News Tribune, October 2, 1918)

Virginia. Spanish Influenza has made its appearance on the Mesaba Range, according to the report of Dr. Miller, City Health Director. The first case is that of Oscar Sjoblom, aged thirty. Dr. John Rajala, who has care of the case, said today he anticipated other cases.
(Duluth News Tribune, October 5, 1918)

There was a man waiting for Andrew Maki when he arrived by wagon in the bustling little mining town of Aurora. The stranger had taken up a seat in Olson's Café, ordered up breakfast, and sat patiently reading the latest edition of the *News Tribune* he'd brought with him from Virginia. Yesterday's paper contained news that eight cases of Spanish Influenza had been diagnosed in Duluth. The previous day, Dr. Fisher, the man in charge of public health, had boasted in the pages of the very same newspaper that Duluth was free of the plague and would likely remain so.

The stranger, a thickly built specimen, had thrown his long winter overcoat over the back of an empty chair across the table from his place setting. The stranger ate quietly as his large fingers thumbed through the sports section of the newspaper. Steam rolled off a cup of hot coffee, coffee the man had spiked with a shot of bourbon, in front of a plate of quickly disappearing eggs and bacon.

"Mrs. Genelli," Andrew said, as he opened the front door to the restaurant and walked in from an unusually warm morning. "Hot enough for you?"

Indian summer, prolonged warm weather that was out of touch with the autumn season, had stalled over Northeastern Minnesota. Temperatures soared into the mid-seventies. Golf courses remained open. People delayed removing their docks from lakes and ponds, relishing the few extra days of summertime before the onset of snow.

"I'm ready for winter," Heidi said cheerfully from behind the lunch counter, as she wiped a water glass with a dishtowel.

Maki strode over the linoleum floor, purposefully missing the white tiles, stepping only on the blacks, until he had crossed the room.

"Give me a kiss, will you?" he asked, bending his stubble-filled face towards the woman.

"What is that on your cheeks and chin, Mr. Maki?" the woman said in mock horror, pecking the bristled surface of his face with disdain.

"A beard. I'm growing a beard. A man needs a beard to shoot a bull moose," Maki proclaimed, hugging the tall woman, collapsing her modest chest in the process.

"I've missed you," he whispered in Finnish. "You don't know how much."

It was Saturday, October 12th, 1918.

"There's a gentleman here to see you," Heidi Genelli whispered back. "I think he's a cop," she added in Finnish, pointing with the hand holding the dishtowel towards the big man in the corner. There were other patrons in the shop, talking quietly in pairs or eating solitary breakfasts with their eyes riveted upon newspapers. No one seemed to notice the stranger.

"Deputy?" Maki asked quietly.

450

"I think so."

The Finn dropped his light summer jacket onto a stool and walked over to the man's table.

"I hear you're looking for Andrew Maki," the Finn announced.

The stranger's broad face, his jowls covered in bright red fur, muttonchops and a handlebar mustache drooping over his mouth, stood up and extended a hand.

"You Maki?"

"I am."

"Sorry to have to do this on a Saturday," the man replied as he reached into the pocket of his coat across the table. The man's fingers removed a legal document, long pages of typewritten words backed by a blue cover. "Summons and Complaint. Cancellation of a Contract for Deed."

Maki accepted the papers and unfolded the legal document so he could read the details.

Horace Ellison was calling the loan on Papoose Lake. The claim in the pleadings was that Andrew Maki hadn't made a payment on the contract since leaving for the Great War. Maki was in default and had sixty days to pay off the entirety of his debt. The unpaid balance and accrued interest, together with sheriff's fees, now totaled over $2,000.00.

"Shit," Maki whispered in Finnish.

"How's that?" the deputy asked.

"Sorry. I swore in Finnish."

"Didn't introduce myself. Pat Flynn. From Virginia. St. Louis County Deputy. Sorry I had to be the bearer of bad news on your day off," the man related, returning to his seat to finish his meal.

Andrew Maki stood in the middle of the café, his heart in his throat, emotions bursting to escape. His face flushed. His heart raced. Heidi Genelli noticed the change in his demeanor and stepped to his side.

"What's the matter?" she asked.

Andrew's eyes blinked, battling tears, an emotional reaction she found unusual from the staid Finn.

"Andrew? What's the trouble?" Heidi asked in Finnish.

"Ellison has called my note. I have sixty days to pay off the property, or my farm will be taken away from me."

The woman sighed and looked over the man's shoulder at the legal documents.

"I have some savings, nearly a thousand in the bank in Virginia," she offered hopefully.

His eyes met hers. There was a sudden glint of love, of gratitude intermixed with anger and injury.

"That's not nearly enough," the Finn said, shoving the papers into the pocket of his wool work pants before walking out wordlessly into the morning.

Chapter 71

Andrew Maki sat in the barber's chair, studying the legal documents that Deputy Flynn had served upon him. There was a realization that Horace Ellison, despite all appearances, had harbored a grudge, had waited for the right circumstance, the right moment, to retaliate for the humiliation of the events of four years previous. There was no question in Maki's mind that the young businessman was still reeling from the effects of being bested in a fistfight.

Horace Ellison, at the time a swaggering braggart of a college boy home for a long weekend from Carlton, an expensive private college in Northfield, Minnesota, had prided himself in his ability to box. He'd taken lessons in the art of pugilistic combat at an exclusive gymnasium catering to rich and powerful men. It had been quite a surprise to the bigger and younger man that any immigrant, much less a Finn, possessed boxing skills superior to his own. Horace Ellison did not learn humility when Andrew Maki's fist crushed Ellison's jaw, injuring more than mere flesh and bone. The wound to Ellison's spirit, to Andrew's thinking, must have boiled beneath the surface, festering, until the right opportunity to settle the account had landed in the young businessman's lap, in the form of the wreck of the *Blue Heron*.

It's hard to believe that he held this in all these years, given the level of animosity that he must feel towards me, the Finn thought, closing his eyes as Homer Burcar, the barber Maki regularly visited when he was in Aurora, applied warm water to his scalp to wash away the dust of the road. *After all this time, now he strikes. I never saw it coming.*

Maki's eyes closed as he sought a simple solution to the legal papers resting on his lap.

"You hear about the lynching?" Homer Burcar said, his scissors beginning to cut the unruly hairs at the base of the Finn's neck. "Seems to me the fellow they're talking about was someone you knew," the barber added, breaking from his duties to retrieve the Duluth paper he'd saved in case Maki came in.

"Lynching?" Maki asked, opening his eyes, massaging his throat with his left hand, working on a catch in his windpipe.

"Read for yourself," Burcar urged, handing the crumpled newspaper to his customer.

The barber resumed his work as the Finn studied the articles on the page.

"Where is it?"

"Right here, in the center of the page," Burcar said, pointing to the passage with the tip of the stainless steel scissors he was using to cut Maki's hair.

Maki read the article.

"Shit," the customer said in Finnish as he turned to look at the barber. "Ouch, you cut me," Maki exclaimed, dropping the newspaper in his lap.

"That's what you get for moving around in the chair, you *hoelzernkop*," Homer Burcar advised. "You're bleeding. I'll get a towel."

The barber retrieved a clean cotton towel and dabbed at a bubble of blood on the back of Maki's suntanned neck. The wound was only a half-inch long and had barely broken the skin. Sunlight filtered into the barber's shop from the late morning sun and landed upon the barber's significant mustache, turning the white hairs into apparitions of silver. Maki's eyes glanced up from the article and noted that Burcar, despite being over eighty years old, moved with supple grace.

"I know enough German to understand what you called me," Maki muttered, checking the back of his neck with his left hand while raising the newspaper from his lap with his right. "My head is not wooden."

"It is if you're stupid enough to leap around when a man is cutting your hair," the barber retorted with a sly grin.

Burcar stepped away to admire his work.

"I know this man. He's a friend. He worked for me at Wolf Lake," the Finn said, his attention riveted on the newspaper account of Arthur Fox's gruesome discovery and

454

the theories advanced by the police and the coroner as to the cause of Olli Kinkkonen's death. "Olli was a true Finn," Maki continued emotionally. "He'd sooner cut off his nose to spite his face than kill himself. No way he'd hang himself out of shame. Doesn't make sense in the context of the article. Says he refused to back down from renouncing his second papers and avoiding the draft. If that's true, having stood his ground, he'd never take his own life."

"Seems sort of odd, you being a war hero and all, that you'd stand up for a slacker," Burcar said, applying lather to the Finn's cheeks and chin in preparation for trimming Maki's beard and moustache. "Got shot at my share during the War Between the States," Burcar added as he slapped a straight razor against the leather strop hanging from the barber's chair. "I was nearly thirty, oldest volunteer in my company, when I made the stand with the other boys of the First Minnesota at Gettysburg. Watched men fall all around me, took out five or six young Rebs, but came out without a scratch," the old man added with satisfaction.

Maki remained silent, considering a response to the slightly built old man, with the fiery eyes and the pent-up energy. A headache had come on while Maki sat in the barber's chair. The dull throb in the back of Maki's head made it difficult for the Finn to concentrate.

"Came here to Minnesota from the Old Country, from Germany, with my parents," Burcar added, his voice interrupting the uneasy silence between the men. "I was only a wee thing. Grew up American, loving this country even though I wasn't born here. Would have taken a bullet, if it came to that, keeping this country together. Don't understand folks like Kinkkonen who aren't willing to die for what their adopted country stands for," the barber concluded, beginning to trim the edges of Maki's beard.

"I'm no war hero," Andrew Maki whispered, his eyes riveted on the newspaper article in front of him. "And Olli Kinkkonen was no coward."

Homer Burcar sensed that there was nothing more to be gained from pushing the issue with the Finn. The barber finished his work in silence, wiped off the excess lather, and accepted four bits from Maki in payment for the haircut and shave.

"See you in a month," the barber called out as the Finn turned to leave the newspaper on a wooden bench near the shop's only door. "Keep the paper," Burcar urged. "Might want to look into the matter when you get down to Duluth."

Andrew Maki tucked the newspaper under his left arm and walked out of the door without saying another word.

Outside, Percherons hitched to Maki's freight wagon waited patiently in front of Olson's Café. Andrew Maki's eyes looked up and down the blacktopped main street of Aurora. A variety of people walked the sidewalks of the town: miners, their clothes filthy with red dirt; women with parcels under their arms, fresh from shopping at the little stores that were squeezed between the bars and saloons along both sides of the thoroughfare; and the occasional couple dressed for an afternoon of revelry in Virginia or Duluth. Those folks who knew one another exchanged pleasantries. No one greeted the Finn as he moved towards the wagon.

Maki was set to go back to work at Wolf Lake Camp as the camp boss on Monday. Despite Maki's consternation over the Laitila affair, George McAdams had insisted that Maki return to his old job. The Finn had little choice. There was nowhere else he could make the same kind of money and still live on Papoose Lake, at least until Horace Ellison snatched it from him in court. The old crew, minus Kinkkonen and Laitila, would be back on Monday. Work in the forest would begin as soon as the ground froze. There was recognition from the Finn that he needed to get back to work, to get his hands dirty and his mind occupied, as a means to forget the bullets, the bombs, and the dead; as a means to end the nightmares that caused him to toss and turn, robbing him of meaningful sleep, nearly every night. Throwing himself back into work would not solve the problem presented by Horace Ellison, however, nor answer the lingering questions in Andrew Maki's mind about the death of his friend at the hands of vigilantes.

Those matters will require further study and creativity to resolve, he thought, his thin face breaking into an inadvertent smile at the sight of Heidi Genelli and her son, exiting Olson's Café.

The woman and child stopped upon seeing Maki approach. Joey Genelli broke into a run. The child's arms pumped with effort as the boy dashed towards the Finn.

Chapter 72

Bemidji. Twenty-five men who registered in September have claimed exemption...on the grounds that they are aliens. Of that number, fifteen are Norwegians, five are Swedes, two are Danes, two are Russians, and one is a Finn.

A man who gave his name as Gunnar Erickson...returned his First Papers to the board and forever relinquished his right to become a United States citizen.
(Duluth News Tribune, October 11, 1918)

Influenza gains in Duluth. Twenty-five cases reported.
(Duluth News Tribune, October 11, 1918)

A reward of $500.00 is offered in a proclamation by Governor J.A.A. Burnquist for information leading to the arrest and conviction of any person who participated in outrages blamed to the secret organization in Duluth known as the Knights of Liberty, who recently, according to mysterious information, tarred and feathered disloyal suspects. The governor's action followed a report from the County Attorney Richard Funck of Duluth because of the suicide of Olli Kinkkonen who was given a coat of tar and feathers.
(Duluth News Tribune, October 6, 1918)

County officials and police authorities in Duluth and Range towns continued yesterday to search for information that would help solve the death of Jimi Zillo, whose body was found a week ago on the Miller Trunk Road, twenty miles outside Duluth, of a gunshot wound to the head. Zillo's head was found severed from his body.
(Duluth News Tribune, October 4, 1918)

"I'm not sure I can assist you, Mrs. Ellison," Judge William A. Cant advised, leaning back in an oak swivel chair, which was situated behind a gargantuan oak desk in the judge's chambers, on the fourth floor of the St. Louis County Courthouse.

Cant's office was on the eastern end of the building. His windows, large and free of draperies, overlooked the hustle and bustle of the port. A pair of Bausch and Lomb binoculars rested on the window ledge, ready for use whenever boats entered or exited the ship canal beneath the Aerial Bridge.

Cant studied the woman. The woman studied him. The intensity of the audience was palpable. Cant's linear face, long sideburns, imperious neck, his light brown hair swept off his forehead, his dark penetrating eyes, were scrutinized by the young woman as silence imposed itself between them.

Elin Ellison shifted her gaze and began to talk. "Judge, you're never one to shy away from trouble, at least that's what I've gleaned from reading about your rulings over the years."

"For example?"

"Your decision on the Finns, of which you are doubtlessly aware I am one. That took courage. What I'm asking now will take similar strength of character."

"Mrs. Ellison, from what I understand, there is an ongoing police investigation into Mr. Kinkkonen's death."

"Into his abduction, yes. His death, no."

"But I'm a judge. It's not my place to conduct investigations. And from what I've read in the papers, the police and the county attorney are convinced Mr. Kinkkonen killed himself."

Elin drew her face closer and fixed her pewter eyes on the judge.

"I knew him, Judge Cant. Not well, but well enough to know he wouldn't hang himself in shame over doing what he thought was right. Someone murdered Mr. Kinkkonen. Maybe their 'discussion' with him got out of hand and his death was an unintentional result of that. Maybe it was intended all along, like that of Bob Prager in Illinois, as an example to all of the other so-called slackers. I don't know. But I'd like the police and the county attorney to at least make an effort to find out."

Cant rubbed his chin and looked out the southern window of his office, the window that faced the hillside. A blue flame burned in a gas fireplace behind a glass door across the room, despite the unnaturally warm day outside.

"I have no reason to go to the county attorney. I don't know any more than what is in the papers," the judge said slowly, his back to the woman.

Elin Ellison nodded her head.

"But I do. Understand that I cannot divulge, as a reporter, the source of what I know. But I believe that a certain element in this town, folks well-known to me and to you, intended Mr. Kinkkonen to be lynched, intended for his death to shock those opposing the war into silence."

Her stomach fluttered. She had no such information. She possessed nothing more than a creosote-soaked handkerchief and a mountain of suspicion. It was a bluff, a bluff calculated to prompt the jurist into action.

"Reporter? What we talk about here today is 'off the record', correct?" the judge asked, concern sneaking into his diction.

"Agreed."

"Which paper do you write for?"

"*Tyomies.*"

"Ah, a radical. Just like your mother," the judge said through a smile as he turned to face back the woman. "Must have some lively discussions with old Karl, I'll wager. What's your take on the Senate rejecting universal suffrage?" Cant asked, blithely changing the subject.

On October 2nd, the United States Senate had rejected President Wilson's latest call for the extension of federal voting rights to women. The ratification of the Nineteenth Amendment was stalled in Congress, narrowly defeated before the upcoming elections.

"It will pass shortly," Elin said confidently. "The last vote was 53 to 31 in favor. Once the elections are over, it will pass," she asserted.

"I believe you are correct," Judge Cant agreed, smiling as he studied the woman's pretty features.

Such a beauty, he thought to himself. *And from what I hear, every bit as formidable as her departed mother. Laina was a sweet woman with a powerful sense of justice*, the judge mused. *Perhaps there is something I can offer to mollify the handsome daughter of Laina Gustafsson.*

"I'll tell you what, Mrs. Ellison. I'll speak to Mr. Funck, the Acting County Attorney. He's a little wet behind the ears, if you know what I mean, but he's an honest man. Perhaps I can convince him to pressure the coroner into holding an inquest. That way, the investigation into Mr. Kinkkonen's demise will be public and open to scrutiny."

"I would appreciate that," Elin whispered. "I would be in your debt."

"I'll see what can be done," Judge Cant said, rising from his seat. "Now, if you'll excuse me, I have special term starting in a few moments."

The judge came out from behind his massive desk, extended his right hand to the woman and assisted her out of her chair. At the doorway leading from the judge's chambers to the courtroom, Elin stopped and turned towards the judge.

"Judge Cant, thank you so much for seeing me," she said softly. "I hope you can convince the county attorney to force an inquest."

The jurist smiled.

"Acting County Attorney. Don't give him a title he hasn't earned yet. I think I can persuade young Mr. Funck to be a bit more inquisitive. Beyond that, we'll simply have to see. Good day, Mrs. Ellison. And say hello to your father. I don't see him up here as often as I used to."

"I'll give him your regards, Judge Cant," the woman said, stepping out into a courtroom that was slowly filling with attorneys waiting for their cases to be called.

Sofia Gustafsson bundled her year-old daughter, Alexis, for the out-of-doors. The woman's forehead was covered in perspiration, sweat from the onset of a high fever, not from exertion. Sofia had been kneading bread dough with the family cook when she had felt the onset of unnatural heat and accompanying dizziness strike. A quick review of Alexis'

461

temperature confirmed that the little girl was burning up with fever as well. There was no hesitation on the part of the mother. She telephoned a taxi and departed for the office of Dr. Arthur Collins, located in the Fidelity Building on Superior Street in downtown Duluth.

"It's 'the Grippe', I'm afraid, Mrs. Gustafsson," Dr. Collins advised after examining mother and child. "Both you and the baby have come down with Spanish Influenza."

The Finnish woman, her classic figure unaffected by the birth of her first child, began to weep.

"There, there, Mrs. Gustafsson. We'll put you and little Alexis in a private room, the best suite at St. Luke's. With rest and proper observation, you'll do just fine," the physician announced, optimism clear in his voice.

"I need to call my husband," Sofia said softly. "Could the nurse watch my baby while I speak to Karl?"

"Certainly. I'll dial the operator," the doctor added sympathetically. "Follow me," he urged. "Nurse Albright, please see to the child," Dr. Collins added, nodding to the registered nurse, who was already in the examination room.

"With pleasure. Alexis is such an easy baby," Nurse Albright responded, taking the child from the mother.

It was Friday, October 11, 1918. The number of cases of Spanish Influenza, a disease primarily of infants and young adults, striking predominantly those between the ages of twenty and forty, was asserting itself. It was not the flu virus itself that made the epidemic of 1918 so deadly. With rest, proper food, and observation, most patients were able to recover. It was the tendency of opportunistic secondary complications, such as bronchitis, which often blossomed into bronchial pneumonia, that made Spanish Influenza deadly. Aspirin, in the form of powder, was often used to treat fever. Epinephrine was prescribed for pneumonia. Oxygen was commonly applied, either by mask or injected under the skin. The exact origin of the disease, a malady that had first manifested itself in crowded Army camps throughout the United States, was never determined, although the first wave of disease was detected at Fort Riley, Kansas on March 9, 1918. Wounded Doughboys returning from France apparently carried the disease back with them from Europe. The outbreak of the epidemic in Duluth would eventually result in the dedication of numerous new funeral homes in the city.

The flu knew no class distinctions. By the end of its reign, Spanish Influenza would claim more than twenty million victims worldwide; more than 600,000 in America alone. Duluth's death toll from the flu would be in the hundreds by the time the epidemic subsided in 1919. Some of those who died were Finns.

Chapter 73

The freight wagon bounced along the gravel surface of the Aurora Road. Andrew Maki drove the borrowed team, the midday sun reflecting off the sweaty backs of the Percherons, his attention concentrated on keeping the animals moving at a steady pace. Heidi Genelli sat next to Maki on the pine seat of the wagon. Joey Genelli sat in the rear, on the wagon's freight deck, surrounded by sacks of flour, sugar, coffee, and boxes filled with canned goods that Maki had purchased for the winter. Though he would take most of his meals at Wolf Lake Camp, Maki's intention was to spend Friday nights in Aurora with Heidi, and Saturday mornings through Monday mornings at his farm. Over the past months, using the meager military pay he'd saved while in France, Maki had purchased laying hens, a rooster, and a pair of feeder pigs. His plan was to slaughter the chickens one at a time as winter progressed and as the hens' egg production declined. He'd keep the rooster.

No sense in killing a perfectly good rooster that would taste perfectly awful, the Finn thought as the wheels of the wagon rolled over stones, holes, and piles of gravel along the Aurora Road. Motorcars using the gravel path between the Village of Aurora and County Road No. 4 often broke down, their axles snapped by the terrain. Horses fared better, though not by a great margin.

I'll get Joey to help me put down the feeder pigs once they reach weight, teach him how to butcher, how to smoke the hams and the bacon, Maki thought, noting that the piglets he'd acquired since coming back home were now close to fifty pounds.

"You're awfully quiet," Heidi observed.

Andrew Maki tried to speak, but was seized by a rough cough. The Finn couldn't reply until he had expelled the phlegm blocking his throat.

"Just thinking about winter," Maki replied, his voice coarsened by mucous.

"You don't sound good," Heidi observed, her eyes drawn to her companion's face. "Your face is as white as a ghost's."

Maki shook his head in disdain. "It's nothing. Just a cold."

The wagon pitched over a large gap in the gravel. Joey fell to one side in the bed of the conveyance. A sack of flour landed on top of the boy.

"You OK back there?" the Finn asked, concern apparent in his words.

"Fine, Mr. Maki," the youth replied, righting the flour sack and himself without assistance.

"Takes strong arms to manhandle a sack of flour," Maki observed, returning his eyes to the road. "He'll be a powerful man when he grows up."

"His father was," Heidi replied. "He could lift a twelve-foot white pine beam and hold it in place by himself," she added, pride colored by the longing apparent in her voice.

"He must have been a fine man," Andrew said, his words distorted by another coughing spell.

"He was. You're sure you're OK?" Heidi Genelli asked solicitously.

"I told you, I'm fine."

The wagon turned onto County Highway No. 4. The roadway improved. No. 4 boasted a smoother surface than the Aurora Road. A horse-drawn blade had graded newly placed gravel. The lack of any significant rain, the recent cloudburst in Aurora having been confined to a path further north, allowed the leveled surface of the road to maintain its integrity. Highway No. 4 was nearly devoid of potholes and pitches, though these defects were present to a considerable extent over the entirety of the Aurora Road.

"Look," Joey exclaimed, pointing an index finger at a clearing in the scrub forest surrounding the road.

The Percherons neighed apprehensively. Whether they detected danger by virtue of their sense of smell or by

465

concerted effort of their weak eyes, the horses sensed the risks presented by a predator.

"Shhhh," Maki said quietly, his voice reduced to a mere whisper. "Whoa, boys," he urged, pulling hard to slow the team, his bare forearms exposed by his rolled-up shirt sleeves as he strained against the leather reins linking the wagon to the horses.

"What is it?" Heidi Genelli asked, lowering her voice, her brown eyes squinting in an attempt to identify the source of the horses' agitation.

"Mountain lion," Maki advised, his left hand dropping to the .25-.35 Winchester repeater he kept tucked beneath the seat of the buckboard to ward off the occasional drunk bent on hooliganism, or to shoot game when animals of merit presented themselves.

"You're kidding, right?" the woman murmured.

The child started to move towards the rear of the wagon.

"Stay put," Maki commanded softly, his voice remaining calm despite the rapid beating of his heart.

The Finn withdrew the Winchester. The big cat stood imperiously on a pile of timber slash, debris left from the final cutting in the section, lifted its head, and sniffed the air. The cat's long, prehensile tail waved back and forth as the animal detected the humans. Maki slid his left hand into the lever action of the Winchester and brought the rifle to his left cheek. His right hand gripped the walnut undercarriage, supporting the gun's barrel.

"Don't," Heidi Genelli said softly, placing her left hand on Andrew Maki's right shoulder. "Why kill it? We may never see another one."

The Finn glanced at the woman before locking his eyes on the cat.

"What?" Maki whispered.

"It's so beautiful," Heidi said, pressing her hand firmly against Andrew Maki's arm. "It's one of God's great mysteries."

Andrew maintained a wary eye on the cougar.

"There'll be no mystery when one of my feeder pigs goes missing in the night and there are cat tracks from the barn to the swamp," he muttered.

"Think about it, Andrew. Is a pig or even ten pigs worth killing an animal, the likes of which we'll never come across again?"

He had to admit that she was right. Mountain lions had once made Northeastern Minnesota part of their range. However, with the coming of the logging camps, the decimation of the old-growth forests, and the rapid settling of the land by immigrants, the caribou had largely, with the exception of isolated animals, disappeared. The moose had retreated into the extreme northern limits of the state, away from the disruptive efforts of man. And the big cats had migrated west, towards the Black Hills of South Dakota, where game remained plentiful.

Maki lowered his rifle and sat quietly beside the woman. His finger remained on the Winchester's trigger, at the ready if the cat threatened the team. But the cat didn't advance towards the horses. Apparently satisfied that the humans posed no threat, the cougar leapt from the brush pile and disappeared into a marsh bordering the cutover.

"That was a mountain lion?" Joey asked from his perch behind the driver's seat.

"It was," Andrew Maki advised.

"You wanted to shoot it?" the child continued.

"Hey, now," the Finn said, urging the nervous team forward. The pair stood motionless. "Come on now, boys," Maki urged, snapping the reins against the animals' flanks. The horses reluctantly raised their hooves and began a slow walk down the road. "I did," Andrew said in answer to the child's question, once the wagon was moving.

"Why didn't you?"

"Your mom," the Finn said, turning his unnaturally pale face to the woman, sweat pouring out from beneath his work Stetson. "She'd rather sacrifice my pigs to that mangy cat than watch me shoot it," the man quipped in Finnish.

"He doesn't know that much Finnish," Heidi said, placing the back of her left hand, the skin cool and dry, her forearm exposed and covered with soft blond hair, against Andrew Maki's cheek.

"I know enough to figure out that Mr. Maki was making fun of you, Mother," the boy added with a sly grin.

"You're burning up with fever," Heidi noted, ignoring her son, her hand recoiling from Andrew Maki's forehead.

"I do feel warm," Maki admitted, his head spinning, his balance becoming questionable.

"You need to get to bed," Heidi Genelli urged, wiping Andrew's forehead with a lace handkerchief pulled from a traveling bag beneath her seat.

Andrew Maki was about to say that he had too much work to do at Papoose Lake, too many things to accomplish before going back to work on Monday, to take to his bed. Instead, Maki's head dropped to his chest, his eyes rolled back, and his hands went limp, releasing the reins.

Chapter 74

Duluth clamps Spanish Influenza lid - 27 cases found. All public buildings, churches, schools, and theaters are now closed.
(Duluth News Tribune, October 12, 1918)

The re-election of Governor Burnquist faces opposition due to the actions of the Minnesota Board of Public Safety. Judge C.W. Stanton of Bemidji supports the governor even though Stanton is a Democrat:
"Every German sympathizer, every IWW member, every discontent of every kind is opposing this re-election...This is but part of the insidious propaganda."
(Duluth News Tribune, October 12, 1918)

The Thompson Dam of the Great Northern Power Company has insufficient water flow due to no rain. The drought is causing water shortages. Electrical rationing has been instituted.
(Duluth News Tribune, October 12, 1918)

Horace Ellison stumbled and then fell on his way to work. His head pounded. His chest wheezed. He was unable to breathe deeply. Fever rose and fell, as if an out-of-control thermostat regulated his body temperature. As he lay on the sidewalk in front of the Lyceum Theater, the building housing Amalgamated Properties, images floated in and out of Ellison's influenza-infected mind: hallucinations of the street, visions of passing motorcars and streetcars racing over the tracks hogging the middle of Superior Street, sparks flying and crackling from the trolley cars' connection to overhead electrical power. Pedestrians, folks who did not know Horace Ellison, stopped and knelt on the cement sidewalk to assist the stricken young man.

"It's the flu," surmised a rough-looking character, obviously a laborer headed to work. "Keep clear of him until

469

we get him some help," the man advised, standing up as he urged others in the crowd to stand back.

"What seems to be the problem?" said a mustached young fellow, a man no older than Horace Ellison, as he pushed his way through the folks assembled around the unconscious victim.

"I think it's the flu," the laborer advised. "I felt his neck for a pulse. It's strong but he's burning up. You should keep your distance," the laborer suggested, noting that the man who'd asked the question was dressed in expensive casual attire.

"I'm a doctor," the man replied, kneeling next to Horace Ellison, feeling the man's neck pulse with two fingers and watching the second hand of a Swiss timepiece as he counted.

"Don't look like a doctor," the laborer said, maintaining distance from the ill man on the sidewalk.

"Supposed to meet my brother for breakfast at the Spalding," the physician explained as he stood up. "You should hang out a shingle," the physician said to the laborer, wiping his hand on the handkerchief he drew from the front pocket of his slacks. "Dr. Everett Pratt," he said, extending his right hand to the laborer. "He's definitely suffering from Spanish Influenza. This man needs to go to the hospital."

"Pleased to meet you. Don't be offended, but I can't afford to get sick, so I'll pass on shaking hands, if you don't mind," the laborer replied in a gruff tone. "Name's Becker. Bob Becker. I'm late for work at the Steam Plant, so if it's all right with you I'll take my leave now."

"I'll stay with the patient," Pratt responded. "Thanks for your assistance, Dr. Becker."

The laborer grinned at the praise and raised his lunch pail in salute as he turned and walked east, towards the steam generation plant.

Elin Ellison was surprised when she arrived at St. Luke's Hospital. Karl Gustafsson had telephoned his daughter and explained that both Sofia and Alexis had taken ill with the flu and were at St. Luke's, under the care of Dr. Collins. Elin did not expect to discover her husband also being treated in St. Luke's for influenza.

"How are they?" Elin asked Karl Gustafsson as she arrived on the ward where her stepmother and half-sister were being kept in isolation.

The lawyer appeared, upon first impression, to be utterly devastated. Whatever Elin thought of her father, for the secret life he had led while her mother was still alive, for his inability to buck himself up and emotionally support Laina as she died, there was, behind a thin wall of contempt and spite, a foundation of love. It was the obligatory love that a child feels for a parent who has perhaps erred but not failed. Karl Gustafsson's massive frame, his large round head, his ample hairless jowls and chin shuddered in agony as he wept in the waiting room.

When Elin addressed her father, he looked up, and in his eyes, in Karl Gustafsson's eyes, she saw real pain.

"Oh, God," he muttered, rising from the wooden bench he was sitting on to embrace his oldest child. "Oh, my God."

Tears, moisture that Elin Ellison did not think would ever be produced by her father's body, rolled off the man's wide face and onto his daughter's winter coat.

"Here, let me get those," Elin said, reaching into her pocket to remove a kerchief. She dabbed Karl's tears, drying the skin of her father's face as she looked intently into his eyes.

"Tell me how they're doing," she said, urging Karl to sit next to her on the hard pew.

Karl Gustafsson took a significant breath.

"The doctor says it's touch and go for the both of them. Sofia is so stubborn. She hates doctors. Used a mid-wife for Alexis' birth. Wouldn't hear of going to the hospital unless it was something serious," Karl Gustafsson said, wiping his face on the sleeve of his sweater as the words rolled off his tongue.

Elin nodded, observing that her father was uncharacteristically dressed in a sweater and casual slacks.

471

Must have been golfing, she surmised. *He hates knickers. Says they make his bottom look huge. He must have been at Northland when he found out about Sofia and Alexis.*

"And the baby?"

Karl Gustafsson grimaced.

"As bad; maybe worse because she's so dehydrated."

Elin stood up and removed her coat.

"Horace is here as well," Karl Gustafsson revealed.

"He stopped by to visit?" Elin inquired as she reclaimed her seat. She found it incredible that her husband would actually be concerned about the wife and child of his father-in-law.

"No, he's here as a patient. Next ward down," Karl explained, his words becoming very soft. "And he's worse off than Sofia is."

The information should have catapulted Elin Ellison from her place on the bench. Instead, she patted the back of her father's broad hand and smiled.

"I'll see him in a bit," she answered.

Karl shook his head. "No, you won't," he replied. "They won't let anyone into the rooms. Too contagious. This bug has wiped out entire Army bases. They're working on a vaccine. Supposed to be ready soon. But for now, they won't let anyone around a confirmed case of the Grippe."

Karl studied the face of his oldest child as he explained the precautions in place.

She's taking this much too calmly, this news about Horace. My fears were right. She doesn't love the man.

Elin smiled and swept a strand of hair away from her finely chiseled nose.

"I best go see how the old boy is doing," she said. "I'll be back in a few moments."

Karl Gustafsson smiled.

"There's no reason to rush," he confided. "None of us are going anywhere."

Chapter 75

Paul Pederson rode north from Wolf Lake Camp on a borrowed roan gelding. The saddle, a hard-worked brown cattleman's seat boasting a roping horn and significant stirrups, creaked and groaned under the Norwegian's weight as the twenty-year-old horse stumbled and scampered over the trail between Wolf Lake and Highway No. 4. Pederson set a breakneck pace to make the nearest telephone in Aurora to call for a doctor; not just any doctor, but Dr. Rajala from Virginia, the man listed in the *News Tribune* as being well-familiar with the treatment of flu victims. Pederson believed it would be easier and faster to find old Doc Miller, Amos Miller, the only physician officing in Aurora, and bring him back to Papoose Lake. Pederson had suggested that he could simply turn the rig, the wagon that Heidi Genelli had guided into Wolf Lake Camp with her son and the ailing Finn, around and head back to Aurora to retrieve Doc Miller.

"I don't want some eighty-year-old horse doctor trying to bleed my fiancé," Heidi had protested. "Or putting leeches on his skin in some antiquated and unproven attempt to remove unhealthy humors," she continued.

"Take my horse," Augustus Mathews, the English blacksmith hired to replace Tim Laitila at Wolf Lake Camp, had offered. "Henry's fast and agile. Tough as nails. He'll get you to town in half the time it'd take by wagon," the man advised. "I'd ride him in, but my leg hasn't quite healed from that kick I took when shoeing Big Blackie." Mathews was referring to the camp's Percheron stud stallion, an animal so mean and disagreeable that the men would have made him into steaks but for Andrew Maki's insistence that no harm come to the animal. Maki's prohibition wasn't based upon affection: the horse stood stud for a minimum of five quality Percheron mares a year, at an average of a hundred dollars a service.

"Thanks," Pederson said.

Once the gelding was saddled and ready to ride, a problem had developed.

"Western?" the Norwegian had asked as he approached the animal. "I've never ridden Western. Why in God's name would an Englishman ride Western?"

Mathews smiled and tapped the felt brim of his overly wide Stetson. "Same reason I wear this hat. I love American cowboys."

The other men gathered around the scene had laughed.

Iner Halvorson, the camp cook, quipped, "Bit far away from cowboy country, aren't we, Mr. Mathews?"

The Brit smiled more broadly.

"It's my intention," he said with British precision, "to eventually live in the Great American West. This bit of drudgery," he continued, waving his arms to encompass the logging camp, "is but a way-station on my journey west."

"But I can't ride Western," Pederson said again, holding the reins of the sleek red quarter horse.

"Ah, but he can ride you," Mathews replied. "He'll accept a plowman's direction, reins in both hands, if that's what you wish."

"You sure?"

"Quite certain," Mathews promised.

"Ride safe, Mr. Pederson," Joey Genelli offered, watching the big lumberjack climb onto the little horse.

Pederson hadn't replied. He had simply nodded and clicked his heels, sending the animal into a smooth trot. The men watched the Norwegian and the cow pony amble down the dusty logging trail, until the man's red flannel shirt disappeared behind the trees.

Inside the camp boss's quarters, Andrew Maki tossed and turned in bed, delirious with fever, overcome by influenza. Heidi Genelli sat in a pine rocking chair next to the man she loved, a washbasin of cool water and a clean rag nearby. She remained ready to wipe the sweat from the man's chalky face. She rocked gently in the chair as she maintained her vigil. The runners of the rocking chair creaked. The woman held a

Finnish Bible in her hands and read verses from the New Testament, from the Love Gospel, the Gospel of John, to herself. Whenever moisture appeared on Andrew's skin, the woman stopped reading and mopped up the sweat with the cloth, tenderness and concern apparent in her every gesture.

My God, Maki dreamed, the fever racking his brain. *I've died. The Germans, men I have no quarrel with, have done me in.* He dreamed, Belleau Wood so clear in the vision, the sounds, smells, and pictures of battle so natural, so real, it was as if he was back at the Front. *No, Sergeant Cukela, don't stand up,* he heard himself shout. *But it was too late. Cukela stood up, exposing his head to a sniper. Crack. The Croatian's brains were splattered on Maki's uniform. The man's blood stained the Finn's face. The picture dissolved and reformed. Now it was Sergeant Gruber who stood up. It was Sergeant Gruber who had his skull exploded by a Mauser bullet.*

A cannon boomed. An airplane droned. The Germans were in Minnesota, conquering the forests, the lakes, the rivers. Sergeant Gruber, his face restored, his life returned, was leading them, leading German soldiers in battle against his former American comrades. Maki raised his rifle. He took aim. His eyes leveled on Gruber. The sergeant's features became those of Olli Kinkkonen, but Maki didn't hesitate. He fired. The result was the same.

Dr. Rajala didn't arrive until late that evening, the evening of October 12. An ominous wind blew into camp after the doctor's arrival. The wind carried with it the smell of charred wood, of burned plaster, of ruined dreams, and scorched flesh. Wildfires raged from Moose Lake, fifty miles south of Duluth, to Grand Lake, twenty miles north of the city, and from just outside Two Harbors, along the North Shore of Lake Superior, to Grand Rapids, over a hundred miles to the west. Smoldering piles of old railroad ties and slash being burned at separate locations along various railroad rights of way had been empowered by zephyrs traveling in excess of thirty miles an hour. Walls of flames merged, diverted, and converged all across Northeastern Minnesota. There was a danger that the cities of Moose Lake, Wrenshall, Barnum, and

Cloquet would be reduced to ash. There was a likelihood that the Village of Proctor and the Township of Herman would have to be evacuated. And there was a wall of fire headed towards the cottages and homes dotting the pastoral shoreline of Pike Lake, twenty miles north of Duluth.

Chapter 76

Nashwauk. Arrested as a deserter from the Canadian Army and as a slacker in the United States, Raymond G. Houle was released here yesterday by Itasca County authorities. It was found he has discharge papers from the Canadian Air Force and was also discharged from the recruiting station in Duluth.

(Duluth News Tribune, October 4, 1918)

Investigations into the death of Olli Kinkkonen and also that of Axel Nyssti and Jimi Zillo were continued by authorities of St. Louis County yesterday. No new developments resulted... Coroner James McAuliffe stated that no inquest could be held over the bodies until sufficient evidence is obtained.

(Duluth News Tribune, October 12, 1918)

John Kuttenen carried construction debris to a large pile located on the rear lawn of the McAdamses's summer home. Kuttenen was a laborer working for Berglund and Peterson, the general contractors building the Pike Lake mansion of the Canadian and his Finnish-American bride. Oscar Berglund and John Kuttenen were the only men left on site. The finishing touches inside the home awaited a crew of five carpenters who would arrive on Monday. The grounds were being tidied because the McAdamses were arriving at noon with the Marshalls, the Fregeaus, and the Walshes to tour the new home. Kuttenen's wife and two small children were happily enjoying their Saturday on the family dairy farm in Brookston, ten miles to the west of Pike Lake. The children and their mother were waiting for Mr. Kuttenen to be released from work by Mr. Berglund.

Maybe we'll go to town, take in a matinee, John Kuttenen thought, unaware that the theaters in Duluth had been closed due to the Spanish Influenza outbreak. *Christ, this ground is dry,* Kuttenen observed as he turned topsoil around the pile of construction debris with a spade to prevent fire from spreading once he lit the pyre. *The humidity must be near zero,* Kuttenen mused, his wild speculation highlighting the arid weather conditions.

In fact, the humidity recorded on October 12, 1918, reached twenty-one percent, the lowest ever recorded in Duluth. The day began with little wind, but as the sun rose, a stiff breeze from the northwest asserted itself. Drought conditions had existed in Northeastern Minnesota since the summer of 1916. Small fires were already burning along the Great Northern railroad tracks above the city of Cloquet, in the form of supervised clearing fires, controlled fires to burn old ties and debris, and unplanned brush and bog fires ignited by sparks thrown by passing locomotives. Along the tracks, stockpiles of pulpwood were neatly stacked, awaiting transport. Woodchips, sawdust, and other flammable debris surrounded these orderly pyres. This wooden litter had been allowed to accumulate during the decades in which logging had been the primary industry of the area.

Near Milepost 62, just north of the hamlet of Brookston on the Great Northern line, where railroad tracks follow the natural arc of the St. Louis River Valley, these conditions were particularly dangerous. Ten miles away, along the north shore of Pike Lake, John Kuttenen pondered whether or not to ignite the gigantic pile of construction debris he had crafted. The conditions near Pike Lake were identical to those found at Milepost 62, conditions that caused the Finnish laborer to think deeply before igniting the pile of brush and timber.

Oscar Berglund walked up to John Kuttenen shortly before the guests were due to arrive. The boss smiled and slapped his employee on the back as he joined Kuttenen next to the neat pyramid of wood the Finn had stacked, a good hundred yards away from the carriage house on the property.

"What d'ya think, John?" Berglund asked, looking to the west, towards the source of the breeze. "Seems a little dicey for burning today."

Kuttenen nodded his head in agreement.

"I'll be back on Monday," the Finn said slowly, the English words formed with difficulty. "I can start 'er up then."

Berglund nodded and grinned.

"Trying to stretch this project out as long as we can, are we, Kuttenen?"

The Finn laughed.

"A man gets hungry in the winter when there's no paycheck," Kuttenen added.

"And the wife gets testy if there's no money for Christmas shopping," Berglund agreed. "Don't worry, we'll have plenty of inside work to keep you busy this winter. You're a good man, John. A hard worker. I'll make sure that family of yours is well-fed."

Kuttenen shook his head in appreciation. "My family will be grateful."

Motorcars parading up the gravel drive attracted Oscar Berglund's attention.

"Sounds like they're here," Berglund observed. "Why don't you take off, get home to that lovely young wife of yours," the boss said. "We can take care of this pile on Monday."

Kuttenen nodded and gathered up his shovel, rake, and tool belt. The Finn walked easily towards a battered old International truck, threw his tools into the bed of the vehicle, opened the door, and climbed into the driver's seat. The electric starter whirled and spun as it sought to engage the motor.

"Sounds like you could use a new coil," Berglund quipped.

"Maybe if my boss paid me a bit more, I could afford one," John Kuttenen joked as the engine finally caught.

Blue smoke boiled out of the truck's tailpipe as the Finn released the clutch and backed the vehicle out of its parking space. Oscar Berglund watched the black truck pull onto the gravel driveway and pass two smart-looking motorcars, filled with revelers intent upon examining his company's handiwork.

Wendy McAdams led the Marshalls and the others around the interior of the home, the grounds, and the outbuildings. The small crowd paused for a considerable time on the sandy beach jutting out from the grassy bank in front of the palatial home, to watch the wind whip Pike Lake into a white-capped frenzy.

"She's a wild one out there today," Charles Marshall said to George McAdams, his eyes scanning the surface of the lake.

"Big bass," George noted, pointing to a large fish hovering in a shadow cast by the dock. "Must be eight or nine pounds. That's one monster of a large mouth."

"Where?" Marshall asked, his eyes squinting as he scanned the lake bottom.

"There," McAdams advised, pointing to a silhouette contrasted against the sand.

"It's a beauty," the theater owner agreed. "Well," Marshall said standing to his full height, a height at which he was still several inches shorter than the Canadian, "time to get back for Miss Walsh's birthday party." Marshall was referring to the occasion that had brought the group to the lake.

"You folks go ahead. Wendy and I'll catch up in a bit," the Canadian advised. "I want to go over some finishing details with Mr. Berglund."

"You bet. See you in a while."

Two days earlier, on Thursday, October 10th, 1918, a passenger train had stopped at Milepost 62 on the Great Northern tracks. A small brush fire broke out while the locomotive idled. Local Finnish farmers culling discarded railroad ties for use as fence posts had recognized the danger and attempted to douse the flames. Other, more formal efforts succeeded, so that by the morning of October 12th, Saturday morning, the accidental fire at Milepost 62 appeared under control. But that Saturday afternoon, as the Marshalls were returning to their cottage and as George and Wendy McAdams were touring their property with Oscar Berglund, northwest winds fanned the smoldering embers at Milepost 62 into an inferno. The renewed fire soon threatened the farms of the very Finns who had fought the early stages of the blaze, the Koskelas and the Knuttis. As the wind picked up strength and as tongues of flame found tinder dry slash and marsh grass, the conflagration, a fire that would eventually become known as the Great Cloquet Fire, was born.

"What the hell?" George McAdams said, pointing to the western sky as he, his builder, and Wendy McAdams exited the front door of the mansion. "Looks like a forest fire."

Oscar Berglund followed the other man's gesture.

"Shit," Berglund said in Swedish, the word completely lost on the Canadian but recognized immediately by Wendy McAdams.

"Mr. Berglund," Wendy McAdams scolded. "Such language."

"Sorry, ma'am. But that looks to be one heck of a fire in the making," the contractor advised. "I've never seen a cloud of smoke like that."

The three people walked down to the lakeshore and observed the gathering concentration of ash and soot.

"That does not look good," Wendy McAdams whispered, as pieces of burned wood and assorted debris began to rain down on the turbulent surface of the lake.

"I'd say we best head back to Duluth," George McAdams advised. "The lake will block the flames if the fire shifts this way, don't you think, Oscar?" the Canadian asked.

The contractor, a man in his late fifties, a few years older than McAdams, nodded. "I believe you're right. I think it best that we make our way back to the city. The lake is wide and deep. It would take a hell of a fire, one I've never seen in my lifetime, to breach such an obstacle."

Oscar Berglund left the premises in his panel truck. George and Wendy McAdams entered their Stutz motorcar and followed the builder's truck down the driveway. The McAdams stopped at the birthday party at the Marshall cottage. Efforts to convince the participants of the party to leave early, to continue their revelry in town, met with polite resistance.

"We've got plenty of time before we have to evacuate, if indeed the fire ever heads this way," Charles Marshall said, sipping a gin and tonic as he stood with his head cocked to view the wall of smoke rising in the distance. "The fire will likely stay to the north and west."

"I'd advise against staying put," George McAdams argued, attempting to convince the theater entrepreneur to gather his crowd and escape while there was time to do so.

George McAdams watched Charles Marshall's young son dance across the lawn after a border collie.

"It's not worth risking the boy," the Canadian whispered.

"I appreciate your concern," Marshall replied. "But I think we'll be fine. The moment things begin to look dicey, I'll pack the party up and hit the road. A motorcar can outrun any fire I've ever come across," the theater owner concluded with confidence.

George McAdams and his wife returned to the Stutz, entered the car, and pulled away from the Marshall cottage.

"I wasn't very persuasive," George said finally, after a long period of silence. "I wish Charles had been more willing to listen."

Wendy McAdams turned her small face towards her husband.

"I don't like the looks of that," she said, pointing her index finger at a mountain of black smoke swirling in the western sky.

"Neither do I," George McAdams agreed. "Neither do I."

Chapter 77

Date of death: between September 18 and September 22, 1918.
*Cause of death: suicide by hanging. Father's name: Matt Kinkkonen.
Mother's name: Katherine Kinkkonen. Occupation: day laborer.
Date of birth: unknown. Personal characteristics: single, white, male.
Informant: Frank G. Pelto. Burial: Park Hill Cemetery, October 6,
1918.*

    (Death Certificate of Olli Kinkkonen)

*Deaths to Marshall, Walsh, Fregeau Families Follows Birthday
Dinner. Shocked and stunned by the swift current of events of the
last two days, which has wiped out neighbors and friends in the
fearful toil taken by Saturday's fire, the tragedy to the Charles A.
Marshall party is on every tongue. Entirely wiped out; the death by
drowning of the Marshall family and wife and two daughters of
James F. Walsh...and the little son of Mr. and Mrs. Francis
Fregeau... is uppermost on the thoughts of all Duluthians.*

    (Duluth News Tribune, October 13, 1918)

*An entire family from Brookston, Mr. John Kuttenen, his wife, and
their two children, who died in the fire, were buried today.*

    (Duluth News Tribune, October 15, 1918)

"There will be no coroner's inquest into the death of your
friend," Karl Gustafsson related to his daughter as they sat on
a wooden bench in St. Luke's Hospital, waiting to hear from
Sofia Gustafsson's physician. It was October 15. The Great
Cloquet Fire had run its course.

    "How's that?" Elin Ellison asked.

    "Judge Cant."

    "Yes?"

    "You went to see Judge Cant about that Finn the
police found hanging from a tree in Lester Park."

"How did you know that?" Elin asked, her eyebrows crinkling as she addressed her father.

"He told me. You think Judge Cant would keep something like that to himself, after all the years he and I have known each other?"

Elin Ellison nodded.

"And?"

"The county attorney did as the judge requested. He asked the coroner to hold an inquest. Seems Coroner McAuliffe wasn't interested."

The woman stood up and walked to a nearby window and looked out onto First Street. Cars and buggies moved in choreographed fashion over the bricked street. Elin's gaze took in the high clouds of the near-winter sky, before becoming fixed on a steam locomotive pulling a string of empty flatbed cars, logging cars, through the East End of Duluth, towards Two Harbors.

"I figured as much."

"Daughter, you can't expect that the coroner is going to go to the bother of exhuming the body of one dissident Finn, who may or may not have died by his own hand, when hospitals, Shrine buildings, and theaters are filled to the brim with victims from the fire and this flu epidemic. Jim McAuliffe's wringing his hands over the situation he finds himself in. Burned babies. Sick mothers. Old folks keeling over dead of the Grippe," Karl Gustafsson observed quietly, tightness beginning to reassert itself in the left side of his chest.

"Mr. Kinkkonen was no dissident," the woman continued as she watched the train chug its way out of town. "He simply didn't want to fight in the war," she said with quiet assurance.

The pain intensified in the lawyer's chest, until it felt like someone was standing on his ribs, restraining his ability to breathe. Karl Gustafsson was about to speak when his right hand clutched the fabric of his golf sweater. The attorney gasped. His fingers dug into the wool of the garment before he fell heavily onto the tile floor.

"Father?" Elin queried, turning in surprise as the man collapsed. "Oh, my God!" she shrieked.

The devastating fire had burned virtually everything in its path between Moose Lake, a small town located on the southern edge of Carlton County, to Woodland, a neighborhood situated on the northeast edge of Duluth. In actuality, the Great Cloquet Fire of 1918 was not a singular wall of flame. The disaster was not a unified holocaust, but the result of multiple blazes concentrated by chance in one geographic region at one moment in history. By the time the separate blazes had been reduced to smoldering coals, more due to the exhaustion of combustible fuel than any fire-fighting accomplished by God or man, all of Cloquet, Brookston, Kettle River, Moose Lake, as well as the Duluth neighborhoods of Woodland and Lester Park, had been reduced to charred rubble. Within Duluth's city limits, one hundred and eleven citizens perished in the conflagration, and over one hundred suffered serious injuries. Locales such as the Town of Herman and the Village of Munger sustained destruction of more than fifty percent. In all, more than 1,500 square miles were burned to a crisp. Four hundred and fifty-three people died as direct victims of the fire; over one hundred perished later from maladies attributable to the blaze. Hundreds of Northeastern Minnesotans were treated for injuries and burns at first aid stations and in hospitals located in Superior and Duluth. Nearly one hundred souls were burned so severely they required morphine for pain. This exhaustive demand for medical expertise, supplies, and bed space came on the heels of the onset of Spanish Influenza. On October 12, 1918, the date of the fire, there were already forty-two cases of the deadly flu being treated in Duluth.

The fire left so many injured and burned, and rendered so many families homeless, that both St. Luke's and St. Mary's Hospitals in Duluth were filled to overflowing, resulting in the use of the National Guard Armory in Duluth as a shelter for less seriously injured patients and those without shelter. In the tiny hamlet of Moose Lake, the number of dead in and around the community was immeasurable. The bodies were gathered together and placed in a mass grave near the railroad tracks cutting through the town, as an emergency means of disposing of the charred corpses.

Charles Marshall had seen to it that his guests left the party on Pike Lake, once it became clear that the fire was not going to detour around the lake. The women and children set out for Duluth in a motorcar driven by Mr. Walsh, but were unable to advance past a line of fire and smoke blocking the Pike Lake Road. Upon turning back, the entire party took to two small prams, which the three men – Mr. Marshall, Mr. Walsh, and Mr. Fregeau – shoved into deep water, just as the flames arrived. Despite the fact that at least three other parties had utilized the same strategy with success, the use of the boats by the Marshall group proved tragic. The prams soon capsized in rough water, the surface of Pike Lake having been whipped to a frenzy by winds gusting over fifty miles per hour. The Marshalls and their infant son perished in the confused darkness, as did both the Walsh girls and the little son of Mr. and Mrs. Fregeau.

Across Pike Lake, the high winds and blowing sparks ignited the grass and brush bordering the McAdams property. The flames advanced. The fire leveled everything in its path: every building, every improvement, every structure that had been erected upon the land. When all that could burn had burned, there remained, where the defiant mansion of George and Wendy McAdams had once loomed above the placid waters of Pike Lake, two brick chimneys and a heap of ash, and nothing more.

"Do something," Elin Ellison cried out as she bent over the rapidly failing body of her father.

At the far end of the hall, near the entrance to the isolation ward where Sofia and Alexis Gustafsson were being treated for influenza, two nurses in starched white skirts and caps noted the woman's distress and came at a run. The first nurse on the scene, a bulldog-faced gray-haired matron, knelt next to the stricken man and held his wrist.

"No pulse," she whispered. "What happened?"

"God, you've got to do something!" Elin screamed out, her fists pounding against the black and white granite tiles of the floor.

"Ma'am," the other nurse, tall, thin, with a narrow lantern jaw and deeply recessed eyes, said calmly, her hand steadying Elin's thrashing shoulders, "we can't help him if you don't tell us what happened."

Elin stopped her hysterics.

"His heart. He has a bad heart."

The thin nurse opened the buttons of Karl's cardigan, pulled up his ribbed undershirt, and placed her stethoscope on the bare skin of the man's chest.

"Heart's still beating," she whispered.

"Pulse is back," the other woman added.

Two orderlies entered the hallway, carrying a canvas stretcher slung between two oak poles.

"Intensive care," the thin nurse ordered as the men stooped to pick up the attorney. "I'll call the doctor."

"They're full down there," one of the orderlies said as he rolled Karl Gustafsson's limp body onto the stretcher.

"Tell 'em to make room," the bulldog snorted. "He was my lawyer."

Elin Ellison looked at the short nurse.

"Is. He is my lawyer," the nurse corrected, patting the younger woman on the shoulder as she followed the other nurse and the patient.

"Where are you taking him?" Elin whispered as she rose from the floor.

"To Intensive Care. Just wait here. I'll send someone up to get you, once he's stable."

Elin nodded and watched the hospital workers ferry her father's ample body away, before walking to the wooden bench where she and her father had been sitting moments before. She resumed her place and placed her hands together in front of her face.

God, she prayed silently in Finnish, *don't let him die.* *Despite all that's come between us, despite Sofia and Alexis, and what he did to Mother, do not let him die.*

She leaned into the wall, allowing the plaster to support the back of her head as tears rained down her cheeks. She made no attempt to wipe the moisture from her face.

I've been such an ass, she thought. *I've already lost my mother. I have no siblings, unless you count Alexis, which is a difficult equation for me to accept. I have no family but him. I've been a fool. He was wrong. What he did was unforgettable, but I could have forgiven. Could have tried to understand. Jesus*, she concluded, *give me another chance to talk to him, to understand.*

The day waned. Outside the hospital, the sky darkened quickly. Night fell over the city, beginning over the hills to the west, then spreading out over the entirety of the St. Louis River Bay, until all of Duluth and Superior were in shadow. Electric and gas street lamps came on sporadically, illuminating the main thoroughfares of the city. The corridors of the hospital grew quiet. Elin's eyes were shut tight, closed against the possibility that her father was dead and that her prayers had been left unanswered.

If that's the case, she thought, *then I have no one to blame but myself. He's a man, not a god. Men are far from perfect. Mother saw that, knew that. She accepted Father despite what she knew. Even when he was reluctant to sit by her and read to her during the last stages of her illness, Mother knew the truth*, Elin considered. *She knew Father still loved her and that he hadn't set out to hurt her. He was afraid, not aloof. That was what Laina had said, was it not? 'Your Father is afraid. That's what keeps him from lingering by my side. It's the cancer. He can't deal with the cancer, with what will come,'* Laina confided.

Elin Ellison sighed and stood up. She nodded her head as she looked out the window and watched the streetlamps shudder in the brisk wind.

Mother is right, the woman silently agreed. *This may be my last chance to set pride and animosity aside and just talk to my father. I can forgive, Jesus. I know I can.*

A slight smile appeared on the pleasant face of Elin Ellison.

But there is no forgiving Horace. Him, there is no redeeming. I think it's time my husband and I had a talk, she thought, nodding once more to herself as she pulled a tar-stained handkerchief from her handbag and held it firmly in her sturdy fingers. *It's time we had a discussion about a number of matters.*

Chapter 78

Winds at Moose Lake fan fire as the burial of the dead goes on.
(Duluth News Tribune-October 17, 1918)

14,000 People were made homeless by the tornado of flame.
(Duluth News Tribune-October 18, 1918)

"It's a total loss," Joe Peterson said as he stood with George and Wendy McAdams, next to the smoldering debris of what had once been the couple's dream home.

"I can see that," George McAdams muttered, tossing a partially burned piece of window trim onto the smoking pile. A slight breeze stirred the air, causing flame to erupt and lap at the fuel supplied by the Canadian. "Christ, anyone can see that."

"George," Wendy admonished, her arm looped through her husband's as they stood next to their builder and surveyed the loss.

"Sorry," George said quietly.

"It's too late to start again this year," Peterson observed. "Snow's on the way. Already some on the ground over by Brainerd. By next week, the ground will be frozen," the contractor added. "But we can always rebuild next year."

"There won't be any next year," George McAdams whispered.

"How's that?"

"The wife and I are moving back home."

"Back home?"

Wendy McAdams smiled and pecked George's right cheek. The difference in their respective heights required the woman to stand on her tiptoes to kiss her husband.

"Port Arthur," Wendy said, her voice airy and light, as if the tragedy of losing one's home and being asked to move

490

to a country, a city she'd only spent a few days in, was an everyday occurrence. "George's home."

"Ah," Peterson acknowledged. "Back to Canada, is it?"

"I have little choice in the matter," McAdams said quietly. "My brother has made a bloody mess of things."

They walked over to the edge of the property, where scorched black lawn sloped to the sandy beach.

Joe Peterson looked across the skim of ice that had formed overnight on Pike Lake, and studied the stricken landscape.

"You could rebuild with the insurance money, you know," Peterson said after a long silence.

The Canadian merely stared at the ice.

"I said..."

McAdams's face flashed scarlet.

Wendy noted the rising color and intervened.

"He heard you, Mr. Peterson. The issue of insurance on the house is something of a sore spot."

Peterson stared at the woman's delicate features, stopping briefly to inventory her long eyelashes and pouty lips.

"There was a mortgage, correct?"

Wendy nodded. Her husband did not attempt to dissuade her from discussing the situation.

"So there was fire insurance?"

Wendy shrugged her shoulders. "One would hope so, wouldn't one? Unfortunately, Adrian, my brother-in-law, the same man trusted to insure George's ship, the *Blue Heron*, and did not, saw fit to make the same error with respect to our home."

"It wasn't insured?"

"It was for about a month, while built the basement, I'd guess," the woman added, turning her husband by the arm and initiating their walk towards their waiting motorcar. "The premium check, one drawn on a Canadian checking account, bounced. Seems my brother-in-law has a gambling problem. High-stakes poker. He cleaned out all the accounts in Canada without so much as an 'I'm sorry' to George."

The Canadian didn't acknowledge his wife's story. He walked slowly, as if carrying a great burden, until they arrived at the Stutz.

"I'm sorry to hear about your misfortune, Mr. and Mrs. McAdams," Joe Peterson said. "Losing a house and not having the insurance to rebuild... well, that's quite a blow."

George McAdams entered the driver's side of the Stutz and started the motor. His wife slipped her left leg into the car before turning her head to speak to the builder.

"But it's nothing compared to what the Kuttenens suffered. Tragedy, that was: an entire family suffocated in their own basement," the woman noted, her words conveying the seriousness the topic required. "He was a friend?"

"He was. John was a good man. Who can say when it's our time? He led his family into the cellar to protect them. Instead, he led them to their deaths. The fire, they say, sucked all the oxygen out of the cellar. Poor boys, poor little boys," the contractor muttered.

Wendy reached over and patted the builder's forearm, his arm covered by a leather coat.

"Take care, Mr. Peterson," the woman said.

"You too, Mrs. McAdams," Peterson replied with a nod, as the woman shut the door to the motorcar.

The Stutz puttered down the drive, past a sooty forest of burned maples and oaks, before accelerating out of view. Peterson opened his jacket and drew a commercial cigarette from the pack in his shirt pocket as he walked back towards the lake, to take one last look at the place where he'd spent most of 1918.

Chapter 79

The body of Charles Marshall, age 47 years old, was recovered yesterday from the waters of Pike Lake.
(Duluth News Tribune-October 25, 1918)

As of yesterday, the total death toll in Duluth from Spanish Influenza is 21. There are presently 364 cases being treated in Duluth.
(Duluth News Tribune-October 31, 1918)

Duluth received its first snowfall of the year. The flu epidemic is near its apex and the public theaters are expected to reopen shortly.
(Duluth News Tribune-November 1, 1918)

Heidi Genelli applied shaving cream to Andrew Maki's face as he sat up in bed, his back propped up by a pillow lodged against a tamarack wall. The woman brought the straight-edged razor across Maki's rough skin with deftness. She did not nick or injure the man as she removed his beard and moustache.

"You do this well," Maki remarked, smiling weakly, his body still timid, his muscle strength impinged by flu.

"It's all about patience," Heidi replied, focusing her eyes on her work.

"And a steady hand," the Finnish logger added.

"That too," she agreed, dipping the blade into a bowl of warm water to remove accumulated hair and lather. "Your friend, Mrs. Ellison..." she began nonchalantly, knowing that the term "friend" did not do the relationship between her fiancé and the other woman justice.

"Yes?"

"The woman her father married –" Heidi stopped, unable to recall the name.

"Sofia. Sofia is her stepmother's name."

"Ah, yes, Sofia. She passed away. From the Grippe," Heidi Genelli continued matter-of-factly, as if the same disease did not afflict the man in bed before her.

"She had a child."

Heidi nodded and began wiping shaving cream from Maki's face with a clean towel.

"A daughter."

"Elin's half-sister," Andrew whispered.

"Yes, her half-sister."

A wave of chills assaulted the logger, compelling him to bury his body in the blankets covering his bed.

"You don't look well," Heidi offered, running her fingers along his temple. "You're clammy again."

"Doc Rajala will be here tomorrow."

The woman nodded. "I have to go into town and work. Paul's bringing me in. You need anything?"

He shook his head in the negative.

"Joey will be here."

"Shouldn't he be in school?"

She smiled and stood up. Her long fingers adjusted her dress, an old frock that she wore when cleaning house.

"He should. His teacher understands. She gave him two weeks' worth of assignments so he can help me out."

"When will you be back?"

"Tomorrow's Saturday. I've hired someone to help father on the weekends. Marge Ensign: good cook, hard worker. Has three boys. Husband ran off with some tart from Biwabik. She needs the money, and we need the help."

Maki's head pounded. His lungs gurgled with fluid accumulating from the pneumonia that had imposed itself upon him and would not depart. His mind wandered as he fought delirium. Aspirin wasn't strong enough to dull the pain, and had no impact upon the bacteria lodged in his lungs.

"You can't afford that."

Heidi lingered at the threshold.

"And you can't afford to be in the hospital in Virginia, like Doctor Rajala ordered. We'll get by. I've got my savings."

Maki's eyes closed and he fell into a light slumber without replying.

494

In the morning, Doc Rajala was unable to rouse the patient. Andrew Maki's condition had deteriorated to the point where he needed round-the-clock professional nursing care and constant monitoring. Paul Pederson was quick to take time off work to drive the patient into Virginia in Maki's freight wagon, the ailing logger covered with a pile of blankets. Two hot water bottles provided heat against the plunging mercury. Joey rode in the wagon to provide companionship and prayers. Doc Rajala's carriage bounced ahead of the freight wagon, Rajala's brown Morgan mare pulling the physician's rig at a trot.

"It doesn't look good," Rajala observed, conferring with Heidi Genelli in the foyer of the isolation unit of the Virginia Municipal Hospital. "His fever is out of control, the fluid is accumulating too fast in his lungs. If something doesn't break in the next day or so, I'm afraid his chances of survival are not good."

The woman's body quivered as the import of the doctor's prognosis became apparent. Heidi Genelli had expected the doctor to reassure her that she would not lose the man she loved.

I'm glad Joey is with his grandfather, she thought, her eyes downcast and beginning to tear. *He doesn't need to hear this.*

Paul Pederson approached the doctor, his dirty Stetson held anxiously in his raw hands, and nodded gingerly.

"He's a tough old bird, ma'am," the Norwegian said. "Andrew is strong. He made it through France. He made it through all that hell, pardon the expression, on account of your love. He's not about to give up now."

The logger patted the woman on the shoulder. They were the same height. As he spoke, Pederson checked to make sure Heidi Genelli was not watching before tossing a threatening glare in the doctor's direction. Doc Rajala winced, as if stung by a bee.

Good, Pederson told himself, *he got the drift. Stop alarming the little lady. Andrew will come through this just fine.*

"Maybe Mr. Pederson's right," the doctor begrudgingly added, as an afterthought. "There's something to be said for inner strength."

"He's not much of a Christian," Heidi Genelli admitted softly. "I mean, he believes, but I wouldn't hazard a guess as to when it was he last took communion."

"That's not the sort of strength I had in mind, ma'am," the physician said, his small black eyes maintaining contact with Pederson's, as if he were taking cues from the logger, "though spirituality is doubtlessly important and a comfort. I was thinking more along the lines of the will to survive, the raw animal power possessed by those men who have been bloodied and lived to tell about it. Sounds like that's what we have here."

Pederson smiled. "A war hero. Andrew's a war hero."

"Well, then," Rajala said, smiling nervously, finally diverting his eyes to the woman. "That settles it. God is not going to take someone who fought for his country and survived the battlefield, at least not quite yet. You two get some rest. I'll go check on the patient."

"Thanks, Doc," Pederson said with a wink. "Let's go get a cup of coffee," the logger suggested, his hat still clenched tightly in his hands, the presence of a woman clearly causing uneasy apprehension now that the two of them were alone.

Chapter 80

Austria deserts Germany - Armistice begins November 4, 1918 at 3:00pm Washington time.
(Duluth News Tribune-November 4, 1918)

WAR IS OVER! ARMISTICE SIGNED! World War will end at 6:00pm Washington time.
(Duluth News Tribune-November 11, 1918)

The total deaths from influenza in Duluth reach seventy-nine. There are 700 active cases being treated.
(Duluth News Tribune-November 12, 1918)

The theaters have reopened. Charlie Chaplin is starring at the Strand Theater in "Shoulder Arms."
(Duluth News Tribune-December 1, 1918)

"How are you, Horace?" Elin Ellison asked as she leaned over her husband's linen-wrapped torso, a cloth mask secured around her face to prevent her from being infected with the Grippe.

The young businessman, his hair matted from perspiration, his eyes glazed and needy, mouthed, "OK."

The woman smiled beneath the mask and patted her husband's forehead with a wet cloth.

"This might not seem the most appropriate time, Horace, my darling, but I have some matters that we need to discuss," she whispered, the strokes of the cloth becoming more vigorous as her emotions rose.

"What?" Horace Ellison gasped.

"I think I'll pull up a chair," Elin said, draping the washcloth over the rail of the hospital bed before crossing the floor and dragging a Craftsman-style oak side chair to Horace's bedside.

"Do you know that I've never really loved you?" she began, her voice not at all bitter, her words containing no spite.

Horace's eyelids flared.

"Yes," he whispered.

"That's good. We need to have an understanding of our positions before I get too far along with what I have to say."

His eyes closed and opened reflexively.

"I love you," he rasped out slowly, "I do."

Elin's left hand patted the exposed skin of her husband's right forearm.

"I understand that might have been true once, but I'm not sure you love me anymore. And that, given what I have to say, is probably for the best."

Elin found that her mouth was dry. The only water in the room was contained in her husband's glass and she was in no position to share it with him. Elin Ellison swallowed her own saliva and continued.

"I know about the other women," she began.

"Elin..."

His attempt to refute the forthcoming accusation was met by his wife touching her index finger to her lips.

"Shush now, Horace. You know better; I know better," she lectured, keeping her voice level.

Elin reached into her purse and retrieved the shards of the medicine bottle that she had discovered in his toiletry kit.

"I certainly didn't give you the clap," she said matter-of-factly, as if she were reading information off one of Margaret Sanger's pamphlets. "So don't try to deny the obvious."

Horace Ellison's eyes closed slowly, as if weighed down by shame. He opened his mouth but was unable to speak.

"No apologies, Horace. They'll serve no useful purpose here. It's not your infidelities that compel me to confront you like this, as you lay here, possibly dying, in the hospital. Do you know the risks of giving gonorrhea to a woman, Horace? The long-term, permanent harm you can do?"

Elin's voice evinced anger and then, as quickly as it had surfaced, the emotion disappeared.

I wish she'd show her rage, Horace Ellison thought, fighting through the veil his illness cast over his ability to think succinctly. *This cold-heartedness; this, I cannot defend against.*

"I thought not," Elin added, calm restored to her demeanor. "I am sterile, Horace. You and your visits to your whores have made me, at twenty-nine years old, incapable of producing children. You have closed up my womb, locked away my capacity to conceive, all because of your insatiable, animal lust."

The accusation stung. Horace determined that he must defend himself. Wasn't it she who had closed off her body to him? Wasn't it she who had become, very soon after their marriage, disinterested and vague about their lovemaking? Hadn't she, in her aloofness, forced his conduct? Horace studied the skin inside his eyelids and sought a defense to her accusations. He could think of nothing to say.

"But none of this, none of what you've done to me, Horace Ellison, compares to the other things you've involved yourself in," she whispered, removing from her handbag the stained handkerchief bearing the initials "H.E.E" monogrammed on it, brandishing it like a captured battle flag under her husband's nose.

"What the hell is that?" Horace Ellison said loudly, his voice suddenly finding strength.

"What is this? Why, it's the handkerchief you used to wipe the tar off your hands after you and your associates tarred and lynched Mr. Kinkkonen, that's what this is, Mr. Ellison."

The man's throat clenched. He could not swallow. He could not breathe. Despite the reaction of his body to her revelation, Horace Ellison did not display his upset.

"You're insane."

"Am I? 'Knights of Liberty', Horace? I know you were at their meetings. I'm not stupid. I know how you and David and the rest of your crowd, the boys whose fathers were able to pull strings and call in favors to keep their sons away from the War, got together to display your patriotism. You yourself, why, Horace, I do believe, escaped induction by virtue of that broken jaw Mr. Alhomaki gave you four or five years back. Am I right? Isn't that how you avoided being shipped to France, tossed into the fray along with all the immigrant boys that you so deeply believe should die for America?"

Horace Ellison snorted air out of his nose like a bull clearing its airway before a charge.

"You're crazy."

"Don't play me for the fool. This isn't axle grease or paint remover or motor oil on your kerchief. It's creosote. You know it and I know it. You helped kill Mr. Kinkkonen. You're in the 'Knights'. You were gone the night of, and the night after, Mr. Kinkkonen's disappearance. And you've got creosote, the very substance used to torment the poor man, on your monogrammed handkerchief. I'd say that's pretty good circumstantial evidence that you helped kill Olli Kinkkonen."

Fever surged through the young tycoon's skin. As suddenly as the fever had come on, chills replaced it. Horace's teeth chattered. His body shook. His lungs rattled when he coughed to clear them. It was obvious that Horace Ellison was a very sick man.

"I didn't kill him."

The words came out slowly, without pretense.

"You were there."

Silence.

"Horace, you profess to be a Christian."

The man's eyelids opened. For the first time in months, Horace Ellison stared into the bright blue irises of his wife's eyes.

Why couldn't you love me? he thought.

"I try," he mumbled.

There was a hint of shame embedded in his response.

"We all sin, Horace."

"Some more than others."

She felt, against her better judgment, a pang of pity for the man she had married for position and convenience. She did not mistake the emotion for love, though the sympathy Elin felt at the moment was more than she had felt for Horace Ellison in a very long time.

"Darling," Elin said softly, placing her face next to her husband's. Her mask touched his cheek as she whispered, "this might be the only time we are able to talk."

The unspoken inference – that Horace Ellison might die of influenza – struck the ailing man like a bullet.

If I tell her the truth, what will she do with the information?

Horace concentrated his gaze on his wife's forehead.

"You were there, weren't you?" Elin asked again.

"Yes."

"Tell me what happened."

"What will you do with the information?"

Indeed. What will I do with the information?

Elin Ellison had been one of a handful of mourners in attendance at the interment of Olli Kinkkonen's body at Park Hill Cemetery on October 6th. Matti Peltoma, two other Finnish immigrant men who had worked the docks with Kinkkonen, Sadie Salmela and Elsie Laine were the others who stood with Elin Ellison beneath the rain-sodden sky, trickles of water running off their faces on that warm Sunday. There had been no man of God present, so Elin, ever the teacher, read a passage from her mother's Finnish Bible, a verse from *First Corinthians*:

But in fact, Christ has been raised from the dead, the first fruits of those who have fallen asleep. For as by a man came death, by a man has come also the resurrection of the dead. For as in Adam all die, so also in Christ shall all be made alive. But each in his own order: Christ the first fruits, then at his coming those who belong to Christ. Then comes the end, when he delivers the Kingdom to God the Father after destroying every rule and every authority and power. For he must reign until he has put all his enemies under his feet.

Elin Ellison did not cry at the grave of the martyred Finn. Despite an overwhelming feeling of loss – not personal loss, but loss of residual innocence – Elin shed no tears, standing in the miserable rain, mourning the passing of a man she barely knew. She had wanted to cry, wanted to let a river of tears cascade out of her in the hopes that the flood would unbind her emotions and make her once again capable of feeling. But such a thing did not happen. She had recited her verse. The Finnish men had assisted the gravediggers in lowering the wooden casket into the hole, and she had departed.

Olli Kinkkonen had been dead for over two months. Her father had informed her that the coroner was in no position to commence an inquest into the circumstances of the man's demise. Suicide was what the death certificate said, and suicide it would remain. Chief of Detectives Lahti, according to Oscar Larson and her father, concurred.

But Elin Ellison needed to know, before severing her ties with the man she had married under the worst of illusions, under the pretense of a creating a social bond to foster financial security, if her husband had played any part in the death of an innocent man. There would be no running to the police. There would be no hysterics. There would only be the acquisition of knowledge.

"Nothing," Elin finally said.

"What?" Horace whispered, his mind having wandered as he waited for his wife to respond.

"I will say nothing. Tell me the truth and it stays here, between us. The law, if I remember my father's instruction on the point, holds that what a husband tells his wife, regardless of the circumstances, is privileged and cannot be used against him. But even if such were not the case, I swear that I have no intention of using what you say against you."

A period of quiet. Nurses' shoes made a pit-pat, pit-pat sound as they struck the tile in the hallway outside the door. Steam hissed from a radiator as Elin Ellison waited for her husband's response.

"It wasn't supposed to end like it did. We were just going to tar and feather him."

"The newspaper mentioned tar and feathering, but my sources indicate there were no feathers found on the body."

"Someone forgot to bring the feathers. I won't tell you who. We were just going to tie the rope around his neck to scare him, to show him we meant business. Then it got all confused. Someone, one of the men who shouldn't have been there, one who wasn't a Knight but who was brought in because of, shall we say, his 'attitude'..." Horace coughed and motioned for a sip of water.

Elin retrieved the water glass and placed the rim of the container against her husband's lips. The man sipped slightly and nodded. Elin placed the container on an adjacent window ledge.

"He was the one who said to string Kinkkonen up. He got angry when the Finn tried to fight back; took exception to it. I couldn't stomach what was happening. I went outside. When I came back in, Kinkkonen was dead. They'd hung him. I tried to stop them, Elin, you've got to believe me; I did. I even wiped tar off his face before I left, wiped it away from his eyes. That's how it got on my handkerchief. I swear, as God is my witness, I had nothing to do with the Finlander's death."

The woman studied her husband's face.

He's telling the truth, Elin thought. *For once in our relationship, one of us is being honest.*

"I believe you," she finally said.

He nodded.

"You're tired. You need rest," Elin observed, "but we have some other less taxing matters to discuss. Are you up to it?"

Horace's throat constricted.

"Yes," he mouthed.

"Andrew Maki."

"That asshole?"

"Watch your tongue."

"I apologize. But it still burns me up when I think of you and him together. What did you see in that immigrant dirt farmer?"

503

Elin shifted on the hard wooden seat of the chair but did not rise to Horace's bait. She had not come to argue.

"It's of no consequence why I fell in love with Anders Alhomaki. The point is, you hold the note on his farm, yes?"

A spasm of coughing ensued. More water was sipped. The spell passed.

"I do. How did you know?"

"Wendy."

"Ah, yes, the fetching Mrs. McAdams. Her husband has had one bad spell of luck lately."

"More like one stupid brother. Regardless, I want, as part of another issue we will be discussing shortly, for you to sign over the contract to Mr. Maki's farm to me."

"Another issue?"

There was a lengthy pause.

"Our divorce."

"Divorce?"

"After what's transpired, I'd say one is warranted, don't you?"

Horace Ellison shifted his body under the sheets.

"What else, besides the Maki land contract and a divorce, do you want?"

"Mr. Gran will be representing me. He'll be drafting the documents and having you served. Until we resolve this matter, you'll need to move out of the house."

"It's my house too, Elin."

"Perhaps. But for now, you'll need to take a room elsewhere."

He nodded.

"We should have never been married," the woman said quietly. "I blame myself, Horace, not you. You thought you could, in time, entice me to love you. I knew better, but was too pig-headed to stop a train I knew I didn't want to ride. I don't fault you for that. For other things, yes, but not for that. I'm willing to work out an equal split, with minimal alimony. One exception is Mr. Maki's note. That you'll give to me as a penalty for your infidelity. Everything else, with one other exception, all the stocks, bonds, property, your share of Amalgamated Properties, we split right down the middle."

The man's eyelids quivered.

The reflex caused the woman to reconsider her demands.

"You said 'one other exception'," he whispered.

"Ah, yes. I almost forgot. I want you to transfer your interest in Wolf Lake Camp to me as well," she said slowly.

"You can't be serious. What will you do with a logging camp?" Horace Ellison asked, his voice weakened by disease.

"These are my terms. I want the mortgages and deeds covering both properties. And I want an amicable divorce: no trial, no contention, just an orderly end to our union. Those are my demands."

Horace lowered his head onto a goose down pillow. Another spasm of hacking ensued.

"The Papoose Lake property isn't worth much, you know," Horace Ellison finally observed, spit dripping from the corner of his mouth.

Elin's mouth curved into a faint smile. She used the washcloth to wipe away the saliva hanging from her husband's lower lip.

"It is to Mr. Maki," the woman asserted. "Get some sleep, Horace. We'll talk in the morning."

Elin Ellison stood to leave. Horace's fingers wrapped around her wrist with a strength that seemed impossible for his condition.

"We could have been something," Horace Ellison whispered.

The pleading was plain on his face.

"Maybe," the woman murmured. "Maybe if I'd been more willing to try," she concluded, gently removing her husband's hand from her narrow wrist, half-believing her falsehood as she left the hospital room.

Chapter 81

Winter came to Northeastern Minnesota with confidence. Squalls of snowflakes assaulted Duluth. Some of the snow was the result of "lake effect": flakes formed when warm winds steal moisture from the surface of Lake Superior, abscond with it, mix the moisture with the cold atmosphere, and then deposit the resulting precipitation on land. The remainder of the storms came out of the south, bearing moisture from the Gulf of Mexico, or from the west, blown into Minnesota by Canadian winds.

Duluth's funeral parlors were busy throughout Thanksgiving, embalming the bodies of those who died from burns received in the Great Fire, and making arrangements for the citizens who had perished from Spanish Influenza's many complications. Forest Hill Cemetery, a pastoral setting surrounded by the Morely Heights and Woodland Neighborhoods of Duluth, was the site of many interments during the days following the Great Cloquet Fire.

Mourners stood in the cold. Members of the crowd held their winter hats fast in gloved and mittened hands. Reverend Sarvela said a few pious words in Finnish. Sobs were heard as a casket was lowered into recently excavated earth. There were folks from all walks of life in attendance, steeled in their grief, quiet in their praise of the departed.

Elin Ellison stood at the front of the mourners, surrounded by distant relations, folks that she'd not seen or spoken to since her mother's passing. Her eyes blinked significantly as she watched the lid of a coffin descend below a berm of wet dirt. An infant cried. Pastor Sarvela nodded to Elin. The young woman, resplendent in her new winter coat, her hair neatly trimmed, her make-up peerless, her face drawn into mournful reflection, stepped forward until she stood alongside the preacher.

Elin carried a small volume of Finnish poetry that she had found amongst her stepmother's belongings. Religion remained difficult for Elin Ellison. There was an acceptance of an afterlife, knowledge that Christ had been a real person, a champion of lost souls. But Elin's faith stumbled and became fraught with questions when divinity was brought into the equation. Still, she found in the end, fragments of belief, some small respite of hope, of faith, that grace, so prominent in the Lutheranism of her heritage, might indeed save her. She faced the crowd and began to read from the volume in her gloved hands. The words Elin Ellison recited were not Biblical but poetic:

> Down from the hill the child came running
> Down to his mother running.
> Spoke, and his eyes were brightly shining:
> I have seen heaven's country.
>
> 'What are you saying, little darling,
> Of the far land of heaven?
> Where did you see the blessed country?
> Tell me, my golden apple.'
>
> Long on the mountain ridgeway standing,
> Casting my gaze north-eastward,
> There I could see a bluish heath, a
> Forest of firs far distant.
>
> Over the trees I saw a hillock,
> Fair where a lovely day shone,
> And to the hillock's top a pathway,
> Covered with golden sand ran.
>
> When I saw this my heart began to
> Pine and my cheek was wetted,
> Nor did I understand my tears, but
> I had seen heaven's country.
>
> 'Not so, my child; in blue skies yonder,
> Heaven's uplifted hall is,

There shine the lamps, the golden crowns, and
There is the seat where God sits.'

Not so, but there upon the skyline
Where the far forest glimmers,
There is the world of happiness, and
There is the blessed country.

As Elin completed the final line of Aleksis Kivi's poem, *The Far Forest*, her tongue nearly tripped over the Finnish words. But she drew upon the internal fortitude that marked her heritage, and concluded the poem without hesitation.

Well-wishers pressed towards the woman once she had returned to her place with the family. Her ears burned when she heard the murmurings of those behind her:

"I wonder what she will do now, now that her father is gone?" or

"Do you think she'll keep the child?"

In front of the mourners, on the level ground of Forest Hill, two pits had been dug for two coffins. The larger of the two had been dug immediately next to the gravestone of Laina Gustafsson. Elin had insisted upon the separation, upon using her father's body as a buffer between the spaces occupied by his two dead wives. Karl Gustafsson's bulk, the enormity of his physical remains, and more importantly, his larger-than-life persona, were necessary, in Elin's mind, to separate the earthly spaces occupied by Laina and the recently departed Sofia. Elin surveyed the reality of her father's death, focusing her silver-blue eyes upon two men using No. 2 shovels, as the workers began to fill in her father's grave, closing off the space between mahogany and sky. Elin's tears ceased, though her ache, the pangs of guilt at never having been able to make amends with her father, the heart attack rendering him unconscious until his body simply willed itself to stop, continued to plague the woman.

"Elin," a female voice said softly.

Elin Ellison turned to face her friend, Wendy McAdams. An infant squirmed in Wendy's arms, bouncing off the woman's obviously pregnant belly. The child's upset

508

immediately turned to joy at the prospect of being returned to her big sister. Wendy McAdams extended her arms, the weight of Alexis Gustafsson obvious by the expression on Wendy's face, and handed the child to Elin.

"That was a moving poem," Wendy McAdams said. "Who is the author?"

"Kivi," Elin whispered, drawing her half-sister against her chest.

"Ah, yes. He died young, didn't he?"

Elin nodded but said nothing more.

Other mourners – Oscar Larson, Victor Gran, Judge Cant, city and county politicians, former clients of her father's – all walked past and extended their condolences, as Wendy McAdams and her husband stood next to the two offspring of Karl Gustafsson and patiently waited for the well-wishers to depart.

"Your father was a good man," Oscar Larson said, his felt hat removed in respect and held strongly in his hands, exposing sandy hair and a receding widow's peak. "If you follow his example, you won't go wrong."

"Thank you, Mr. Larson," Elin whispered, the baby fidgeting in her arms as they stood beneath the open blue sky, scattered patches of snow interrupting the brown of the graveyard's grounds.

Victor Gran was next. The Finnish lawyer's angular face, accented by the round frames of his eyeglasses, increased the aura of stern resolve emanating from the man.

I hired him because he reminds me of Lenin, Elin thought as her lawyer offered his condolences and patted Alexis on the child's winter bonnet. *He's the exact opposite of Lenin in terms of his politics, but that is of no consequence, so long as he keeps Horace in line and brings our divorce to a speedy conclusion.*

"It's unseemly to discuss business on such an occasion," Gran whispered in Elin Ellison's ear. "But, to my surprise, your husband has accepted your proposal. Without objection. We can talk later this week. Just stop in. Anytime. I'll make myself available. I have no appearances in court until Friday," Gran concluded with a patronizing smile.

Elin Ellison nodded, but did not reply.

The lawyer handed the woman an envelope.

Elin shifted the child to free a hand to receive the parcel. "What's this?"

"Your husband said you'd know," Gran said.

Elin smiled wearily and kissed the attorney on the cheek. "I'll be in to see you."

Horace Ellison and his parents remained at the rear of the throng. They had attended the funeral and committal ceremony as a courtesy. Horace did not linger or personalize the event by speaking to Elin. There was little left to be said between husband and wife. Horace's lungs had cleared. He'd been released from the hospital, free of Spanish Influenza, just as a new vaccine was being tested, a vaccine that markedly reduced the number of new cases.

Elin cradled her sister in her arms and walked towards Pastor Sarvela. She stopped immediately in front of the cleric.

"Thank you, reverend, for all your support," Elin managed to say, the words, difficult; the circumstances, disheartening.

"There were no relatives here from your stepmother's side?" the minister asked.

"She came from Finland as an orphan with an old maternal aunt. The aunt is still alive, but lives in a retirement home in Memphis. I wrote to her. She did not write back."

"You will keep the child?"

Elin nodded.

In the beginning, when the reality of Sofia's death first manifested itself, when it became obvious that the woman's lungs had filled with fluid and that the pneumonia could not be abated, this but a day after Karl Gustafsson's sudden cardiac arrest, Elin quarreled with herself as to what should be done.

Sofia was the cause of my mother's upset, Elin Ellison had thought vindictively. *I have no business raising the offspring of the woman who destroyed my parents' marriage. Her mother was an orphan: let the child become one as well. Better to let the child be*

510

raised in such a place, surrounded by folks who care, than by me. What do I know of children?

But then, once the infant's symptoms abated, a nurse at St. Luke's had thrust the child into Elin's arms. The instant she held her half-sister, Elin Ellison understood. Raising Alexis would provide the means for Elin and Karl to finally achieve peace.

Elin gave up her reporting position at *Tyomies* and dedicated herself to learning, from women she knew with small children, the intricacies of caring for an infant. Elin became, once the issue had been decided within herself, a wonderful caregiver and big sister. And the child, without doing more than existing, became a source of comfort, laughter, and joy for the woman.

"You're doing a marvelous job," Wendy McAdams offered as they moved quickly towards a waiting taxicab. "You'll have to come to Port Arthur when little George is born and give me some lessons," the woman said, patting her belly.

Elin smiled and looked into the face of her friend. Wendy's delicate features had widened with pregnancy. Her elfin nose and chiseled cheekbones were less distinct. Her body was swelling noticeably, and the burgeoning fetus, but three months along, was already pressing against nerves in Wendy's low back, making walking on uneven terrain problematic.

"Alexis and I would be glad to come for a visit in the spring, when the lake is calm and the weather safe for a trip north."

George McAdams walked behind his wife and her friend, hat tilted back on his head, revealing the hints of gray that were beginning to replace his scarlet locks.

"It would be our pleasure to have you, Mrs. Ellison, for as long as you want to stay," George advised. "We've got the room. The old place we bought on the hill overlooking Port Arthur has six bedrooms. I daresay we won't be able to fill all those rooms up by next summer," he quipped, patting his waddling wife on her rear.

"George, you're at a funeral. Mind your manners," Wendy scolded, no real anger behind the admonition.

They passed Horace Ellison and his parents. Nods, but not words, were exchanged.

The cabbie opened the doors to the automobile and assisted the women and the baby into the rear of the Ford. George McAdams claimed the front passenger's seat. The motor puttered, tires spun, and the car moved away from the gravesite on a gravel access road leading back to Woodland Avenue.

As the motorcar negotiated the decline towards downtown Duluth, it passed obvious signs of the Great Fire. Nearly every tree, including those shading Glen Avon Presbyterian Church, the largest structure along Woodland Avenue, bore evidence of the fire's power. The trunks of the great elms lining the avenue, though scarred by flame, had survived to bear silent witness to the complete and utter destruction the fire had wrought further up the hill, at the end of Woodland Avenue, where nearly every tree, structure, and blade of grass had been incinerated.

"Will you be seeing Mr. Maki before you leave?" Elin Ellison asked as the car bounced onto Sixth Avenue East and began its final descent towards Lake Superior.

"I planned on it," George McAdams replied from the front seat.

Elin raised her eyes from the legal papers she was studying and folded the documents before replacing them in the envelope she'd received from Victor Gran, an envelope bearing the return address of Amalgamated Properties.

"Would you see that Mr. Maki gets this?" Elin asked, handing the envelope to the Canadian.

George McAdams accepted the envelope, unbuttoned his winter coat, and placed the document in the inside pocket of his suit coat.

"What's in the envelope?" Wendy McAdams asked tenuously, cognizant that she had no right to inquire into her friend's personal affairs.

"Recompense," Elin said curtly, the tone of her voice clearly implying that she would say nothing more on the matter.

Chapter 82

Wolf Lake Camp was their destination. George McAdams and his wife caught a Duluth, Missabe, and Northern passenger train in the Village of Proctor. The locomotive traversed the fire-scarred landscape between Duluth and Virginia. The train's path dissected a countryside filled with blackened stumps and half-burned trees. Snow covered the besooted ground, rendering the countryside a disturbing portrait in black and white. No evergreens remained to provide contrast. No red barns or green farmhouses had survived the Great Cloquet Fire to add color to the scenery.

In Virginia, the couple hired a driver and a Ford truck, the tires equipped with chains for the winter, for the final leg of the trip to Wolf Lake. George McAdams's fortunes had not improved to the extent that he was free to be extravagant, but renting a vehicle was the only way that George and Wendy McAdams could complete their errand. After visiting Wolf Lake Camp, the couple would board a Duluth, Winnipeg, and Pacific passenger train in Virginia and ride the DWP to Fort Francis, Ontario. In Fort Francis, they would catch a Canadian Pacific passenger train and travel east, to their new home in Port Arthur.

George McAdams had liquidated all of his American holdings in the face of the loss of the *Blue Heron* and the mansion. He'd scraped together enough cash to convince the family of Tim Laitila to settle their wrongful death lawsuit against him. Oscar Larson had the papers signed and ready for filing with Judge Cant. The case would be dismissed within the week, leaving George McAdams free to return to Port Arthur to reclaim the reins of control over whatever Canadian assets Adrian McAdams had not squandered.

"It's cold," Wendy said as the truck bounded over the frozen surface of County Highway No. 4, towards the logging camp.

"Five below zero, ma'am," the driver announced, "last I looked."

The woman collapsed into the solid frame of her husband and dug her mittened hands into the pockets of her woolen coat.

"We'll be there soon, dear," George McAdams said.

The truck passed acre after acre of logged-over land, slash and limbs piled high along the ditches of the roadway as they drove east, towards the camp.

This is how it all started, George McAdams mused, noting that the brush piles dotting the landscape were tinder dry.

The vehicle shuddered and waddled over potholes along the access road into the camp.

"Keep this up," Wendy McAdams quipped as she patted her pregnant belly through her coat, "and little George won't be able to hang on."

"He's a Scot," George replied, his eyes looking out the window, studying the buildings of the logging camp as the truck pulled in front of the camp's dining hall. "He'll be fine."

"He's also a Finn," the woman responded without missing a beat, "so at least we know he'll be intelligent."

George laughed.

"I do believe you're right, Mrs. McAdams. I do believe our son will take after his mother with respect to his intellect."

"And if the child is a girl?" the woman asked as she accepted the driver's hand and exited the truck to breathe the frigid air of Northeastern Minnesota.

"She'll be both beautiful and quick-witted," the Canadian added, exiting the Ford.

"How long do you think you'll be?" asked the driver, a short, portly man, his round face boasting an ebony beard flecked with silver.

"Not long. A few moments, nothing more. We need to be back in Virginia to take the evening train to Fort Francis," George advised.

"I'll just wander off a bit," the driver said, drawing a shabby Mackinaw around his rotund torso.

"Don't get lost," McAdams joked to the driver as McAdams led his wife into the Wolf Lake Camp dining hall.

The cook found Andrew Maki working on ledgers in the camp office and retrieved him. The logger, his face looking gaunt and tired from his recent illness, his clothing hanging from a frame reduced by disease, smiled broadly when he saw his friend and his friend's wife:

"Mr. and Mrs. McAdams, what a pleasant surprise. I see Inver has provided hot coffee and some of his famous pastries. May I join you?"

The camp boss moved slowly. His knees creaked as he stepped across the slab wood floor of the dining hall. The men shook hands vigorously.

"You remember Wendy?" George McAdams asked absently, realizing after he'd inquired that Andrew Maki had known Wendy McAdams far longer than George McAdams had.

"Silly George," Wendy interjected, leaning her blossoming form into Maki and pecking him on the cheek. "I knew Andrew before you could find Duluth on a map."

They sat and made small talk. Andrew asked about Wendy's pregnancy. He inquired about Elin and her family, having read the twin obituaries of Karl and Sofia Gustafsson in the *Duluth News Tribune* on his last visit to Burcar's Barber Shop in Aurora.

"How is Elin?" Andrew Maki asked shyly, his black eyes darting about the room.

Maki was unwilling to allow his friends to see still-kindled desire for the woman on his face.

"She's in New York," Wendy said quietly. "With Alexis."

"New York?"

George McAdams took a deep gulp of tarry black coffee and allowed his wife to converse.

"She's staying with Alice Silvey, a friend of her mother's. You remember, the widow whose husband died on the *Titanic*?"

Andrew shook his head in the negative.

516

"In any event, she's gone back to school. Columbia. She's hoping to be accepted into the university's doctor of literature program next autumn. Her divorce settlement from Horace was very generous."

Maki nodded. "At least he did one thing right. Never did like that boy."

George McAdams chortled. "Like him? Hell, Andrew, you broke his bloody jaw."

Wendy's eyes narrowed. "George."

"Sorry, dear."

Wood cracked in the kitchen's cook stove. The thick warmth of the fire battled cold air infiltrating the porous building from the outside.

"And Mrs. Genelli?" Wendy McAdams asked, her dark brown eyes twinkling with interest.

The logger smiled shyly.

"We're getting married in June."

George McAdams reached across the table and slapped the smaller man's back.

"It's about time. Best thing I ever did. Keeps you young, trying to please a wife," McAdams said. "Keeps you humble, too," he added, to appease his spouse.

Maki chuckled.

"I was hoping you'd be the best man. Nothing fancy. Just a small ceremony with a Catholic priest out at the farm, down by the lake. Just Heidi's family, you, and Wendy."

McAdams slapped Maki's upper back with more vigor.

"Damn, you're full of surprises. I'd be honored."

"So I can count on two McAdamses being here on June 10th?"

"Three," Wendy reminded Maki, using the Finnish word for the number.

"Three," Andrew agreed.

George nodded towards his wife. "Time's getting short."

"In a hurry?" Maki asked.

"We're taking the train to Fort Francis and then on to Port Arthur. I've concluded my business here. Wrapped it all up. The boat and the house wiped me out. And my good-for-

517

nothing brother Adrian can't be trusted to pull his own ass out of the toilet," the big man muttered, animosity obvious in his words.

"George," Wendy McAdams cautioned.

"Sorry."

"Who's going to run this place?" Andrew asked, raising his left hand into the thick warm air for emphasis.

Wendy retrieved a battered, letter-size envelope from her purse, placed it on the rough-sawn surface of the pine table, and pushed it to Maki.

"What's this?"

"Open it," the woman instructed.

Maki's calloused hands turned the envelope over. His eyes focused on the printed return address. He instantly recognized the company name.

"What the hell," he mumbled, his fingers struggling to open the flap.

"Here," George said, handing his friend a jack knife retrieved from a pants pocket.

Andrew opened the knife and slid the dull blade along the envelope's top edge. Maki's fingers fumbled with the papers inside the envelope, drawing them out with difficulty before unfolding the paperwork and placing it on the surface of the table in front of him.

Inside the envelope there were two pieces of paper, deeds to land, warranty deeds free and clear of any encumbrances or liens.

"What the hell?"

"Andrew," the woman admonished gently. "You're starting to sound like my husband."

Maki read and re-read the English typed into the open spaces on the printed forms.

"She is giving you the land," George McAdams whispered. The Canadian had peeked at the documents during the long drive from Virginia and had carefully resealed the envelope to preserve Elin Ellison's surprise. "You are now the proud owner of your own farm and Wolf Lake Logging Camp."

Chapter 83

When their bodies finally came together on the lumpy mattress of Andrew Maki's handcrafted double bed in the little log cabin on the shores of Papoose Lake after the wedding ceremony, their son Joey away, visiting his grandfather, Jerome Seppo, in Aurora for two weeks over summer vacation, their union was not what Andrew Maki had expected. Their marital embrace was not as Andrew's fevered linkings with Elin Gustafsson had been, a rushed dash culminating in exhilaration, but rather a slow, comforting stroll that satisfied and sated Andrew for days.

Maki's canoe moved quietly over placid water. Redwing blackbirds flitted in the distance, their aerodynamic bodies darting and weaving between tufts of yellow saw grass that lined the shoreline of Papoose Lake. Dusk settled over the land. A male ruffed grouse drummed, beating its wings on a hollow log in hopes of attracting a mate. An orange sun hung low over trees to the west, and caused purple and magenta disruptions in an otherwise blue and cloudless sky. Andrew Maki stroked his paddle easily, propelling the canvas and cedar Old Town canoe across the lake in silent precision. His wife, pregnant at age thirty-three, a circumstance that gave Andrew Maki renewed vigor and hope, dangled the fingers of her right hand over the varnished gunwale of the canoe, touching the inky black water of the dying lake.

"What are you thinking?" Heidi Maki asked.

She was becoming accustomed to silence in their marriage. Andrew was not, as her first husband Joseph Genelli had been, an idle chatterer. Andrew Maki was, in all ways, a serious man, a man made more serious by the war he had fought and by the life that he had lived.

"Kinkkonen," the Finn replied, using a J-stroke to turn the bow of the canoe.

"Why?"

A fish, likely a snaky pike, skinny and full of bones, jumped in a tangle of lily pads off to the left of the canoe's bow. Concentric rings moved out from the epicenter of the disturbance.

"I'm not sure. His face just comes to me without any real prompting at the oddest times," the logger replied in Finnish.

Jerome Seppo was now the sole owner of Olson's Café. He was running it with the assistance of Marge Ensign, the woman Heidi Maki had hired to work as the weekend cook in order to allow Heidi to care for Andrew during Andrew's long illness. Now, if the rumors were true, Jerome Seppo and his new employee were cooking more than flapjacks and eggs in Mr. Seppo's bedroom above the café. The sale of Heidi's interest in the restaurant to her father had allowed Heidi Maki to begin working side by side with her new husband as the manager of the Wolf Lake Camp kitchen.

During their short time living together, Heidi Maki had learned that Andrew was routinely visited by ghosts, by spirits and specters of men and women he'd known over the course of his life. It would not, during the duration of their marriage, be at all unusual for Andrew to suddenly leave an arduous task before completion, simply to attend to a vision that had manifested itself in his mind.

"Is there something you want to talk about, something you need to discuss regarding Mr. Kinkkonen?" she asked as the canoe drifted.

Andrew shook his head and dipped the wide blade of his canoe paddle into the tannin-hued water.

"Look," Andrew whispered, pointing with an index finger to a cluster of alders hugging the marshy shoreline opposite the Maki farm.

The woman squinted.

"I don't see anything."

"There," Andrew gestured, his canoe paddle resting across the wool pants covering his legs.

Water fell from the paddle's blade into the bottom of the canoe.

Drip. Drip. Drip.

A branch moved. An animal appeared from behind the foliage.

"What is it?" Heidi Maki asked in a whisper.

"Your cat," Andrew Maki murmured as a cougar stepped out of the brush, assured itself of safety, and began to lap fetid water with its long, pink tongue.

The animal's piercing eyes focused upon the canoe as it drank deeply from the lake. A cougar kitten appeared next to its mother and timidly flicked its tongue at the black water.

"Your cat is back," Andrew repeated quietly as the Finn and his wife watched the predators drink their fill, "and she has company."

Epilogue
June, 2003

A young woman stands at the edge of a bluff overlooking the Atlantic Ocean. She is lithe, well proportioned, and college-educated, thanks to sacrifices made by her parents. There are allusions to money in her family's past, money lost during the Great Depression. Her great-grandfather suffered the humiliation of watching his logging empire disappear into bankruptcy. Details of her family's descent into poverty are routinely recounted by distant relatives at family reunions, back in Thunder Bay, Ontario, the place she calls home.

She has come to Halifax, Nova Scotia, to pay her respects. A graduate student working on her doctorate in genetics at Lakehead University in Thunder Bay, she relishes the salty air of the Maritimes. She has journeyed east, through Ontario and Quebec, in hopes of achieving closure. A sense of unfinished business lingers. This anomaly in her ordered and scientific world began to germinate the very moment she was approached by Mr. Parr, the lead investigator on the *Titanic* DNA Recovery Team, a consortium of scientists and student assistants from Lakehead University, Genesis Genomics, Inc. and Geomarine Associates.

Molly McAdams had recently completed a Bachelor's degree in Applied Molecular Science at Lakehead University. Her favorite instructor recognized the young woman's interest in forensic DNA. Molly's mentor, a professor of chemistry, knew Mr. Parr was seeking to employ graduate students who were willing to work hard for little pay. One interview, the submission of her application to Lakehead's graduate program in genetics, and the position was hers.

The first speculation had been that the remains retrieved by the research team from Burial Plot No. 4, mere shards of bone and bits of teeth, were those of a two-year-old Swedish child, Gosta Leonard Paisson. Using mitochondrial DNA, the artifacts from Burial Plot No. 4, when compared to maternal DNA retrieved from descendents of the Swedish child, defied such a link. Suspicion mounted that the bone chips and partial teeth, taken as they were from beneath the monument erected by the sailors of the Canadian rescue ship, *Mackay-Bennett*, were likely from the body of Eino Panula, the youngest of John Panula's five sons who died in the sinking.

Forensic dentistry confirmed that the tooth fragments removed from the Halifax graveyard were from a child less than a year in age. This determination focused the team's genetic investigation on the youngest Panula child, just eleven months old on the date of the tragedy. Lakehead University scientists obtained blood and tissue samples from relatives of Maria Panula living in Finland. Molly's careful analysis of the maternal DNA samples convinced the team's principals as to the identity of the child who had been buried with such tender care in the hardscrabble soil of Nova Scotia back in 1912.

On November 6, 2002, Lakehead University announced to the world what Molly McAdams and her colleagues had discerned in their laboratories: the remains of the child buried beneath the maritime monument in the Halifax graveyard were those of Eino Panula.

Molly's eyes follow the rise and fall of the sea as waves shimmer and roll. She searches the eastern horizon for the impossibly distant coastline of Europe. The geneticist knows the stories. She has listened, from an early age, to tales describing how her Finnish ancestors crossed the inexhaustible expanse of the North Atlantic to come to North America in the late 1890s. Her father, Erik, has explained in great and serious detail how Molly's Great Grandmother Wendla, known as Wendy, a young Finnish beauty whose profile, as preserved in old photographs, is reminiscent of Molly's, had married a rich Canadian and moved to what was then Port Arthur. In Port Arthur, as reported with great flourish by the less squeamish members of Molly's paternal family, George McAdams eventually lost everything he owned to speculation before passing away due to complications from emphysema. George's death at age seventy-five left Wendla McAdams and her three children, including Erik's father and Molly's grandfather, Dennis McAdams, to fend for themselves.

Wendy McAdams found employment as a cook at Hoito, a communal dining hall located in the Finnish Labour Temple in the Finntown neighborhood of Port Arthur. Wendy remained employed at Hoito through the late 1960s, up until the moment she died of a fatal stroke in Hoito's kitchen at seventy-nine years old. Her son Dennis married when he was eighteen. Dennis's marriage produced Molly's father, Erik. Erik McAdams married Lisa Uttenkot. Their union conceived Molly and her younger sister, Abbie. Abbie, though barely twenty-one, is already married. Molly is not. Molly has prospects, male friends who are both interesting and interested. Nevertheless, Molly finds herself propelled towards her doctorate by an insatiable need to succeed, a drive her father ascribes to Great Grandfather George, the family's only brilliant success and also its most luminous failure.

How was it for them? Molly asks herself, pulling the drawstring of her fleece jacket tight around her narrow waist to defeat the ocean's chill. *What was it that made them leave their families and their homes for this place, this land?*

While preparing to work on the DNA team, Molly Elin McAdams, her middle name a relic passed down to each first-born McAdams woman born after Great Grandmother Wendla, watched the movie *Titanic* a half-dozen times. She read the histories and consulted the maps. Despite her studies, it is beyond Molly's youth and her relative affluence, affluence hard won and gingerly given by her father and mother, to understand the reasons behind her ancestors' emigration from the boreal forests of Finland for unproven opportunities in North America.

Molly lingers near a precipice jutting out over the churning sea, the press release announcing Lakehead University's dramatic discovery relegated to history, her doctoral thesis nearly completed. The young scientist remains uncertain as she curls her blue-jean-covered legs beneath her rump to sit on moss-covered ground. Human mortality tugs at her and forces her to admit that the accolades are wonderful, but... The thought stops there, interrupted by visions of history.

He was only a baby, Molly McAdams recalls, watching a white-feathered gull wheel against the charcoal sky stalled above Nova Scotia, the wind buffeting bird and clouds, preventing progress for either. *The future was his,* Molly continues. *Why didn't his mother save him? Why didn't she put him in that lifeboat?*

Molly wants to scream out. She wants to reveal the injustice of Maria Panula's selfish decision to the world. Instead of vocalizing her rage, Molly McAdams maintains silence, cognizant that she has not earned the right to play judge.

"Five boys," Molly McAdams whispers.

A gust of wind tosses strands of golden hair across the woman's smooth cheeks. Molly pushes the hair away from her face with the back of her hand before focusing her eyes upon rows of distant headstones marking the graves in which immigrant passengers from the *Titanic* remain at permanent rest. Eino Panula's family has left him here, in his grave beneath the monolith. There is, in the family's estimation, no need to disturb things that have been.

Lines of Finnish poetry intrude upon the young woman's mind as she ponders the voyage her ancestors made across the wide sea. Molly McAdams doesn't read or speak Finnish, but she has memorized the entirety of the poem in English, the language used when her mother recited the verse to Molly and her sister at bedtime:

> *There is a road none has trodden*
> *before you.*
> *Perhaps it is yours.*
> *If you find it, it is yours.*
> *It does not exist but does when you tread it.*
> *When you look round it is gone.*

How you got here no one knows,
least of all yourself.
Whoever thought shadows lack color
has never lived with shadows.
Death's black shadows are blue, or dark blue.
There are light yellow shadows that escaped from
childhood wallpaper.

When only the invisible was real, like
the grownups behind the drapery in the hall.
As soon as Papa disappeared it was blue, the
color when shadows dance.
In our wood cellar there was a special kind of shadows
you got splinters in your fingers from.
They are there still.

I live my life among the living and the dead
shadows.
The living shadows keep the dead shadows
in the dance.
The dead love the dance of the living.
Because time had abandoned them, as the light leaves
us we stop dancing.

*

Like the beach we practice talking
with our mouth full of stones.
A low rattle at sunset.

"Five boys," Molly McAdams repeats, dollops of cold water
moistening the white hair that covers her forearms like down,
the precipitation the result of an unexpected cloud burst.

Sitting on lichen-softened Nova Scotian earth, her
eyes closed to the weather, her head tilted to accept what she
cannot change, water splashes Molly McAdams's young face.
She considers the rain to be an omen, to be an indication that
life will always have something new to offer.

Her clothing becomes saturated. Her blond hair
becomes limp from the moisture. She opens her eyelids to take
in the ocean, the birds, and the storm before uncoiling her legs
and rising from the ground to begin her long journey home.

Notes

Historical fiction requires that some modicum of truth be contained in the facts and settings surrounding the fantasy world created by the author. Hopefully, the author has accomplished these somewhat divergent goals, to entertain and to enlighten, without causing the reader to yawn in boredom because the plot and characters have disappeared in a quagmire of trivia, or to rage out loud at a factual inaccuracy found buried somewhere in this tale.

This is a story. However, that having been said, certain individuals appearing in this work are indeed based upon real human beings who walked, talked, loved, and died during the early Twentieth Century. The thoughts, words, and actions this author ascribes to these "real" individuals are indeed fiction. I have attempted to respect the families and legacies of historical figures as best I could, while using these folks to propel the story forward. Hopefully, the "real" individuals upon whom the characters in this novel are based have been treated fairly, as fairly as possible given the distance of time from their contemporary setting. While a historical novel is not a place to write accurate or detailed biographies of the "real" people who pop up within a book's pages, it may be of some interest to the reader to know what happened to certain characters who made appearances in this, the author's third novel. What follow are bits and pieces of biography regarding the historical figures appearing in this book.

Olli Kinkkonen

So far as I am aware, the question of whether or not Olli Kinkkonen died by his own hand or was the victim of a lynching remains unresolved. The dates and information contained in this manuscript regarding Mr. Kinkkonen are what I could glean from a review of contemporary newspaper accounts of Mr. Kinkkonen's death, as well as some additional brief descriptions of his demise in other published materials. Others will hopefully resolve the question of whether Mr. Kinkkonen hanged himself or was assisted in that regard.

Oscar Larson

Mr. Larson was born in Uleaborg, Finland in 1871. He immigrated to the United States and began his law practice in Upper Peninsula Michigan, before coming to Duluth in 1908. He ran for the United States House of Representatives as a Republican, becoming the first native-born Finn to be elected to Congress. A personal friend of Theodore Roosevelt (Roosevelt stayed at Larson's home in Duluth while campaigning as a "Bull Mooser" in 1912) and Herbert Hoover (who came to Duluth in 1921 to personally campaign for Larson), Congressman Larson served two terms in the House of Representatives (1921-1925) before returning to Duluth to resume the practice of law. He died on August 1, 1957, at the age of eighty-six years old, survived by a son and two daughters.

Victor Gran

Victor Gran immigrated to Duluth from Finland with his parents at the age of five. He engaged in the private practice of law in Duluth until appointed Assistant Attorney General by J.A.A. Burnquist in 1939. Gran served from 1939-1955 in that capacity before returning to Duluth. Victor Gran ran unsuccessfully for the state trial court bench in 1936, but was elected St. Louis County Court Commissioner in 1958 at the ripe old age of 79. A vigorous advocate for his fellow Finns, Gran locked horns in court with Oscar Larson on numerous occasions. He died in Duluth on October 1, 1964, at the age of 85, leaving two sons and a daughter.

Major Louis Cukela

Though the incidents contained in this novel revolving around Louis Cukela's contacts with Andrew Maki are fiction, Major Louis Cukela was indeed a Marine who enlisted to fight in the Great War, after having been honorably discharged from the United States Army. For his acts of heroism in engagements occurring during the Battle of Soissons, Major Cukela was awarded double (both Army and Navy) Congressional Medals of Honor. Following the end of the war, Major Cukela continued his military career, serving in many posts with the Marines until his death on August 10, 1956.

Major Edward Cole

Cole commanded the 6th Machine Gun Battalion, 4th Brigade of Marines, 2nd Division American Expeditionary Force, from the inception of the unit in 1917 until his death during the Battle of Belleau Wood on June 18, 1918. He received the Navy Cross for his service.

Gunnery Sergeant Fred Stockham

As depicted in this novel, Marine Sergeant Stockham removed his gas mask during the Battle of Belleau Wood and saved the life of a fellow soldier by placing the mask over the stricken soldier's face. Stockham died from ingestion of gas on June 22, 1918 at the age of 37. He was awarded the Medal of Honor for his heroism and sacrifice.

Governor J. A.A. Burnquist

Burnquist served the State of Minnesota as a Republican member of the Minnesota House of Representatives, Lieutenant Governor, and as the 19th Governor of the state (1915-1921), before concluding his distinguished career as the Attorney General for the State of Minnesota. He died on January 12th, 1961, at the age of 82.

Margaret Sanger

The leader of the American birth control movement and the founder of the predecessor organization to Planned Parenthood, Sanger spent thirty days in jail for providing birth control advice to poor women in New York City. She won an appeal and continued to strive to educate women on birth control issues until her death in 1966.

Elizabeth Gurley Flynn

An agitator and organizer for the Industrial Workers of the World (IWW), Flynn eventually joined the Communist party. She wrote her autobiography, *Rebel Girl*, while serving a prison sentence during the McCarthy Era. She continued to be active in the Communist party until her death in 1964 at the age of 74.

Judge William A. Cant

Integral to many of the important decisions during the three decades Judge Cant served on the bench was his keen understanding of fundamental fairness. Though the language of Cant's 1907 decision regarding John Svan's right to apply for citizenship appears to include racist references, the reality is that his decision paved the way for immigrant Finns to receive fair treatment from the United States Government. Judge Cant also played an important, though unsuccessful, role in the 1920 lynching of three black circus workers in Duluth. Judge Cant sought to thwart the lynchings by placing himself in front of a crowd bent on murder, and by advising those in attendance that what they were about to do was wrong. His words went unheeded and three innocent men died. (For a detailed analysis of the 1920 lynchings, read *The Lynchings in Duluth*, by Michael Fedo. See below in the Sources section for further information.)

Judge Cant was a young lawyer when he ran for and won a seat in the Minnesota House in 1895. Later that same year he was appointed City Attorney for the city of Duluth. The following year, William Cant was elected to the Minnesota District Court bench. Judge Cant served four full terms and a portion of a fifth as a state trial court judge, before resigning in 1923 to accept an appointment as a United States District Court Judge. The appointment came after Judge Cant's acclaimed decision that held the railroads responsible for the Great Cloquet Fire. He served on the federal bench until his death of influenza at St. Luke's Hospital in 1933. He was survived by five children.

Harry L. Smith, MD

Dr. Smith provided medical expertise to the American Expeditionary Force as a member of the United States Army Medical Corps. He survived the Great War and returned to the United States, where he had a long and distinguished career practicing medicine at the Mayo Clinic in Rochester, Minnesota.

The Reverend Heikki Sarvela

Reverend Heikki (Henry) Sarvela was born and ordained in Finland. He served numerous congregations as a Lutheran missionary before settling in Duluth in 1891. By 1899, Rev. Sarvela had established the Independent Finnish Evangelical Church located on St. Croix Avenue. In 1912, the mission became affiliated with the Suomi Synod. Sarvela served the church as its pastor until 1923 when, ever the missionary, he started another Suomi Synod church in West Duluth. Heikki Sarvela's forty plus years as an ordained pastor allowed him to provide spiritual guidance to Finnish Lutherans in South Dakota, Canada, Northern Michigan, and Minnesota. His career culminated in 1930 when he was awarded the Order of the White Rose, Finland's highest honor, by the president of that country.

Reverend Sarvela died in Duluth on February 21, 1931, survived by his widow, four sons and a daughter.

Sources

Books

Aurora, Minnesota - The First Century, 1903-2003. 2003. Vivid Design.

Bosley, Keith, Editor and Translator. 1997. *Skating on the Sea: Poetry from Finland.* Bloodaxe Books.

Caroll, Francis M. and Franklin R. Raiter. 1984. *The Fires of Autumn.* Minnesota Historical Society Press.

Fedo, Michael. 2000. *The Lynchings in Duluth*. Minnesota Historical Press.

Lemberg, Lauri. Translated by M.L. Eldridge. 1992. *St. Croix Avenue*. Tyomies Society.

Lindsell, Harold. 1952. *Harper Study Bible*. Harper and Row.

Lydecker, R., Editor. 1976. *Duluth, Sketches of the Past*. American Revolution Bicentennial Commission.

Maki, V.C. 2000. *Ready to Descend: The Journals of Matti Pelto*. Sampo Publishing.

Norton, Maryanne C., and Aubut, Sheldon T. 2001. *Images of America: Duluth, Minnesota*. Arcadia Publishing.

Ryan, J.C. 1980. *Early Loggers in Minnesota*, (Volumes I-IV). Minnesota Timber Producers' Association.

Wargelin, John. 1924. *The Americanization of the Finns*. The Finnish Lutheran Book Concern.

Wasastjerna, H.R., Editor. Toivo Rosvall, Translator. 1957. *The History of the Finns in Minnesota*. Minnesota Finnish-American Historical Society.

Wuorinen, John W. 1938. *The Finns in Delaware*. Columbia University Press.

Websites

www.military.com (Louis Cukela information)

www.scuttlebutsmallchow.com/cole (Major Cole information)

www.msc.navy.mil/inventory/citations/stockham (Sergeant
Stockham information)

www.minnesotapolitics.net/governors/19burnquist (Joseph
Burnquist information)

www.bioguide.congress.gov (Oscar Larson information)

www.encarta.msn.com and
www.nyu.edu/projects/sanger/msbio (Margaret Sanger
information)

www.college.hmco.com/history/readerscomp and
www.spartacus.schoolnet.co.uk/USAflynn (Elizabeth Gurley
Flynn information)

www.titanic.com; www.lakeheadu.ca; www.encyclopedia-
titanica.org; www.utu.fi/erill/instmigr/art/titanic;
www.uta.fi/~kt22588/titanic; www.ebcom.com/jrudolph/turja
www.ivory.lm.com/~cass/Finntitanic (*Titanic* information)

www.yale.edu/ynhti/curriculum/units/1982/6/82.06.03.x;
www.sexuality.about.com/library/weekly/aa082399;
www.purehealthsystems.com/colloidal-silver;
www.bartleby.com/65/go/gonorrhe;
www.longevinst.org/nlt/newsletter18 (Venereal disease
information)

www.condor.depaul.edu/~lincoln/dischi;
www.pbs.org/wgbh/amex/influenza;
www.stanford.edu/group/virus/uda/fluscimed; (Spanish
Influenza information)

www.genealogia.fi/emi/art/article213e;
www.news.mpr.org/features/199706/10;
www.utu.fi/erill/instmgr/art/farmwomen;
www.colonialswedes.org/churches; (Finnish immigration
information)

www.firstworldwar.com;
www.lib.byu.edu/~rdh/wwi/memoir/Ambco/officer3;
www.1stmarinedivisionassociation.org/world-war-one/WWI;
www.worldwar1.com;
www.multied.com/navy/transport/dekalb;
www.scuttlebuttsmallchow.com/dekalb;
www.qmfound.com/army_rations_historical_background;
(World War I information)

www.news.mpr.org/programs/specials/lynching/olli;
www.northstarcompass.org/nsc9909/finns;
www.members.aol.com/wdwylie3/1910-1919; (Olli Kinkkonen
information)

www.members.aol.com/wdwylie3/1910-1919;
www.law.umkc.edu/faculty/projects/ftrials/saccoV/redscare;
www.web.mala.bc.ca/davies/h324war/prager.lynching.1918;
(Slacker information)

www.genealogia.fi/emi/art/article/164e;
www.globalgourmet.com/destinations/finland;
www.personalweb.smcvt/tmatikainen/finnishfood;
www.travellady.com/articles/article-finland;
www.cyberbohemia.com/pages/historyofnordic; (Finnish
food and cultural information)

www.mnhs.org/places/nationalregister/shipwrecks/niagara;
www.d.umd.edu/~pcollins/sugarloaf/history;
www.dnr.state.mn.us/canoeing/cloquetriver;
www.wildnorth.org/heritage5;
www.gilbertmn.org/city_history;
www.nrhp.mnhs.org;www.rangecities.com/cty/virginia;
www.vaillod.com/keweenaw/sailor; (Minnesota history)

www.valpo.edu/about_valpo/history (Valparaiso University
history)

www.michmarkers.com/pages/SO211; (Suomi College
history)

www.potowmack.org/conscri1; (Selective Service cases of
1918)

www.lib.duke.edu/forest/Publications/mccollister.pdf;
http://www.mnhs.org/places/sites/fhc/logdrives;
http://www.d.umn.edu/cla/faculty/troufs/Buffalo; (Logging
and Wanigan history)

www.encarta.msn;
www.geocities.com/captiolhill/5202/rebelgirl;
www.aflcio.org/aboutaflcio/history/history/hill;
www.newyouth.com/archives/music/joehillbio; (IWW
history)

Videos

    For the Common Good, © 2000 T. Selinski Productions,
Tyomies Society

Additional Author Comments Regarding Sources

Two Internet sources proved invaluable to me in writing this
work of fiction. The opening sequences could not have been
written without the historical background supplied by
www.encyclopedia-titanica.org. Readers are encouraged to
check out this marvelous compendium of *Titanic* history for
themselves.

    The second site, equally as impressive as the first,
upon which I relied heavily for details regarding the Great
War, may be found at www.firstworldwar.com. Readers with
an interest in World War I are urged to log onto this site and
explore the wealth of data, photographs, and ancillary
materials contained there.

    Finally, without the fine resources of the Duluth
Public Library and the helpful, courteous staff of the main
library facility, this book could not have been written. Nearly

all the references to Duluth, Minnesota, circa 1908-1918 came from my review of the microfilmed copies of the following newspapers maintained at the Duluth Public Library: *Duluth News Tribune, Duluth Herald, The Truth, The Labor World,* and *The Ripsaw.*

About the Author

Mark Munger is a life-long resident of Northeastern Minnesota. Mark, his wife, René, and their four sons live on the banks of the wild and scenic Cloquet River north of Duluth. When not writing fiction, Mark enjoys hunting, fishing, skiing, chasing kids, and working as a District Court Judge.

The Author and his son Christian, at Indian Lake, ready to begin
a fifty-mile canoe trip down the Cloquet River.

Other Works by the Author

The Legacy (ISBN 0972005021; Cloquet River Press)

Set against the backdrop of WWII Yugoslavia and present-day Minnesota, this debut novel combines elements of military history, romance, thriller, and mystery. Rated 3 and 1/2 daggers out of 4 by *The Mystery Review Quarterly*.
Trade Paperback - $19.95 USA, $26.95 CAN

River Stories (ISBN 0972005013; Cloquet River Press)

A collection of essays describing life in Northern Minnesota with a strong emphasis on the out-of-doors, the rearing of children, and the environment. A mixture of humor and thought-provoking prose gleaned from the author's columns in *The Hermantown Star*.
Trade Paperback - $19.95 USA, $26.95 CAN

Ordinary Lives (ISBN 0972005005; Cloquet River Press)

Creative fiction from one of Northern Minnesota's newest writers, these stories touch upon all elements of the human condition and leave the reader asking for more.
Trade Paperback - $17.95 USA, $22.95 CAN

Pigs, a Trial Lawyer's Story (ISBN 097200503x; Cloquet River Press)

A story of a young trial attorney, a giant corporation, marital infidelity, moral conflict, and choices made, **Pigs** takes place against the backdrop of Western Minnesota's beautiful Smokey Hills. This tale is being compared by reviewers to Grisham's best.
Trade Paperback - $19.95 USA, $28.95 CAN